SUCCESSFUL INVESTING

A Complete Guide to Your Financial Future

Fourth Edition/Revised and Updated

BY THE STAFF OF

Babson-United Investment Advisors, Inc.

*With Introductory Chapters on
the Art of Prudent Investing by*

DAVID R. SARGENT
CHAIRMAN, INVESTMENT COMMITTEE

Editor **CAROLYN M. FINNEGAN**

A FIRESIDE BOOK
Published by Simon & Schuster, Inc.
New York, London, Toronto, Sydney, Tokyo

Copyright © 1979, 1981, 1983, 1987 by
United Business Service Company, Inc.
All rights reserved
including the right of reproduction
in whole or in part in any form.
FIRST FIRESIDE EDITION, 1987
Published by Simon & Schuster, Inc.
Simon & Schuster Building
Rockefeller Center
1230 Avenue of the Americas
New York, NY 10020

FIRESIDE and colophon are registered trademarks of
Simon & Schuster, Inc.
Designed by Irving Perkins Associates
Manufactured in the United States of America
10 9 8 7 6 5 4 3 2 1

Library of Congress Cataloging in Publication Data

Successful investing.

"A Fireside book."
Includes index.
1. Investments.   2. Finance, Personal.
I. Sargent, David R.   II. Finnegan, Carolyn M.
III. Babson-United Investment Advisors.
HG4521.S823   1987   332.6′78   87-19736
ISBN 0-671-64762-8

Contents

How to Use This Book   13

PART I   *The Art of Prudent Investing*

CHAPTER 1   *Overview*   17
Lessons Not Learned / The Power of Positive Thinking / Beware the Ideologues / Be Positive, Be Patient / What's in This Book for Me?

CHAPTER 2   *On Planning Your Investments*   24
Where Should You Save? / Why You Can't Ignore Stocks / Stock Values Go Up and Up

CHAPTER 3   *Investment Risks—Defined and Contained*   31
The Inflation Risk / The Interest-Rate Risk / The Market Risk / How Much Risk for You? / Spreading Your Risks

CHAPTER 4   *Building Your Portfolio*   39
Investing Defensively / Investing Bit by Bit / Investing to Preserve Capital / There Are Men, Too / Don't Marry Your Stocks / Adjust for Your Changing Needs / Keep Good Records

PART II   *Your Investment Alternatives*

CHAPTER 5   *Equity Investments: "A Piece of the Action"*   51
The Concept of Ownership / Common Stocks: Rights and Risks / Picking the Right Stocks / Watch Dividend Performance / How Stock Splits Work / How to "Value" a Stock / Be Aware of the Risks / Preferred Stocks / Rights and Warrants / Puts and Calls

CHAPTER 6   *How to Find Growth Stocks*   62
What Makes a Growth Stock / Growth Stocks and Economic Trends / Timing Your Buys / Timing Your Sells

CHAPTER 7   *Common Stocks for Income*   67
Look Beyond Current Yield / Get a Line on Telephone Stocks / Plug into Electric Utilities / Tap a Water Company / Inflation and Income Stocks

CHAPTER 8   *Corporate Bonds*   73
Simply Stated, They're Loans / The "Mechanics" of Bonds / Marketplace Determines Yield / Yields Fluctuate / Different Kinds of Yields / Bonds—Why and When?

CHAPTER 9   *Convertible Securities*   82
How They Work / The Conversion Premium / How and When to Convert / Their Uses—and Limits

CHAPTER 10   *Investing in Uncle Sam*   88
How "Governments" Work / Bills, Notes, and Bonds / Hold That Tiger / The Treasury STRIPS / Federal Agency Bonds / A Word on Taxability

8 / Contents

CHAPTER 11   *Investing in Tax-Exempts*   95
When Are Tax-Exempts Profitable? / What Kinds of Bonds Are There? / New Muni Bond Types / Marketability Can Be a Problem / Insured Bonds Have an Edge / How Do You Judge Them? / Which Ones to Buy? / When Shouldn't You Use Them?

CHAPTER 12   *Mutual Funds*   106
What Is a Mutual Fund? / Closed-Ends and Open-Ends / Load Versus No-Load Funds / Advantages of Mutual Funds / Cost of Ownership / When a No-Load Isn't a No-Load / Reading the Prospectus / The Pulse of Portfolio Turnover / An Important "Don't" / Funds in Your Future? / What Kind of Fund? / Closed Funds and Clones / Again . . . Diversify

CHAPTER 13   *Special-Purpose Investment Funds*   122
Convertible Funds / Gold Funds / Foreign Funds / Ginnie Mae Funds / Index Funds / Money-Market Funds / Municipal Bond Funds / Option-Income Funds / Sector Funds / Social-Action Funds / Unit Trusts

CHAPTER 14   *Options*   134
CBOE: Order from Chaos / Call Options / When to Buy and When to Sell Calls / Options and Margin Requirements / Avoiding Unwanted Exercise Notices / Put Options / Buying Puts—When and Why / Writing Puts / A Growing Market / Summing Up

CHAPTER 15   *Commodities*   146
Historical Evolution / The Commodity Exchange / Organization of the Exchanges / The Clearinghouse / The Standard Commodity Contract / Margins / Leverage / Open Interest / Hedging / The Short Hedge / The Long Hedge / The Trading Floor / Government Regulation

CHAPTER 16   *Stock Index Futures and Other Financial Hybrids*   163
A Short History / The Mechanics of Futures / Playing in the Big Leagues / Informational Tools / Putting Up Cash

CHAPTER 17   *Gold, Inflation, and Your Dollars*   170
The Gold Standard / Gold and the Dollar / The Dollar Is Cut Free / U.S. on the Bargain Counter / Investing in Gold / Investment Outlook: So-So / The Glitter of the Kaffirs / The Krugerrand and Others

CHAPTER 18   *Real Estate*   181
Successes—and Failures / Investing in Raw Land / Rental Property / Business Property / Real Estate Investment Trusts / Real Estate Syndicates / Real Estate Investments and Taxes / What Can and Has Gone Wrong

PART III *How to Make Your Choices*

CHAPTER 19 *Forecasting with the Cyclical Indicators* 195
Leading Indicators: A Dozen Precursors / Coincident Indicators: Four-Track Broad-Based Activities / Lagging Indicators: Six Tend to Trail Behind

CHAPTER 20 *Measuring the Market's Ups and Downs* 203
How to "Build" an Index / Different Indexes Yield Different Results / The "Dow" / The S&P 500 / Other Indexes / Indexes Are Useful—to a Point

CHAPTER 21 *Getting the Picture from Charts* 211
Practical Application / Charts and Your Investments / Plotting the Percentages / Not Only for Technicians

CHAPTER 22 *Technical Analysis* 220
Definitions / More Than Charts and Figures / Some Technical Indicators / Irregular Forecasting Methods / Interpreting Chart Patterns / The Dow Theory / In Conclusion

CHAPTER 23 *How to Read an Annual Report* 242
What Is in an Annual Report / The Balance Sheet / Analyzing a Balance Sheet / The Income Statement / Analyzing the Income Statement / Other Lodes to Mine / Analyzing a Common Stock / The Footnotes Are Important / The Accountants' Report

CHAPTER 24 *Analyzing Specific Industries* 262
The Basic Industries (automobiles and trucks, chemicals, coal, construction, machinery and machine tools, metals, oil and natural gas, paper and forest products, textiles) / Science and Technology (aerospace, data processing, electronics and electrical equipment, health care) / Transportation Industries (airlines, railroads, trucking)

CHAPTER 25 *More on Specific Industries* 284
Consumer Products and Leisure Time (food processing, lodging, the media, motion pictures, personal care, recreation equipment, retailing) / Financial Services (banking, insurance, savings and loan associations) / Public Utilities (electric utilities, natural gas pipelines and distributors, telephone companies)

CHAPTER 26 *Cashing In on the Future* 301
Innovation Versus Invention / The Effects of "Future Shock" / Why Some Companies Succeed / Watch for Trends / Profits in "Cleaning Up" / Cashing In on "Getting There" / Making Money on Money / Some Guidelines

CHAPTER 27 *Where to Get Advice* 309
Your Broker and the Bank / Standard & Poor's and Moody's / Advisory Services / The Financial Press / Magazines / Government Publications / Investment Counselors

10 / Contents

PART IV *Mastering the Strategies and Tactics*

CHAPTER 28 *Five Rules for Investors* 319
Set Your Goals / Buy the Best-Known Companies / Invest for the Long Term / Avoid Fads / Diversify

CHAPTER 29 *How the Stock Market Works* 328
The Role of Investment Bankers / The New York Stock Exchange / AMEX and the Regional Exchanges / A Central Securities Market / Types of Orders / Special Timing Situations / Buying Low and "Taking Profits" / Dollar Cost Averaging / In Conclusion

CHAPTER 30 *Capitalizing on Special Situations* 342
Mergers, Acquisitions, and Takeovers / Spin-Offs and Turnarounds / New Products / Investing "At Home"

CHAPTER 31 *How to Use Options in Trading* 350
Buying Calls / Selling Calls / Trading Puts / Hedging with Options / Spreads—Bullish and Bearish / Risk Versus Reward

CHAPTER 32 *Investing in Commodity Futures* 358
Should You Speculate? / Choosing a Broker and Account Executive / Keeping Things Straight / The Kinds of Orders / Buying, Selling, and Delivery / Three Classes of Commissions / Market Quotes and Price Forecasting / Your Trading Plan

PART V *Taking Care of the Housekeeping*

CHAPTER 33 *Choosing a Broker* 373
Full-Service Houses / Discount Brokers / How Much Should I Pay? / Special Programs Available / Making the Choice

CHAPTER 34 *Safeguarding Your Securities* 380
Holding Your Securities / How SIPC Protects You / Good Records Are Important / If Certificates Are Lost or Destroyed / Are Old Certificates Valuable? / Minority Shareholder Rights

CHAPTER 35 *Running Your Investment Program* 389
Dividend Reinvestment Plans / Mutual Fund Programs / Stock Dividends and Rights / U.S. Savings Bonds / Other U.S. Obligations / Deregulation and Savings

CHAPTER 36 *Tax Pointers for Investors* 399
Don't Let the Tax Tail Wag the Investment Dog / Give Uncle Sam His Due / Don't Go to the Showers on a "Wash Sale" / Don't Trip Over the Calendar / Don't Compare Stock Loss Apples with Tax Saving Oranges / Year-End Tactics / Charitable Gifts Aid Donor and Donee

PART VI *Investments and Your Financial Plan*

CHAPTER 37 *Are Your Affairs in Order?* 407
*Finding Your Net Worth | Where Does the Money Go? |
Controlling the Outgo | Providing for Illness, Disability,
and Death | A Record-Keeping Checklist*

CHAPTER 38 *Investing for a College Education* 415
Keeping the Tax Man at Bay | Doing It with Trusts

CHAPTER 39 *Countdown to Retirement* 419
*How Much to Save? | Savings Alternatives | Making Sav-
ings Grow | Equities Have a Unique Advantage | Supple-
menting Retirement Income*

CHAPTER 40 *Employee Benefit Plans* 427
*ERISA Sets New Standards | Pension Benefits Insured |
What's What in Pension Plans | Some Companies Provide
Several Plans | Calculating Your Benefits | The Tax Re-
form Act of 1986 and Pension Plans | Collecting Plan Bene-
fits*

CHAPTER 41 *Keogh Plans* 435
*How Keogh Plans Work | Investment Alternatives | Col-
lecting Your "Benefits" | Withdrawal Options | Distribu-
tions After Death | Summing Up*

CHAPTER 42 *Individual Retirement Accounts* 442
*How IRAs Work | A New Class of IRAs | Flexible Invest-
ment Options | Employer-Sponsored IRAs—SEPs | Note
the Penalties | You'll Pay Taxes—Eventually | Nondeduct-
ible Contributions Complicate Distributions | IRA Is Soon
Exhausted | Unisex Actuarial Table | Using Tax-Free
"Rollovers" | Some Rules on Rollovers*

CHAPTER 43 *Annuities as Retirement Fund Vehicles* 455
*Annuities as Savings Vehicles | How an Annuity "Pays"
You | How Much Will It Pay? | Should You Use Annui-
ties? | Consider a "Private Annuity" | Proceed Carefully*

CHAPTER 44 *Estate Planning* 463
*Keeping Your Will Current | Choosing an Executor | Can
You Use a Trust? | Pros and Cons of Joint Ownership |
How Gifts and Estates Are Taxed | Marital Deduction | A
Program of Planned Gifts*

CHAPTER 45 *After Retirement* 473
*Social Security | Annuities | Savings Accounts | U.S. Sav-
ings Bonds | Corporate Bonds | Real Estate | Common
Stocks | Consuming Your Capital | In Conclusion*

PART VII *Speaking the Language of the Bulls and the Bears*

*An extensive glossary of investment, economic, business,
legal, and financial terms of importance to investors.* 489

Index 517

Editor's Note

SUCCESSFUL INVESTING IS an art as well as a science. First, though, before the artistry can be acquired, the science of investing must be mastered. To invest successfully requires time, patience, and a willingness to dig out information. The beginner must learn the fundamentals; the seasoned investors must keep abreast of new developments.

In this book we present basic information on all aspects of investing to acquaint the novice with this fascinating world. For the old hand we delve into the hows and whys of some arcane new and not so new securities. We also demystify a few of the more involved investment strategies. Whether your investment goal is safety, income, or capital growth, you will learn how to invest successfully to attain these goals. We cover in detail how the massive Tax Reform Act of 1986 affects investment and financial planning decisions.

Compiling a book such as this and keeping it current with changes in the investment world and in tax law requires the expertise of many people. We have approached the task on a team basis. The members of the professional staff of Babson-United Investment Advisors who have contributed to this work bring to it a diversity of backgrounds.

In addition to their experience in the field of investments, the contributing authors have impressive credentials. One has a doctorate in economics. Several have master's degrees in business administration. Many are Chartered Financial Analysts, and one is a Certified Financial Planner. Collectively these authors have more than 275 years in the fields of business, investment, finance, and academia.

While we have attempted to avoid material that will become dated, it is virtually impossible for a truly useful reference book to elude this trap. We do not venture opinions on the investment potential of any specific company. References to particular corporations are included for the purposes of illustration and emphasis.

Happy reading . . . and successful investing.

Carolyn M. Finnegan, *Editor*

Charts appearing in this book are from Securities Research Company, a division of Babson-United Investment Advisors.

How to Use This Book

THE EFFECTIVENESS OF a reference book can be nullified if the user can't quickly and easily find the information he or she seeks. Recognizing this, we have provided you with a detailed table of contents and a thorough and extensive index. A quick scan of the table of contents shows you the breadth of the subjects covered in this book. The index pinpoints any references to subjects which interest you.

The book is arranged in broad segments, each containing several chapters. A beginner would be wise to start at Chapter 1 and work his way through to the end. Experienced investors may prefer to use this book as a reference source. The table of contents will help the latter find sections that cover subjects on which they need information. Each chapter and segment leads the reader in a logical sequence to the next.

Here is a synopsis of each of the book's seven sections:

Part I—The Art of Prudent Investing—can best be described as an expression of investment philosophy. David R. Sargent, Chairman of the Investment Committee, Babson-United Investment Advisors, sums up in this section the investment theses that have shaped the company's advice for over sixty years. Buy for the long term. Buy common stocks for capital growth. Buy them for increasing dividend patterns. Select your investments with care, then hold them. Avoid fads. Be content to amass capital slowly—but surely.

Part II—Your Investment Alternatives—describes each of the various securities from which you may choose: stocks, bonds, con-

13

vertibles, Treasuries, municipals, mutual funds, options, commodities, index and financial futures, gold, and real estate. In these chapters we explain how each of these securities works, which investment goals they facilitate, and their advantages and disadvantages.

Part III—How to Make Your Choices—discusses the various investment analysis tools used by professionals. You discover how the various market averages are compiled and in what ways they differ. You can learn how to read charts and economic indicators. Annual reports are dissected for your edification. To select stocks, you should first know something about industry groups. Several chapters are devoted to industries—from smokestack to high tech, from food to water. In addition, we tell you about other sources of investment information.

Part IV—Mastering the Strategies and Tactics—this "how-to" segment shows you when to use options, why people trade commodities, and how to spot special situations. The functions of the exchanges, brokers, and investment bankers are outlined; the various types of buy and sell orders are explained. We also give you five succinct investing rules to follow.

Part V—Taking Care of the Housekeeping—explains how to decide whether you need a discount or a full-service broker. It also tells you what to do if you lose a stock or bond certificate. Dividend reinvestment plans and other periodic investment plans are detailed. The relationship between taxes and your investment program is clarified.

Part VI—Investments and Your Financial Plan—helps you plan for your future financial security. You learn what needs to be done in advance of death to assist survivors. Planning programs for a secure retirement are included. The advantages of employee benefit, IRA, and Keogh plans are detailed, especially in light of the Tax Reform Act of 1986. The hows and whys of annuities are explained. You can learn about several techniques for estate and family financial planning.

Part VII—Speaking the Language of the Bulls and the Bears—is an extensive glossary of investment, economic, business, legal, and financial terms.

PART I

The Art of Prudent Investing

CHAPTER 1

Overview

MOST PEOPLE WANT to remain poor, and do. They deliberately avoid financial prosperity. Think of the number who rent apartments instead of buying houses, for example, when everyone alive today should know that home prices have risen every year since memory begins, except for a brief period during the Depression of the 1930s, and in the early '80s when prices ran through the roof only to be curbed some by soaring mortgage rates.

The mortgaged householder can deduct his interest payments and real estate taxes from his income before taxes, so Uncle Sam is really helping him pay his "rent." The real rent payer pays his share of his landlord's interest and taxes but gets no deduction; the landlord gets it. The landlord gets the profit on the apartment or house as it rises in value. So does the homeowner. What does the rent payer get from a boom in property values? An increase in rent.

Yet millions of people pay rent, by preference. Other millions borrow but once. They take out a mortgage to finance their first home, because there's no other way to get a home, then bear down to pay off that mortgage. "Neither a borrower nor a lender be," advised their mothers, so they push to retire the mortgage early. Think of all the World War II GIs who sacrificed to get rid of their GI mortgages and the 4 percent rate they carried. What do mortgage lenders now demand? Three or four times that amount. Few of us today are likely ever to see a 4 percent mortgage money again.

Lessons Not Learned

Even those who have profited from the post–World War II plunge into real estate have not learned much of a lesson. How many people do you know with two houses, one for living and one for investment? The writer had a friend with a paid-off mortgage and a swollen passbook account. When the house next door came on the market we urged the friend to borrow and buy it for investment. The advantages were easy to see—deductible tax and interest costs, plus depreciation and a steady flow of rental income. Long term there was the virtual assurance of profit through capital gain.

What was the response? A sardonic smile and the cynical remark, "No thanks, and I suppose the next urging from you will be to buy stocks instead." True, that's what we did urge, the point being to buy something, for the road to wealth must in great part be traversed via the ownership of things—real estate, businesses, equities, and the like. The more you buy with bank money the more leverage you have, and the faster the progress can be. But buying things with borrowed money does involve risk, and we'll talk more on that later in this book.

Why don't people buy things? Why do they tend to squirrel money away into "safe" places like the local savings and loan association? Why do they determinedly turn their backs on the chance to make money? Because they are pessimists. They fear the future. They don't believe things will work out. They give everything a negative interpretation. They lack faith. "I would never open a store on that corner." "Convertibles are too dangerous. What if you rolled over?" (How many convertibles have you seen roll over? How many sedans, for that matter?) "Flying scares me." "The weather has been so bad this winter that corporate earnings are sure to suffer—and if this cold weather does break, the floods could be disastrous."

Worry, worry, worry. The Arabs have us by the throat. Inflation is heating up again. Interest rates are sure to rise. Consumer debt is too high. The budget deficit will surely swamp us. Who can afford to buy a house or car at these prices?

There is always something to worry about, and concentrating on such uncertainties or unfavorable possibilities prevents action. People don't make decisions, investments, or money. A pity.

The Power of Positive Thinking

The optimist, statistically a rare bird, has a leg up. He assumes from the start that as America was here when he was born, it probably will be when he dies. If he's wrong in this main assumption, he will lose more important things than his money. He looks around for opportunities. When the dollar is at an all-time high against European currencies, he takes a trip to the Continent and buys a Mercedes while there—a bargain! He doesn't simply mutter darkly, "Foreign trade has had it," and keep his cash in the bank.

Consumers generally do exactly the opposite, which is the very worst thing for them to do. When inflation threatens, they cram their extra money into bank accounts. If the stock market falls, optimists look for bargains while the pessimists are predicting even lower prices. Most people never seem to learn from the turtle that you cannot make any progress unless you stick your neck out.

The optimist can, and often does, go too far. He might expect to get rich quick. He often thinks he can pick stock market winners, and has been known to get so far out on a borrowed-money limb as to be cut off by a falling stock market or interrupted cash flow. Despite experience that tells him there are no wizards on Main Street, he frequently believes there are some on Wall Street.

For you, the key is to think positively. But temper your optimism with prudence. Weigh the possible gains and risks, then go ahead, making haste slowly. That's the road to riches.

People tend to think alike. When times are prosperous,

everyone feels good, usually too good, and lots is done to excess. Too much borrowing, spending, and speculating often bring on a corrective recession of some sort in business, and folks turn to living sensibly. But they feel worse. They don't feel as if they are living sensibly, but more as if they are being forced to live at penurious levels.

Investors felt this way in the early 1980s after the stock market had stumbled along for several years between 800 and 1,000 on the Dow Jones Industrial Average. Despite the steady rise in corporate earnings and dividends, the feeling grew that something serious was the matter. A longtime subscriber wrote us, "I have been with United Business Service for more than twenty years and never before have written to ask a question. Over the years, you at UBS have generally taken the position that in the longer range, investments in sound American companies will provide the best hedge against inflation and the route to happiness and prosperity. Looking backward, you have always cited ample proof in support of your positions, but my question is, looking forward, are we seeing the end of an era, a whole new ball game to which old rules and precedents no longer apply?"

He continued, "Should we all be in gold, or other things that the political sector can't take away from us by destroying their value? Or should we be short in the market, or just hiding in our cellars, waiting for the holocaust? We have to remember that the mighty Roman Empire was not destroyed by the barbarians, as some would have us think; it was destroyed by the politicians and the citizens who no longer fought to preserve their rights."

Beware the Ideologues

As we wrote to him then, "Such fears are fanned by magazine articles which claim among other things that corporate profits are illusory, that if the replacement costs of plant and equipment currently being depreciated were considered in setting up depreciation charges, there would be no corporate profits. This widely discussed canard always appears in inflationary and worrisome times, when the market is low. No one worries about accounting procedures in roaring bull markets."

The last time this fear of replacement costs of plant and equipment surfaced was in the late 1940s as a result of war-induced inflationary surges in price. What actually followed, of course, was one of the biggest jumps in corporate profits ever and an all-time-great bull market which swept the Dow from under 200 in 1949 to more than 500 in 1956.

Or take the article by two professors who write convincingly of the end of the private corporation, the victim of too much government. The SEC, FTC, FDA, EPA, and Justice Department, not to mention a horde of lesser controllers at state and local levels, are regulating business into oblivion, they argue. The authors simply ignore the more than twofold increase in corporate profits and dividends over this last decade of increasing federal, state, and local concern for what business does to and for the nation.

It is amusing, as an aside, to note how often those who deplore any restrictions of the marketplace are those who never themselves took a chance therein. They write off the sad demise of the free enterprise system as they peer out safely from within the tenured walls of academia and non-profit organizations.

In the same league are, of course, the gold and silver bugs. These are essentially ideological in their approach to economics: "Gold has intrinsic value. Silver almost does, too. So switch from depreciating dollars and pounds and hie to the precious metals." The stark fact that such metals are simply commodities and are worth only what the marketplace says they are worth is beyond belief to such ideologues.

Gold was a great hedge against inflation when it was turned loose on the market and soared from $35 to $195 per ounce. It was not when it fell back to $110 or less in the next two and a half years. The yellow metal also did well for holders when it bounced back up again from there to the dizzying height of $875 per ounce in early 1980. Lots of gold buyers were bruised, however, when the metal fell to $500 that spring.

The truth is, the future is always impossible to foresee. Who could have predicted double-digit inflation, the hostage crisis, the surprise attack on Libya, a budget deficit of around $200 billion?

During these unsettled years our big corporations and their shareholders have prospered, a fact that was reflected in the performance of the Dow, which broke into new high ground in early 1985 and then kept rising. This prosperity should continue in the next decade. Meantime, as the following chart shows, stocks have remained historically undervalued. If corporate merger mania is any indication of relative stock values, then stocks must be very cheap indeed!

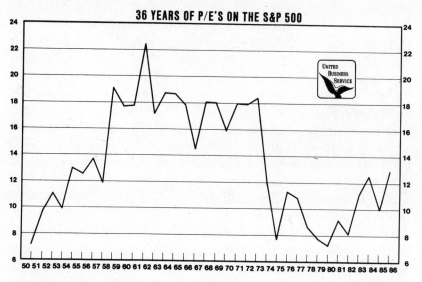

36 YEARS OF P/E'S ON THE S&P 500

Be Positive, Be Patient

The moral is, of course, to think positively (with prudence), and when everyone else is waiting for the future to become obvious, buy the good stocks you see on the bargain counter. But you must be patient, too. Sometimes the stocks you buy will move up rapidly, but more than likely they won't. The time factor is always unknown. Just buy the shares of a company that has a good record and seems to have as good a prospect, and sit with it.

One Wall Street sage once admitted that he'd made more money with the seat of his pants than with his security analysis. In short, buying and holding beats trading over the long term. Below are a couple of true-life examples of what one sensible lady did with her patience and positive thinking.

She bought 100 shares of Dresser Industries in March 1954 for $2,339. This was split two for one twice, giving her a total of 400 shares. She bought another 300 shares in September 1966 for $7,590, and another 200 in March 1974 for $9,950. The total holding was then 900 shares. After she had given away 200 of her lowest-cost shares, her remaining 700 were split two for one, giving her 1,400 shares with a total value of $56,000 as of the end of 1977. Another two-for-one split in 1980 meant 2,800 shares, worth $50,400 at the market's bottom in 1982, and $58,800 three years later when she sold the shares. Her net cost was $18,700.

Her experience with Emerson Electric was even more impressive. She bought 100 shares in December 1949 for $1,200 and another 100 through rights in April 1953, for $1,810. After several stock splits, she had 2,432 shares by early 1987 worth $255,000. Her total cost, $3,010, was substantially less than the annual dividend of $4,864.

She always told us she was too busy running the farm to trade. "I just buy and hold," she said. Too bad more people don't do likewise.

What's in This Book for Me?

The purpose of this book is to acquaint the unacquainted with the path to financial prosperity and to encourage the timid to take a chance. We'll look at all sorts of investment vehicles, as the Wall Street sophisticates call them—stocks, bonds, convertibles, Governments, municipals, mutual funds, etc.—with an eye to showing you what's available, what they're good for, and how to tell which ones are for you.

CHAPTER 2

On Planning Your Investments

MOST PEOPLE ARE, and sadly will forever be, planless. Or, if they have a plan, it will be a one-track route to a passbook account or to the local broker. Few are the savers who sit down and consider first what their dollars should do for them and second, given those needs, what their options are. All too often the savings habit perpetrated on the hapless individual in his prepubertal elementary school years by the local savings institution is simply carried over into adulthood. The Lord's Prayer, the Pledge of Allegiance, and a passbook account are all part of the good clean life.

Life insurance is introduced later to the adult who in money matters really doesn't know much more than he did in the third grade. He succumbs to "You do care for your wife and kids, don't you?" or "This policy will get you to a happy retirement in Florida when both you and it mature and are ready for endless summer."

No one usually comes around to explain the leverage in real estate or the growth potential in common stocks. The nearest the average person gets to the vast, complex, and at times lucrative bond market is a recommendation from the personnel department that he consider a payroll deduction for EE Savings Bonds. The exhortation to buy EE bonds was made even when long-term Treasury bonds could be bought at the local bank around the corner to yield double what EE bonds did.

The truth is, most of those giving such advice don't know much about money or savings and rarely have financial plans of their own. They, too, stumble from one financial misconception to the next. So have a plan. Figure out what you need and what's available, then set up a program that approaches both. This should be a loose, easily adjustable program for the removal from the spending stream of a few dollars, more or less regularly, and the storage of these dollars in places where they should do the most good for all concerned.

Where Should You Save?

Let's look at some of the options casually referred to above. First, the passbook account. Great for the beginning. The interest rate is modest, but you can have the money anytime (with the passbook and proper identification, of course). The savings bank is perfect for the dollar you may need tomorrow or next fall. But for the long pull, forget it.

Inflation takes the joy out of saving. When this writer joined the working world almost four decades ago, the clerical starting wage in Boston was around $22 per week. Today it is over $190 and one could suspect that today's beginner is not much wealthier than yesterday's. Thus, the poor soul who squeezed a dollar out of a meager pay envelope forty years ago for a savings account would be withdrawing a dollar worth 17¢ today. So the savings account, whatever its other blessings are, is no long-term investment.

Neither is insurance, and for the same reason—inflation. Insurance is for protection, whether from the premature demise of the principal breadwinner in the family or the flaming destruction of the family home. So buy it that way, for protection against financial loss and not as an investment, and you'll be OK.

Real estate can be a good investment. Rarely have real estate prices *on average* fallen: The only time in recent memory was in the early 1980s when prices fell back moderately from absurdly inflated levels. Many bankers found themselves holding sour mortgages on property that had dropped in value. However, to make wise individual investments in real estate, you have to know the territory, and for the average person that generally is limited to his own backyard.

Thus, for practical purposes, most of us buy the house we live in, and maybe one in the country, but that's about it, and properly so. We have more about real estate later on in this book, but for now we can probably agree simply that it is not a major investment preoccupation for most of us.

There are other choices for those with miserly inclinations. French peasants buy gold napoleons and bury them in the backyard, a relatively tiresome practice for the average American family that moves every few years. Furthermore, there is no interest income here and an obvious risk of theft in this break-and-enter society of ours. Certainly you have read of the man who kept his packages of tens and twenties in an old stove until a kindly neighbor came in and used the stove to burn the trash.

The small investor can have difficulty with bonds, if only because they tend to come in relatively large dollar amounts. Bond dealers prefer to work with $25,000 units and really jack up the price when you talk about anything under $10,000. But the larger investor should review the opportunities in the bond market, particularly when income is of paramount concern.

We'll deal in depth with all sorts of bonds—corporate, government, municipal, convertible, deep-discount—later in this book, but for now we'll treat them generally as one savings option. Bonds are a loan by you to the issuer. That issuer agrees to pay you a fixed rate of interest and to give you your money back on a certain future date.

This means that a bond has much the same weakness as a savings bank account. It leaves you vulnerable to the ravages of inflation. The dollar you get back is nowhere near as good as the one you originally lent or deposited. It won't buy as much. A good bond will usually give you a better return than the savings account, but the bond will move up and down as interest rates fluctuate. So the savings account and a quality bond are at about a standoff with one another and, because of their vulnerability to inflation, not particularly attractive for very much of your long-term savings dollars.

Why You Can't Ignore Stocks

Short of diamonds, art, or some other esoteric storehouse of value, there's not much left in the way of choices for the saver but common stocks. Lots of people stay away from common stocks because they always go up and down in value, sometimes with alarming speed. Stocks can also at times fall to zero and disappear, a most disheartening experience for the holder.

All of us have heard of people who "lost everything" in the great stock market crash of 1929. Few of us hear of the good solid investment gains enjoyed by thousands upon thousands of sensible buyers of good common stocks. Like a happy family life, a good investment experience does not make prime-time TV.

So we tend to hear the horror stories of stock ownership, and, unless educated to the contrary, we stay away from common stocks. It is a shame, for the investment in common stocks is about the only way most savers can hope to offset inflation. Sometimes stocks do not rise enough to match the loss in purchasing power of the dollar, and sometimes in a roaring bull market stock values soar far ahead of the inflation rate.

Stocks were a marvelous inflation hedge during much of the 1950s and 1960s, when the market rose impressively and inflation ran at a modest 2 to 3 percent annual rate. Any long-term chart of the Dow Jones will show that. Any chart will also show that the market did not do so well versus inflation in the 1970s. For a number of years the Dow Jones Industrial Average ranged along between 800 and 1,000, taking stockholders nowhere, while the rate of inflation ran at 6 percent or better. (In 1974, the inflation rate soared to 11 percent and in early 1980 nearly doubled that pace as it hit 18 percent.)

But what most stock-fearing savers fail to realize is that there is more to owning stock than profits or losses. There is dividend income, which tends to rise yearly. Back in 1977 our *United Business and Investment Report,* which is now the *United & Babson Investment Report,* carried the following editorial to illustrate that point, and it bears repeating here:

According to the 1976 economic figures, all we lost last year [to the ravages of inflation] out of our dollar saved was about a nickel. The consumer price index rose but 4.8%.

This compares well with the more than 9% experience in 1975 and seems but a trifling amount when compared to the whopping "double-digit" rate of 1974. But even 4.8% goes a long way toward obliterating the savings bank return on a dollar saved, and it also puts a big hole in the 8.5% return available on an A-rated bond.

	Dividends	
	Then	Now
American Electric Power	$2.00	$2.10
American Tel. & Tel.	3.40	4.20
Exxon Corp.	2.65	3.00
Middle South Utilities	1.26	1.38
Mountain States Telephone	1.52	1.88
Tenneco Inc.	1.76	1.88
U.S. Fidelity & Guaranty	2.48	2.64
Washington Water Power	1.56	1.76

Inflation doesn't do any particular favors for common stock dividends either, but it can be offset by dividend increases. Just by way of illustration, consider the experience of the portfolio recommended [in 1975, as shown in the table].

Each company increased the dividend—some by just a little, but the overall rise was 13.3%, nearly three times the rate of inflation. And these increases are not the last to expect, for these companies characteristically boost dividend rates frequently.

Exxon and American Telephone have increased their rates seven times in the past decade while American Electric Power and Middle South can claim ten. Washington Water Power is the champ in this group with twelve boosts in ten years.

The moral is clear. Even if the Dow has trouble clearing 1000, rising dividend payments will take much of the sting out of inflation.*

Stock Values Go Up and Up

Another thing folks tend to overlook is that the intrinsic values behind good stocks go up along with dividends. As

* *United Business and Investment Report,* February 22, 1977.

the economy of this country grows, so do the sales and earnings of our leading corporations. Gross national product, for instance, amounted to $233 billion in 1947. Forty years later, the figure was $4.4 trillion. Part of this impressive change was inflation, of course, but part also represented incredible industrial growth and a huge surge in the standard of living.

Naturally, business participated in this growth. Some would even claim that business created this materialist surge. In any event, stockholders participated in it, while savings bank depositors did not. Emerson Electric, for example, reported revenues of $23 million and net income of $1.4 million in 1947, versus revenues of $4,953 and net of $409 million for the year ended September 30, 1986. Small wonder that the stock sold at less than $1 (adjusted for all splits) a share then compared with $85 at the end of 1986. Yet the stock is selling at a reasonable multiple of under 17 times earnings.

Other companies have fared as well or better. Consider this random sample of the performance of some well-known blue chips over the last ten years. Note how values rose for these companies. Yet, in some cases, stock prices have not increased commensurately with the gains in revenues and profits.

	Revenues*		Earnings†		Stock Price‡	
	1976	1986	1976	1986	1976	1986
Abbott Labs	$1,085	$ 3,800	$0.41	$2.32	6	47
Anheuser-Busch	1,441	7,677	0.21	1.69	4	26
DuPont, E.I.	8,361	27,148	3.10	6.24	44	86
Merck & Company	1,661	4,129	1.69	4.85	32	124
Minnesota Mining	3,514	8,602	2.94	6.80	57	118
Procter & Gamble	6,513§	15,439§	2.43§	4.20§	47	79

* Millions of dollars.
† Per share adjusted for all stock dividends and splits and fully diluted.
‡ Stock prices at year end.
§ Year ended 6/30.

Of course, having determined that common stocks represent your best long-term investment savings option, you shouldn't just trot down to your corner broker and start investing in stocks. You can, to be sure, but you shouldn't. You need a plan that accommodates such variables as your income, your family responsibilities, your housing needs, reasonable insurance protection, short-term spending protection (savings accounts), and long-term investment objectives (college, retirement, etc.).

Rough these figures out and you'll have an idea of what part of your spending stream is savable, and how much of that you will likely have available for the purchase of common stocks over the years ahead.

CHAPTER 3

Investment Risks—
Defined and Contained

"I ABHOR RISK," wrote the senior legal type for a large life insurance company. "I want to know that a dollar saved today will be around tomorrow and the day after that." So his savings plan was strict and sober—straight life, paid-up annuities, and, of course, plenty in the local savings bank. "No use putting all your eggs in one basket." That is the picture of the supercautious saver.

His pattern and program of saving might be OK if his circumstances were acutely straitened. Let's suppose a man has a limited amount saved and limited life expectancy, plus a large and young family. Under such circumstances, there is little hope of recouping any dollars lost. His needs will be large and long-term, while his source of income is likely to be near-term. Obviously, such a fellow would have to play his investment savings cards close to his chest.

But if he is not in such dire straits, he would be foolish to stay so close to the ground. A small flight, so to speak, into common stocks would give him some hope of protection from inflation. Put another way, where savings are concerned, there's always an element of risk. Money in common stocks can swell or shrink as the market rises and falls. Money in bonds can do much the same as interest rates wax and wane. Money in the local savings and loan association can shrink in value as inflation pushes up the cost of living.

31

If risk is inevitable, it is worth studying. What sorts of risks are there, how should they be offset, how much can you take in the way of chance, what is tolerable and intolerable as far as a risk is concerned, and is one man's risk another man's opportunity? In this chapter we will run through some of the typical risks all of us face today. Then we will show you some ways to balance them. We'll also try to show you how to recognize your risks and opportunities and, more important, how to determine just how much risk you can and should assume.

The Inflation Risk

First, what sorts of risks are there? The biggest risk to anyone, of course, is his own mortality. This the intelligent soul tries to keep under reasonable control with moderate living habits, good medical care, and, if he's inclined, prayer. But financial risks are more complicated. Savers are perpetually on the horns of this dilemma. If they buy securities, the market for them may go down, and their savings will shrink. If they don't buy securities, if they just hold on to their dollars, they'll stand a good chance of seeing those dollars shrink in purchasing power, if not in numbers. Outside of your own perishability, inflation is likely to be the major threat to your security and to that of every other denizen of the Western world.

Inflation is *the* enemy. It is the biggest and surest risk most of us ever face, for no currency in the financial history of mankind has failed to lose purchasing power over the years, sometimes at a furious rate, as in Germany right after World War I, and at other times quite sedately, as in the early 1950s in this country, when the dollar lost only about 2 percent of its value annually to higher prices. In fact, during that period the late Professor Sumner Schlicter of Harvard Business School argued for more inflation as an economic stimulant and a producer of a faster rise in the standard of living.

It is doubtful if even Dr. Schlicter would have liked the raging inflationary pace of the post–Vietnam War era, when the nation struggled with price inflation rates of 7 to 13 percent. It is equally doubtful that we'll ever again get back to the Eisenhower era's 2 percent, which became so dull to some. Even partway back, to an annual 4 to 5 percent rate, means some real problems.

The table here shows what a 5 percent rate will do over forty-five years, the working lifetime of the average man or woman.

	Start*	After 45 Years
Bread	$ 1.25	$ 11.23
Round steak	2.45	22.01
5 lbs. potatoes	1.30	11.69
Butter	1.90	17.07
4 rolls toilet paper	1.20	10.78
Suit	225.00	2021.63
Dress	90.00	808.65
House	88,500.00	795,173.00
Chevette	6,900.00	61,996.55
Gas, unleaded	1.22	10.96

* Boston prices in 1986.

To keep pace with this, a $5 hourly wage would become $44.93 after forty-five years. Clearly, investments that did not have a chance to move along too would be disastrous.

The Interest-Rate Risk

Though inflation is the major risk, there are other, usually smaller, risks in setting out to defeat or even partially offset that primary threat. Prices of stocks and bonds fluctuate, for example, and when they fall below your purchase price, the loss seems real even though it is only on paper. Some people can't take such losses, even temporary ones, on paper. Our "I abhor risk" friend is one. Others can, and thus they are able to use stocks and bonds to beat inflation.

Let's take a look at the risk in bonds. First, a bond is simply a certificate which represents a loan you have made to a company, say General Motors, or to the United States government, a state, or a city. One obvious risk is that the borrower might not pay you back. This is unlikely, given the nature of the borrowing organizations suggested above, and has happened infrequently in modern times. Furthermore, bonds are rated. So you have a good idea before you buy one how much chance there is of anything occurring like default—failure to repay principal or interest.

The real risk in a bond is a rise in interest rates. Bonds are issued initially at a fixed rate of interest. But from there on—until they are close to maturity—they trade at a price where the current yield is equal to that of the bond market generally. General Motors Acceptance Corporation 9⅝'s of 1989 will sell at 100 if interest rates generally are running close to the 9⅝ percent coupon rate (or the $96.25 annual interest payment on the $1,000 face value bonds). But if rates rise to 12 percent generally, the bond price will fall to around 92⅝ ($926), so the $96.25 payment will represent a 9 percent yield to maturity for a new investor adding such a bond to his portfolio. Conversely, if interest rates should fall to 7 percent, the GMAC 9⅝'s would rise to 109 ($1,090) or thereabouts, the increase needed to make the $96.25 interest payment produce a yield to maturity of 7 percent.

Since the prospect of profit is not a very scary one, we'll concentrate on the risk of loss of principal due to rising interest rates. This risk can be greatly reduced by keeping the maturity of the bond you buy short. For example, the GMAC bond discussed above matures in 1989 and was a ten-year bond at issue. This means you get the bond's face value back in a few short years, regardless of where interest rates are then. Thus, if interest rates are up between the time you buy and the time the bond matures you can simply ignore the paper loss, knowing that when the maturity date comes you will get your money back.

The other risk in bonds is that inflation protection is small. You "lend" 100-cent dollars and get back maybe 80-cent or 90-cent dollars when the bond matures, depending on the degree to which inflation has eaten away at the dollar's purchasing power during the years you held the bond. A portion of this loss, to be sure, is offset by the coupon, because the interest rate offered on a bond reflects in part the general level of inflation. We'll have much more on bonds later in this book, so we can end here by simply stating that the risks in bonds—default, premature call, rising interest rates, and inflation—are by no means intolerable.

The Market Risk

Everyone knows that the risk in common stocks can be enormous. We have already noted how the stock market crash of 1929 beggared many investors overnight. In fact, most people think the risk in stocks is so great that buying stocks is just like betting on horses. They believe that savers go to the bank and gamblers to the stock market. While nearly everyone is familiar with the 1929 experience, how many of them know that thousands of investors who held common stocks in 1929 still held them in 1939 and were doing very well indeed?

That is because good stocks—the shares of our leading corporations, like Abbott Labs, General Electric, Emerson Electric, etc.—go down in a bad market, but not out. When investment sentiment, the business cycle, or whatever improves, good stocks come back. So the little old lady in Boston's Back Bay who held American Telephone, United Fruit, United Shoe, General Electric, and the like in 1929 was doing all right in 1939. Her shares had come back in price, and in most cases her dividends were better.

If the big risk in stocks is a rising and falling market, it can largely be offset by long-term holding. Don't worry when the market goes down. It will eventually come back, and your good stocks will come with it. A second risk in stocks is the soundness of the companies they represent.

A national figure once made the unfortunate comment, "If you've seen one slum you've seen them all." You will be no more correct if you consider one stock to be just like another. Stocks vary widely in appeal, popularity, price stability, and dividend characteristics, as well as in risk and reward. Before entering the stock market with your dollar saved, you should review these differences carefully, for on Wall Street what's good for the goose isn't necessarily good for the gander.

How Much Risk for You?

Which brings us to you and your risk-taking ability. We touched on this earlier in this chapter. If the money you save is small in amount and your needs pressing and near-term, you have to be a lot more careful than if you are in the opposite and more enviable position. If you barely have your son's tuition in hand and the bill is due in six months, you don't put the money in *any* common stock, not even a blue chip. Who knows what surprise could come around the corner to upset the stock market, albeit temporarily, and leave your tuition fund badly dented?

On the other hand, if you have your son's tuition in hand and he's only seven years old, you would be foolish not to buy some Exxon or GE with it. By the time he gets to college, it could be two or three times as big (so also the tuition bill). Better yet, you may have saved even more, so you can let your GE or Exxon stock ride to even higher long-term levels.

In the final analysis, the amount of risk you take depends on you and your circumstances. The richer, younger, and less depended upon by others can take bigger chances than the poorer, older, and more leaned on, obviously. The commission salesman should save more carefully than the tenured academician. The fellow with six kids has to play it safer than the man with none and a working wife.

Put another way, invest in stocks only that money you do not expect to need in the foreseeable future. Start with the shares of the best companies, picking those that represent the fastest-growing areas of the economy, rather than the clearly more mature industries—health care rather than autos, for instance.

Spreading Your Risks

By all means, diversify. This means spreading your money over a number of different companies and industries. You never get rich quickly this way, for one stock will sag when another soars. Neither will you go broke, for the same obvious reason. A Wall Street tycoon once said the way to make money was to put all of your eggs in one basket and then to "watch the basket like hell." Well, maybe it worked for him, but for the rest of us diversification is a must.

It makes saving more fun, too. To hold the shares of a number of companies is entertaining. It makes you feel like part of the big world. You can stick out your chest when "your" company comes up with a promising method for treating cancer, and can shrink in shame when your company is caught dumping chemical wastes. Owning stocks puts you right out there in big business with the millionaires, tycoons, and corporate brass who make things happen.

There are other risks within the stock market beyond that of price or rising and falling markets. There is the risk of obsolescence—of corporate management or products. Things go out of style. Video games did that in the early 1980s. Or conditions change to make a product less attractive to the buying public. This happened to recreational vehicles when the Arabs quadrupled the price of oil. The private auto put street railways and many railroads out of business. There are things we consider commonplace today which will be uncommonly unnecessary tomorrow.

There is risk in too much of a good thing. The first discount stores were highly successful. Soon they became chains, then more chains. After a while there were too many of them and lots went under. If an industry appears to be "the rage," stay away. Political shifts can add risk, too. Think twice before investing in a company doing business abroad. It's one thing to make pharmaceuticals in England, France, or Germany. It's quite another to mine copper in Peru, drill oil in Indonesia, or refine chrome in Zimbabwe.

Politicians are important at home, too. Electric utilities know this all too well. All of them have to appeal to various governmental agencies for rate increases. The company with a friendly regulatory climate is usually a much better investment than one in the opposite situation. Similarly, think twice before investing in an industry whose product runs counter to national policy. Producers of nuclear generators, asbestos, and some chemicals have suffered as a result of this in recent years. Lastly, remember, politicians have an unnerving way of reversing themselves, to the endless discomfort of some companies and their shareholders.

No discussion of risk is complete without an avuncular admonition to common stock buyers that life itself, as well as the stock market, is risky. Just as you adjust to the adverse mortal possibilities as you live out your three score and ten, you have to adjust to the risks inherent in stock ownership. Don't worry about a sharp drop in the Dow. Don't be rattled by the television anchorman's sonorous announcement on the evening news that "stocks fell sharply today on Wall Street."

Just remember that if you buy the "best," stay reasonably diversified, and hold for the long pull, you are bound to win. The country is growing, the economy is expanding, and our leading companies are going right along, too. So also will their shareholders, with ever-rising dividend income and stock prices.

CHAPTER 4

Building Your Portfolio

THERE ARE TWO ways to build your portfolio—all at once or gradually. Most of us have to use the latter method as we painfully extract a few dollars at irregular intervals from our family's spending stream. Those who get to do it all at once are usually widows who are the beneficiaries of their husbands' insurance policies.

Investing Defensively

We'll show you how to do it both ways in this chapter. We'll also show how people with different circumstances can meet those varied circumstances with differing investment portfolios. Let's start with a "for instance." A woman came to us in 1948 as a middle-aged widow whose children were grown and gone. She was housemother at a local college (no coed dorms in those days) and had, therefore, "free" board and room and little need for her modest salary. Neither did she have much in the way of assets. So she had to be careful with her savings and yet could buy stocks because she appeared likely to have no immediate need for the dollars she could save. We told her to buy a stock each time she had saved $500 or $1,000, and gave her suggestions of very good companies in relatively "defensive" industries. Until she retired in 1958, she followed our plan.

By "defensive" we mean rather steady businesses which are relatively unaffected by the ups and downs of the business cycle. A good example of this is a telephone company. People seem to use the telephone in good times and bad. Revenues for the industry never go down, and when their costs go up and threaten earnings, the companies simply seek —and almost always get—rate relief. So their earnings records are excellent and their dividends secure.

Ma Bell, for example, was famous during the depressed 1930s for paying her $9 dividend each year while many companies were falling by the wayside. In recent years she has done even better by shareholders, with regular dividend boosts until the divestiture in 1983. Even the split-up was a boon for Telephone investors. Rochester Telephone has boosted its rate yearly over the last dozen years. Another good record is that of Centel Corporation, whose dividend rate in 1985 was 112 percent above the 1975 level. Such increases take care of a lot of inflation.

Other defensive industries include the big retail chains (Federated Department Stores), small loan companies (Beneficial), food suppliers (CPC International), household products (Colgate, Procter & Gamble), banks, and, believe it or not, tobacco companies. These are industries whose products are in relatively steady demand. You rarely cut toothpaste purchases because times are tough, and, as the record shows, smokers smoke no matter what. This group is further favored by the steady rise in population and average hourly income. This means there is a yearly gain in the number of dollars flowing their way.

Then there is always the neighborhood power company. These are in much the same position as the telephone people. Revenues rise regularly along with rates, and sufficiently faster than costs to permit almost annual dividend increases. So we urged our widow to buy some of the more interesting electric utility issues, those of companies serving the more rapidly growing sections of the country.

After a decade her portfolio, into which she had put about $13,000, contained these companies:

Company	1948 Value	1958 Value	1981 Value	33-Year Gain (%)
American Cyanamid	$ 1,560	$ 8,259	$ 9,234	+ 491.9
American Tel. & Tel.	1,650	2,475	3,765	+ 128.2
Beneficial Industrial Loan	1,817	6,081	7,607	+ 318.7
Federated Dept. Stores	700	3,330	9,720	+1,288.6
General Motors	1,180	5,940	5,050	+ 328.0
Lowenstein & Sons	440	791	1,166	+ 165.0
National Lead	1,020	10,281	11,595	+1,036.8
Northern States Power	1,044	2,552	3,096	+ 196.6
Phillips Petroleum	580	1,930	5,917	+ 920.2
Tennesee Gas Trans.	1,584	7,078	9,521	+ 501.1
Texas Utilities	1,040	5,219	6,654	+ 539.8
Yale & Towne	550	2,023	11,865	+2,057.3
TOTALS	$12,585	$55,959	$85,190	+ 576.9

She already had a decent capital gain on these securities in 1958, and an even more impressive one by 1981, when her estate was evaluated after her death. Stock dividends and splits played a big part in the growth of her portfolio. In fact, only one of her holdings failed to split its share in those thirty-three years. Over the years, too, her dividend income kept pace, increasing 533 percent from $907 in 1948 to $5,739 in 1981. Interestingly enough, the yield on the total portfolio backed off slightly to 7 percent from 7.2 percent in 1948. Only when bond yields got up to 9 percent and 10 percent and her eightieth birthday passed did she capitulate to anything of a fixed-income nature. Incidentally, Beneficial Industrial Loan is now Beneficial Corporation, Tennessee Gas is Tenneco, National Lead is NL Industries, Lowenstein & Sons is M. Lowenstein Corporation, and Yale & Towne is Eaton Corporation.

Investing Bit by Bit

Here's another "for instance," from a California woman who really had it made, financially anyway. She wrote to us:

I do not know much about the stock market but it has always fascinated me and I want to get into it. This is my situation.

I am female, 52 years of age (but I look 45), working for the State of California at $1,000 a month. I hope to retire in ten years if not before.

I have no properties and rent for $200 per month. My expenses are nil. I can live on $400 per month because I am single and have men friends who pay for all entertainment and most of my meals. My auto is paid for. I can live on the balance of my paycheck after all deductions are made plus income from a note.

I am deferring $700 a month on the State deferred income plan which is deposited with the Great Western Savings & Loan. The State also offers the T. Rowe Price Growth Stock, Inc., and Price New Income Fund, Inc. According to your reports these are excellent mutual funds. Would you advise me to diversify and take some of that $700 and invest it in Rowe?

I also have a $10,000 note out which pays 10% annually and can be recovered at any time. I would like to invest this money also.

I have $3,000 in savings for emergencies. I have good medical coverage through the State.

I am sure there are a lot of other gals like me who need guidance on how to invest their incomes so they will be able to be independent in their later years. Any advice you can give me would be appreciated.

Obviously, here is someone who should buy stocks. Her savings program is impressive, yet it offers no protection against inflation. The $700 per month deferred income could shrink substantially in purchasing power by her sixty-second birthday. So would the note she had out. So we told her to switch her monthly savings to the T. Rowe Price Growth Stock Fund, a no-load mutual fund with a broadly diversified list of leading common stocks in the underlying portfolio.

Because the fund was huge, $900 million under management at the time, we told her it would probably continue to bump along about with the market, no great shakes maybe, but lots better than Great Western Savings & Loan could offer. Then we suggested that as additional cash became available for investment, she should buy a few stocks of her own. She would, in effect, be building her own mutual fund.

We further pointed out that she didn't have to be too conservative in her stock selections, because her current money needs were slight. After all, think of all the free meals she could boast of. So the list we sent along to this woman was not quite as somber as the one to our housemother friend. Here it is:

Abbott Laboratories	Minnesota Mining (3M)
American Express	Schlumberger Ltd.
Anheuser-Busch	Unisys

"Start with the A's and buy them alphabetically, or in any other order that pleases," said we, "for they are all good long-term growth stocks. Abbott Labs is big in health care, an industry that prospers in good times and bad. American Express and Anheuser must be familiar to you. Burroughs [now Unisys] is computers; 3M is tapes, adhesives, graphic systems, abrasives, and the like. Schlumberger is huge in oil field services and is a growing factor in electronics as well."

We never learned whether our "youthful" correspondent did what we suggested, but we certainly hope so. That is one of the drawbacks to life as an investment advisor. Folks generally never tell you whether they have followed your advice or not, unless of course it didn't work out very well. As elsewhere in the human condition, nothing flies as fast as word to the advisor that his advice has caused losses. (John Milton put it better: "For evil news rides post, while good news baits.")

Investing to Preserve Capital

In another instance, a widow came to us with a $50,000 insurance check, a $10,000 passbook account, and about $7,500 in common stocks, one of which was a no-income highly leveraged fund managed by Scudder. She was in her fifties, which meant a life expectancy of another twenty-five years or so, had her own mortgage-free home, and had no job. Her situation was a great deal different from the California woman's discussed above.

For one thing, she had no men friends to buy her meals. With no job, neither did she have the many attendant fringes that employment usually involves. She needed eating money now and could take few chances. So we told her to split her investment funds in two, putting half in bonds and half in stocks. This program would offer more income now, of course, for the average high-grade bond yield in these inflationary times runs nearly twice that of common stocks. The trade-off, quite obviously, is that the portfolio half in bonds offers the holder only half as much protection against inflation as the all-stock program.

We will not go into the bond solutions required, except to say we kept the maturities fairly short, ten to twelve years. As for stocks, we split again about evenly between growth and income issues. Our widow's current income needs were just too pressing to allow as much emphasis on long-term growth as we would have liked.

Of the stocks she received from her husband's estate—Tenneco, Unisys, Georgia-Pacific, American Telephone, and Scudder Duo-Vest—we sold only the fund, because it was oriented toward capital gains and offered no income. Clearly it was not for her. Tenneco and Telephone would give her good income, and the other two, good long-term growth possibilities. We added to Tenneco and Telephone and bought other issues to the tune of $28,000, with about the same amount in bonds. The excess over the $50,000 insurance check came out of the savings account. We thought $4,000–$5,000 in savings ample for an emergency fund.

When all was said and done our widow's portfolio looked like this:

No. Shares	Cost	Value	Dividend	Yield
100 American Natural Resources	41	$ 4,100	$ 264	6.4%
40 American Tel. & Tel.	60	2,400	152	6.3
200 Bank of America	24	4,800	160	3.3
100 Georgia-Pacific	33	3,300	80	2.4
200 Koppers	23	4,600	180	3.9
200 Louisiana Land & Exploration	28	5,600	240	4.3
100 Tenneco	34	3,400	188	5.5
200 Texaco	27	5,400	400	7.4
20 Unisys	90	1,800	14	0.8
		$35,400	$1,678	4.7%
5 high-grade bonds		$27,000	$2,295	8.5%
savings account		$ 4,500	$ 225	5.0%
Totals		$66,900	$4,198	6.3%

You can see here how the bonds "sweetened" the income. You can see also how we stuck to big-name issues and balanced between income and growth potential. It's obvious why we sold the Scudder and why we did not buy more of Unisys. It is probably also easy to justify our reduction in the savings account in light of the large investment in high-grade bonds, which are almost as easily available if a financial pinch develops.

There Are Men, Too

Men invest too, of course, and some of them have the same opportunities and restrictions as the women we have used as examples. Others are in a different environment and can take real chances in the hopes of big gains. Income they have in surplus; dividends they do not need. A high-income small-town family attorney came to us over a period of years, and after a while he had this list of stocks:

Abbott Labs	Georgia-Pacific
American Home Products	Heinz, H.J.
Burlington Northern	MAPCO Inc.
Caterpillar Tractor	Mesa Petroleum
Dayton Hudson	PepsiCo Inc.
EG&G, Inc.	Questar Corp.
Eastman Kodak	Westinghouse Electric
General Cinema	

A review of these names will show some to be solid blue chips (Abbott Labs, American Home Products, Heinz), some to be chancy (Caterpillar, Georgia-Pacific), and some to be in the middle (Burlington Northern, General Cinema). Although the dividends on these shares went up over the years, the average yearly percentage return never ran much over 3 percent.

Some of the blue chips gave our man grief, too, at times. Probably his biggest heartbreaker was Eastman Kodak, which he bought at 60 and saw soar to double his cost and then plunge to less than 30, before moving up again. But on the average his well-diversified portfolio did what he wanted it to do—produce capital gains and minimum income.

Don't Marry Your Stocks

The last pearls of wisdom we have to offer on building your portfolio are on how to watch it after it is built. Even though you subscribe to the "buy good stocks and hold them long term" philosophy of investment, there are times when stocks should be sold. You do not do so when you think the market in general will go down, but you do when there is evidence that a company's position is deteriorating, its market is shrinking, its products are becoming obsolete, or some other demonstrably unfavorable situation is developing.

Let's try an example. Suppose you had owned an oil service company such as Halliburton back in 1980, when it looked like the sky was the limit. Yet these stocks peaked by the end of that year and have trended lower ever since. Suddenly there was an oil glut—supply had outdistanced demand. A number of factors were involved—energy conservation efforts, conversion to alternative fuels, a world-wide economic slump, and confusion among OPEC members. Would you have been astute enough to foresee that this was no temporary aberration but the start of a long-term downtrend?

While the oil drillers and service companies faltered, others prospered from the weakness in oil prices. Industries that were heavy energy consumers—the airlines, utilities, and certain chemicals—profited from lower operating expenditures. Again, it doesn't take genius to see such shifts. Often the changes are much subtler and harder to see, but when you see them it is wise to move.

Adjust for Your Changing Needs

Another cause for switching is when a stock no longer fills your financial bill. While our lawyer friend is a big earner, it is fine for him to hold low-yield stocks. But what about the same fellow in retirement? Taking chances on stocks when you are young is one thing; it's quite another in those golden years. As your need for safety and income increases, you gradually switch from the Mesa Petroleums to the Tennecos. It is only good sense to do so.

Keep Good Records

Last, it is imperative to keep records. There are all sorts of record-keeping books available, and it is easy to log the number of shares you have and what you paid for them. There is a place to put down the dividend payment dates, amount paid, etc. The tough thing is to make yourself do it. But without such records you are at the mercy of the company's computer as far as your dividends are concerned—and at the mercy of the Internal Revenue Service when you sell.

To sum up, building your own portfolio is easy, it can be fun, and it certainly will be rewarding. First, figure out who you are, financially speaking, then put together a list of securities that brew up into your cup of tea. After that, ride with your portfolio long term, making changes only as they appear necessary. It is a great way to financial independence.

PART II

Your Investment Alternatives

CHAPTER 5

Equity Investments: "A Piece of the Action"

IF EVER THERE was an affordable and convenient way for most of us to participate directly in the free enterprise system, it is through the acquisition and holding of common stocks. Your single share of General Motors represents an actual ownership stake in that industrial behemoth. As even a most fractional owner, you enjoy certain rights—and you assume certain risks. We'll get into those rights and risks in this chapter as we explore the pros and cons of investment in common stocks. We'll also introduce you to ways other than common stock ownership that allow you to establish equity positions in a company: preferred stock, convertibles, warrants, rights, and put and call options.

The Concept of Ownership

Let's expand a bit on the ownership concept, zeroing in first on common stocks. Your share of common stock represents something of intrinsic value, a piece of equity in the company. As that intrinsic value rises and falls, so does the worth of your investment. You have committed a portion of your wealth to the fortunes of the company. If you have chosen the company wisely—or fortuitously—each dollar in-

51

vested has the potential of rising exponentially in value as the company prospers. You are not merely being paid for the privilege of letting the company borrow your dollars.

Because your investment is in something of intrinsic value, you have in effect untied it from monetary value. When you convert it back to monetary value by selling it, you will get what it is intrinsically worth in current dollars—or at least what a buyer perceives as its worth. This is completely without regard to what it was worth in dollars when you acquired it. If the company has been growing as fast as the economy in general, or faster, the intrinsic value likewise will have grown. The dollars you receive when you sell will have buying power equal to or greater than that of the dollars you used to purchase the investment.

Contrast that with the situation when you merely lend your dollars to the company via purchase of a corporate bond. In effect, when you redeem your "loan," you get the same number of dollars back. In the meantime the buying power of those dollars may have shrunk, leaving you with less valuable dollars.

It is important that you have a firm grasp of the equity concept and comprehend the difference between being an owner and being a lender in order to understand the value of common stocks as a hedge against inflation. By being an owner, you tie your investment more closely to ongoing economic conditions, whereas by being a lender you keep your dollar tied to a post sunk into the ground on the day you made the loan. The latter can go only as far as its short leash allows.

It is also important that you understand the risk-reward differences between ownership and lending. As an owner, just as you stand to gain when the business prospers, you stand to lose your stake if it should collapse. You are also at the mercy of the market when you sell your equity, for, in the final analysis, it is worth what the market says it is worth, regardless of its intrinsic value.

As a lender, your assets are protected against such loss (unless, of course, the business fails completely and defaults on the loan), but you replace that risk with the risk that the worth of your dollar and what it earns will not keep pace with rising prices.

Common Stocks: Rights and Risks

A corporation offers shares of its common stock to the public as a means of raising capital. If it is a company's initial offering, or if it is an offering of previously unissued shares, it is called a primary issue. Shares which are outstanding and offered in a block by one or more holders are referred to as secondary offerings; proceeds of these do not accrue to the company. In return for your investment, you receive a stock certificate that along with providing evidence of ownership has other legal characteristics. The certificate contains a serial number, the name of the registrar or transfer agent, and the par or stated value of the stock. It should be noted here that in the case of common stocks, par value has little, if any, relationship to the market value of the stock. The certificate also informs you that as a shareholder you have no financial obligation to the corporation. This means that should some corporate liability arise, that liability would not extend to you.

Along with certain legal protection, you enjoy various rights as a shareholder. First, unless you hold stock that is specifically designated as nonvoting, you have voting rights, meaning you are entitled to vote on such things as the selection of an accounting firm and merger proposals. Most of these matters are dealt with at a company's annual meeting. Since you could own shares in dozens of corporations, you could spend a good part of your time attending such meetings. As this is usually neither possible nor desirable, when an important matter is to be voted, a corporation distributes a proxy statement to its shareholders. This is a legal document which permits you to choose someone (a proxy) to vote for you. It is usually mailed to the stockholder, along with information pertaining to the particular matters to be voted on. A card is included where you can indicate your preference in the matter at hand.

As a shareholder you are also entitled to receive dividends on a pro rata basis. A corporation is not legally obligated to pay a dividend on its common stock, but when the directors declare a dividend, every shareholder receives an equal amount per share of the stock.

Also, as a stockholder you retain the right to protect your proportionate interest in the corporation. For instance, if you own 100 shares of a company which at some point, say, decides to increase the amount of its outstanding stock by 15 percent, you have a preemptive right to purchase 15 additional shares. If you decide to exercise this right, your initial proportionate share of ownership in the corporation has not been reduced despite the increase in the number of shares outstanding. Those rights, by the way, have a value of their own; should you choose not to exercise them, you can sell them to someone else. This usually must be done within a certain time or the rights expire. More on rights and their cousins, warrants, later.

Finally, although you have no legal financial obligation to the corporation, in cases of bankruptcy or liquidation the corporation has an obligation to its common stockholders. In such cases, the corporation's first responsibility is to its creditors—to those who have lent it money. After they have been paid, the holders of preferred stock are entitled to the par or stated value of their shares; that's one reason it is called "preferred" stock. If anything remains, it is then divided among the common stockholders on a pro rata basis.

Picking the Right Stocks

OK, you ask, now that I know what a common stock is, how do I go about choosing from among the thousands of stocks available? How do I determine in which corporations I want to own shares?

The answer is the key to successful investing—choosing stocks that meet your individual investment needs. It is not an altogether simple task, as any professional analyst, portfolio manager, or investment advisor will tell you. However, in the case of common stocks, understanding a few basic characteristics can be beneficial in helping you make your investment decisions.

First, you should know that the two most important aspects of a common stock's value are quality and earnings. Determining the quality of a common stock is more difficult than determining the quality of, say, a bond. But a common stock is usually graded on the basis of the corporation's historical earnings performance as well as its future earnings outlook. Has it shown healthy growth in the past? Have earnings been stable? What are its prospects in the years ahead? The stock's performance in the market is an important criterion, too. Does its price tend to remain relatively stable or does it tend to be volatile?

Watch Dividend Performance

Of more than passing interest to the common stockholder, naturally, is the company's performance on dividends. As we said earlier, a corporation is not legally required to pay dividends on its common stock. However, since the regular payment of a dividend increases the attractiveness of its stock, a corporation tries to provide them whenever possible. The most common form is a cash payment. Such payments are usually made quarterly, but they can also be made more or less frequently. The corporation's directors decide how much will be paid.

At this point it might be helpful to define some of the terms that are used in conjunction with dividend payments. First, the directors *declare* a dividend of a specific amount. The dividend is said to be payable to *holders of record* (in other words, owners of the stock) as of a certain date. The *payment date* is the actual date that you, as a shareholder, will receive the dividend. The *ex-dividend date* determines whether the buyer or the seller receives the dividend.

As a shareholder, you should also be aware of two other types of distribution: the *stock dividend* and the *stock split*. Neither of these actually changes your proportionate ownership in the corporation. A stock dividend is stated as a percent dividend. For example, a corporation declares a 2 percent stock dividend. If your initial holding amounted to 100 shares, you would own 102 shares after the dividend was paid.

How Stock Splits Work

Now take the case of a stock split. Say a corporation declares a two-for-one split. This means that if you were originally holding 100 shares you would have 200 shares after the split. But since all the other shareholders would likewise have twice as many shares, your relative ownership position remains the same. The value of your investment would not change, either, for the new shares would trade at half the cost of the old ones. Reducing this trading price, in fact, is the main reason for stock splits; a corporation generally uses a split to trim the stock's price to what it considers to be a more marketable trading range. It is important to keep in mind that when you receive a stock dividend or when your stock is split, your interest in the corporation has been neither increased nor decreased. Also, the total value of the stock has not been affected, nor has the earning power of the corporation been diminished.

How to "Value" a Stock

Speaking of value, how can you place a specific "value" on a common stock? How do you determine at what price the stock should be bought? When can it be considered overvalued and best sold? Let's talk more about a point we mentioned earlier—the discrepancy that sometimes exists between a stock's "intrinsic" value and the value that the stock market places on it. In determining a stock's intrinsic value, you look at such things as the corporation's balance sheet (assets, liabilities), its debt, capital requirements, earnings, dividends, future prospects, and management. In choosing a stock, you try to pick one whose intrinsic value appears greater than the value the market has currently placed on it. Other factors sometimes used to evaluate a stock are book value (net worth), liquidating value, and price-earnings ratios. We give you a much more detailed description of these tools and how to use them in Chapter 23.

Be Aware of the Risks

Let's now talk more about some of the risks involved in investing in common stocks. One of the largest is also the most difficult to combat, for it frequently is fickle, unpredictable, and illogical. That factor is market psychology. Generally speaking, a rising trend in prices will occur when there is an attitude of optimism (economic, political, social) on the part of investors (the market). On the other hand, declines occur when investors take a pessimistic stance. Changes in basic market psychology can be seen in the fluctuations that occur from day to day in the stock market.

On a more individual level, as mentioned previously, a particular stock's price will be affected by such things as earnings, dividends, and future prospects. The risk lies in the fact that these elements change and that unforeseeable events occur. Take, as an extreme example, the case of Union Carbide. The tragic toxic gas leak at its Bhopal, India, plant claimed more than 2,000 lives and injured thousands more. Within days of the announcement, the stock had lost 40 percent of its market value. How the company and the stock will fare by the time the courts are finally through and all the claims are settled is anyone's guess.

So you can see how abruptly the tide may turn for certain corporations. Of course the higher the quality of the stock, the less is the inherent risk. The high-quality stocks tend to be much less volatile, and while "quick" profits will probably not be forthcoming, what is saved on the nerves might be worth it to some investors.

Preferred Stocks

The more conservative investor might be better able to sleep at night with preferred stocks instead of common. Preferred stocks reside in a sort of no-man's-land between bonds and common stocks. Some would say these hybrids embrace the least favorable characteristics of both, for they have neither the enforceable claim of a bond nor the share in profits of a common stock. Although preferred stock is an equity security representing ownership in a corporation, holders do not have a vote (except under certain conditions), nor do they have preemptive rights.

"Preferreds" must have some redeeming features, or they long ago would have passed into oblivion. For individual investors, that appeal is seated in the generous returns usually available in preferreds. Though the dividend may not enjoy the same guarantee that bond interest does, it takes preference over common stock payments. This is a right that usually is stated in the issuing company's charter, as is the right of the preferred holder to corporate assets in liquidation ahead of the common stockholder. But for the corporate investor, new-money preferreds (those issued since 1942) offer a tax break. In order to avoid double taxation, a taxable corporation may deduct 80 percent of dividend income derived from investments in other taxable corporations.

Adjustable-rate preferreds, a more recent innovation, have proved very popular with corporate investors. These hybrid securities pay dividends that are tied to a Treasury index and are adjusted quarterly. The payment rate has a floor below which it won't fall and a ceiling determining the highest amount that will be paid. So these preferreds, although still classed as fixed-rate investments, pay a variable rate.

The market behavior of straight preferreds and adjustable-rate preferreds is much the same as that of bonds; both are fixed-income investments and therefore are interest-rate-sensitive. This is not the case with convertible preferreds. Their market price pattern more closely follows that of the common stock because they may be exchanged for shares of common. We mentioned above that preferred shareholders in certain cases may be allowed a vote. That generally happens when the preferred dividend has been omitted for a stated number of quarters. Still other types of preferred stock may accumulate unpaid dividends which have to be cleared before common dividends are paid.

More recently, utilities—the principal issuers of this genre —have offered preferred stocks with sinking funds, giving holders the illusion of eventually getting their money back. Under the terms of the sinking fund, the issuing corporation will retire a stated percentage or dollar amount of the total issue each year until the entire issue is retired. This fund may be satisfied by open-market purchases made when the issue was trading well below par value. The shares are held in the company treasury to satisfy future sinking-fund requirements. Thus, a shareholder could hold the preferred to the bitter end without a single share's being called early. Of course he would be free at any time to sell the shares on the open market.

Rights and Warrants

In counterpoint to the staid preferreds is an array of more speculative equity-related investments—rights, warrants, and options. Let's look first at rights and warrants. As is true of common stocks, a corporation issues rights and warrants to obtain additional capital. To obtain it quickly, a rights offering is usually made. Under the terms of a rights offering, a shareholder is entitled to purchase a limited amount of additional stock at a preferential subscription price during a fixed period of time (usually within a month of issuance). During this period the stockholder can either exercise his rights and buy the stock, or he can sell his rights to others, who, in turn, may exercise them or sell them. Or, if he is careless, he can merely allow the rights to expire unexercised or unsold. Money down the drain. It is in the buying and selling of rights and warrants that the speculation occurs.

Warrants, like rights, give the shareholder the privilege of purchasing additional shares of stock at a fixed price during a specific period of time (usually several years in the future). As mentioned previously, common stock prices tend to fluctuate widely over a period of time. There is considerable risk involved in trading either rights or warrants, but because rights involve a shorter period of time, they are of a less speculative nature.

Here is an example to help you understand how warrants work and how they are evaluated by the market. XYZ Corporation's common stock has a current market price of $40 a share. XYZ issues warrants that will permit owners to purchase one share of common at $35. At these prices the warrant has a theoretical value of $5 (current market price of common minus subscription price). If the common should double in price to $80 a share, the warrant should be worth $45 ($80 less $35). As you can see, a far greater percentage gain would have been made if you had owned the warrant (800 percent) than if you had held the common (100 percent).

Warrants generally sell at premiums over their theoretical value in rising markets, reflecting their greater leverage. By the same token, if the common begins to fall, the warrant generally falls at a more rapid clip.

As a buyer of rights or warrants, you assume all the risks without the benefits of the common stock ownership. You are entitled to no dividends; you have no voting rights or any of the other rights of the common stockholder. In other words, you do not participate in the ownership of a corporation. Any return you receive on this type of investment is based solely on price appreciation.

Puts and Calls

Now let's look at another method of investing also linked to the price action of common stocks: put and call options. A put is an option to *sell* a specified number of common stock shares at a specified price (the striking price) during a specified period. A call is an option to *buy* a specified number of shares at a specified price within a specified period of time. Put and call options may be both sold (written) and bought, and we discuss them in greater detail in Chapter 14.

The major attraction of option trading is the great leverage it provides. An option can be bought or sold at a fraction of the cost of its underlying stock (usually 3 to 8 percent), and small swings in the price of that stock can generate larger gains or losses for the option trader. The field, therefore, has been a magnet for speculators.

But conservative investors, if they know what they are doing, can make use of options, too: in guaranteeing market position and obtaining stock at what may amount to a discount price, in hedging against unpredictable turns in an uncertain market, and in generating greater income. We'll tell you more about how to do it in Chapter 31.

Meanwhile, as a general rule, we think your best bet in staking out a position in the equity markets is through common stocks. In the next two chapters we give you more specific information about how to find the stocks you need to fulfill your investment aims.

CHAPTER 6

How to Find Growth Stocks

LET'S ASSUME THAT at this point in your life you do not need any extra income, and you are beginning to think about funds for the kids' college education and your own retirement. With the evils of inflation hacking away at your hard-earned savings, you want today's invested dollars to grow sufficiently to meet your future needs. What you are looking for is a good growth stock.

"Fine," you say. "How do I tell a good growth stock from any other stock? Where do I look for them? How do I evaluate them?"

What Makes a Growth Stock

Let's take a look at some of the characteristics that distinguish a growth stock from the other general categories of stocks, those that emphasize dividend payments (income stocks) and those whose prices tend to rise and fall in line with the economic cycle (cyclicals). For a start, we can tell you that growth stocks are generally found in companies that offer products and services with particularly favorable long-term growth potential. Managements tend to be aggressive and are constantly searching for new products and eying growing markets. As such, they place a good deal of emphasis on research and new-product development. Also, they generally exhibit an ability to achieve consistent and above-average sales and earnings growth.

On the other hand, dividend growth might be less dramatic because a good portion of earnings is plowed back into the company rather than paid out to investors. Thus, a growth stock more often than not will have a below-average yield. It should be pointed out, however, that a low yield today could mean a higher return tomorrow. By reinvesting its earnings, the company hopes to increase its profits over the years, which in turn means higher dividends for investors. For instance, between 1970 and 1985 Disney (Walt) increased its dividend payment by 1,900 percent, yet the stock's current yield remained below 2 percent.

Growth Stocks and Economic Trends

One of the most difficult tasks in choosing a growth stock is knowing what areas of the economy do in fact possess unusual growth potential. It's difficult, but by no means impossible. In the absence of a crystal ball, you have in your daily newspaper one of your best information sources. What phases of life does it discuss the most? What are people talking about? What trends are developing in our society? What deep-rooted changes are emerging?

One increasingly obvious example of an expanding technology is the area of data processing. Automatic Data Processing, a $1 billion concern, is the largest independent purveyor of data services in the country. Currently in its twenty-fifth successive year of uninterrupted growth, ADP has succeeded largely by concentrating on the service sectors of the economy—banks, insurance agents, securities brokers, auto repair shops. The company provides payroll, accounting, reporting, and other services to small- and medium-sized businesses on a client-to-client basis. Its revenue stream is steady, continually growing, and its markets far from saturated.

The company's success—earnings have grown at close to a

20 percent compound rate during the 1975–85 decade—has not gone unnoticed. The stock is widely held by institutions and its price-earnings ratio remains higher than average.

So, through just this one example—and there are countless others—you see the rewards that can be reaped from finding an area with future promise and being patient enough to stay with it.

Timing Your Buys

With growth stocks, as with any other investment, timing is an important key to success. You have to determine the best time to buy—and to sell. While there is no sure formula, a few considerations should prove helpful. The ideal time to buy is when a company is still in its early stages of development. There is, of course, more than average risk involved, since emerging companies are smaller and less known, and their success has not been firmly established. But their stocks do tend to be more reasonably priced than those of companies that have carved a niche.

On the other hand, a company's chronological age is not necessarily significant. Some well-established corporations fit the criteria for a growth stock because of their proven ability to introduce new product lines and find new markets. A good example is Philip Morris. For years growth had been based on cigarette sales. Then in 1969 it embarked on an expansion program, acquiring Miller Brewing. Within a decade this cigarette maker had taken over three more companies—a wine maker, a paper company, and the Seven-Up soft-drink bottler. Philip Morris applied its skills as a marketer of consumer products to these new lines, boosting the company's growth rate from 15 percent to more than 20 percent annually. Even more recently Philip Morris entered the food-packaging business in a big way, acquiring giant General Foods. While the merger may cool the company's growth rate over the next few years, it should still be at a respectable 16 to 18 percent pace. This example vividly demonstrates that a company's growth has less to do with its age than its ability to recognize growing product areas and then to capitalize on them.

Of course an investor must be willing to pay a premium for a well-established growth company, such as Abbott Labs, International Business Machines, Merck, and Procter & Gamble, which sold at twenty-five to forty-five times earnings in 1972. But these same companies are also sensitive to market declines—as amply demonstrated by their price-earnings ratios, which fell to around 10 a decade later. The key is to choose a stock with an above-average growth record which is selling at a reasonable multiple of earnings. While this takes a bit of searching, it can be done.

Finding the answers to a few simple questions should make the selection easier. Does the company have a product or service with exceptional long-term potential? Does management reinvest earnings? Is a reasonable return on capital realized? Is capitalization of a size that will allow for future expansion? Does management have a piece of the action via stock ownership? What portion of net goes to research and development? Is the price-earnings multiple reasonable vis-à-vis the company's record and potential? If most of these questions rate a positive answer, you may well have uncovered a worthwhile growth situation.

Timing Your Sells

Even long-term growth stocks should be sold at certain times and in some situations. Performance of the market as a whole is not generally one of the criteria. Major market turns are difficult to spot and they seldom coincide with the tops and bottoms in an individual issue. The 1981–82 downturn, which decimated the highfliers, caused little more than a dip in the long-term uptrend of many blue chips. What you should be on the watch for are changes in the prospects for a firm—new competition, new laws, new products. If something in the fundamental outlook for a corporation develops, a switch may be indicated.

There are many examples of this principle at work, but one of the best was Scott Paper back in the 1960s. Scott was the foremost maker of premium tissue and toweling. The company's record was one of dynamic growth. The stock was a blue chip growth favorite and sold at lofty price-earnings ratios. The company had a huge and growing market pretty much to itself. Then Procter & Gamble moved in. It bought a Midwestern outfit named Charmin and took off after Scott's tissue and toweling customers. This shook the Scott management at the time. To have the expert marketers at P&G after your customers would scare anyone.

Here, then, was a perfect example of fundamental change. Scott went from being virtually alone in a rich market to being eyeball to eyeball with one of the world's toughest competitors. The market saw this and the Scott price-earnings multiple tumbled. Investors who sold then were doing the right thing for logical reasons. The fundamentals of Scott had changed.

In conclusion, if your investment objective is to beat inflation, then growth stocks could be the route for you. But remember, patience may be required. The table here illustrates comparative short- and long-term performances of cyclical and growth stocks over a ten-year period. As you see, the rewards for perseverance can be great.

	Price			*Price*		
	Aug. 1982	*June 1983*	*% Change*	*Mar. 1977*	*Mar. 1987*	*% Change*
Growth Stocks						
Abbott Laboratories	34	48	+ 41	6	62	+ 925
Capital Cities Comm.	75	150	+100	25	347	+1284
Dayton Hudson	21	38	+ 81	9	46	+ 411
Heinz, H.J.	21	29	+ 38	5	48	+ 933
Hewlett-Packard	27	44	+ 63	9	57	+ 533
Philip Morris	55	60	+ 9	15	87	+ 480
Average			+ 58			+ 838
Cyclical Stocks						
Aluminum Co. Amer.	29	40	+ 38	29	44	+ 52
Dow Chemical	25	34	+ 36	39	81	+ 107
General Motors	48	72	+ 50	66	78	+ 18
Int'l. Paper	42	53	+ 26	58	108	+ 86
Union Carbide	47	70	+ 49	19	29	+ 53
U.S. Steel	18	25	+ 39	48	28	− 42
Average			+ 41			+ 42

CHAPTER 7

Common Stocks for Income

IN THE PREVIOUS chapter you learned the benefits of investing in growth stocks. But what if your prime objective is income —you're looking for a little extra "bread money"? Many retired people with fixed incomes find themselves in this category. While bonds and preferred stocks are popular investment vehicles for those seeking income and safety, you should not make the mistake of ignoring common stocks as a valuable means of obtaining extra income. Many of these issues provide high current yields and have the potential for future dividend increases as opposed to the fixed rate of return on bonds and preferreds. They offer the possibility of some capital growth as well.

Although the need for additional income might be of the utmost importance, with the cost of living constantly edging upward, albeit at changing rates, you should not pick a stock solely on the basis of current dividends. You won't gain any ground by purchasing one of today's high yielders if there is little potential for future dividend increases.

Look Beyond Current Yield

There is, of course, more risk involved with a common stock than, say, a bond, but the risk can be reduced by choos-

67

ing stocks that have exhibited steady and dependable earnings and dividend growth over the years. The key, again, is not just to look at current yield. You must look to the past record, too. Is there a long history of consistent dividend payments? What has the dividend growth record been like? What are the prospects for dividend growth in the future? Again, careful attention must be given to price. What is the stock's price-earnings ratio? Is it high or low in terms of current earnings and future prospects and in terms of other stocks in its industry? Like any other common stock investment, an income stock should be chosen on the basis of quality and growth, and not just because it is enjoying a high level of current income.

Actually, choosing income stocks is a relatively easy matter compared to selecting growth stocks. First you look for a business that is steady, something that by nature tends to do well despite the prevailing economic climate.

Get a Line on Telephone Stocks

The telephone business is a fair representative of this type of industry. We pointed out in an earlier chapter how people tend to use the telephone as much in bad times as good. With the rapid pace of technological progress in the last decade, all areas of the communications field have excellent growth prospects and are experiencing steadily increasing demand for their basic services.

The only major problems the telephone business encounters come from inflation and politics. The former pushes up costs of both labor (through increases in wage levels) and capital (through higher interest rates). Politics enters when the company seeks rate relief from the squeeze of rising costs. In the wake of the consumer movement, regulatory authorities frequently think first of the consumer's reluctance to pay more for telephone service and second, if at all, of the stockholder's right to a fair return on his investment. After all, in the popular lexicon, the user is poor, the stockholder rich. But these problems have been surmounted time and again, so the earnings-dividend experience of telephone companies' shareholders has been passing fair.

Politics also resulted in the 1982 antitrust agreement between American Telephone & Telegraph and the Justice Department. It divided huge Ma Bell into one high-tech communications concern and seven regional telephone holding companies in order to encourage competition in both areas. As a result of the divestiture, income investors have seven more telephone utilities from which to choose.

In addition to the former Bell System affiliates, there are a number of attractive independent telcos. Many of the latter have consistently raised dividend payments, year after year. For example, Centel boosted its dividend about 8 percent compounded annually over the 1970–85 period, while in the same time frame, Rochester Telephone upped its rate over 10 percent compounded. So when you are putting together an income portfolio look at all the possibilities. Some well-situated telephone companies are:

ALLTEL Corp.	Northern Telecom
Bell Atlantic	Pacific Telesis
Centel Corp.	Rochester Telephone

Plug into Electric Utilities

Like the telephones, electric utilities make good sense as income investments. We say this even though they are having trouble these days from environmentalists and from nuclear-plant shutdowns, skyrocketing construction costs, and consumer-conscious public utility commissions. In spite of these problems, the industry's leading companies have enviable dividend records.

The table below lists dividend payments of the FPL Group over a twenty-year period. It shows why utility stocks have appeal for income year in and year out, even when the stock market fails to behave.

In short, the 1967 buyer of the FPL Group common enjoyed dividend increases every year. By 1986, the dividend had increased by close to 400 percent. When this increase is compared with that of the consumer price index, the most widely used measure of inflation, it shows that this utility's dividends handily outpaced the rise of prices in general. During the two decades, the dividend compounded at an 8.3 percent annual rate while the consumer price index moved ahead at a 6.1 percent annual compound rate.

Year	Dividend	Year	Dividend
1967	$0.42	1977	$0.83
1968	0.45	1978	1.00
1969	0.48	1979	1.16
1970	0.51	1980	1.32
1971	0.53	1981	1.48
1972	0.55	1982	1.64
1973	0.58	1983	1.77
1974	0.68	1984	1.86
1975	0.72	1985	1.96
1976	0.78	1986	2.04

This type of inflation-beating dividend growth has been exhibited by several other of the companies listed below. If electric utility stocks appeal to you as income possibilities, any of these perennial favorites would bear investigation.

Central Louisiana Electric	Southern California Edison
FPL Group	Southwestern Public Service
Florida Progress	TECO Energy
Hawaiian Electric	Tucson Electric Power
New England Electric	Wisconsin Energy

Tap a Water Company

One little-known and often overlooked group that offers steady income plus some hope of profit over the long pull is the water utilities. Just as certain as death and taxes is our steady uptrend in water consumption. This has been regularly reflected in a similar annual increase in water utility revenues and, in most cases, earnings. Of course water company profits per share are unlikely to explode, but no matter how bad the times, neither are they likely to dry up. Water is just about the last commodity we would forgo. While consumer activists often oppose rate increases requested by telephone, electric, and natural gas utilities, water service is generally too cheap to get excited about. The fact is, however, that water rates have been rising at a much faster pace than inflation recently. The rate increases reflect higher levels of capital expenditures, maintenance costs, and treatment expenses necessary to keep up with increasing demand.

After years of ignoring the group, investors have begun to take a second look. Not only do they see a conservative management, but also an underlying value in the group's real estate holdings. Yields on the water-service stocks are not as generous as those of other types of utilities. But with dividends rising at close to a 10 percent annual pace, a shareholder should be well satisfied. The following water companies are worth checking:

American Water Works	Philadelphia Suburban
Consumers Water	Southern Calif. Water
E'Town Corp.	United Water Resources

Other industry groups come and go as candidates for an income list. When in disfavor, stocks in some industrial groups can sell to yield more than twice what they do when they have caught the public favor. It's perfectly logical to buy temporarily unpopular stocks for income as long as you can be reasonably certain that the dividend is safe and that the company has a good earnings-dividend record. Do not, however, buy a stock for high yield when the earnings-dividend performance is erratic, for that very irregularity may account for the temporarily generous return. The market will be telling you in those instances that it "ain't safe."

Inflation and Income Stocks

A word is warranted at this point on inflation and income stocks. One of the reasons income stocks return a high yield in times of rising prices is the very inflation itself. When inflation intensifies, stock prices fall at first, particularly those of income-type stocks. They fall with the bond markets as lenders say, in effect, "If you want my money now you will have to pay me a decent return, plus what those dollars will likely depreciate per year."

A high prime rate reflects just this equation—so much for a "real" return and so much to offset inflation. The income group generally comes to terms with current inflationary reality. For instance, many of the growing electric utilities yielded less than 5 percent for years. But when inflation reached the double-digit level, yields on utilities rose to 10 and 15 percent. Even after inflation had cooled to 4 and 5 percent and stayed there, yields on utilities were slow to return to their earlier level. Thus, inflation expectations were factored into utility returns for a couple of years after the fact.

CHAPTER 8

Corporate Bonds

A GOOD MANY conservative investors have long believed that the only really "safe" security is a corporate bond, and would never think of putting their money into anything else. However, the increasingly high interest rates available on bonds in the early 1980s, as well as an uncertain economic climate, won a lot of theretofore more venturesome investors into that camp.

Nevertheless, many common stock investors still blanch at the thought of investing in bonds, and one reason is that fixed-income securities represent unfamiliar territory. We shall seek to span that knowledge gap in this chapter. There is no real mystery to bonds. Neither are bonds always as "safe" as they seem, and we'll get into that a bit here, too.

Simply Stated, They're Loans

Stripped of their esoterica, bonds are no more than credit instruments and merely represent a loan by the investor to the issuing company. When a corporation wishes to build a plant or finance equipment purchases, it may do so by floating a bond issue, which is no more than taking out a loan composed of tradable evidences of debt.

There are several reasons why a corporation will choose to sell bonds rather than offer the public more shares of common stock. For one thing, the registration procedures and expenses of issuing bonds generally are less burdensome than those involved in issuing stock. For another, the company might not wish to dilute any further the equity of outstanding common shares. Or the company's assessment of the existing investment and economic climate tells it that bonds would be easier to sell than stock, or less costly in the long run.

Corporate bonds come in several styles. They can be mortgage bonds backed by liens on specific assets. They can be issued for specific purposes, as when railroads or airlines float equipment trust certificates. Most frequently, however, they are in the form of debentures, which means they are backed solely by a pledge of the earning power of the corporation rather than by a lien on specific corporate property.

However, these mortgage bonds, trust certificates, and debentures share many common characteristics. They all are, as we said above, tradable evidences of debt; they usually come in denominations of $1,000, and so can be readily bought and sold by investors. They generally carry a fixed interest rate (coupon) on their face. They all have a predetermined expiration date when the loan must be repaid (maturity).

The precise nature of the bond and the specific terms of the "loan" agreement are contained in the bond indenture. Besides noting the type of bond being issued and fixing the coupon and maturity date, the indenture might also reserve the issuing company's right to retire, or "call," the bond at a specified date and price in advance of maturity. It might also note whether all bonds of the particular series will mature at once or serially, i.e., in stated amounts annually. It would give specifics on how the bonds could be called. Sometimes, if an entire issue is not called, those bonds chosen for retirement are picked on the basis of serial number; often they are chosen by lot. The indenture also will identify the name and address of the trustee, usually a bank. The trustee administers and oversees the bond issue, making sure all terms and conditions are met, interest payments are made on time, and the like.

The "Mechanics" of Bonds

Bonds may be issued in "registered" form, which means the name and address of the current owner are kept on file by the corporation. The issuer sends periodic interest payments directly to the owner, and no one else may offer the bond for sale or redemption. The registered owner of a called bond is notified directly. This is the safest and most convenient way for you as an investor to hold bonds. Although bonds can no longer be issued in "bearer" form, there are thousands of older issues still available. Bearer bonds, in effect, are owned by whoever has them in his possession. Thus, they are virtually the same as cash. No proof of ownership need be demonstrated to redeem them or to collect interest. Interest is indeed collected by snipping little coupons from the bond certificate at stated intervals in that stereotyped procedure that conjures up images of wealthy little old ladies and gents stooping over a table in a vault doing just that. After they're clipped, the coupons can be presented to a bank for payment. Because ownership of bearer bonds and interest payments on them are difficult for the IRS to trace, they have been used by some for tax avoidance. For this reason Congress as part of the Tax Equity and Fiscal Responsibility Act of 1982 banned any new offerings of bearer bonds after 1982.

Bonds are issued and traded in $1,000 denominations and quoted in terms of "par" (100). Thus, a bond quoted at 98 sells at $980, one quoted at 101½ sells at $1,015, etc. Because bond interest is fixed, prices must adjust up or down to reflect prevailing interest rates. Sometimes such an adjustment is made even as the bond is being issued. Suppose an issuing company wants the bonds to pay only 6 percent interest, while the prevailing interest rate is 6.25. As an inducement, instead of selling the bond for $1,000 and being committed to pay $62.50 a year in interest for the life of the bond, the company will sell it initially for $960 and pay $60 a year in interest. This will give the buyer an effective rate of 6.25 percent as long as he holds the bond. That is called an "original issue discount." Though the buyer paid only $960 for the bond, he will collect $1,000 when it matures. The difference is reported as income ratably over the life of the issue, with the holder's cost basis rising each year by that amount of reported income.

Marketplace Determines Yield

Once the bond has been issued, whether it sold initially at par or at a discount, the marketplace takes charge of its price fluctuations. Suppose you buy a bond at par that pays 7.5 percent interest. Each year as long as you hold the bond you will receive a $75 interest payment. If bond yields in general rise to 8 percent, your 7.5 percent bond will drop in current value to $940, because that's all a potential buyer would be willing to pay, in order to reap the 8 percent he could get elsewhere. On the other hand, if bond yields generally dropped to 7 percent, you could get $1,070 if you sold your bond. For the sake of simplicity these examples ignore the effect that years to maturity may also exert on the price of a bond. A bond that sells below par is said to be selling at a "discount." One that sells above par is said to be selling at a "premium."

In order to avoid paying out the high rates of interest prevalent in the early 1980s, corporations began offering deep-discount bonds with zero coupon rates. For example, J.C. Penney, the first company to exploit this idea, brought out a bond priced at $332.47, which will provide initial investors with a 14.25 percent yield when it is redeemed at its face value ($1,000) at maturity in 1989. However, because the bond holder is taxed on a portion of the discount each year, as if it were earned income, these bonds are suitable for individual investors *only in tax-sheltered accounts,* such as Keogh plans and individual retirement accounts.

Yields Fluctuate

Over the past four decades, the overall trend in bond yields definitely has been upward. Back in 1950, Moody's Aaa Corporate Bond Composite Index returned less than 3 percent. By 1982 that yield had jumped to nearly 17 percent, reflecting expectations of continued inflation. Four years later, when inflation appeared to be well controlled, the Moody's Aaa yield had backed off to under 9 percent. There are times when interest rates go down sharply, usually when the economy enters a recession. Bond prices then move up quickly. When interest rates stop falling, though, the advance in bond prices slows markedly, then stops, too.

International economics will play an indirect role in bond prices and interest rates in the years ahead. Currency fluctuations facilitated by floating exchange rates, and our inevitable entanglement in the web of worldwide politics and economic cycles, will pose ongoing uncertainties.

How do you as a bond buyer protect yourself in such an investment and economic climate? One way is to buy shorter-term bonds, sticking pretty much to those with maturities of ten years or less. Such bonds tend to hold price fluctuations to more moderate proportions. Another way is to manage your bond portfolio such that you are not left holding outdated bonds at deep discounts. Try to keep your portfolio heavily represented in bonds with coupon rates closely approximating prevailing interest rates.

How do you judge a bond's quality? If you're up to it, you can examine the corporation's debt structure, its financial statements, its credit rating, and other complex factors and make an assessment on your own. More likely you'll do what most of the rest of us do—you'll look to the rating services and bow to their judgment. There are two that are widely quoted: Moody's Investors Service and Standard & Poor's.

Both use similar criteria in determining the relative quality of bonds available for public sale, those representing the least risk to the investor being rated highest. Consequently, U.S. Treasury issues backed by the federal government's awesome taxing power are at the top of the pile. Close behind are those of the various federal agencies which, though they are not specifically backed by the government, carry the weight of moral obligation of the government not to allow them to go into default.

Some corporate bonds carry the highest AAA or Aaa rating, too: Aetna, Exxon, and several of the Bell System spin-offs are examples. However, 1985 was a hard year on the credit ratings. According to S&P, the number of debt issues downgraded more than doubled, from 125 in 1984 to 272 in 1985. Credit quality deteriorated, particularly in the corporate sector, while utility and transportation companies improved their financial positions. As bonds go down the rating scale, risk rises. In compensation for that added risk, investors demand a higher yield. The higher the bond's rating, the more closely its yield will tend to reflect changes in interest rates in general. On the other hand, yields on bonds carrying lower ratings will be much more heavily influenced by changes in the credit rating or profitability of the issuer.

This table shows you the rating scales used by Standard & Poor's and Moody's (in addition each uses qualifiers, + or − by Standard and Poor's, and 1, 2, or 3 by Moody's):

Standard & Poor's		Moody's Investors Service
AAA	Highest quality	Aaa
AA	High quality	Aa
A	Good quality	A
BBB	Medium grade, some speculative aspects	Baa
BB ⎱ B ⎰	Speculative, but with some defensive qualities	Ba
CCC ⎱ CC ⎰	Highly speculative	B
C	Bonds on which no interest is being paid or which already may be in default	Caa
D	Lowest rating	C

Both rating services are highly regarded in the financial community, and either one can be relied upon as you make your bond-buying decisions. However, for the purposes of uniformity, we shall use the Standard & Poor's ratings throughout this book.

Generally speaking, most investors buying for income should go no lower than Baa- or BBB-rated bonds. If you go much lower than that, you put your capital in jeopardy; and, after all, the primary reason you're interested in investing in bonds is to protect that capital. Examining authorities, for example, consider issues carrying one of the top four ratings to be suitable for bank investments. Trust departments, being more conservative, stay with bonds rated A or better. Any additional yield provided by more speculative issues would be more than offset by the additional risk undertaken.

Different Kinds of Yields

As we noted earlier, bonds are issued with a specific interest rate printed on the face of the certificate. This is called the "stated," or "nominal," income. However, as we also noted, the price you actually pay for the bond, whether at its issue or in the aftermarket, determines the true yield the bond is earning for you. This yield, the amount of annual interest payment in relation to the price you paid, is called the "yield on cost." Another important figure is "current yield"—the coupon rate divided by the current trading price for the bond. If a bond stands a chance of being called before maturity, there is a "yield to call date" to consider. Finally, there is a "yield to maturity."

If you buy a bond at par when it is issued and hold it until it matures or is called and you get your principal back, all four yields will be the same. However, that's not a likely sequence, so you have to apply one or another of the available yields to your investment to determine its standing in your portfolio.

Generally speaking, the current yield will give you the truest reading, for it tells you how much income that holding is generating in comparison with other income investments.

If you hold the bond until it is called or until it matures, the yield to call date or yield to maturity will be of some consequence to you. That's because these figures take into account the premium or discount at which a bond is trading and the fact that this premium or discount must be amortized from purchase date to maturity.

For instance, if a bond trades at 107, you pay a $70 premium. When the bond is called or matures, you will sustain a $70 loss, since you will receive only the $1,000 face value of the bond for which you paid $1,070. That $70 may be offset against the income you will receive over the life of the bond. On the other hand, if you bought the bond at 93, you would receive a $70 profit when the bond is retired.

These yield-to-call or yield-to-maturity figures allow you to make a quick comparison of the bond's possible return with the potential return of all other bonds carrying an endless variety of coupon rates, maturity and call dates, and prices. The computation is more involved than most of us want to bother with, so we consult tables that have been especially constructed to provide this information. Your broker should be willing to look it up if you ask. These yields, as well as current yields, are frequently included in a newspaper's listing of bond quotations.

Bonds—Why and When?

Bonds have appeal, despite their tendency to fluctuate in price as interest rates change, because they do offer better defensive qualities than common stocks; hence, they really can represent an anchor to windward in your investment program. Because their return is fixed, they can provide a firm dollar foundation on which to build an income portfolio. That fixed return is useful, too, if you should wish to use securities as collateral for a loan. Often bankers will lend you a greater percentage of the market value of a bond than they will on the common stock of the same corporation.

But the fixed return of bonds also represents their greatest drawback. This is particularly so in an inflationary environment such as we have seen in recent years and which we can expect to continue into the foreseeable future. The continual erosion in the dollar's purchasing power has raised havoc with fixed-income investments, and today's investor cannot begin to keep pace with rising prices if he stakes his entire claim on fixed-income securities. That's why it is our judgment that bonds should compose no more than a modest portion—perhaps 30 percent at most—of your portfolio.

Because conditions change, no bond, not even those of the very highest quality, can be put away and forgotten. Contrary to many investors' impressions, bond holdings should be watched closely, less for changes in quality or interest-payment reliability than for shifts in the overall level of interest rates. Federal Reserve policy, the availability of credit, the volume of bank loans, corporate liquidity, and a host of other outside factors all have an important bearing on the prevailing level of interest rates, and these have a far greater and more frequent impact on high-grade bond prices than changes in the interest-paying ability and credit rating of the issuer.

Consequently, if you choose to include bonds in your investment program, you have to remain alert and ready to shift positions according to your perception of overall interest rates and bond market trends.

CHAPTER 9

Convertible Securities

SOME STOCKS, AS we have seen, offer the double attraction of good yield plus moderate capital gains potential. So does another form of investment security—the convertible.

Logically enough, the convertible derives its name from the fact that it can be converted into, or exchanged for, another investment security—common stock in all but the rarest of cases. Also, it can come in the form of a bond or preferred stock. In either event, the convertible can be swapped for a specified number of common shares—often within a specified time period, after which the conversion privilege is "no longer" and the bond or preferred sells on its merits as a fixed-income investment.

To some degree, at least, the convertible enables the investor to have his cake and eat it, too. If the common stock goes up, the convertible will go up—though probably at a slightly slower gait, and provided that the common is not selling many points above the conversion price (more on that below). Of course, stocks also go down, but the convertible almost always provides a better yield than the stock it can be swapped for, and this higher return limits its downside risk. If it is high enough, it can even provide a "floor" beneath which the convertible will not fall, no matter what the stock does.

This is a rather esoteric area of investment, abounding with terms such as "conversion basis," "conversion value," "premium," "parity," etc. It's really not very complicated, but much of it seems to be a mystery to the average investor —the person who just might find the convertible much to his liking if he understood what it was all about.

How They Work

So, let's try to unravel the mystery. Below we have tabulated four convertibles—two bonds and two preferred stocks —using prices and yields that were prevailing in mid-1986. The table is of the type you can expect to find whenever convertibles are touted by investment advisors, brokers, and the like.

First of all, remember that the Kmart and USAir bonds, like all bonds, are quoted on the basis of 100, though they bear face values of $1,000; hence, one USAir convertible would actually cost $1,120 rather than $112. Now let's look at the individual columns in the table.

	Price	Yield	Com-mon Stock Price	Con-version Basis (Shares)*	Con-ver-sion Value†	Com-mon Stock Yield
Bonds						
Kmart 6s, 1999	145	4.1	51	28.17	144	2.8
USAir Group 8s, 2009	112	7.1	32	29.00	93	0.4
Preferred Stocks						
Anheuser-Busch $3.60	98	3.7	50	1.935	97	1.6
Union Pacific $7.25	117	6.2	54	2.000	108	3.3

* Number of common shares which would be acquired if conversion privilege were exercised.

† Market price of common stock multiplied by number of shares to be obtained in conversion.

Price and yield, of course, require no explanation. Under *conversion basis,* we have the number of common shares you will receive for each bond or each preferred share if you convert. In the case of the USAir bonds, each can be swapped for 29 shares of common. The holder of Anheuser-Busch $3.60 preferred can exchange each share for 1.935 in common.

The *conversion value* is simply the number of common shares you can acquire through conversion (or conversion basis) times the price of the common. In other words, it's the value of what you will get if you convert. Again, in the case of USAir, the conversion value is 93 (29 shares times 32, the market price of the common). With Anheuser common selling at 50, the conversion value of the $3.60 preferred is 97 (1.935 x 50).

Common stock yields, as seen in the table, are lower than the returns generated by the convertibles listed above. If the yields were higher, in all likelihood it would pay you to convert.

The Conversion Premium

Before we get into the techniques of how to convert, it would behoove us to discuss the all-important conversion premium. The premium is simply the percentage by which the price of the bond or preferred exceeds its conversion value. If the price is equal to conversion value, then the convertible is selling at conversion parity. If by some quirk the bond or preferred is trading below its conversion value, it is at a discount.

Therefore, the premium is just that. It's simply what you pay for the conversion privilege, over and above the value of the common stock into which you can convert. For Anheuser preferred, you pay 98 for the right to swap for stock worth 97. Thus, the premium is only 1 percent (98 ÷ 97). Of course you are also paying the premium for the "right" to receive higher income. The 3.7 percent yield on Anheuser preferred is almost double that on the common.

In buying convertibles, the size of the premium is always an important consideration. Generally it isn't a good idea to pay a premium of more than 20 percent, but there are no ironclad rules. For example, USAir 8s sell at the full 20 percent premium (112 ÷ 93), yet have investment merit. The bond's 7.1 percent yield is generous by contrast to the meager return on the common and carries less risk as well. Thus, it offers the holder a means of participating in an interesting growth situation while reaping an attractive return. Such opportunity is not always available.

Conversely, K mart 6s are trading at conversion, perhaps reflecting their very insignificant yield advantage over the common. Union Pacific $7.25 convertible preferred commands a modest 8 percent premium but provides about twice the yield of its common counterpart.

Generally speaking, a convertible is not much better or worse than the stock it can be swapped for. While such factors as premiums, yields, expiration of conversion privilege, etc. must be carefully weighed, it is the investment appeal of the company and its common stock that overshadows everything in importance.

How and When to Convert

Some mention should perhaps be made of how convertibles can be converted, and when it is especially advisable to do so. Most convertible certificates, be they bonds or preferreds, carry on their reverse sides a small section which the owner must fill in and sign (everything is well explained) and then send along to the company's transfer agent—the address of which is given. If there is no such section on the back of the certificate, the holder can either contact the company directly or turn it all over to his broker.

As to *when* it's best to convert, it pretty well boils down to this: So long as the convertible provides better income, stay with it. But when dividends on the common stock are raised to the point that you can improve your income by converting, then do so. Of course, there is no guarantee that dividends will continue to be paid at the new higher rate. That's up to the company directors from quarter to quarter. But if prospects are good, as they should be if dividends have just been increased, it's most likely that payments will be maintained at the new rate.

A good example of a time-to-convert situation was provided by J.P. Morgan late in 1984. Shortly after the November interest payment on the 4¾s of 1998, a dividend increase was announced for the common shares. By swapping for the common, a bondholder could increase his or her income. For each $1,000 bond paying $47.50 per year, 25 shares of common paying $55.00 a year could be obtained by converting. At that time the bond was selling close to conversion parity, so no principal loss was incurred as a result of converting.

There is, of course, another time when conversion is called for, and that's when the conversion privilege is about to expire. This may happen when an issue is called for redemption, but in some cases the convertible "lives on" as a straight bond or preferred after the exchange period has run its course.

Again, an example might clarify matters. In September 1980, Burlington Northern called for redemption its $2.85 convertible preferred, at a price of $52.40 a share, on October 10. Through October 9, each preferred share could be converted into 1.778 shares of common, which was then selling at around 41. Obviously, it was more to the holder's advantage to convert the preferred (then around 73) than to wait for it to be called.

In this case, however, conversion meant a reduction in current income, since Burlington's indicated common dividend was only $1.25 annually. Thus, the holder had another option. He could sell the preferred and buy something else. But whatever his preference, he had to act by October 9, when the conversion privilege expired. Otherwise he was out roughly $20 a share.

Their Uses—and Limits

Convertibles, like stocks, come in all sizes and colors. Some are issued by strong, growing companies and carry high-quality ratings. Some are highly speculative. Clearly, a bond or preferred selling closely in line with its conversion value is much more appealing than one selling well above. In the latter case, the conversion privilege may never be of any real value. The attraction of convertibles—which are, after all, fixed-income securities—may also be influenced by the level of interest rates.

Well-chosen convertibles can provide inflation protection, long-term growth, relatively better price protection on the downside, and, in almost all cases, greater income than the underlying common stocks. A successful investor once described them as "like spinning a coin and saying, 'Heads, I might lose a little; tails, I could win a fortune.' " Maybe that's an overly rosy assessment, but convertibles do deserve consideration by the patient investor.

CHAPTER 10

Investing in Uncle Sam

You would be hard put to find anyone but an unrecon-
structed pessimist to argue with the statement that obligations of the United States government are just about the
safest investments in the world as far as preservation of your
dollar is concerned. As long as Uncle Sam retains control of
the presses that print the money, there is virtually no doubt
that interest and principal on these obligations will be paid
when due.

The safety of "Governments" in terms of preserving the
buying power of that invested capital is quite another thing.
When inflation ran at annual rates of 9 percent and upward,
and yields on these government securities remained moderate by comparison, the purchasing power of the assets committed to them continued to shrink. In other words, you pay
for one kind of "safety" with another. It's that trade-off of
risks we talked about in earlier chapters.

An understanding of these risks and trade-offs is necessary
if you consider U.S. government obligations as candidates for
your investment program. Sometimes they do indeed have a
valid place—because you want some safety of capital, or you
want an assured rate of return for a specified period, or you
have a tax problem they can help solve.

When the New York Stock Exchange was founded in 1792,

its main business was dealing in U.S. government issues. Ever since then, they have been actively traded and enjoy the best market of any security in this country and probably in the world. Millions of dollars' worth can be bought and sold in a few minutes. Most of the trading is now done in the over-the-counter market, though these issues are listed on the New York Stock Exchange.

How "Governments" Work

"Governments" come in a wide variety of sizes, shapes, and styles. Before we get into their specifics, let's take a short detour and explore the structure through which they are issued and administered. All securities that are issued directly by the federal government come from the Department of the Treasury. Hence, they are also frequently called "Treasuries." The Treasury sells these securities to raise money to pay its bills, either in anticipation of tax revenues or because such revenues are insufficient to cover the bills.

The government also buys as well as sells these securities to help control the supply of money floating around in the economy. But that job is done by the Federal Reserve Board, a fiefdom unto itself, charged with the well-nigh impossible task of keeping the country's monetary and credit machinery chugging smoothly across the balance beam between too much growth and too much inflation. When the Fed wants to shrink the size of the money supply, it sells securities, thus taking out of circulation the money investors use to buy those securities. Conversely, if it wants to expand the money supply, it buys up these obligations, releasing dollars into the nation's spending stream.

The Fed also acts as the nation's central banker. It does this through the twelve Federal Reserve banks spread out around the country. These banks administer the Federal Reserve Board's monetary, credit, and banking policies. They also serve as the "bank" for the Treasury Department by handling the details of selling and purchasing its various marketable securities. You can deal directly with your nearest Federal Reserve Bank if you wish to buy or redeem U.S.

government obligations. (More on the specifics of buying and selling them is included in Chapter 35.)

Bills, Notes, and Bonds

Back to those securities. Although they provide an almost endless variety of yields, maturities, and denominations, Treasury obligations are divided basically into three categories: bills, notes, and bonds.

Each week the Treasury auctions off thirteen- and twenty-six-week bills and, every four weeks, fifty-two-week bills. The bills are sold at a discount from par, the difference representing the interest to the buyer. Until 1970, these bills came in denominations as low as $1,000. But when a surge in short-term interest rates lured millions of dollars from savings accounts into Treasury bills that year, the minimum denomination was jacked up to $10,000 to keep small investors from draining thrift institutions dry. Because of their relatively short maturity, T-bills present practically no market risk.

If you can't come up with the $10,000 entry fee for bills and you find Treasuries attractive for short-term investments, take a look at Treasury notes. They range in maturities from two to ten years. Although the minimum denomination varies with each offering, notes are issued in denominations as low as $1,000. Their yields, too, are generally comparable with those provided by bills.

For longer-term investment, Treasury bonds are available. They are issued in varying maturities longer than ten years, depending on the Treasury's financing needs at the time of offering. They come in registered or book-entry form and in denominations ranging from $1,000 to $1 million.

Some U.S. obligations are callable at par before maturity, on four months' notice. This fact is indicated in their description—for example, the 4¼s of 1987–92.

Besides these marketable issues, the government offers a variety of other special-interest securities. The most common are U.S. Savings Bonds. If you're old enough, you'll remember them as the "war bonds" of World War II. For many years these were available in the E and H series, but now they are sold only in the EE and HH series. A full discussion of their special features appears in Chapter 35.

United States Retirement Plan bonds, which were available in denominations as low as $50, were no longer sold after mid-1982. Interest on those Retirement Plan bonds still outstanding is compounded semiannually and is payable when the bonds are redeemed. In accordance with Keogh and IRA rules, redemption may not take place before age fifty-nine and a half without tax penalties to the owner, unless he can demonstrate complete disability. Federal income tax is deferred on these issues until they are redeemed. They are exempt from state and local income taxes.

Hold That Tiger

In response to investor acceptance of the zero-coupon bond concept, several large brokerage companies offered similar investments, using Treasury bonds. Merrill Lynch's Treasury Investment Growth Receipts (TIGRs) were the first to come on the market and their acronym caught on, so now these securities are known as "tigers," "cats," and "lions." You buy the tiger, maturing in six to twenty years, at a substantial discount from face value. These receipts are backed by Treasury bonds, so they are considered safer than their corporate counterparts. At maturity you receive face value, and the difference between amount and cost is treated as income. Because taxes are payable annually on that future interest, tigers are suitable for tax-sheltered investments, such as IRAs and Keoghs.

The Treasury STRIPS

Early in 1985, the Treasury initiated its own program of stripping and selling ten-year notes and bonds. The acronym STRIPS stands for Separate Trading of Registered Interest and Principal of Securities. Individuals can't buy these zeros directly from the Treasury but must obtain them from a bank or other depository institution. STRIPS are sold in book form only, in a minimum denomination of $1,000, which represents the maturity value, not the cost, per bond.

Federal Agency Bonds

In addition to these direct obligations of the United States, there are a wide variety of securities called "instrumentalities of the United States government." These are securities issued by official or quasi-official offshoots of the government called federal "agencies." These agencies were first used in the 1920s to provide capital for federally sponsored activities or federally guaranteed programs outside the regular budgetary structure.

Their growth mushroomed in the 1970s and continues to accelerate in the 1980s. As recently as 1965, interest-bearing obligations of agencies and government-sponsored enterprises amounted to about $17 billion. Only eight years later, in 1973, the total had soared to more than $70 billion. By 1986, it had passed $536 billion and was still climbing.

Many obligations of these agencies do not carry a direct federal guarantee. But a strong moral obligation is attached to honoring them, and it is improbable that the government would ever allow a default on any of them, a point that has been tested by the farm crisis. Therefore, from the standpoint of safety of principal, they are virtually as solid as obligations specifically guaranteed by the government.

The government-sponsored enterprises are Farm Credit System, Federal Home Loan Banks, Federal Home Loan Mortgage Corporation, Federal National Mortgage Association, Student Loan Marketing Association, and the U.S. Postal System. Federal agencies include the Export-Import Bank, General Services Administration, Government National Mortgage Association, Maritime Administration, and the Tennessee Valley Authority.

In 1973, Congress created the Federal Financing Bank in an attempt to bring a measure of order to the chaotic structure of federal agency financing. Its aim was to provide a single vehicle through which the smaller agencies could raise capital. Debt issued by the FFB was $4.5 billion in 1974, its first year of operation; it had reached $122 billion by 1986.

At times these quasi-governmental securities have provided noticeably higher yields than direct obligations of the United States. When this occurs, these issues bear serious consideration. Generally, though, the spread is rather small.

As a result of serious problems in the farm belt, the farmer-owned Federal Farm Credit System reported a $2.7 billion loss for 1985 and nonearning loans of $5.3 billion (8 percent of its loan portfolio). Despite its shaky financial condition, long-term System bonds were yielding only 50 to 75 basis points (½ to ¾ of 1 percent) more than comparable Treasuries. Short-term issues were just a few basis points higher. Until Congress voted to allow the Farm Credit System to tap the Treasury for bailout funds, the spread had been as high as 130 basis points. In anticipation of the government's continued backing, the market does not now see undue risk in System bonds, hence the narrow yield spread.

A Word on Taxability

Before leaving Governments, we should take note of the tax implications attached to them. Income earned on them is fully taxable at the federal level. However, interest on Treasuries and most agency obligations is exempt from state and local income and property taxation. Interest on Federal Home Loan Mortgage Corporation, Federal National Mortgage Association, Government National Mortgage Association, and Export-Import Bank obligations is not state and local tax-exempt. The state and local tax situation is a point to consider when comparing Governments with corporate bonds and other taxable securities, particularly if you live in a high-tax state.

Although their income may escape state and local taxes, U.S. government and agency securities are subject to excise, gift, estate, and inheritance taxes levied by the states. They are also subject to federal income tax on capital gains and gift and estate taxes.

We should not neglect to mention here a class of Treasury

bonds which bear a special privilege with regard to federal estate taxes. This feature, which allows them to be applied at par against the estate tax obligation even if they were bought at a discount, has earned them the nickname of "flower bonds." Although law prohibits issue of any new bonds carrying this special feature and none have been issued since 1971, there are still several outstanding, should you wish to acquire some in the course of your estate planning. Here is a list of flower bonds still available:

3½s of February 1990	4⅛s of May 1989–94
4¼s of August 1987–92	3s of February 1995
4s of February 1988–93	3¼s of November 1998

Since government obligations are at the top of the quality list, their market action depends wholly upon fluctuations prevailing in interest rates. The volatility of that price action is determined largely by the amount of time to maturity; the shorter the maturity the narrower will be the price swing. As a bond approaches maturity, its price will begin to stabilize right around par. Prices of obligations subject to call will be influenced by that factor. For example, in times of falling interest rates, high-grade bonds will tend to rise in price but their call price also will limit the extent of such advances; noncallable issues, on the other hand, will not be so constrained.

To preserve investment flexibility, we recommend that if you include Governments in your portfolio you choose those with maturities of ten years or less. This will help minimize the market risk should you find it desirable or necessary to sell them before they mature.

But keep in mind that despite the ultimate safety of U.S. government and agency obligations in terms of marketability and preservation of capital, they possess the same serious drawbacks in protecting against inflation as do other bonds, because both income and principal are fixed.

CHAPTER 11

Investing in Tax-Exempts

THE MUNICIPAL BOND market has irrevocably changed as a result of the Tax Reform Act of 1986. The use of tax-exempts to fund some state and locally sponsored projects has been restricted, while the stripping of municipal bonds is permitted by TRA '86. Consequently several new municipal bond products have been introduced, giving this market a whole new look. In addition to the tried-and-true tax-exempt municipal bonds, there are now taxable municipals, stripped municipals, annual-payment M-CATS, and munis collateralized with Treasuries. The tax exemption on "munis," as they are collectively known, provides a means for state and local governments to raise capital at lower interest costs. Because munis are tax-exempt they are attractive to investors in higher tax brackets despite their below-market interest.

When Are Tax-Exempts Profitable?

When does it become more profitable for you as an investor to buy tax-exempts than to hold taxables? The answer depends on three things: your tax bracket, the prevailing yield on taxable securities, and the going rate on tax-exempts. A

95

table and a simple mathematical formula are presented below to help you decide when you should switch to munis.

When we say tax bracket, we do not mean the percentage of your income you actually pay to Uncle Sam, but the amount you would pay on every dollar earned above your present taxable income, based on the Internal Revenue Service tax tables. Thus, if you are in the 33 percent bracket (reflecting the 5 percent surcharge when income exceeds certain levels), 33 cents of your next dollar of income will go to pay federal taxes.

Besides your own tax bracket, the relationship between yields on taxable and nontaxable securities will determine their relative merits. On average, tax-exempts yield somewhere around 70 percent of what taxable bonds yield. The following chart traces the generally stable relationship between taxable and tax-exempt bond yields from mid-1984 to mid-1986.

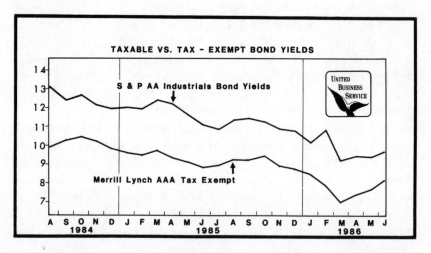

Although this relationship was fairly stable during the period depicted on the chart, there have been times when this was not the case. In the 1975 aftermath of New York City's near default, tax-exempts took a real beating, pushing their yields to within 85 percent of those on taxable bonds. This stimulated widespread investor interest in munis. To accommodate those lacking the wherewithal to buy bonds outright and/or those who wished to diversify assets, tax exempt unit trusts sprang to the forefront. Municipal bond funds did not appear until a propitious change was made in the tax laws, allowing them to pass interest through tax exempt to fund holders.

There remains the broad question of deciding when tax-exempts are of value in your portfolio. The table below shows how the advantages of tax-exempt securities are increased by a tax-bracket increase.

TAX-EXEMPT AND TAXABLE YIELDS COMPARED

Tax bracket	*Tax-Exempt Yield of:*									
	5.5	*6.0*	*6.5*	*7.0*	*7.5*	*8.0*	*8.5*	*9.0*	*9.5*	*10.0*
	is equivalent to taxable yield of:									
28%	7.6	8.3	9.0	9.7	10.4	11.1	11.8	12.5	13.2	13.9
33%	8.2	8.9	9.7	10.4	11.2	11.9	12.7	13.4	14.2	14.9
35%	8.5	9.2	10.0	10.8	11.5	12.3	13.1	13.8	14.6	15.4
38.5%	8.9	10.0	10.6	11.4	12.2	13.0	13.8	14.6	15.4	16.2

If you want to work the figures out for yourself, here's the formula. To determine the equivalent taxable yield on a municipal bond, divide the stated interest by 1.00 minus your tax bracket. Thus, for someone in the 33 percent bracket a yield of 7 percent from a tax-exempt bond would be equivalent to a 10.4 percent yield on a taxable bond.

$$\frac{0.07}{1.00 - 0.33} = .104$$

What Kinds of Bonds Are There?

The safest of all tax-exempt securities are those offered by municipalities under the Department of Housing and Urban Development (HUD) and guaranteed by federal subsidies. Don't confuse these bonds with those issued by the various state housing authorities, which have neither federal nor state backing.

General obligation bonds, also called "full faith and credit bonds," are next safest because they have the full taxing power of the state or municipality behind them. However, they run the gamut from safe to moderately speculative, depending on the solvency of the issuing body.

Revenue bonds, which depend on such things as tolls and user fees for their income, are more risky because they do not have taxing power behind them. If their fees do not generate the necessary income to service the obligations, they can go into default.

Tax revenue bonds and tax anticipation notes are offered by communities in expectation of incoming revenues. They are usually short term and have low interest rates. However, their short maturities and high quality make them attractive to commercial banks. Generally, they trade at roughly half the rate available on taxable commercial paper.

Industrial revenue bonds (IRBs, also called industrial development bonds) are first cousins to revenue bonds. IRBs are issued by a state or community authority to build a facility for a company whose lease payments cover interest and principal. The corporation puts its credit on the line but in return gets financing at tax-exempt rates. They were created to provide incentives for investment in local economic development projects and particularly to attract capital for installing pollution-control equipment in existing plants. Because corporations are easier to analyze than municipalities, IRB offerings generally are snapped up quickly.

The popularity of industrial revenue bonds with both issuers and investors led Congress to restrict their use. Too many questionable projects were being funded with tax-exempt bonds at the expense of federal revenue. Now only a limited amount of so-called private-activity bonds can be issued tax exempt annually. The 1987 cap for each state is the greater of $250 million or $75 per resident. These amounts are reduced to $150 million and $50 per resident thereafter. Above these limits, municipalities will have to fund projects with taxable issues. In any case, all municipal bonds issued prior to mid-August 1986 retain their tax-exempt status. Public-purpose municipal bonds, i.e., those serving a bona fide public need and issued after that date, will also be fully tax exempt.

New Muni Bond Types

Taxable municipal bond offerings have been limited, selling primarily to institutional investors. Interest rates on these bonds are more generous than on similar corporate issues. Despite the high ratings accorded them, they are usually not the direct obligation of the issuing municipality. Backing from third parties, such as insurance companies, obscures the responsibility issue. Individuals should be very cautious with these relatively untested debt issues.

Stripped municipal bonds were permitted for the first time by the technical corrections segment of TRA 1986, which removed prohibitions on their stripping. With this stricture lifted, Wall Street began scurrying to offer stripped or zero-coupon tax-exempts. M-CATS (municipal certificates of accrual) were first marketed by Salomon Brothers. But Merrill Lynch & Co. and Goldman, Sachs & Co. are also active marketers of stripped munis. Interest income on these deep-discount zero-coupon bonds is not received until they mature. Zero-coupon municipal bonds are attractive investment alternatives for parents who must pay tax on the unearned income of their children aged fourteen or under.

Annual-income stripped municipals are another innovation from the staff at Salomon Brothers. Coupons are stripped from a municipal bond selling at a premium. One of the two semiannual interest payments will be made to buyers of these annual-income issues. The remaining coupons stay with the principal. This maneuver converts a bond selling at a premium into one that sells at par. Since most investors prefer not to pay a premium for municipal bonds, annual-income muni strips should sell well.

Collateralized municipal receipts are packaged with serial maturities of one to "X" number of years. The offering municipalities collateralize the bonds with Treasury issues in order to take the debt off their books before the bonds can be refunded. Thus, the receipts are backed by prerefunded bonds. Muni receipts are suitable for individuals seeking high quality and safety.

Marketability Can Be a Problem

There is no central marketplace for the half trillion dollars' worth of outstanding municipal debt. Bonds are traded by telephone among countless brokerage dealers. There are no commissions, but neither are the prices of most bonds listed anywhere. You are at the complete mercy of the dealers, who inventory bonds for their own accounts and have a major stake in profiting from markups and discounts.

Moreover, there is no strict definition of a round lot in this market. It is whatever amount is large enough to get the dealer to narrow his spread between bid and asked prices. Although $25,000 is considered a round lot, sometimes $50,000 or $100,000 is the standard.

With many thousands of issuing entities continually floating and retiring bonds of varying maturities and interest rates, the factors affecting these securities reach infinite proportions. Because institutional and individual investors frequently purchase and hold these securities for long periods, the market is not nearly as liquid as that for common stocks or corporate bonds.

Potential municipal investors should consider marketability in making purchases. Generally speaking, it is best to avoid small-town securities that might be difficult to sell without a price concession should you need to dispose of them prior to maturity.

Issues floated by larger governmental subdivisions are rated by Moody's and Standard & Poor's. They also appear regularly in the Blue List, an inventory of bond offerings published each trading day by Standard & Poor's and circulated among municipal bond dealers. The obligations of many smaller towns, school and utility districts, and authorities, on the other hand, will appear in the listings only infrequently. Generally speaking, any muni bearing a rating of A or better may be considered safe.

Insured Bonds Have an Edge

In the early 1970s, AMBAC Indemnity Corp. began offering bond holders protection against the possible risk of default. Since then several other companies have entered the field, and municipal bond insurance has become a well-accepted feature in the tax-exempt field. In 1985, some $47 billion of municipal bonds were issued carrying this protection.

There are four major insurers—AMBAC Indemnity Corp., Bond Investors Guaranty (BIGI), Financial Guaranty Insurance Co. (FGIC), and Municipal Bond Investors Assurance Corp. (MBIA). Each of these represents a consortium of private insurance companies. For example, investors in FGIC include GE Credit, General Re Corp., J.P. Morgan, Kemper Group, Merrill Lynch, and Shearson Lehman Brothers.

These four insurance providers are rated triple A by Moody's Investor Services and Standard & Poor's. Therefore, bond issues underwritten by them carry a similar rating. However, the underlying bond, if uninsured, would rate lower, perhaps double A. Insurance is not without cost to the investor. Yields on insured bonds are 10 to 50 basis points (.1 to .5 percent) under those on uncovered issues. How the insurer is organized bears on the yield differential. AMBAC, BIGI, and FGIC were set up with a one-time capital infusion from their investors, whereas MBIA represents an ongoing association of insurance companies. Because investors think MBIA-backed bonds are less risky, they yield less than those backed by the other insurers.

If the insurer's rating is lowered, the bonds insured by it are also downgraded. Crum & Foster, parent of municipal bond insurer Industrial Indemnity (II), was dropped from AAA to AA by S&P. As a result, some $6 billion of II-insured muni bonds were downgraded to AA. While insurance is useful at times—AMBAC paid up on defaulted WPPSS bonds—the investor should look for issues that carry high ratings on their own merits, irrespective of insurance coverage.

How Do You Judge Them?

There is a great deal more to picking municipal bonds than selecting the largest yield and collecting income. Auditing standards for municipalities are inferior when compared with those of the corporate world. Though financial statements are improving, issuers frequently publish inadequate reports. Moreover, ratings can sometimes be unreliable measures of credit risks.

Therefore, you are much more on your own as you evaluate tax-exempts than you are with corporates. Good information is hard to find, so the rating services are a helpful starting point. But you should get a prospectus on any bond you are considering for purchase, and you should watch financial statements for news of litigation or legislation that might influence the quality of the bond.

Beyond that, what should you look for in a municipal bond? With general obligation debt, the object is to discover how heavily indebted the issuing municipality already is relative to its real assets and its economic power. Important considerations must include an assessment of the area's largest employers and taxpayers, population growth, personal income levels, and operating revenues.

If you look at revenue bonds, pinpoint the sources of income. As a rule of thumb, be sure there is at least $1.20 in income for every $1.00 in debt service (interest costs). If revenues tend to be highly cyclical, you might want to add a larger cushion. Then try to determine the order of liens, see what is pledged to whom.

Revenue bonds include water and power issues backed by receipts from users (industrial, commercial, and residential customers of the utility). Besides a company's financial track record, you must also assess the rate-relief history of the state's regulatory agency.

Revenue bonds, bridge and turnpike bonds, airport and sports-complex bonds, and local housing authority bonds fall within the private-purpose category. Tax exemption of interest on such issues already in existence prior to the passage of TRA 1986 is grandfathered. However, all but a limited quantity of newly issued bonds in this category now carry taxable interest.

Bonds floated by hospitals, which historically have derived about 90 percent of their revenues from Medicare and Medicaid programs, now entail increased risk. With the institution of congressionally mandated cost cutting in these health care programs, hospital revenues have been hurt. Skyrocketing malpractice awards are another cloud on the horizon. Increasingly, hospitals are being taken over by private hospital management companies, thereby reducing supplies of these bonds.

We should not proceed without mentioning specifically the bonds of Puerto Rico. Its economy has strengthened in recent years; unemployment rates are down and production up. Puerto Rican bonds possess a feature that should not be overlooked: Income from them is exempt not only from federal taxes but also from taxes in all states and municipalities. Look for A- or AA-rated issues when selecting them.

Which Ones to Buy?

Once you've decided that tax-exempts belong in your investment program, you're faced with the decision of how to stake your claim. Do you want to hold the bonds themselves or leave the selection to the professionals? If you choose to go with the pros, do you want an unmanaged unit trust or a managed municipal bond fund?

If you don't feel confident of your expertise and you have no advisor to consult, or if you have less than $25,000 to invest, you might do best to stick with the funds. Many offer minimum investments as small as $1,000, and for that you get a broadly diversified portfolio, which minimizes your risk.

Bond fund or unit trust, what's the difference? A bond fund has no set expiration date; maturing bonds are sold or replaced and the fund continues in existence long after its original portfolio has matured or changed. Not so with a unit trust, which consists of a set portfolio split into $1,000 units. As the components of its portfolio mature, unit holders receive their prorated share of the principal.

If you are going to invest in tax-exempt bond funds or unit trusts, you should try to reap the fullest measure from the tax exemption. This means you must explore your own state's and municipality's tax treatment of them. All states but Illinois, Iowa, Kansas, Oklahoma, and Wisconsin exempt interest generated by bonds issued within the state. If your state is one that exempts interest only on its own bonds, you should try to find home grown bonds, issued by your state of residence. If you live in Indiana, New Mexico, or Utah, interest is tax free on all municipal bonds regardless of the issuing state.

You have to watch this angle when investing in unit trusts or bond funds. While these funds are allowed by federal law to pass the tax exemption on to you, some state and local governments have not gone along. This means they tax all the income generated by the fund—including that from bonds issued within your state. If local or state law penalizes you on that score, think about going with the bonds themselves instead of the bond fund. Or look for a unit trust wholly invested in bonds from your own state. There will be no tax problem with these.

Single-state municipal unit trusts are getting increasing attention from sponsors and investors alike. State tax bills will account for a larger share of individuals' tax burdens now that federal tax rates have been lowered. Therefore, investments that help reduce the state tax take are of interest to many taxpayers. However, with sponsors vying with one another for a shrinking pool of tax-exempt municipal bonds (as a result of the previously discussed tax law changes), these UITs may be heading for problems. Only in states that are prolific bond issuers and that have high marginal tax rates do single-state UITs make economic sense.

When Shouldn't You Use Them?

There are times when municipal bonds do not fit the investment needs even of those whose income is most heavily taxed. Since munis are subject to gift, estate, and inheritance taxes, they have some drawbacks in estate planning. A forced sale in an estate settlement could result in loss of principal, particularly in the case of a municipal for which no ready market exists. Younger beneficiaries might rather have investments with greater appreciation potential.

Taxpayers who are subject to the alternative minimum tax should choose tax-exempt bonds with care. Interest on non-essential function tax-exempt bonds issued after mid-August 1986 was added as a tax preference item beginning in 1987. And for Social Security recipients, tax-exempt interest is added to adjusted gross income to determine whether a portion of the SS benefit is taxable.

Although the deduction for consumer and personal loans will be phased out by 1991, a decreasing portion of it will be deductible until then. If you have such loans outstanding, interest deductions on them could be jeopardized to the extent that it matches income from municipals. The IRS disallows such deductions where it can show a connection between the loan and the purchase of tax-exempts. Losing even a partial interest deduction could make the difference between winning and losing on a tax-free investment.

If your income fluctuates a great deal, tax-exempt bonds might help you one year but hurt the next. However, if you anticipate substantial growth in your income over the next several years, you might want to acquire municipals during times of high interest rates, when their yields are attractive.

In the final analysis, though, tax-exempts are vulnerable to the same criticisms we voiced earlier about other fixed-income investments. If they possess any protection against inflation, it is strictly limited. In fact, in a highly inflationary environment, they can lose ground. The prospect so alluring to many taxpayers—depriving Uncle Sam of some tax revenue—must be weighed against the possibility of obtaining greater gains elsewhere. Giving Caesar his due can frequently be more profitable in the long run.

Mutual Funds

THE CONCEPT OF forming a company to execute in collective investment the pooled assets of like-minded investors is a relatively recent development. As early as 1823 a New England life insurance company possessed features that resembled those of an investment company. The first recorded precursor to what we know today as mutual funds was organized a few years later by King William I of the Netherlands.

But it wasn't until 1868 that the first bona fide "mutual fund'" came upon the scene. In that year the Foreign and Colonial Government Trust was formed in London to provide "the investor of moderate means the same advantages as the large capitalists, in diminishing the risk of investing in Foreign and Colonial Government stocks, by spreading the investment over a number of different stocks."

If the mutual fund idea was rooted in Europe, it blossomed into full flower across the Atlantic. The first bud appeared in the United States in 1893 with the appearance of the Boston Personal Property Trust. It was followed in 1904 by the Railway and Light Securities Company. Both were organized as closed-end investment companies. In 1954, the latter converted to an open-end investment company and became the Colonial Fund, under which name it still operates. We shall distinguish between closed-end and open-end funds and define other terms in a moment. First let's complete our historical perspective.

The early 1920s witnessed the appearance of the mutual fund as we know it today, offering a self-liquidating feature, prudent investment policies and restrictions, diversification, a published portfolio, and an uncomplicated capital structure. Massachusetts Investors Trust, the first of the modern genre, was introduced in March 1924. Then came State Street Investment Corporation, also in 1924. These were followed in 1925 by Incorporated Investors, now Putnam Investors Fund. From modest beginnings, these three funds have become giants with assets in the hundreds of millions of dollars.

By 1929, there were nineteen open-end funds with assets totaling only about $140 million. Growth was slow through the Depression of the 1930s, so that by 1940 combined assets of mutual funds were less than $500 million. The next three decades witnessed phenomenal growth, and by the end of 1972 net assets of the industry had mushroomed to $60 billion, representing more than ten million shareholder accounts. Falling markets and net redemptions served to lower the total to only $34 million in 1974. By early 1987, industry assets stood at $464 billion, well above the $137 billion figure a year earlier. Money-market funds and short-term municipal bond funds had another $244 billion in assets. Mutual fund sales in early 1986 were at record levels, with much of the buying coming from IRA investors.

It should be noted that while the mutual funds have been credited from time to time as having a significant influence on the direction of the stock market, their assets generally have accounted for less than 8 percent of the market value of all stocks listed on the New York Stock Exchange.

What Is a Mutual Fund?

Now let's get a handle on what a mutual fund is—and what it isn't. Legally speaking, there is no such thing as a "mutual fund." That's merely a name coined to embrace a variety of investment companies and investment trusts created for the mutual investment under professional management of assets contributed by several individuals. A mutual fund—or, more technically, an investment company—is a corporation; and, as with other corporations, the individual investor's interest in it is represented by shares of stock. If the assets under management increase in value, the investor's capital will increase accordingly. Should the assets' value decline, the prorated net value of each share will likewise decline.

A mutual fund thus is basically different from, say, a savings account, where a depositor is guaranteed a fixed rate of return and will be able to withdraw all of his principal when he desires. A mutual fund investor is an owner, not a lender; he shares in the profits and losses and in the income and expenses.

However, there are some differences in the way they are taxed that distinguish investment companies from other corporations. Where all of the income from a conventional corporation is subject to federal income taxation, investment company income which is passed to shareholders is not taxed at the corporate level. In order to qualify for investment company status, a fund must comply with the provisions of the Investment Company Act of 1940. That comprehensive piece of legislation provides the foundation for regulation of the mutual fund industry and establishes standards of income distribution and diversification of assets.

Briefly, to operate as a regulated investment company and enjoy the tax benefits attached thereto, a fund must distribute at least 90 percent of its income each year to its shareholders. The remaining 10 percent or less is used to cover operating expenses and other overhead and is subject to corporation taxes. Shareholders pay income taxes at their own individual rates on the income passed along to them.

To assure diversification and to prevent the possibility that an investment company would acquire a controlling interest in a corporation, the law prohibits it from investing more than 5 percent of the value of its total assets in the securities of any single company or from holding more than 10 percent of the voting securities of any one company.

Closed-Ends and Open-Ends

The first mutual funds were closed-end funds. Closed-end funds, which today are known as publicly traded investment funds, differ in a number of respects from open-end funds. The primary difference, though, is in the way the shares of the fund are created.

In a publicly traded fund, the number of shares to be offered for sale is fixed at the outset; the fund operators may not create new shares on demand. An open-end fund, on the other hand, may create and sell its shares on a continuous basis; if an investor wishes to purchase fund shares, the new shares are created as needed.

Another important difference is that open-end funds stand ready to buy back, or redeem, outstanding shares at a price based on the market value of the portfolio at the time of redemption. Publicly traded funds do not buy back their shares from investors. Investors, in fact, have no direct buying or selling contact with the publicly traded fund except when reinvesting distributions in additional shares. Instead, they buy and sell fund shares on a securities exchange or in the over-the-counter market, just as they would do with any common stock. The broker who handles the transaction charges the same commission as he does for any similar transaction involving common stock.

Load Versus No-Load Funds

Open-end funds fall into two major categories: load funds and no-loads. They resemble each other in every way but one. Load funds are sold with a sales commission (the "load"), typically about 8.5 percent. This figure is expressed as a percentage of the total purchase price; that is to say, net asset value plus the sales charge. Thus, as compared with stock commissions, which are based on the sums actually invested, the sales charge for mutual funds is understated. For example, if you purchased shares in a load fund for $1,000, only $915 would actually be invested in securities.

The remaining $85 would go to the sales organization. If you divide that $85 by $915, the amount invested, you get 9.3 percent. Looking at it another way, if you want a full $1,000 in securities earning money for you, you must pay the fund a total of $1,093.

In respect to performance, there is no appreciable difference between that of the load funds and of the no-loads. Why, then, should you as an investor pay the load? Mutual fund salespersons will proffer any number of arguments to justify the load. Probably the most common is that over the long run the growth of the fund will reduce the effective cost of the sales charge to a minimum. In rebuttal, you can't always count on such growth, even over a relatively long period. Even if you amortize the load over a nine-year period, it amounts to about 1 percent a year. And over time the sales charge actually becomes more and more detrimental to performance because of the effect of compounding. The longer you plan to hold your mutual fund investment, the greater the advantage of purchasing a no-load. Because of compounding, the no-load will produce a significantly higher total return over the long haul.

Another argument put forth in defense of the load is that it carries an element of service for the investor. The salesperson or broker to whom the load is paid stands ready to answer questions, give advice, and help iron out any kinks that might develop with regard to your fund account. You have to ask yourself whether the cost of such an implied service is justified. In the final analysis, the price of a fund, whether you pay a sales commission or not, is secondary to choosing a fund with a good long-term performance record and investment aims in accord with your own.

Advantages of Mutual Funds

There are a number of sound reasons why small investors and large investors lacking access to investment counsel should explore the advantages of buying and holding mutual funds. Among them:

PROFESSIONAL MANAGEMENT. When you buy a fund you benefit from the expertise of full-time money managers who watch over the fund's portfolio and make all the necessary decisions as to what to buy, sell, or hold. Of course the experts can make mistakes—some of them are beauties—and, as is true among doctors and lawyers, some mutual fund managers are bright, others are not. In general, however, the leading funds are run by high-caliber people with substantial experience in investments.

DIVISION OF RISK. A typical fund spreads your investment dollar over many different industry and company stocks and securities. Thus a disaster in any one or a few of them does not mean a calamity for the fund as a whole. For example, a fund such as T. Rowe Price Growth Stock, with about $1 billion in assets, invests in more than 60 different stocks, none of which accounts for more than 5 percent of the fund's total market value at the time of purchase.

INFORMATION. How a mutual fund has performed is a matter of record. Mutual funds are unique in that they publish information as to their performance and it is readily available. Thus the layman, by reading the prospectus and shareholder reports, can compare one fund with another and make a decision as to which to buy. This is not the situation, say, with bank trust departments and stockbrokers.

FREEDOM FROM EMOTIONAL INVOLVEMENT. All too often the individual investor is swayed by the influence of one or a few well-motivated but poorly informed friends who are only too free with their stock market advice. Also, lacking expert knowledge, the individual may make investment decisions at times on the basis of headlines, rumors, and the fears and emotions of the moment. Investing in the stock market is for cool heads only, and it is one place where a little of the wrong knowledge can lead to big losses. When you buy good mutual funds, you can sit back and relax and, to paraphrase the Greyhound ad, leave the driving to them. The time and effort needed to choose and follow a good fund and keep on top of its fortunes, compared with the time and effort required for keeping track of individual stocks, is as minutes are to hours.

FREEDOM FROM HOUSEKEEPING. Aside from the emotional aspect of investing, there's the problem of mechanics. If you own stocks, you have to protect the certificates unless your stocks are held by your broker in "street name." There may be proxies to sign, rights to exercise, decisions to exercise or sell warrants, and on and on. Then there's the headache at income tax time. At the end of each year, mutual funds provide shareholders with information as to the total of dividends and other distributions made during the year and certain pertinent tax information. On a day-to-day basis, the status and value of your mutual fund account can be determined at a glance from the mutual fund quotations in your newspaper.

AUTOMATIC REINVESTMENT OF INCOME DIVIDENDS AND CAPITAL GAINS DISTRIBUTIONS. One of the principal advantages of mutual fund investment is that dividends can be automatically converted to additional shares, thus compounding your investment. Contrast this with the situation when you own a few thousand dollars' worth of each of several stocks. The dividend checks might be so modest that it would be difficult or expensive to reinvest them in additional shares. All too often dividend checks are frittered away, and the investment loses the benefit of compounding. The reinvestment feature of mutual funds is a form of forced saving and can make a big difference over the long run.

INSTANT DIVERSIFICATION. It often takes as little as $250 to start a mutual fund account. Additional investments can likewise be made in small amounts and at any time. When you buy shares in a mutual fund you buy a pro rata share of many different corporations in a number of different industries. To achieve similar diversification as an individual investor even in a small way would entail considerable time, to say nothing of commission expenses. Furthermore, funds purchase stocks in such large quantities that they almost always qualify for minimum sales commissions.

EXCHANGE PRIVILEGES. Most of the larger investment companies sponsor a variety of funds which offer a broad range of investment objectives, services, and programs. Thus a shareholder whose investment goals have changed may be able to switch part or all of his principal from one fund to another within the same "family." In addition, this exchange may be done by mail, telegram, or even telephone. The exchange privilege is only one of a number of shareholder services that make mutual funds an increasingly useful adjunct to financial planning. Tax-sheltered retirement plans and systematic investing and withdrawal plans are other features of the modern mutual fund, making it a comprehensive and convenient investment for the individual of moderate means.

Cost of Ownership

Every form of investment has its negative side, mutual funds included. Fund ownership is no free ride; there are costs and fees. We've already discussed the sales charge in the case of load funds. Not so obvious are management fees, which average about 0.5 percent per year of assets for load and no-load funds alike. In some instances the management fee is reduced as the fund's net asset value increases. Besides the management fee, there are a number of smaller charges for administrative services, directors' compensation, shareholder servicing, custodian fees, legal fees, reports to stockholders, and the like.

The total of the management fee and the housekeeping costs expressed as a percentage of net assets constitutes the fund's expense ratio. These ratios vary considerably depending on the size of the fund and other factors. For example, at T. Rowe Price Growth Stock they have averaged about 0.5 percent annually in recent years. Aside from efficient management, the low expense ratio reflects the benefits of size, for this is a fund with assets numbering in the hundreds of millions of dollars. Contrast that with the 1.5 percent and more per year for Nautilus Fund. Since many expenses are fixed, they understandably represent a larger portion of the cost of running a small fund than of a large fund. What you look for is a declining trend in the expense ratio as assets grow over the years. Otherwise the fund is not managed efficiently, and expenses may become a heavy drain on performance.

When a No-Load Isn't a No-Load

Recently many funds which began as no-loads have been reborn as low-loads. A low-load fund typically charges a fee of 3 percent or less. Low-load fees are used to cover the costs of marketing the fund to new investors; they are not used to pay brokers' commissions. Increasingly all funds, loads and no-loads alike, have added several fees and charges of which you should be aware.

DEFERRED SALES CHARGE. Also called a back-end load, this fee is used by funds to discourage frequent exchanges or early liquidation of shares. Sales charges are assessed when shares are sold before a certain time period has elapsed. For example, Dean Witter charges a deferred load of 1 to 5 percent when shares are liquidated within six years of purchase. The fee is on a sliding scale so that the longer the shares are held the lower the fee. Deferred sales charges are often used to pay brokers' commissions on portfolio transactions.

REDEMPTION FEE. This fee, generally 1 to 2 percent, serves to inhibit switching of the fund shares. Redemption fees normally disappear after the first year of holding.

12b-1 PLAN. Since 1980, a plan called *12b-1* has been used to help investment companies underwrite the costs of marketing and distributing their funds. The fee can also be used to pay brokerage costs. Although fee amounts are not often disclosed in a prospectus or financial statement, the fact that a 12b-1 is used will be noted somewhere in the prospectus. There is no maximum allowable charge under these plans, but generally fees are less than 1 percent of assets per year. Be forewarned that 12b-1 plans often are used by companies that levy deferred sales charges.

Reading the Prospectus

The Securities Act of 1933 requires delivery of a prospectus (essentially an abbreviated form of registration statement) prior to or with any solicitation of an order for mutual fund shares. The prospectus "tells it all"—something about management and its background, such unfavorable facts as there may be, including litigation and problems with the Securities and Exchange Commission, as well as a host of figures relating to income and expenses, dividends and gains (or losses), portfolio turnover, assets and liabilities, and the portfolio of investments.

In most cases, the funds have taken great pains to word their prospectuses in such a way that the average investor, with careful reading, can find out more about a fund's potential than he can glean from a similar reading of the annual report of an industrial corporation. Only when you buy a new issue, with its accompanying prospectus, are you in a position to learn as much about a corporate common stock.

The prospectus opens with a statement about the fund's primary objective. Thus the prospectus of Financial Industrial Income Fund states: "[The] investment objective is to emphasize current income while secondarily striving to attain capital growth."

The prospectus then elaborates on the fund's investment aims and gives information as to the minimum starting investment ($1,000 in the case of Financial Industrial Income) and the minimum subsequent investment, which is generally $50 or less. Early in the prospectus is a statement of per-share income and capital changes for each of the past ten years. That will give you an idea of the fund's investment income and expenses, its dividends, and its net realized and unrealized gains (or losses) on securities. The statistical tables that accompany this information show changes in net asset value and various financial ratios, such as the ratio of expenses to average net assets, and the ratio of net investment income to average net assets. It may also show portfolio turnover.

The prospectus goes on to outline the fund's investment

limitations. For example, among other restrictions, Financial Industrial Income may not "sell short or buy on margin unless it is a temporary measure for clearance of purchases of securities. . . . Buy or sell commodities, commodity contracts, or real estate (however, securities of companies investing in real estate may be purchased). . . . Invest in any company for the purpose of control or management. . . . Buy other than readily marketable securities. . . . Purchase securities if the purchase would cause the fund to have more than 5 percent of the value of its total assets invested in the securities of any one company, or to own more than 10 percent of the voting securities of any one company, or to own more than 10 percent of the voting securities of any one company (except obligations issued or guaranteed by the U.S. Government)."

Next comes information about the fund's investment advisor, plus the names and backgrounds of officers and directors. Information on the "how-to's" follows: how to purchase shares, how to redeem shares, how to exchange shares, and how to transfer shares. Then come statements about the fund's dividend policies, dates dividends are paid from investment income if and when earned, and perhaps a few remarks on the tax status of dividends and capital gains distributions.

The prospectus winds up with a statement about the fund's investments, including a breakdown as to the proportion of the portfolio in common stocks and bonds as well as the number of shares and the market value of each holding as of the statement date. The prospectus may also provide the cost of each investment, thus enabling the reader to see at a glance how the portfolio is doing. Other statements about assets and liabilities, along with notes to the financial statements, bring up the rear.

The Pulse of Portfolio Turnover

The frequency with which securities are bought and sold is a vital measure of a fund's health. By itself, however, it does not tell all you need to know to evaluate a fund's prospects. You might call it a financial heartbeat. A rapid heartbeat may be shown by a vigorous individual enjoying healthful exercise, and in someone else it may be symptomatic of a morbid condition. Similarly, a performance fund may show a substantial portfolio turnover rate and good performance all at the same time; a similar turnover rate for a fund that never goes anywhere suggests both poor portfolio management and a heavy drain on net assets from brokerage commissions and related expenses. The table on this page will give you some idea of the wide variance there is among funds as to expenses and portfolio turnover rates.

1986 FACTS ON 25 REPRESENTATIVE MUTUAL FUNDS

Fund	• Total Assets	Fund Type*	Expense Ratio	Turnover Rate %	% Load
Amer. Capital Harbor Fund	$241 mil.	GI	0.63	89.0	8.5
Amer. Capital Venture	413	AG	0.68	101.0	8.5
Columbia Growth	301	G	1.06	92.6	NL
Decatur Income	1100	GI	0.65	75.0	8.5
Eaton Vance Nautilus	23	AG	1.78	14.0	8.5
Evergreen Fund	589	G	1.52	41.0	NL
Fidelity Equity Income	2,882	GI	0.66	118.0	2.0
Fidelity High Yield Muni	1,861	TE	0.56	57.0	NL
Fidelity Magellan	6,038	AG	1.12	126.0	3.0
Franklin U.S. Gov't. Sec.	1,355	I	0.57	9.3	4.0
Guardian Mutual Fund	553	GI	0.76	57.0	NL
Int'l. Investors	801	S	0.81	5.1	8.5
Legg Mason Value Trust	312	G	2.10†	32.6	NL
MFS MMB Trust	644	I	0.75	101.0	4.75
Merrill Lynch Pacific Fund	235	Int	1.12	30.8	6.5
Mutual Qualified Income	513	GI	0.70	95.9	NL
Mutual Shares Corp.	1,264	GI	0.67	91.4	NL
Nicholas II Fund	310	G	1.11	10.0	NL
Northeast Investors Trust	270	I	2.00	37.3	NL
Nova Fund	25	AG	1.50	88.5	NL
OTC Securities	197	G	1.25	28.0	8.5
Pioneer II	2,693	GI	0.71	18.0	8.5
Templeton World	2,982	Int	0.82	15.8	8.5
Twentieth Century Select	1,738	AG	1.01	119.0	NL
Vanguard Wellesley Income	295	I	0.60	‡	NL

• Assets 3/31/86. * AG—Aggressive Growth; G—Growth; GI—Growth and Income; I—Income; Int—International; S—Specialized; TE—Tax-Exempt. † Includes 1% distribution fee. ‡ 32% for stocks and 14% for bonds.

An Important "Don't"

There is nothing to be gained by acquiring mutual fund shares immediately prior to dividends or capital gains distributions. On the contrary, to do so can hurt you.

Here's how: Apart from the ups and downs of the stock market, asset value gradually increases to the extent that portfolio securities are a source of interest and dividend income to the fund. If portfolio holdings appreciate, so much the better, for this also builds up asset value. To the extent such appreciation is realized, it becomes a source of capital gains distributions. Dividends from investment income and capital gains distributions are paid to the shareholder who buys the shares before the ex-dividend date. In other words, the ex-dividend date is the day on and after which the buyer of a share is not entitled to a previously declared dividend.

An investor who purchases fund shares shortly before an ex-dividend date will receive the dividend, to be sure, but it will be a hollow benefit. The pitfalls are spelled out in the prospectus, but while some funds take pains to explain the matter in some detail, others slough it off as a minor detail. This is unfortunate, because in a strong market the payments can be big and the tax consequences important.

Here's how one fund explained it:

Prior to purchasing shares of a fund, the impact of dividends or capital gains distributions which are expected to be announced or have been announced but not paid should be carefully considered. Any such dividends or capital gains distributions paid shortly after a purchase of shares by an investor prior to the record date will have the effect of reducing the per share net asset value of his shares by the amount of the dividends or distributions. All or a portion of such dividends or distributions, although in effect a return of capital, are subject to taxes, which may be at ordinary income tax rates. The individual should consult his own tax advisor for any special advice.

No one wants to pay taxes on someone else's gains, yet that is the situation if shares are purchased just prior to a capital gains distribution. Moreover, in the case of a load fund, the total sales charges would be needlessly high.

Funds in Your Future?

There you have some of the basics about mutual funds—where they came from, how they work, what to look for in evaluating one, how to read a prospectus. As you must have concluded from the foregoing, it's not exactly a matter of running your finger down a list of funds, finding one whose name intrigues you, and buying it to hold for keeps.

As with any investment decision, you have to know first what your own objectives are. Then you must find the proper vehicle—or, more frequently, vehicles—for meeting those objectives. Mutual funds can and do play an important part in achieving the investment goals of millions of Americans. How well funds do for you as an individual investor depends in large measure on how skillfully you have chosen the funds in your portfolio.

Just as you must evaluate other investments as to quality and the type and extent of risk each embodies, you must do the same with mutual funds. Some funds are better managed than others. Some place more emphasis on safety of principal than others. Some trade off quality of their holdings for higher yields or the chance of greater growth.

What Kind of Fund?

If you are a risk taker at heart and like a fast ride for your buck, look at the performance funds. If you buy for the long haul and have in mind a nest egg for retirement many years hence, you should stick with the sound-quality growth funds. If you want some current income while waiting for the day you cash in your shares, you should try to find funds that combine good current income with a potential for growth. Finally, if income is all-important to you and you will settle for little or no growth in the process, bond funds may be for you.

Often people find that their investment objectives change over time. Different stages of life—young adulthood, child rearing, mid-life, retirement, old age—all make different financial demands. Mutual fund families offer a ready method of accommodating changing investment needs. A family is a group of funds, each with a different objective, sponsored by a single investment company; three well-known ones are Fidelity, Vanguard, and T. Price Rowe. Most load-fund sponsors allow exchanges from fund to fund at minimal (usually $5) charge. Fund switching can also be used to take advantage of stock market cycles. And a money-market fund can be used to give conventional mutual fund investments added liquidity. When you need to cash in shares, a process which normally can take ten days or more, simply instruct the fund sponsor to move the desired amount from the stock or bond fund to the money-market account. The transferred funds are then accessible simply by writing a money-market check.

Closed Funds and Clones

As a mutual fund attracts investments, it gets larger and larger. Eventually it may become so sizable that its management may have difficulty moving in and out of stock positions at satisfactory prices. Fulfilling the fund's investment objectives can become tough sledding. For this reason some popular funds have been closed to new investors. Present shareholders' money continues to be managed as before. Dividends can be reinvested, and new money may be added to their accounts. Sometimes the fund will reopen after a time, or the sponsor may simply opt to start a clone. A clone is a mutual fund whose investment objectives closely resemble those of some other, established fund from the same sponsor. Clones often sport familiar names onto which Roman numerals have been tacked to indicate generation: Pioneer II, Nicholas II, and Option Income Portfolio II are examples. Once spawned, the offspring may or may not mimic the performance of its parent.

A Sample of Mutual Funds by Investment Objectives

Growth Funds

Columbia Growth	Nicholas II
Evergreen Fund	OTC Securities
Guardian Mutual	Templeton Growth

High-Income Funds

Fidelity High Income	Northeast Investors Trust
Fidelity High Yield Municipals	Pacific American Income
Franklin U.S. Govt. Securities	Wellesley Income

Growth and Income Funds

American Capital Harbor Fund	Fidelity Equity-Income
Decatur Income	Mutual Qualified Income
Evergreen Total Return	

Speculative/Aggressive Growth Funds

Fidelity Magellan	Nova Fund
IDS Progressive	Quasar Associates
Janus Fund	Twentieth Century Select

Again . . . Diversify

For the same reason you choose a mutual fund to diversify your portfolio and thereby spread your risks, you should not put all of your investment eggs in the same mutual fund basket, either. By avoiding that trap, you will cut your losses should a fund you are holding undergo a management crisis, lose its "magic touch," or just plain hit a patch of poor luck.

CHAPTER 13

Special-Purpose Investment Funds

COLLECTIVELY, MUTUAL FUNDS compose a dynamic, ever-evolving industry. Sponsors have been resourceful in bringing out new products to fit changing market conditions. In recent years, new types of funds have been devised, particularly in the income area, although narrowly aimed industry-specific funds have been another recent phenomenon.

This section is devoted to a rundown of funds which meet specialized investment objectives. Few of these funds can stand alone in an investment progam, but they can be used with other funds or securities to "fine-tune" your portfolio to your particular financial needs.

Convertible Funds

Though convertible bonds and preferred stocks are insignificant in numbers of issues compared to Wall Street's aggregate, mutual funds investing in these securities offer reliable income and the opportunity for healthy capital gains. *Convertible bonds* are securities which at the option of the bondholder may be converted into the common stock of the issuing corporation. This conversion takes place at a prescribed price or ratio. *Convertible preferred stock* is likewise convertible into common shares of the issuer. The market for convertibles is generally strongest when stocks are rising and interest rates are high. But during weak markets convertibles offer special appeal because they retain their value better than the underlying common stock.

It makes sense to purchase convertible funds after the underlying stock prices have fallen. That's when the bargains are found. There are several funds that have a sizable percentage of their assets in convertible securities, among them American Capital Convertible Securities, American Capital Harbor, Bancroft Convertible, and Castle Convertible. As a group, these funds have provided healthy long-term performances both in terms of capital gains and income.

Gold Funds

Some investors choose investments in gold stocks as a hedge in times of war, social upheavals, inflation, or other dire distresses. During 1973–74, when inflation was rampant and foreign exchange rates fluctuating, gold-bullion and gold-mining shares lured large numbers of speculators and individuals seeking to protect the purchasing power of their savings. Aside from their disaster-hedge value to pessimists, gold and gold-fund shares have little usefulness except as speculation on the value of gold itself. Gold funds are rife with volatility, heaped with political and economic hazards, and burdened with the unpredictability of the production process itself. To wit, the performance of gold funds is ragged, generally even poor. But if an investment in gold will give you peace of mind, or if gold-market timing is your interest, try International Investors fund, Fidelity Select Gold Fund, Keystone Precious Metals Holdings, the Financial Portfolios Gold Fund, or the Vanguard Specialized Gold Portfolio. We talk more about gold in Chapter 17.

Foreign Funds

An investment made on a foreign stock market can produce gains in two ways. The first is by a simple increase in the price of the foreign shares. Often foreign markets are out of step with American ones. The Japanese economy, for example, grew twice as fast as the American economy from 1953 to 1983. Because foreign market cycles frequently lag American ones, they often heat up when the U.S. market is cooling down, and therefore provide additional opportunities for investors. The second means of profiting from foreign investments is through disparities in the relative exchange rates for U.S. and foreign currencies. If an American investor puts $2,000 into the German stock market and the value of the deutsche mark rises by 10 percent relative to the dollar, then the value of the German shares rises to $2,200 when converted back into U.S. dollars. As you can see, such exchange-rate windfalls have nothing to do with the underlying value of stocks themselves. When the dollar is rising relative to a foreign currency, foreign investments will lose value when translated into dollars; when the dollar falls, they will gain value in U.S. dollars.

The two components, share value and exchange rates, must be considered together to determine whether a foreign investment is a money-maker. During 1984 many foreign stock markets outperformed the U.S. market in terms of their own currency. For the American investor, though, the strength of the dollar effectively wiped out most of the very large overseas gains. But for those who hung on, 1985 was a different story; a declining dollar permitted the favorable conversion of profits acquired the year before.

Since foreign markets are often remote, volatile, and less closely regulated than Wall Street, the best way for most people to participate in them is through an international mutual fund. Such funds may either hold stocks from the most promising markets around the globe, as do Templeton's World and Putnam's International, or they may be comprised of stocks from one region or market, as are the Japan Fund and Merrill Lynch's Pacific. Other leading foreign funds include Templeton Growth and Global II, Fidelity Overseas, G.T. Pacific, and Vanguard World International Portfolio.

Ginnie Mae Funds

When interest rates are down, Ginnie Maes heat up. But Ginnie Maes, often touted as offering unbeatable safety and yield, are both more complex and more unpredictable than they seem at first glance. The Government National Mortgage Association (GNMA), or Ginnie Mae, as it is affectionately known, specializes in mortgage pass-through certificates backed by the full faith and credit of the U.S. government. Ginnie Maes represent shares in pools of mortgages, issued either by the Federal Housing Administration or the Veterans Administration and insured by GNMA. GNMA guarantees the homeowners' mortgage payments, both principal and interest, and passes them through to investors each month, even if a homeowner defaults. A growing number of fund sponsors, recognizing the popularity of Ginnie Maes, have begun offering GNMA mutual funds. Because the yield on government-backed Ginnie Maes is often 2 percent higher than on an equivalent Treasury issue, they are attractive to many income investors.

A Ginnie Mae mutual fund is the easiest way to invest in these certificates for several reasons. First, the average minimum investment in a Ginnie Mae fund is $1,000, versus $25,000 for a GNMA certificate. Then, too, the professional management of a mutual fund is especially advantageous in mortgage security investing because the average investor has neither the time nor the expertise to analyze and track rates on different Ginnie Mae pools. Also, since mortgage-backed securities, unlike other fixed-income investments, return dribbles of principal along with monthly interest payments, reinvestment can be irksome. Ginnie Mae funds automatically reinvest these payments of principal and they will reinvest interest, too, upon request.

The following funds invest solely in GNMA certificates: Franklin U.S. Government Securities, and Lexington, Pilgrim, and Vanguard GNMA funds. Other funds—Alliance Mortgage Securities, Fidelity Mortgage Securities, USAA Income, and Van Kampen Merritt U.S. Government—invest in Federal National Mortgage Association (FNMA) and Federal

Home Loan Mortgage Corporation (FHLMC) issues in addition to GNMAs. While FNMA and FHLMC are federally chartered, their securities, which aren't government backed, offer slightly higher yields.

Index Funds

The Vanguard Group introduced the first index fund to be offered to the public, First Index Investment Trust, in August 1976. This fund seeks to provide investment results corresponding to the price and yield performance of the Standard & Poor's 500 Composite Stock Index. To achieve this end the trust holds all of the issues in the S&P.

Although First Index Investment Trust tracks the S&P, there are many mutual funds that have outperformed it over the long term. If you are content to ride the coattails of the Standard & Poor's 500 and have no expectations of doing better than this average, then an index fund may be satisfactory. However, if you have loftier goals and a conviction that good judgment pays off in above-average performance, then your investment dollars should be in a managed mutual fund.

Money-Market Funds

A soft stock market and hefty returns of 10 percent or more combined to give money-market funds a lot of appeal when they were introduced in 1974. Two dozen or so were started that year, and investors salted away more than $3 billion in them by the end of 1975. Increasingly, small businesses, corporations, and individuals found these funds convenient repositories for their cash reserves. In terms of sales, number of funds, and total accounts outstanding, the growth of the money-market fund has no parallel in the investment industry. At year end 1974, there were but fifteen money-market funds, with total assets of $1.7 billion. By 1986, there were over 350 such funds (including institutional funds), holding assets totaling in excess of $240 billion. Among the largest of the conventional money mutuals are Merrill Lynch's CMA

Money and Ready Assets funds, Dreyfus Liquid Assets, Dean Witter Sears Liquid Assets, and Fidelity Cash Reserves.

What makes money-market funds so attractive to so many? Safety of principal. Money-market funds are the only investment vehicles which maintain a constant price, usually $1.00 per share. To obtain this constant share value, money funds use various investment means, including bank CDs with short, often two-week, maturities, U.S. Treasury bills, bankers' acceptances, and prime commercial paper. Some funds, which take slightly more risk for the chance at slightly higher yields, utilize repurchase agreements (repos), nonprime commercial paper, letters of credit, and Yankee and Euro dollars (domestic deposits in foreign banks).

Besides safety of principal, money-market funds have two other attractive characteristics. They provide automatic dividend reinvestment and cashlike liquidity. Check-writing privileges make money-market investments as easy to tap as conventional checking accounts—although most funds have a $500 minimum per check. Also, exchange privileges with other mutual funds in the same fund family—e.g., Fidelity's Cash Reserves may be exchanged for shares of another Fidelity fund or vice versa—allow investors to implement changing financial objectives and to gain access to equity fund assets easily.

If the promise of tax-free income is worth sacrificing a point or two of yield, a tax-exempt money-market fund may be the answer. Such funds invest in short-term issues by, or on behalf of, state and local governments. Tax-free yields are available from Merrill Lynch CMA Tax-Exempt, Fidelity Tax-Exempt MMT, Dreyfus Tax-Exempt, and Municipal Cash Reserve Management, among others.

When ironclad safety is a must, a fund which invests solely in Treasuries is your ticket. Capital Preservation Fund, Dreyfus Money Market Instruments Government Fund, Merrill Lynch Government Securities, Neuberger & Berman Government MF, T. Rowe Price U.S. Treasury Money Fund are just a few of the Treasury-only funds. Other funds, which invest in agency as well as Treasury debt, include Cash Equivalent Government Only Fund, Dean Witter Sears U.S.

Government MMT, Liberty Government Money Market Trust, and Shearson Government & Agency Fund.

Municipal Bond Funds

Until the Tax Reform Act of 1976, there was no way a conventional mutual fund could pass along to investors the tax-exempt status of interest earned on municipal bonds held in their portfolios. Unit trusts, reviewed below, were able to pass through this tax exemption, but it was necessary to change the tax laws to cover conventional mutuals. Once an appropriate law was passed, mutual fund sponsors lost little time in introducing managed municipal bond funds. Within a few years, more than 30 such funds were offering shares to the public. Today there are more than 150 muni funds, with total assets in excess of $32 billion.

The tax-exempt bond mutuals have drawn their share of critics. Some say that they are not the straightforward, safe investments they were at their inception. Seesawing interest rates and huge numbers of poorly rated bonds have introduced new risks into these vehicles. Today municipal bond funds fall into a variety of risk categories ranging from ultra-conservative *insured* to high-yielding *"junk."* Low-risk funds include Merrill Lynch Municipal Bond Fund Insured Portfolio and the Vanguard Insured Long-Term Portfolio. Both purchase munis insured by AMBAC Indemnity Corporation and the Municipal Bond Investors Assurance. At the price of assuming a little more risk, slightly higher yields can be obtained from the Stein Roe Tax-Exempt Bond Fund and MFS Managed Municipal Bond Trust. These funds invest primarily in municipals rated A or better by Moody's or Standard & Poor's. Most volatile, but highest yielding, are "junk" funds, which invest in low- to medium-quality municipal issues. Two such funds are Colonial Tax-Exempt High Yield and Fidelity High Yield Municipals.

Another variation on the municipal bond fund theme is the single-state or single-city fund, which is exempt not only from federal taxes but also from the issuing state's or city's taxes. These have become very popular in heavily taxed states such as California or municipalities such as New York City.

Municipal bond mutual funds are available in both no-load and low-load varieties (commonly charging 4 to 4¾ percent). Dividends accrue daily and are distributed monthly or quarterly or are automatically reinvested, whichever is elected. Many also offer exchange privileges with their other funds.

Option-Income Funds

The primary investment objective of option-income funds is to provide shareholders with a high level of current income. To achieve this goal, the funds write covered call options on a diversified portfolio of common stocks, the majority of which are dividend paying.

When a mutual fund writes such an option, it agrees to sell by a certain date shares of its stock to the purchaser for a specified price in excess of the market price at the time the option is written. These options often expire without being exercised, because the stock fails to reach the exercise price by expiration date.

In exchange for this promise to sell, the fund receives a premium from the purchaser of the call option. Premiums are distributed to shareholders on a quarterly basis and are considered to be short-term capital gains. When these premiums are added to the portfolio's common stock dividends, the total return often exceeds 12 percent per annum.

You've seen how you can win with option income. Now let's look at how you can lose. Option writing imposes a sharp limitation on potential profits. If a fund sells options during a rapidly rising market, the income earned from premiums is often far less than the amount forfeited through missed stock appreciation. As a simple example, consider a mutual fund which owns 100 shares of General Electric selling at $53 per share. To earn extra income, the fund decides to write an option at $55 on its GE holdings for a premium of $275. If the stock's value rises above the prearranged price of $55 prior to the expiration date, the option will undoubtedly be exercised (the fund will have to deliver its 100 shares). While the fund will pocket the difference between the amount at which it purchased GE and the price at which it was called away plus the premium received for selling the call, it will not share in the capital gains should the stock continue to climb in value.

When stock prices are falling, writing covered calls can help offset a portfolio's losses. Option-income funds are far less volatile than the market as a whole. However, the premiums paid for options are at their lowest during bear markets. The environment in which option-income funds perform best is one which is relatively stable—rising or falling only gradually.

Leaders in this category include Putnam Option Income I, Kemper Option Income, Franklin Option Income, Colonial Option Income Portfolio, and Oppenheimer Premium Income.

Sector Funds

Sector funds invest in the stocks of a single industry or market segment. Fidelity's Select Portfolios Fund, first introduced in 1981, is the father of the portfolio-type sector mutuals. It gave investors the choice of four different portfolios and the ability to switch among them. By late 1986 the number of funds in Select Portfolios had swelled to twenty-five. Other mutual fund companies, Vanguard and Financial Group among them, have joined the sector game.

Sector fund investing is risky; it is best reserved for the knowledgeable, active, aggressive investor. These single-industry funds are becoming more and more specialized. The sector supermarket now spans the alphabet from air transport to utilities. So although Fidelity and Vanguard may nearly always have a sector fund or two in the top ten performers, very rarely are they the same ones from period to period. If the potential for huge profits and the ability to control your investments are irresistible to you, we suggest utilizing Fidelity's original six sector portfolios: Energy, Financial, Health Care, Precious Metals, Technology, and Utilities.

They are more diversified than newer ones and require less day-to-day vigilance.

In order to profit from market segment funds, one must be savvy enough to invest in a sector before it heats up and disciplined enough to get out before it loses steam. How does one get in and out at the right time? The majority of investors and professionals have learned that they don't, at least not with any degree of consistency.

If an investor believes a particular industry group has long-term growth potential, should he purchase a corresponding sector-portfolio fund? Probably not. When one sector is hot, its assets generally increase, and when it is not, shareholders abandon it for the current darling. This ebb and flow of money can cause the portfolio manager to sell a stock prematurely to cover redemptions, or he may be forced to hold too much cash. Neither scenario bodes well for the long-term investor. For long-term holding, a sector fund which is not part of a portfolio is a better bet. Technology enthusiasts might try Nova Fund or Merrill Lynch Sci/Tech Holdings. Pro Medical Technology and Putnam Health Sciences are good choices for the health/medical industry investor.

Social-Action Funds

A number of funds have emerged that cater to investors' wishes to take political stands or precipitate social change. Such funds use a predetermined philosophical screen to select stocks for their portfolios. Commonly such funds will not invest in companies doing business in South Africa, using nuclear power generators, or manufacturing armaments. In the past these funds have had returns generally similar to or better than those of the Standard & Poor's 500. Leading social-action funds include Calvert Social Investment Managed Growth Portfolio, Dreyfus Third Century Fund, New Alternatives Fund, Pax World Fund, and the entire Pioneer family of funds, which refrains from investments in liquor, tobacco, and gambling issues. Calvert and Working Assets also manage socially responsible money-market funds.

Unit Trusts

Unit trusts are similar to conventional funds in the sense that they allow investors to obtain a share of a widely diversified portfolio, thereby benefiting from lower risk through diversification. However, they differ in one very important respect. The portfolios of unit trusts are fixed; no new bonds are added after the initial offering. No trading of the portfolio bonds is allowed—the funds exist as self-liquidating trusts until all or most of the bonds reach maturity or are retired.

The proceeds from trust securities that mature or are called are distributed rather than reinvested. Unit trusts offer monthly, quarterly, or semiannual distributions or income reinvestment in a money-market mutual fund and/or open-end bond fund managed by the sponsor. The trustee also furnishes statements for tax purposes. Pay careful attention to these, as trust distributions can represent a return of principal as well as interest income. Return of principal is not taxable and should usually be saved for future reinvestment.

Shares in the trusts are called units. Unit prices will fluctuate with interest rates and market conditions and will reflect portions of principal which have been called or matured. Unit trusts yield an average of 1 to 2 percent more than comparable diversified municipal bond funds because trust expenses are lower. Although they are under no obligation to do so, sponsors maintain a secondary market in their units. Should a unit be redeemed before maturity, its value is generally based on the bid prices of underlying bonds.

Taxable corporate and federal tax-exempt municipal unit trusts are regularly launched by brokers and dealers such as Merrill Lynch and John Nuveen; minimum investment amounts range from $1,000 to $5,000. When a unit trust comes to market, its stated return takes into account both a front-end sales charge ranging from 3.9 to 5 percent and estimated annual expenses per unit. Unit trusts are available both as intermediate-term investments, with bond lives from five to fifteen years, and as long-term investments, having fifteen- to forty-year maturities. Because the trusts are self-liquidating, over time the ever-smaller portfolio will reduce income payments.

Unit trusts, like municipal bond funds, are offered in single-state and insured forms. The single-state tax-exempt feature is a boon in high-tax states. However, insurance is an expensive balm for the skittish. But if insurance appeals to you, be sure to purchase a product, like Nuveen's insured trusts, in which each bond is permanently insured by the Municipal Bond Investors Assurance (MBIA). Such bonds receive AAA ratings from Standard & Poor's. This kind of insurance is called "insured to maturity" and is superior to "while-in-trust-only" coverage. "While-in-trust-only" coverage ceases when bonds are sold, and thereafter cast-off bonds are priced according to their intrinsic credit worth.

CHAPTER 14

Options

To UNDERSTAND OPTIONS and to be able to employ this knowledge for profit is to be the object of awe among the uninitiated who mill and churn in the courtyards of the temples of investment. To presume to do so without proper understanding is to invite almost certain financial disaster.

Fewer still are those who possess the capacity to convey this esoteric and mysterious wisdom by means of spoken or written word. It is thus with due humility that we embark on this chapter.

The first step in your rite of passage is an introduction to the colorful language of options. Puts. Calls. Strips. Straps. Straddles. Spreads. Naked Options. Naked short puts. Trapezoidal hedges. The list goes on.

The basic concept of options is simple enough. They are used in many businesses as a matter of course. Option contracts are nothing more than obligations to buy or sell a given piece of property at a stated price within a specified time period. A real estate purchase and sale agreement is something like an option contract, and if you've ever bought or sold a house, chances are you used one.

CBOE: Order from Chaos

Until the Chicago Board Options Exchange (CBOE) opened its doors in April 1973, trading in puts and calls was a haphazard venture. Each contract was individually negotiated by brokers for the buyer and seller. Once an investor was into a contract there was little opportunity for his transferring it to a third party.

Initially, the CBOE traded only call options, and those on only 16 stocks. By mid-1977, it was listing options for stocks of more than 100 companies, each offering three expiration dates and at least as many different striking prices. We'll define these terms as the explanation proceeds.

Investors, always eager for new ways to make a killing, latched on to options with such enthusiasm and with such obvious profit to the CBOE that other exchanges soon were clamoring for a piece of the action. By 1980, the American, Pacific, and Philadelphia stock exchanges were sitting comfortably on the options bandwagon. The Big Board, too, is negotiating to get a piece of the option action. All told, puts and calls are listed on more than 400 issues.

The CBOE introduced, and the other three option exchanges adopted, a systematized method of setting striking prices and expiration dates for contracts. The exchanges also provide liquidity and visibility for option transactions.

Purchases and sales are handled in much the same way as they are for common stocks. An order is placed with your broker and is executed on the floor of the exchange. Once an order between a buyer and seller is matched, their connection is severed and the Options Clearing Corporation steps in to become buyer to the seller and seller to the buyer. In this way both parties to the contract are free to take whatever subsequent action they choose, independent of one another. Thus, contracts may be closed out at any time prior to expiration by making an offsetting trade. Furthermore, the Options Clearing Corporation, which serves all the option exchanges, guarantees that stock will be delivered if the option is exercised *and* that the seller will be paid.

While the various option exchanges are auction markets,

not all of them use the CBOE system of competitive market makers. This was a major innovation of the new exchange. The two functions normally handled by the specialist were separated. A board broker took over the brokerage function of executing limit orders placed by floor brokers. Competing market makers were assigned to take over the specialist function of trading for their own accounts to stabilize the market. This tends to make the CBOE a more efficient market, with premiums cleaving closely to supply and demand balances.

Now, into the mechanics.

Call Options

A call is an option to buy 100 shares of the underlying stock at a specified price, known as the "exercise price" or "striking price," within a specified time period. Unless the Clearing Corporation makes a change to reflect a stock split, one option contract is for 100 shares of the underlying security. Striking prices are set at 5-point intervals on or around the trading price for stocks selling below 50 and usually at 10-point intervals for those above 50. A new option series is initiated nine months prior to its expiration date, so that at any given time three contracts with the same exercise price are available on one underlying stock, with maturities three months apart. Options with the same expiration date may be offered with several different striking prices.

When the striking price is above the current trading price, the call is said to be trading "out of the money." A strike below market price would mean the call was "in the money." When market and striking prices jibe, the option is "at the money." Although premiums—the price you actually pay for the option—generally run from 5 to 12 percent of the price of the underlying stock at the time of the option's introduction, this figure then varies with supply and demand and with time. Options are a wasting asset; i.e., they have a value for their limited life span, beyond which they are worthless.

If the premium, which is paid to the seller (also called the "writer") of the option, and the option striking price are equal to the current price of the stock, that option is said to be trading "at parity." The premium tends to move point for point with the share price only when the option is at parity. Prior to that the premium rises less than point for point, since the leverage value is reduced at parity and thus the demand for that call dries up.

In a rising market, the demand for options increases as the number of sellers decreases. This increase in demand under normal circumstances tends to enlarge the premium. In a declining market, the reverse is true, causing the premium to narrow.

The relationship between the striking price and the stock price has an important influence on the size of the premium. A call with a striking price of 40 on a stock trading at 50 is understandably worth more than a call with a strike of 60. A call approaching its expiration date with little chance of being exercised at a profit will move down in value and expire worthless.

Another factor which influences the call premium is an approaching ex-dividend date. It is just prior to this date that options are most frequently exercised by option buyers eager to collect the dividend. In order to prevent the stock from being called away, the writer may buy an offsetting call to close out his contract. This tends to enlarge the premium prior to the ex-dividend date as demand exceeds supply.

These various influences can be clearly seen in the chart of a common stock and two of its call options on page 138. The space between the dashed and solid lines represents the amount by which the call is trading above parity, or its tangible value. The effect of time is obvious; the "fat" in the premium is trimmed away as the calls approach expiration. In fact, the April call traded below its tangible value (parity) about a month prior to expiration, a clear warning to option writers that exercise was a strong probability. The October call, trading well above its parity value until June, shows very succinctly the vital influence of time in the level of a premium.

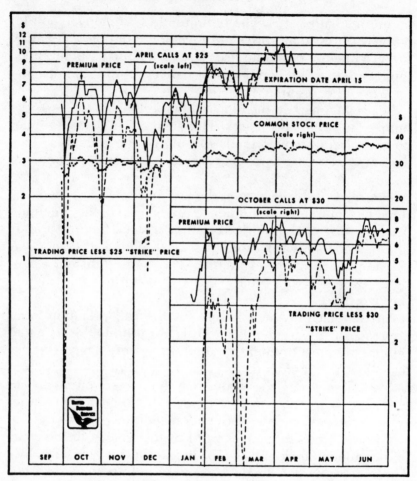

When to Buy and When to Sell Calls

The call option *buyer* is looking for a rise in the price of the underlying security. If the stock moves up, he may choose to exercise the call and buy the stock at its strike price, which would then be below the current market price. Or he could liquidate the call by selling one bearing the same date and striking price. It is the latter transaction that is most commonly used, since this does not entail the expenditure of additional capital.

If the option is covered prior to expiration, a short- or long-term capital gain is realized, depending on whether or not the holding period exceeds six months. However, if the buyer chooses instead to exercise the option and actually acquire the shares, no taxable event will have occurred as long as he keeps the shares. But his cost basis for these shares will be increased by the premium paid for the option. Thus, if the call was bought at a premium of 5 and exercised at 30, the cost basis will be 35 and the exercise date becomes the purchase date for tax purposes.

When the underlying security moves contrary to expectations and it becomes clear that a loss is inevitable, the call buyer is usually best off to take some action rather than allowing the option to expire worthless. He should make a closing sale transaction in order to reduce the extent of the loss. However, he should be sure to make his move before the proceeds from the sale sink below what he would have to pay the broker in commissions. Either an expiration or a closing sale is a short- or long-term capital loss. A covering transaction that would reduce the loss may or may not be possible, depending on whether a buyer exists for that particular series.

A *writer* (seller) of covered options is generally interested in generating a greater return from his long-term holdings than would be possible from dividends alone. When a call is written against securities already owned, it is referred to as "covered."

Writing "naked" options, where the underlying stock is not owned by the seller, is quite another matter. This highly speculative technique will produce a profit if the stock declines or remains constant, but the profit is limited to the amount of the premium received. On the other hand, if the stock rises, the potential for loss is unlimited, as it is on a short sale. Then the writer must either make a closing purchase transaction to liquidate his contract or buy shares at market to cover when the call is exercised.

The premium paid to an option writer is not reported as income when received. If the option expires unexercised, the premium is taxed as a short-term capital gain in the year of exercise. If a covering option is bought, the difference is a short-term gain or loss. However, under certain special circumstances, a loss on a covered call may be long term.

Options and Margin Requirements

Option-writing programs, covered or otherwise, are executed in margin accounts. Margin agreements give the broker a lien on the assets in the account and assure the proper delivery of shares or cash as required. Options currently have no loan value in a margin account. Writers of naked options must maintain sufficient cash or loan value in their accounts to fulfill their obligation in the event of a call.

In a sideways or declining market, when profits are difficult to come by, an option-writing program can generate additional cash flow from a portfolio. However, the market does not always perform as expected, and the call writer may be faced with delivering securities he would prefer to hold. Rather than incurring a large capital gains tax liability, he could purchase new shares to satisfy the call obligation.

Avoiding Unwanted Exercise Notices

A call can be exercised at any time up to expiration; the writer has *no* choice in the matter but to give up the shares he promised to sell. If he really doesn't want to sell, he can watch for and heed certain early warning signals. The chance of exercise is higher prior to an ex-dividend date, since the buyer will want to own the stock and collect the dividend. Also, as a call reaches parity, the instance of exercise increases, and, of course, a profitable call would never be allowed to expire unexercised.

To avoid having to deliver shares, an investor must make a closing purchase transaction in the same call series before an exercise notice is received. Exercise notices are assigned on a random basis and delivered to member firms by the Options Clearing Corporation. Brokerage firms may use either a random selection method or may assign exercise notices on a first-in, first-out basis. You should check to find out which method your broker uses, since it could have a strong bearing on when to close out a questionable option. Once an exercise notice is received, the writer's choices are narrowed—the underlying stock must be delivered, be it shares already owned or new shares purchased to cover. At that point, the offsetting option transaction is no longer possible as a means of liquidating the call.

It is usually more profitable to write call options in a declining or trendless market than in a rising market. An up market favors the call buyer. While an "in-the-money" call may earn the writer a larger immediate cash advance, this type of contract stands a greater chance of being exercised. Similarly, for a call buyer an "out-of-the-money" option is the least costly but also the most likely to expire worthless.

Balancing these risk-reward factors when there may be a dozen or more choices for one stock is not easy. One good rule of thumb is not to reach too far but to settle for the middle of the road, particularly in writing calls.

Put Options

Having completed a strikingly successful four-year trial of trading call options, the exchanges won permission from the Securities and Exchange Commission in June 1977 to begin a pilot program of offering put options. Initially trading was limited to twenty-four issues, but puts are now available on the same issues that have listed call options.

Contrary to what you might think, puts are not simply the reverse side of calls. They are totally separate and distinct transactions. Where a call option gives the buyer the right to purchase shares of the underlying stock from the writer, a put option gives him the right to sell (or "put to") the writer those shares.

Let's take a closer look at how puts work. A trader who expects the stock market to decline might buy a put option on stock he holds to limit his potential loss. Remember the put gives him the right to sell those shares at a specified price. Generally this is done by buying the put with a striking price at or above the current market price. If the market price declines below that level, he can exercise the put to cut his losses. Of course in his expectation of a market decline he could have written a call option on the stocks he was holding, as we explained in the preceding section. Conversely, should the trader expect a rise in the stock market, he could write a put or buy a call.

Buying Puts—When and Why

Buying a "covered" put—one purchased against stock actually owned—allows the trader to put a floor on his losses should the market decline, a point we made a moment ago. However, he might also buy a put without actually owning the underlying shares and make money in a falling market. In this case, if the market declined according to his expectations (before his initial put expired) he would sell a put of the same series and expiration date. At that point, the put he sold would be commanding a higher premium than the premium he paid at purchase. The difference in these premium prices would represent his profit.

In exercising a covered put, a buyer need not necessarily deliver the shares he actually holds, though of course he has the right to do so. If he expects the market to recover and wishes to retain his position in that stock, he might do as the buyer of the uncovered put did and write a put with a higher premium to close out his contract.

If the market goes up contrary to the put buyer's expectations, the loss is limited to the cost of the put—the premium. Just as the buyer of a call option need not let it expire worthless, a put buyer may limit his loss if the stock rises by selling the put at a lower premium than he originally paid. In general, this is a prudent policy. In this case the loss is limited to the difference between the premium paid and the premium received on the covering trade.

There are tax implications in put trading that you should understand before embarking on such a program.

Writing Puts

The writer (seller) of a put is taking a greater risk if the market moves down against him. In this event he will be required to take delivery and come up with the cash for shares at a price well above market. This disconcerting situation could occur at any time up to the expiration date of the option contract. The cost basis on these shares will be the exercise price minus the premium received.

The put seller may be motivated by a desire to generate cash in a trendless market. The put expires worthless and the writer pockets his premium. He may also wish to acquire stock at a price below the current market. In this case he writes a put with a striking price at market and pockets the premium. When the stock drops, the put buyer exercises his option to deliver the shares. Thus, the writer acquires stock below market, the cost being the strike price minus the put premium. Puts should only be written against sufficient cash to purchase the shares when exercise occurs.

Unlike call premiums, which rise as the share price rises, put premiums rise when the share price drops. Thus, for a put to be "in the money" the strike price must be above the market price, and to be "out of the money" the strike price must be below the market price for the shares. Premiums tend to be higher for the more volatile stocks, which also holds true for call premiums. Time has the same value with puts as with calls.

A Growing Market

In 1974, the first full year of an organized options market, more than 300,000 contracts were written and only one in six was exercised. Two years later, eight times as many contracts were written, 2.6 million. Whether it was because conditions were more favorable or traders more discriminating, one contract in three was exercised that year.

Although widespread institutional participation is a factor in the growth of options trading, this was not always the case.

Aside from the strictures that were placed on money managers and pension fund administrators by the prudent man provisions of the Employee Retirement Income Security Act of 1974 (ERISA), institutions theretofore had been held back by tax considerations. Mutual funds must derive at least 90 percent of income from investments to qualify for pass-through tax exemptions. Until the Tax Reform Act of 1976, option premiums were treated as ordinary business income, not investment income. After that such premiums were specifically classed as capital gains. This development cleared the way not only for institutional option writing programs but also for the introduction of a new group of mutual funds called "option income funds."

Summing Up

Broadly speaking, options may be used to guarantee market position, to obtain stock at below-market prices, to limit losses, to hedge against unpredictable turns in an uncertain market, and to generate income or cash flow.

To help you get a handle on these somewhat confusing trading techniques and to help clarify for you the risk-reward parameters of options trading, the table opposite places these concepts in perspective.

Utilizing options as a part of your investment program can be conservative investment strategy. Conversely, it can be as speculative as short selling, with an unlimited loss potential. It is not a technique which should be attempted without full understanding of its uses, values, and risks. For a more detailed discussion of the myriad strategies possible with options see Chapter 31.

Market action necessary for profitable option trades:

Call Options	*Put Options*
Buyer: Rising market	Buyer: Declining market
Seller: Declining or sideways market	Seller: Rising or sideways market

Market action that will result in losses on option trades:

Call Options	*Put Options*
Buyer: Sideways or declining market	Buyer: Sideways or rising market
Seller: Rising market	Seller: Declining market

The amount of risk or reward in a given option position:

Option Contract Position	*Possible Loss*	*Possible Gain*
Call buyer	Cost of premium	Unlimited
Call seller, covered	Cost of buy-back*	Premium received
Call seller, naked	Unlimited	Premium received
Put buyer	Cost of premium	Unlimited
Put seller	Cost to buy in*	Premium received
Spreads, straddles, or combinations	Unlimited†	Unlimited†

* For the writer of a covered call or a put, the extent of the loss may be limited by making an offsetting sale. If no covering option is purchased, the loss is more a matter of lost opportunity than of cash loss; the option seller cannot participate in a rise on the call side and must take delivery of shares at a price above market on a put.

† Depending on type of spread, straddle, or combination transacted.

CHAPTER 15

Commodities

MENTION THE WORD "commodities" to the average investor, and if there isn't a totally blank look on his face, chances are his reaction to the topic will be strongly negative. Either he will know someone who has lost heavily, or he will regale you with a horror story or two about a hapless investor who awoke one morning to find a truckload of eggs or a few thousand bushels of grain on his doorstep. He may even have read about the great salad-oil swindle, the losses in cocoa and silver trading that destroyed an American-owned Swiss bank, or the shellacking a large U.S. grain exporter took in the soybean market. He may even have lost money himself on a flier.

To our Mr. Average Investor, the commodity market is a hot ticket and not for him—and quite possibly he is correct. After all, many of these stories are rooted in fact. Tino De-Angelis did bankrupt one of the leading brokerage houses of the day (Ira Haupt) with his watered-down salad-oil tanks back in 1963. In the process, he gave the American Express Company a major fright as well. Paul Erdman became a successful author after his Swiss subsidiary of the United California Bank of Los Angeles lost 200 million Swiss francs— $80 million at the exchange rates of the day—trading in cocoa and silver in 1969–70. An American grain company,

Cook Industries, dropped $60 million in the soybean pits in 1976–77—running neck and neck with the Hunt family, who a few years later lost hundreds of millions of dollars when the silver market collapsed. Moreover, many an untimely delivery, although not on anyone's front doorstep, has bloodied a speculator or two caught napping. So if our average investor gets just a little nervous thinking about commodities, it is understandable. There are few quicker ways to part an investor from his money than the futures market.

Man's urge to speculate, however, is well documented throughout history. Thus, while the average investor is quite right to stand at arm's length, those among us with the willingness to apply common sense, a good deal of discipline, a little scholarship, and some spare cash will find the futures game not beyond their ability to understand or trade. They will also find it highly exciting, potentially very profitable, and in some cases not much more dangerous than the stock market. Now let us look more closely at this wild horse called the commodity or futures market and see what it is all about.

Historical Evolution

The futures market that is so widely traded today in reality is an offshoot of the cash or "on-the-spot" market that traces its roots back to the early Greek and Roman trading empires or perhaps further, since there is evidence that the Sumerians had a rudimentary system of credit backed by grains or metals 3,000 years before Christ.

Many of the basic rules of futures trading are clearly traceable to the law merchants' code that evolved out of the well-organized European medieval fairs. Highly complex futures trading systems also existed in Japan in the 1600s. But the rapidly expanding commerce of the city of Chicago in the 1850s was the primary catalyst that led to the development of the modern commodity exchange and to the popularity of trading in "time" or "forward" contracts.

The Civil War was a particularly important formative period. Rising grain demand and price fluctuation stimulated use of forward contracting on the Chicago Board of Trade, a cash grain-trading exchange formed in 1848 to handle and promote Chicago's booming commerce.

Time or forward contracting was not an idea born in the United States, however. It evolved from "to arrive" contracts, which, in turn, were refinements of *lettre de faire* documents used in the twelfth century and earlier. Forward contracting was not quite futures trading, although the distinction is slight. The earlier types of contracting, including forward contracting, were entered into for the express purpose of receiving title at some specified date to the actual goods. The parties to these documents were connected to the business, and nearly all such financial agreements ended in transfer of titles and delivery of the base commodity.

When war conditions, harvest glut, and winter shortages of grains began to create large price fluctuations as well as highly attractive profit situations, it was only natural that the more adventurous investors outside of the commodity business would be attracted. They were. But then the game changed. The new players were not interested in making or taking delivery, but rather in assuming a risk to reap a profit. As a result, each contract passed through many hands. Thus the concept of trading for purposes other than taking title became firmly, though unofficially, established in Chicago during the Civil War years. With speculators now involved, and deliveries the exception rather than the rule, forward trading became the futures trading of today.

In late 1865, shortly after the end of the war, the Chicago Board of Trade passed its first rules on the subject of time trading, providing, among other things, standardization of delivery, margin deposits, and prescribed terms of payments. In practice, if not in name, forward or time contracting merged into futures trading and the era of the modern commodity exchange had begun.

The Commodity Exchange

The modern-day commodity exchange and futures trading have evolved over a long period to fit the developing commercial needs of the country. Each exchange, however, evolved on a separate, if somewhat parallel, track, and each is highly individualistic. Generally, the older exchanges are state chartered. The Chicago Board of Trade was chartered by the Illinois State Legislature in 1848 and is the oldest and largest of the U.S. exchanges. The newer exchanges are organized under membership corporation laws.

Despite the individualistic nature and variety in size of the dozen or more active domestic exchanges, they are all fundamentally similar. The primary objective of the modern commodity futures exchange is to provide and regulate a marketplace for members to trade in futures contracts. Basically this entails providing the physical trading space, establishing the rules and regulations to conduct trading, setting the operating hours, providing the information for the standardized contract, seeing that prices and market information are recorded and disseminated to guarantee the financial obligations of exchange members in connection with futures commitments, and settling disputes between members. In addition to their futures trading activities, some exchanges also provide extensive cash market services such as sampling, grading, weighing, and inspection.

Organization of the Exchanges

U.S. commodity exchanges are voluntary associations of persons interested in buying and selling commodities. Whether the exchange is state chartered or corporately organized, in the U.S. only individuals are eligible to become members. There are no company memberships. In practice, companies often do control a membership. Many members are employees of large companies whose businesses are closely linked to exchange commodities—large brokerage houses, grain processors, meat packers, and exporters. The company furnishes the money to purchase the membership provided the individual agrees to give it up if he leaves their employ.

Only members can trade on a commodity exchange, and therein lies one of the two principal reasons for buying a seat on an exchange—access to the trading floor. The floor trader pays only clearing costs (which will be explained later) and receives a commission from nonmembers to fill orders. The other reason to purchase a seat is economic, provided one is a large enough trader to justify the costs involved. Membership for trader-members unable or unwilling to become floor traders entitles them to a reduced commission rate.

To provide the facilities and services required, commodity exchanges need some source of revenue. U.S. exchanges are nonprofit organizations that exist only to facilitate futures trading of members, not to make money. But they do have expenses to meet, and must remain as solvent as possible. This is generally accomplished through a combination of investments, dues, fees for services, and, if necessary, member assessments.

The Clearinghouse

Guaranteeing the financial commitment that each member makes when buying or selling a commodity futures contract is an important but difficult task. To do this, exchanges have developed corporations called clearinghouses to take the opposite side of all trades and to guarantee all contracts. The clearinghouse, in effect, becomes the buyer to all sellers, and the seller to all buyers. By so doing, it is able to ensure that each contract will be honored. The section on margins later in this chapter explains how the clearinghouse maintains financial integrity for each contract.

The clearing procedure begins at the end of each trading day. All exchange members send their trading cards to their respective clearing member. There is a card for each side of a transaction containing the details of the trade. The clearing member posts this information on trade confirmation cards and forwards them to the clearinghouse. The clearinghouse takes the confirmation cards from all the clearing members and matches up each purchase and sale for names, prices, delivery months, and quantities. The match-up must be exact. If there are any discrepancies, the clearinghouse makes up a duplicate unmatched notice, called an out-trade, and sends a copy back to the two parties to resolve. Most out-trades are resolved. If they cannot be resolved by the start of the next day's trading, the clearinghouse rejects the un-matched trade. Rejected out-trades then go into the ex-change's arbitration process for final settlement.

Not all members of an exchange belong to the clearing-house, but all clearinghouse members must be members of the exchange. The clearinghouse is a stock company, and clearinghouse members buy stock in relationship to the amount of clearing business they do. All trades must be cleared through a clearinghouse member. In addition to pur-chases of stock, a substantial cash deposit must be made to the guarantee fund of the clearinghouse corporation. Like the exchange itself, the clearinghouse is a nonprofit organi-zation and generates its operating capital through fees and from interest on invested capital.

The Standard Commodity Contract

Another, equally important creation of the exchange is the standard commodity contract. "To arrive" trading, the fore-runner of forward and then futures trading, was replete with pitfalls for everyone. Shipments came in all sizes and grades, depending on what the seller happened to have on hand, and settlement was a nightmare. Each transaction needed to be individually negotiated as to the specific terms of payment, delivery point, and so on.

To put everyone on an equal footing and to simplify trad-ing, the standardized contract was developed. Traders now only need to be concerned with the price and number of contracts during trading hours.

In brief, each commodity contract represents a firm legal agreement between the buyer or seller and the exchange's clearing house. The buyer agrees to accept delivery on a specified amount of a commodity when the contract is ten-dered (delivered). Conversely, the seller agrees to deliver the commodity detailed in the contract sometime during the delivery month. Only a small percentage of contracts are ac-tually delivered, since the bulk of traders in a futures con-tract are either speculators who have no need for cash commodities, or hedgers (producers or consumers of the commodity) who are using the market to shift risk temporarily to the speculator. Indeed, the risk-shifting function of the futures market is one of its main economic justifications.

With few contracts being settled by delivery, a method is needed to dissolve the contractual obligation. A simple one is used. The buyer or seller takes an equal, but opposite, position in the same delivery month. This is called offsetting, and negates the original purchase or sale. It can be done at any time before the contract goes off the board (terminates). During its lifetime, a commodity contract, despite its deliverability, is merely a bookkeeping entry. A commodity contract, therefore, is not a tangible item like a stock certificate, and when you first buy and then sell or sell and then buy the same contract, the net result is zero.

There are many commodities traded, and each has specific requirements to maximize its usefulness to the people who are in the cash business—the farmers, packers, manufacturers, and others, collectively known as the "trade." This is an important consideration even though most contracts are offset before delivery. No one is 100 percent sure of what makes one cash commodity a successful futures market while another fails. There are guidelines: a large supply and demand that is uncertain, adaptability to standardization and grade, relatively free flow of supply to terminals, and a low degree of perishability, to mention a few. But there are exceptions to these guidelines, especially with regard to perishability. One thing is clear, however; trade acceptability is a significant factor for success. If the trade cannot economically use the contract to hedge, it is less likely to survive.

The details vary for each commodity, but in general a contract will cover the following items: (1) The quantity (trading unit) being traded. (2) The grade. (3) Termination of trading and delivery date. (4) Daily minimum and maximum price fluctuations allowed. (5) Description of par delivery grade, the grade of commodity specified for delivery. (6) Premiums and discounts for nonpar delivery. (7) Trading limits—number of contracts that can be bought and sold in one day. (8) Position limits—the number of contracts a trader can hold in one single delivery month, and in all months together. (9) Delivery points. Essentially, every facet of entering into, making, and taking delivery of or exiting from the commodity futures market is covered in a standard contract.

Margins

In the earlier description of exchange operations, the subsidiary clearing house emerged as the party to all commodity transactions; that is, it became the buyer to all sellers and the seller to all buyers. From this vantage point, the clearing house can and does control the financial integrity of its members and their contract commitments. We have already mentioned that each clearing house member buys stock and deposits a large amount of cash into the corporation's guarantee fund. Each member is also required to post a performance bond to the clearing house for each net open position. This payment is called margin and affects not only clearing house members but nonmembers as well.

There are four basic classifications of margin. The first is called *standing margin* and is the amount of money a clearing house member keeps on deposit (to assure settlement of the contract) with the clearing house for each net open position (long or short) at the end of the trading day. If the member firm, for example, has 500 long May copper and 500 short May copper, its net position is zero and, theoretically, no standing margin is required. (In practice, a clearing house member would always keep a sizable deposit in his account whether it is needed or not.) On the other hand, if there were only 400 long May copper, the firm would be net short 100 contracts and would be required to post standing margin to cover this net open position. Standing margins are fixed by the governing board of the clearing house and must be current before each day's trading begins.

The second type also affects the clearing house member and is called a *variation margin*. If a market is particularly active and moves against the member's position, his standing margin would need to be supplemented to keep it at full value. The clearing house can call for variation margin money at any time to cover price changes, and the member must provide the money by certified check within one hour.

Like most cost-of-business items, margins are passed

through the system to the nonmembers of the clearing house and on to the nonmembers of the exchange. Although the clearing house sets the rate that member firms pay, what they in turn request from individual traders is left to their discretion. This, incidentally, accounts for the differences you will encounter when asking different brokers about margins on the same commodity.

Use of the word "margin" to describe up-front money in commodities differs significantly, by the way, from its use in the stock market for speculator-investor accounts. Stock margins are the minimum amounts of money an investor can put down to buy shares. He then must borrow the balance of the cost of the stock from the broker to complete the transaction. As a result, the stock investor pays the broker interest on the borrowed funds until the position is terminated or the "loan" is paid off.

In contrast, commodity margins at the brokerage level are similar to those at the clearing house level—they are primarily a performance bond to assure proper settlement of the contract. The commodity broker does not put up the difference between margin and the value of the commodity contract as does the stockbroker, so no interest is required of the commodity investor.

The first level of margin at the customer end is called *original margin.* Unlike a stockbroker, a commodity broker will not buy or sell a commodity before he has your money in hand; there is no five-day settlement period. Typically margins will run between 5 and 10 percent of the face value of a commodity. But they can be much higher, depending on the volatility of the commodity and how close the specific contract is to expiration. For example, most margins are increased when the contract reaches its delivery month.

Since it would be inconvenient for brokers to demand hourly variations in margin from their clients, but since it could be dangerous for them not to adjust for adverse price changes, brokers usually take a range approach. At the upper end is the original margin, and at the lower end is *maintenance margin.* You need original margin to initiate the trade, but the broker will not ask for additional money until your account falls to the maintenance level. At that point the bro-

ker will send a written notice, or margin call, to you requesting enough money to bring the entire position back up to the
original margin level. If you are unable or unwilling to meet
the margin call, the broker can close out the position.

Leverage

The commodity margin system is a particularly important
aspect of futures trading, for it provides the main attraction
for speculators—leverage. With a margin rate of 10 percent,
it takes only a 10 percent change in the commodity's price to
give the speculator a 100 percent gain or loss in his trading
equity. The speculator is also permitted to use equity gains
in open trades to purchase additional positions at no cost. For
example, assume the margin on one hog contract (30,000
pounds) is $1,200, and the current commodity price is 40¢ a
pound. If the price of hogs should advance to 44¢ a pound,
the equity gain would be $1,200. Until the trade is offset, the
$1,200 would be only a paper profit. However, if he wishes,
the trader can buy a second hog contract at 44¢ without adding any extra money. The paper profit would cover the second margin requirement. With two positions working for
him, the hog market need only advance to 46¢ a pound to
give the speculator enough for a third position. Leverage, of
course, is a two-edged sword. A decline of 3¢ a pound would
leave the trader with virtually no gain; a decline of 4¢ would
leave him with a loss.

Open Interest

When a trader buys or sells a contract, until he offsets the
trade or settles it through delivery, he is said to have an
"open position." In each market there will be a number of
these open positions, and collectively they are referred to as
the commodity's "open interest." Open interest is reported
along with the volume of sales and the prices each day. Since
there are always two sides to each contract—a long interest
(representing contracts that have been bought) and a short

interest (those that have been sold)—a figure of 100 for open interest would mean there are 100 longs and 100 shorts currently holding positions in that commodity.

Hedging

We have talked mostly about the speculator up to this point. But futures markets are real, not just artificially created arenas for gambling. They are backed by cash commodities, and grew out of the need of the producers and manufacturers engaged in processing the commodity to protect themselves from adverse price changes. The use of the commodity market by the people in the business or trade is called hedging, and is the backbone of the futures industry. A hedger, then, is an individual or company that either has the commodity to deliver or wishes to receive delivery of the commodity. Whether they actually make or receive delivery is immaterial. A hedge, or hedging, is taking a position in the futures market that is equal to but opposite from an existing or soon-to-exist position in the cash market. To facilitate hedging activity, a must for a successful futures market, exchanges usually set margins for bona fide hedgers below those for speculative accounts, give them lower commission rates, and eliminate position limits.

Because hedging involves the cash market, the hedger is not concerned with changes in the futures price per se. His interest is with the relationship between the cash price and the futures price. This mathematical difference between the two prices is called the "basis." Usually, the basis is given as an amount above or below the futures prices. If a farmer can get $2.50 per bushel for corn at his local elevator, and corn for December delivery is selling for $2.75 on the Chicago Board of Trade, the farmer's basis that day would be "25 under."

In a normal or carrying-charge market, the difference between the cash prices and the delivery of grain in the futures (the basis) will reflect insurance and interest costs. Occasionally an agricultural commodity market will be inverted; i.e., the cash price will be above the futures. This generally occurs when there is a near-term shortage in the commodity and buyers are willing to pay a premium to obtain supplies.

Hedging is an extremely complicated topic—and beyond the survey nature of this chapter. However, generally, a hedger is interested in eliminating as much of the risk associated with price fluctuation as he can, and he does this by putting on long or short hedges in various combinations. So that you will have some idea of what a hedging operation is about, we have conjured up two highly simplified hypothetical examples to illustrate a short and a long hedge.

The Short Hedge

It is July, and farmer Jones has planted 1,000 acres of corn that he expects will be ready for harvest in September. The weather has been good, and his yield history suggests that he will get 100 bushels per acre, or 100,000 bushels by harvest. His production costs are running about $2.00 per bushel. Unfortunately for our farmer, the crop looks good all over the state, and it appears that prices will fall by harvesttime. Currently the local elevator is buying corn for $2.35 per bushel. Farmer Jones looks at the futures market and sees that corn deliverable in December is selling for $2.55 per bushel. That makes his basis 20 under.

If the forecasters are correct and corn does fall, Mr. Jones could end up, not only with less profit, but possibly no profit at all if the market dips below $2.00 per bushel. To protect his current margin of profit of 35¢ a bushel (production cost of $2.00 subtracted from elevator price of $2.35), farmer Jones decides to put on a short (selling) hedge. He sells twenty contracts (grain contracts are in units of 5,000 bushels each) of December corn at $2.55 per bushel. Now, no matter what happens to the actual price of corn, if the basis holds up, farmer Jones will have his 35¢ a bushel. If the cash market falls, what he loses at the elevator or terminal when he sells his corn will be offset by an equal gain in his short futures position. If the price of corn should go up, the loss in the futures position would be offset by the gain in the cash price. The table on page 159 illustrates the principle.

The Long Hedge

Assume once again that it is July. ABC Milling has just landed a large contract to supply a local bakery with flour. A price has been agreed upon for the flour, but the baker wants half of it delivered next January. ABC Milling based production costs and the flour sales price on the current cash wheat price of $2.75 per bushel. January delivery, however, means ABC will need to buy additional wheat in December. To protect itself against adverse price changes over the five-month period, the milling company turns to the futures market. The price for a December contract is $3.00 per bushel, which gives ABC a basis of 25 under. By purchasing (long hedging) enough December wheat contracts to fulfill its raw material needs, the milling company, like farmer Jones, can eliminate much of the risk of changing prices.

The two examples assume that the basis is flat and that the hedges performed perfectly, although in practice they seldom do. As the price goes up and down, the basis also changes, sometimes narrowing, sometimes expanding. These contractions in the basis can be quite costly if they move against the hedger's position. Furthermore, the above examples assume the hedger is seeking only protection from price changes. Recent studies indicate hedgers expect to profit from a hedge in the same manner that a speculator expects to profit from an outright futures position. Thomas A. Hieronymus makes a convincing argument that hedging is, in fact, another form of speculation.*

The Trading Floor

Naturally, the trading area for each commodity will differ from exchange to exchange. Nonetheless, they all have common elements. On the floor will be a specific area designated where each commodity trades. These individual trading

* *Economics of Futures Trading—For Commercial and Personal Profit,* Commodity Research Bureau, New York, 1971.

PROFIT-LOSS EFFECT ON A SHORT HEDGE UNDER VARYING MARKET CONDITIONS

(This illustration assumes that corn costs farmer $2.00 per bushel to produce.)

	Unhedged	Hedged			
		Effects of a hedged position in a changing market if basis* remains stable		Effects of a hedged position in a changing market if basis* changes	
	Profit (Loss)		Profit (Loss)		Profit (Loss)
Sale now at market price of $2.35	35¢	Cash price $2.35	35¢	Cash price $2.35	35¢
		Futures price $2.55	0¢	Futures price $2.60	(5¢)
				(basis: 25 under)	
		Net	35¢	Net	30¢
Sale in December at market price of $2.10	10¢	Cash price $2.10	10¢	Cash price $2.10	10¢
		Futures price $2.30	25¢	Futures price $2.25	30¢
				(basis: 15 under)	
		Net	35¢	Net	40¢
Sale in December at market price of $2.60	60¢	Cash price $2.60	60¢		
		Futures price $2.80	(25¢)		
		Net	35¢		
Sale in December at market price of $1.95	(5¢)				

*Basis is difference between market price and futures price.

159

areas within the larger complex are called "pits" (or sometimes "rings"), and there is only one to a commodity. Some are elaborate octagonal platforms with ascending steps on the outside and descending steps on the inside. Others are simply handrails formed into a circle. There is a telephone area near the pits for floor brokers (or their telephone people) to receive orders from the firms they represent. There is, in close proximity, a table or platform containing one or more market reporters. Their job is to monitor the changing price picture, then to transmit it to the exchange's quote board system and to the ticker services, which send prices all around the country and abroad. There is a quote board system—easily viewed panels or blackboards containing the size and price of the last trade for each contract.

Now that you are familiar with the structure of a modern commodity exchange, let us look at what happens when the bell rings and commodity trading's special brand of pandemonium takes over. For the sake of simplicity, the following description of a commodity trade is a composite of several markets. Procedures differ from exchange to exchange, but the path an order takes is basically similar in all markets.

It all begins when trader Joe decides to enter the futures market. We will assume he is not a member of the exchange and that he wants to buy 10 contracts of May XYZ commodity at 45. His first step is to call his account executive and give him the buy order. The AE writes out the buy slip for 10 May XYZ at 45 and then sends the order ticket to the brokerage firm's order room. The order room time-stamps the slip and then calls or wires the information to the exchange that handles XYZ commodity. At the exchange, the order is received, time-stamped, and passed on to the floor broker's telephone person, stationed at one of the many phones on the trading floor. The phone attendant writes up the order and sends it by messenger or hand signal to the floor traders. All commodity trading is done by public outcry. Needless to say, with several hundred brokers on the bigger exchanges aggressively shouting at one another, it is sometimes difficult to execute orders. To supplement the yelling, therefore, hand signals are also used. There are hand signals for both prices and quantity. The combination of shouting and hand waving often gives a commodity pit a frantic look, but it is remarkably orderly and efficient.

The floor broker, with order in hand, then goes to the necessary pit and via voice and hand signal makes trader Joe's bid. Fortunately for trader Joe (or possibly not), another floor broker has a matching sale order and shouts or signals, "Sold." Meanwhile the market reporter notes the transaction and sends it off to the quote board, and to the ticker system if it is different from the last trade. The two brokers get together and fill out their trading cards before moving back into the pit to fill another order. Trader Joe's floor broker also sends the completed order ticket to the floor phone person, who sends it back through the system to trader Joe. The time between the receipt of the order and its execution is only a few minutes.

Government Regulation

Where large sums of money are at stake, man can be very creative and devious in his pursuit of it. Thus, along with the advantages of having a futures market for agricultural products, Americans also have suffered through an assortment of abuses, most notably those involving the cornering of markets and manipulation of prices by wealthy traders.

The first federal foray into regulating the commodity futures market came in 1884. Since then, there has been a steady stream of legislation passed largely on a "crisis" basis; when the horse has bolted, Congress has locked the door. The Grain Futures Act came in 1922. This act was amended and strengthened somewhat in 1936 and renamed the Commodity Exchange Act; it also extended federal regulations to nongrain commodities. The act created the Commodity Exchange Authority (CEA), which applied its rather limited powers to futures trading until 1974. That year Congress created a stronger watchdog, one tailored after the Securities and Exchange Commission, which regulates the stock market.

Called the Commodity Futures Trading Commission (CFTC), this regulatory agency is armed with a much broader mandate than its predecessor, and over the past few years it has slowly been expanding its authority into every aspect of the futures industry. The latter, meanwhile, has not been idle. The futures industry has set up the National Futures Association (NFA) along the lines of the National Association of Securities Dealers, the watchdog of the securities industry. The NFA became operational on October 1, 1982, and it has steadily expanded its responsibilities. At present this self-regulatory organization looks after the standards of professional conduct and the financial health of the various individuals and organizations that make up its membership. This includes all segments of the industry since members are not allowed to do business with nonmembers. Thus, if a person or organization does not remain qualified for NFA membership, they are prevented from dealing with the public in a business that involves buying and selling futures or futures option contracts.

CHAPTER 16

Stock Index Futures and Other Financial Hybrids

OVER THE LAST decade, a number of arcane financial products have developed which initially were of interest primarily to professional investors. However, with the number of such products increasing, individual investors have taken notice and become more interested in investigating these new instruments. What are these products? They include futures contracts on a variety of stock market indexes and on currencies, Treasury securities, bank CDs, GNMAs, and even the consumer price index, as well as option contracts on fixed-interest financials and market indexes.

A Short History

The first of these products to appear were currency futures on Japanese yen, British pounds, Canadian dollars, etc. The Chicago Mercantile Exchange formed a branch, the International Monetary Market (IMM), to introduce and trade futures on various currencies in the early 1970s. Futures were offered by the IMM on three-month T-bills in 1976 and by the Chicago Board of Trade on Treasury notes in 1979. This latter exchange listed GNMA and bank CD futures in 1981.

Jurisdictional disputes between the Securities and Exchange Commission (SEC) and the Commodity Futures Trading Commission (CFTC), as well as turf wars between the various exchanges, impeded the development of futures contracts on stock market indexes and on financially based options contracts. However, in February 1982, the Kansas City Board of Trade introduced the first stock market index future on the Value Line Index, which is composed of about 1,700 stocks. Shortly thereafter, the Chicago Mercantile Exchange came along with its contract on Standard & Poor's 500-Stock Index, followed by an S&P 250-Stock Index.

The New York Futures Exchange opened trading for futures on the NYSE Composite Stock Index (1,500 or so issues) in mid-1982. Subsequently the CFTC approved this exchange's listing of futures on the NYSE industrial, utility, and financial indexes. Approval was also given the Chicago Mercantile Exchange to trade futures on six-month T-bills to supplement those already listed on three-month T-bills.

Although options on Treasury bond futures began trading late in 1982 on the CBT, option exchanges ran up against a regulatory territorial controversy in their struggle to list options on financial and index futures. Congressional approval giving the SEC authority to regulate these contracts was required before trading on them could commence on the various option exchanges.

Since 1982 financial futures and options have proliferated as a result of the increased interest in them, particularly from institutional investors. In the country's largest futures market, the Treasury bond pit of the Chicago Board of Trade, some $15 billion worth of contracts trade daily, more than twice the volume of the underlying securities themselves. At present, investors can choose from a rapidly growing assortment of financial instruments, including contracts on NASDAQ 100 futures; S&P 100, 500, and transportation indexes; technology stock index options; and futures on zero-coupon Treasury bonds, European currency units, and the Commodity Research Bureau Index.

The Mechanics of Futures

Each of the index futures functions essentially as does a hog, silver, cocoa, or any other futures market (see Chapter 15). Although originally a standardized contract was established for market indexes at $500 times the underlying index, recently $250 and $100 contracts have been introduced. Thus, a one-point move in the index means a $500 change in the value of the future contract on it. Since each market index is composed of several hundred stocks, normal delivery, in kind, would be difficult. Therefore, these futures, unlike other futures markets, are settled in cash. But cash delivery does not mean that the entire price of the contract (around $80,000 for Value Line Index, $70,000 for S&P 500, and $40,000 for NYSE Composite) is required for settlement. Rather, only an amount equal to the change in value on the final day of the contract changes hands—a two-point price change times the standard $500 would mean a $1,000 settlement.

Both financial and index futures contract months are conveniently set at the calendar quarter. However, financials differ from index futures in that their standardized contracts are individually determined by each exchange and range from $50,000 to $1 million. Contracts on the fixed-rate financials are pegged to an 8 percent nominal yield. Anyone contemplating trading in these markets should familiarize himself with the exact terms of the particular instrument, including daily price limits, premiums, time limits, etc.

Playing in the Big Leagues

The entry fee for trading in these markets varies, typically from 5 to 10 percent of the value of the contract. This can range anywhere from $2,000 to $6,500, depending on the futures market in which you are dealing. However, should the market go against you, you may get a margin call and have to add more cash along the way. Furthermore, these arenas are dominated by professional traders, institutional investors, and experts in the financial markets. So be fore-warned: You'll be competing with big-league pros. These experts use financial futures, and more recently index fu-tures, to hedge their positions. Banks may employ them as a means to protect themselves against future interest-rate changes. Portfolio managers turn to the futures market to pro-tect clients' assets against precipitous market declines. And cagey speculators may trade index futures, rather than stocks, while holding portfolios of low-risk Treasury securities.

Informational Tools

How can you use these contracts? Even if you choose not to put up your cash, you can still derive use from the futures market in the form of information. A typical day's listing might look like this:

	S&P 500	NYSE Composite	KC Value Line
June	242.45	139.70	244.06
Sept.	244.65	141.00	245.05
Dec.	246.95	142.30	247.00
Mar.	249.40	143.60	248.70
Actual	241.35	138.88	242.31

You will note that the futures are all selling at a premium to the actual indexes, reflecting the fact that owning them is more convenient than owning the equivalent stocks. When this premium disappears it may indicate that investors are bearish. When the more distant months are selling at a premium to near months it may indicate rising investor ex-pectations. Similar inferences can be gleaned from the fixed-rate financial contracts. On the day depicted above, the discounts on T-bills were 7 percent higher on contract months a year away than on those on current rates. You can use these markets as a bellwether of investor expec-tations, but keep in mind that investors are not always reli-able prognosticators.

Because trading volume of futures and index options has

increased so rapidly, they have begun to call the stock market's turn, thus reducing further the reliability of the stock market as an indicator. More important, much of this trading is done by large institutions executing complex trading strategies that involve both index futures and their underlying stocks. So-called basis or program trading seeks to take advantage of disparities between the index future and its component stocks (or "cash" index).

For example, a trader might purchase $50 or $100 million worth of S&P 500 contracts when they are trading at a discount to the cash index and are considered to be underpriced. He would simultaneously sell the cash index stocks themselves, taking the difference as profit once the two prices converged in subsequent trading. These strategies can yield low-risk returns, often several points above those possible with just the underlying basket of stocks.

Since such trades can involve several hundred stocks and millions of dollars, and usually are prearranged to be executed at set prices, they can trigger sharp price swings in the market. These in turn can set off other programs, causing the process to snowball. Indeed, the record-setting 51-point rise in the Dow Industrial Average on January 24, 1987, followed the next day by a record 44-point drop, was largely attributed to program trading by institutions and arbitrageurs.

These trading progams, which have undoubtedly added volatility to both the futures and stock markets, have been heavily criticized and are the subject of a 1987 SEC report. Individual investors should definitely be aware of such influences, paying particular attention to the one Friday each quarter when stock options, futures, and stock index options expire. The so-called triple witching hour (the last hour of trading) can bring extremely frenzied and erratic trading activity. As a result of the SEC report, the triple witching hour has been modified by changing contract expirations to first and last hours of trading.

Putting Up Cash

Now, after watching these markets for a while and learning all you can about them in the meantime, you are ready to take the big step and put up some cash. What are the types of transactions you might want to make? The simplest, but riskiest, role is that of the speculator. You select an investment on the basis of what you think the market or interest rates are going to do. If you expect a downturn, you go short; if you foresee a rise, you go long. As with options, the attraction in these instruments for the speculator is the leverage attainable. For a 10 percent cash outlay (some brokers may require more), you participate in market swings via index futures. To invest in the actual stocks themselves you must put up 50 percent of the value. With futures a 10 percent rise in the underlying index would translate to a 100 percent increase in your cash position, assuming you put up 10 percent of the contract's value initially.

Using futures to hedge risk is generally done by professionals. It may be done to protect your portfolio against unexpected downturns in the market as a whole. Your choice of which index to use would be contingent on the type of stocks and the size of the portfolio you hold. The Value Line futures would most closely approximate a speculative portfolio. The S&P 500 would be more akin to a portfolio heavily weighted in energy and energy-related issues, business equipment, drugs, and utilities. To execute an appropriate hedge you would sell short the requisite number of contracts to equal the value of your portfolio. For example, say you have speculative holdings with a market value of $130,000. To cover your portfolio you would sell short two Value Line contracts, the index most closely related to your stocks. Since each point drop in the index is worth $500, two contracts will cover you for $1,000 per point and be equivalent to a short sale on $134,000 in stock when the index is at 134.

While these new products offer sophisticated investors new and flexible ways to play the market, they should not be approached without knowledge or, failing that, expert guidance. Some brokerage houses are incorporating the use of futures hedges in managed accounts. However, these generally have a minimum account level of $300,000 or even more. If you are interested in more information, ask your broker to send you any booklets available or write to the Chicago Board of Trade, LaSalle at Jackson, Chicago, IL 60604 for additional facts on using financial and stock market index futures.

CHAPTER 17

Gold, Inflation, and Your Dollars

GOLD HAS BEEN popular with humankind almost as long as the species has existed. It has been used to beautify, buoy, and bribe for centuries. It has been at center stage in the human drama from time immemorial. "Saint-seducing gold," Shakespeare called it in *Romeo and Juliet*. "Though wisdom cannot be gotten for gold, still less can it be gotten without it," said Samuel Butler a couple of centuries later.

The chance for finding gold opened up the American West, and the subsequent preoccupation of this nation with the yellow metal gave William Jennings Bryan the opportunity to declaim, at the National Democratic Convention in Chicago in July 1896, "You shall not press down upon the brow of labor this crown of thorns. You shall not crucify mankind upon a cross of gold."

The Gold Standard

Enhancing the elevated status of gold has been the low status of official money, particularly paper money. Thanks to the widespread inability of governments to live within their incomes, currencies have always depreciated, and often even disappeared. The German mark did so twice within one human lifetime. How many banks have failed in the Western world since 1900, taking depositors' money into oblivion? The runaway inflation in Germany after World War I simply eliminated the hardworking, rigorously saving middle class and paved the way for social and political disasters of far worse proportions.

Anyone who has had the foresight or ability to convert bank deposits or currency to gold during such periods of financial holocaust has survived. Those who "trusted" the system and its money perished. Small wonder, then, that the financial vicissitudes of the twentieth century further elevated gold in the minds and hearts of men. It was tangible, had "intrinsic value," and was a permanent haven for wealth.

So strong was the faith in gold and so weak the trust in paper money that the latter had to be tied to the former to have any credibility. Europe and the United States went on a so-called gold standard, meaning that a dollar, pound, or franc was worth a specific amount of the metal. As long as this was the case, the paper money became as good, or almost as good, as gold. The trouble with the gold standard was the cost it exacted in terms of economic, social, and political upheaval.

Here's the way the gold standard works, in theory. As a nation prospers on the upside of a business cycle, domestic wages and prices tend to rise to a point where some other nation has a competitive advantage in the domestic market. Domestic consumers then begin to buy imported products. The exporting nation exchanges the currency received from the sale of its goods for gold, which it takes home.

As the domestic market loses gold—the base of the domestic money supply—that money supply shrinks. A smaller money supply turns the business cycle down, a depression ensues, and wages and prices fall as unemployment and the number of idle plants rise. Domestic prices then become competitive in foreign markets and domestic companies begin to prosper by selling in those foreign markets.

Foreign currencies are swapped for foreign gold, which is brought home and monetized. Paper money is printed to match it, and the money supply is increased, which leads to boom conditions again. Wages and prices move up as prosperity returns, only to make domestic products vulnerable to foreign competition once again, and the boom ends in another bust.

Obviously, no social or political fabric could stand one wrenching depression and soaring boom after another. Thus, the gold standard was really honored more in the breach than in the observance early in this century. The Great Depression really did it in, and the United States under President Franklin D. Roosevelt finally abandoned it in 1933.

Gold and the Dollar

The United States led the Western world out of the Depression, whether thanks to FDR or to the consequences of Hitler's imperialistic designs for Germany. The dollar was the world currency, having replaced the British pound during World War II. It was pegged to other currencies and to gold at $35 per ounce. Any foreign nation that did not want the dollars earned from sales of goods to us could turn them into gold. Few did. It was American products they wanted, first to rebuild their war-shattered countries, then to give them the consumer prosperity we had long taken for granted.

During that period we could, generally speaking, go wherever we wished, using the English language and the American dollar almost as handily in Manila or Madrid as in Muncie or Mamaroneck. In addition, we sold our excess steel and radios to the world's "natives" and bought what we wished of their coffee, copra, and copper. If we failed to buy enough from them, their prices fell and near starvation followed. Even Europe was sufficiently dependent on the U.S. economy to give credence to the statement that "when the United States gets the sniffles, Europe gets pneumonia."

U.S. trade dominance immediately following World War II produced a flow of gold to this country. The yellow metal was a luxury Europe could scarcely afford when its citizens were clamoring first for food, clothing, and shelter, and later for autos, dishwashers, and color TVs. In the years following World War II, we had most of the world's gold in expensive underground quarters at Fort Knox, Kentucky. Even big gold-producing countries such as South Africa and the Soviet Union turned their gold into dollars so they could buy U.S. products and technology. So in those years, when a few foreign countries sidled up to our gold window with some excess dollars to swap, hardly anyone paid any attention.

But things began to change in these early postwar years, too. First came the Marshall Plan, which funneled U.S. dollars into the rebuilding of European facilities.

Second was the "trade, not aid" philosophy developed by the Eisenhower administration, which encouraged our purchase of European and "third world" products as a way of stimulating those countries' economic growth enough to diminish their need for our aid. All of this worked, helped in no small way by the unswervingly hard work of the ordinary men and women of Germany and Japan. Thanks to their "grit" and our enlightened economic policy, Europe and Japan rose from the rubble of war to economic heights in a far shorter time than anyone predicted. It wasn't long, in national terms, before Germany and Japan became real competitors with the United States in world markets.

During the decade or two immediately following World War II, we sold, or exported, much more than we bought, or imported, in the world marketplace. This excess of exports over imports was used to finance U.S. troops stationed in Europe. We also used the excess to finance the building of Caterpillar Tractor plants in Scotland and Burroughs facilities in France. But as the prosperity we had encouraged, and in part financed, waxed, the need for our dollars to buy goods from us waned.

Our so-called trade surplus—the excess of exports over imports—narrowed and financed less and less. By the time the Vietnam war had escalated, we were spending more for foreign military actions than the U.S. economy earned in the world market. Our balance-of-payments surplus became a deficit. This meant a growing number of dollars were being held abroad, dollars that foreigners increasingly had no need to spend here for the things we made.

Thus, the move to exchange dollars for gold steadily gained momentum. Our gold reserves sank drastically, causing great alarm. The first to panic were those with no trust in "paper money." As far as they were concerned, erosion of the U.S. store of gold was fast reducing the value of dollars to mere paper.

Then came the smart money men. These were the financial experts in the big multinational companies who dealt daily in large amounts of pounds, yen, lira, and marks, as well as dollars. If the dollar was losing its international appeal, they reasoned, why shouldn't we keep as much of our working capital in other, more popular, and stronger currencies? So they swapped dollars. Then came all sorts of speculators, big and little, all trying to "make a buck" (if you will!) selling dollars.

The Dollar Is Cut Free

By the summer of 1971, the dollar was in real trouble. The Nixon administration realized this and did three things. First, it closed the gold window. Second, it unpegged the dollar. From now on, said the White House, in effect, gold buyers can pay what they wish for the yellow metal; the price of gold will have no bearing on the dollar. The price of both gold and dollars in foreign currencies fluctuated according to the dictates of supply and demand. Third, it slapped controls on domestic wages and prices in a frontal assault on the raging inflation that was plaguing the U.S. economy. This was in part to help consumers at home, but also to show Europeans and others that we were facing our inflation and balance-of-payments problems.

Because of this inflation at home and the adverse balance of payments, the dollar had really become overvalued. In part, too, the dollar had started out overvalued after World War II to help our "trade, not aid" policy. An overvalued currency is one that buys more in a foreign country than it does at home. By 1971 this overvaluation of the dollar had become so obvious that everyone had to recognize it, and did.

Gold rose immediately from $35 an ounce, the price for nearly four decades, to $42 or so, a gain of 20 percent. Also escalating were the West German mark, the yen, and most other free-world currencies. The dollar was allowed to move with supply and demand instead of being artificially adjusted by the high priests of the international monetary world, the central bankers.

Recurring "panics" occurred, including a substantial one in early 1973, when Treasury Secretary George Shultz announced a major easing of wage and price controls, following a big jump in farm and food prices for two months in a row. This immediately rekindled fears in the hearts of European central bankers of more inflation here, and the dollar fell apart. Gold leaped to around $126 an ounce or more, and Wall Street got the jitters.

U.S. on the Bargain Counter

Sink the market did, although the declining dollar was far from the only reason. For the next few weeks the dollar became truly undervalued—you could buy more of life's needs in New York with dollars than you could with an equivalent amount of marks in Frankfurt or francs in Paris. This was a good thing for us. Detroit sold more cars; West Germany sold fewer.

Everything we had here really ended up on the bargain counter for foreigners, all because the dollar "collapsed." The dollar remained free to float at levels dictated by supply and demand, clearly the healthiest thing for the economy. Finally the stock market took heart, or at least began to worry about other things as investors saw that a declining dollar did not hurt them. Meantime, gold stocks—the shares of gold-mining companies—had gone through the roof.

Investing in Gold

When Washington unpegged the dollar from gold in 1971, gold-mining stocks nearly doubled in price within a couple of years. A glance at the chart on the next page shows what happened when supply and demand were allowed to set the price. The big surge in 1973–74 reflected in part the rise to world economic prominence of the members of the Organization of Petroleum Exporting Countries (OPEC). When the OPEC oil price was quadrupled, the flow of money—Western money—into their coffers was quadrupled, too.

In 1974, the U.S. Congress made it legal once again for Americans to own gold. Currency speculators rushed out and bought a lot of yellow metal, pushing the price of gold to almost $195 an ounce by the end of 1974 and giving the mining companies a nice surge in earnings. Then the gold-bullion bubble burst, as bubbles always do, and prices plummeted to a low of $103 in August 1976. Obviously, gold wasn't much of an inflation hedge in that twenty-month period.

Gold went through another cycle in the late 1970s and early 1980s. This one sent the yellow metal to an incredible price of $850 per ounce for a few minutes in January 1980. This proved to be the high-water mark. As the chart (opposite) illustrates, gold stocks reached a peak in October 1980, nine months after the price of gold topped out. The price of gold shares continued to ebb as gold itself fell, reaching a low point below $300 in mid-1982, about one-third of what it had been at the high. After rising to around $500 in early 1983, the price of gold moved gradually lower, trading in a narrow range between $315 and $350. In view of the explosive racial situation in South Africa, the world's largest (48 percent) gold producer, the price of gold could be adversely affected.

Although the love for gold dies hard in the breasts of central bankers, French peasants, and others who have a cynical distrust of the ability of political institutions to balance budgets, gold is no longer of monetary importance. Gold-mining countries such as the Soviet Union, South Africa, and Canada will continue to sell the metal in order to finance imports. The International Monetary Fund and the U.S. Treasury will remain on the sell side of gold markets. The yellow metal is a commodity now, just as copper, corn, and soybeans are.

Admittedly, gold differs from other commodities in the way people are willing to squirrel it away. Most aboveground gold is just that, hidden away for a rainy day. Who among us would be willing to store tons of soybeans or copper ingots forever? If people should ever lose this mystic love for the yellow metal, the price could plunge over the long term, for industry use represents only a fraction of the available supply. Nevertheless, gold will tend to move up when inflation fears are rampant and down when world finances appear to be under control. All the hoarders are not yet gone. The long-term balance of market forces favors higher gold prices.

GOLD MINING STOCKS

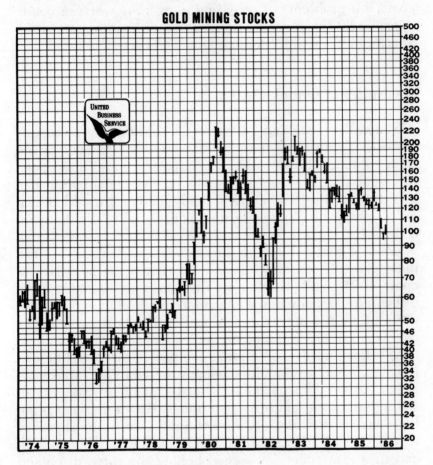

Industrial demand for gold (which accounts for one-third of U.S. consumption) flows and ebbs in line with the economic ups and downs in the U.S. and other Western nations. Gold is an excellent electrical conductor and a well-nigh indispensable ingredient of the supersensitive electronic technology of our times. Therefore, gold-mining shares are likely to continue in a volatile pattern, reflecting the many factors which influence the price of gold.

The market performance of the shares will be enhanced by inflation jitters and depressed by labor and political turmoil in gold-producing nations. They will reflect generally the things that help or hinder all freely traded common stocks. One might guess that earnings progress for this industry, given the problems of dirty and dangerous working conditions, might be substantially slower than that for companies in computers, health care, banking, and brewing.

Investment Outlook: So-So

Generally speaking, therefore, gold-mining company shares have no more than average appeal. However, if you wish to speculate in gold, if you prefer the yellow metal to greenbacks, do so in mining-company shares rather than gold bullion itself. There is a ready market for gold stocks, easy storage of the certificates, and, usually, dividend income.

Owning gold bullion, on the other hand, is expensive. You must pay to store and insure it. It represents negative income, if you will. It offers no dividends and is much more difficult to market when you want to sell. Following is a brief description of what we regard as the four best gold-mining company issues, all traded on the New York Stock Exchange.

ASA Ltd., unlike the mining companies discussed below, is a closed-end investment company, based in Johannesburg, South Africa. The portfolio is made up of investments in some two dozen South African mines. Given the race problems and politics of the Union of South Africa, the shares of ASA Ltd. carry extreme risk. The stock is extremely volatile and in recent years has lagged behind the three discussed below.

Campbell Red Lake Mines Ltd., controlled by Dome Mines, is a leading low-cost Canadian gold producer. Output has grown impressively over the past several years, yet ore reserves as of the end of 1984 totaled 2,026,000 tons. (Ore reserves are important for any extractive company.) Earnings reflect output, costs, and price. Because of the volatility of bullion prices, profits per share have bounced about in recent years, dividends have been erratic, and the shares themselves have swung over a wide price range.

Dome Mines Ltd. is a large and relatively high-cost Canadian gold-mining company but does have a substantial investment in two low-cost producers, Campbell Red Lake and Sigma Mines. Reserves of ore totaled 2,629,000 tons as of December 1984 for the Dome properties, to which must be added those of Campbell Red Lake (see above), and 984,000 tons for Sigma. Market performance of the shares in recent years has been almost identical with that of Campbell Red Lake common and should continue so over the foreseeable future.

Homestake Mining Company is the largest U.S. producer. Operating results for the company are affected in a major way by lead and zinc prices, since these metals account for nearly 70 percent of operating profits. Silver and uranium mining also are part of the Homestake picture. Nevertheless, Homestake common tends to move with other gold issues and should continue to do so. Reserves of all metals mined are ample.

The Glitter of the Kaffirs

Not satisfied with risking all on the gold-mining shares listed on the NYSE, which represent mostly Western Hemisphere mines, some traders and eternally gullible investors are tempted by shares of South African gold producers. Our advice, in a word, is *don't.*

These stocks, called "kaffirs" (for the native tribes in the area), offer all the risks of Dome and Campbell Red Lake, plus a tinderbox racial situation. In addition, good reliable information on reserves, taxes, and routine operating statistics is dated and very hard to come by. For this reason, these stocks are much cheaper in relation to earnings. Their values plummeted much faster than those on NYSE issues and for the metal itself. If you must gamble on gold, use the NYSE-listed issues.

The Krugerrand and Others

Until November 1985, the Republic of South Africa offered for sale gold coin-shaped ingots weighing one-tenth, one-quarter, one-half, and one troy ounce, the basic weight on which gold prices are quoted. Subsequently, the South African government suspended minting of the Krugerrand because of a large surplus of the coins. The surplus resulted from bans on the importation of the coins imposed by the United States and many other countries as a protest against South Africa's apartheid policies.

What do the boycott and the suspension of Krugerrand minting mean to individuals who already own the gold coins? Not much. Many coin dealers still handle Krugerrand trading. So if you decide to sell the coins you now own, and there really is no need to do so immediately, you should obtain a price at or near that day's gold trading price.

In order to take advantage of the void created by the Krugerrand's boycott, the United States has begun minting gold coins in four weights, from one-tenth to one ounce. Canada has for some time offered its gold maple-leaf coin in these same weights. Other gold coins include the Mexican 50 peso, the Austrian 100 corona, and the Hungarian koruna, each of which weighs about an ounce. The Austrian four-ducat coin weighs about half an ounce. You can frequently purchase these coins at a premium from dealers in the fifteen states that exempt gold coins from sales tax.

In general, gold coins offer little appeal as a serious investment. They generate no income and are subject to relatively wide price swings. Coins can be lost, misplaced, and stolen. Our opinion is that you should let someone else have them. The game just isn't worth the candle.

CHAPTER 18

Real Estate

"OF ALL MILLIONAIRES, ninety percent became so through owning real estate," Andrew Carnegie, the steel tycoon, once observed. He went on to advise: "The wise young man or wage earner should invest his money in real estate." This country's history is generously peppered with examples of the fortunes that can be made in pursuit of that investment. John Jacob Astor became the richest man in America in the early 1800s as the "landlord of New York." William J. Levitt foresaw the need for low-cost housing for GIs returning home from World War II and mass-produced houses for them into the Levittowns that have become a part of our landscape and language, making himself comfortably well off in the process. William Zeckendorf fathered scores of flamboyant real estate projects, wheeling and dealing himself into and out of several fortunes.

Not all of us need aspire to such heights to enjoy the fruits of real estate investment. Even if you confine your involvement to owning your own home, you stand to add substantially to your net worth as you dutifully make mortgage payments over the months and years. Home ownership, in fact, is the most common form of real estate "investment." For most homeowners, their house represents their largest single asset. Furthermore, it is likely to be an appreciating asset in dollar terms, for it represents a tangible entity with intrinsic value. It tends to hold its true worth, regardless of what inflation does to the buying power of the dollar. In many cases it tends to rise in "real" value as well, particularly if it is well located and of a type eagerly sought by potential buyers.

Another type of home ownership that is gaining in popularity, particularly with the rise in housing and energy costs, involves taking a stake in multifamily residential property. There are two basic forms: cooperative apartments and condominiums. With a cooperative, you own a share of the entire property. Whatever tax considerations apply to the whole package apply to you as well. With a condominium, you own your unit outright, just as if it were a single-family residence, and have your own individual tax considerations. In addition, you hold a joint interest in the common parts of the property. In both a cooperative and a condominium, you share in the maintenance costs of the common property through assessments which you have a legal obligation to pay. As with a single-family house, you build equity as you make your monthly mortgage payments, and if the property is well maintained and favorably situated, your stake should rise in value over the years.

But beyond the appeal of home ownership, one basic reason for the popularity of real estate as an investment vehicle is the federal government's use of its powers to provide incentives for good-quality housing for all. Recent legislative history is dotted with incentive-inducing provisions. The Housing Acts of 1949, 1965, and 1968, for example, provided mortgage insurance programs, rent subsidies, and the massive urban renewal programs. In 1978, Congress enacted a 10 percent tax credit for investments in historic rehabilitation, which it upped to 25 percent in 1981. As a result of the generous tax credit, some $11 billion have been invested in restoring 17,000 buildings. The 1986 tax revision eliminated most incentives for all but historic rehab investments, but even these were reduced. The tax credit was lowered to 20 percent and is denied to investors whose income is $250,000 or over. Furthermore, the interaction between various aspects of the tax code limit the credit that an investor can take on his tax to $25,000. The new rules will be fully phased in by 1994.

Successes—and Failures

There have been astounding successes and resounding failures in real estate investment in recent years. Two of the strongest areas—farmland and the single-family home— were able to provide excellent protection against a sharply rising cost of living until the early 1980s. In some parts of the country, single-family home values continued to rise, but in other areas prices made little progress. Farmland values began to stabilize in 1986, after having been hard hit in the first half of the decade.

Favorably located real estate has always been a profitable area of investment. It should become even more so in years to come as the earth's resources continue to shrink in proportion to its population. Demographic factors indicate that a strong demand for housing will continue into the 1990s. Some of the demand will come from replacement of aging or dilapidated homes, urban renewal, and the acquisition of second homes.

Regardless of your investment objective, real estate can be a contender for inclusion in your portfolio. The following paragraphs discuss some of the more important forms and their investment characteristics.

Investing in Raw Land

Land investment can encompass anything from the most arid prairie land to fertile farming acreage. Speculation in land has provided magnificent fortunes—but also sizable losses. A speculator in land is looking ahead to some possible change in the usage of the piece of property. Either it must be seen to have potential for homes or it must promise to provide some form of future income. Potential industrial, commercial, residential, or recreational uses can have a major impact on land values.

Speculating in raw land is extremely difficult, and dreams of quick profits can obscure the all too numerous pitfalls. Raw land not only provides no current income but for such things as financing and taxes, it entails additional costs while it is being held. This means that such an investment must appreciate in value by at least 10 percent a year just to break even. That can be an especially tall order. Furthermore, raw land is an extremely illiquid investment and should never be purchased with funds that might be needed quickly. In addition to these drawbacks, you may find you have to work hard to make your speculation succeed. You might have to exert influence over zoning or even a community's total master plan.

If you are undeterred by these potential obstacles, your best approach is to stay close to home, where you can more easily appraise development and growth prospects. There are land development companies that purport to provide real estate investments for you. These programs have been sprinkled with more than their fair share of development problems. At times promised amenities have been nonexistent or slow in coming or have been delayed or stopped altogether by environmental concerns over the proposed development plan. Government regulation has not always fully protected investors. Do not expect that your investment in raw land will be a quick road to riches.

Rental Property

Apartment living offers an appealing life-style for a growing number of Americans discouraged by the ever-rising cost of owning a residence or who simply prefer the convenience. Investing in rental property thus constitutes a large and expanding market that ranges all the way from leasing a single-family home to participations in large apartment complexes with all the amenities—swimming pools, tennis courts, and sauna baths. Investment in rental property can bring substantial economic benefits, though there are often numerous management headaches as well. As a landlord, you face the problems of keeping up with maintenance, finding tenants, collecting the rent, and handling complaints about the all-night parties in 4B. If you're not up to those tasks, you can hire someone to manage the property for you, but this cuts into your profits and may have unfavorable tax implications.

In seeking a rental property, it is well to keep in mind the rule of thumb that monthly rental income should total about 1 percent of the purchase price—as a bare minimum. This effectively removes most single-family homes and as a practical matter makes it hard to justify anything less than three units.

There are some distinct advantages to this form of investment. Apartments can generally be financed with a relatively small down payment of 20 to 30 percent of the purchase price, affording considerable leverage on the investment. The down payment is generally smaller if you make the building your home, too. Indeed, leverage is one of the major benefits of investing in rental property, for it magnifies your rate of return on the appreciating value of the property.

In purchasing rental property, make your selections carefully. Avoid those that show evidence of structural flaws or other conditions which might cause hefty maintenance expenses later on. Location is another important consideration. The deterioration of a neighborhood could seriously erode your capital and diminish the property's earning power. Don't be afraid to get a professional appraisal of the property's worth, either.

You should study the rental market in the area you are considering to be reasonably sure you won't be stuck for long with empty units. There will be vacancies from time to time, to be sure, but too many will play havoc with your bottom line.

Finally, study the revised tax rules in light of your financial and tax situation to determine whether you can gain any advantage from investing in rental property. If your income exceeds $150,000, rental losses in excess of rental income can't be used to offset other income. Loss of this tax break could make the difference in whether the rental investment is feasible.

Business Property

Investing in business property takes several forms. Office buildings, shopping centers, and warehouses are among the most familiar alternatives. When considering these investments, bear in mind that overbuilding has depressed this market. Business property provides certain advantages over rental apartments. The commercial tenant is generally more stable and is looking for a location around which he can build a profitable business. He takes better care of his property and, barring extreme financial emergency, pays his rent on time. Some of the drawbacks include the more expensive maintenance services you as a landlord must provide. Vacancies are usually harder to fill and may require such things as the dismantling of a customized office.

One approach to investing in business property is to buy and convert a marginal suburban retail operation into an office building. This has worked successfully for a good many real estate investors. Some developers have gone one step further. When conditions warrant they then convert the rental offices to condominiums, selling the space to their former tenants or to new occupants.

In the past the potential for tax recapture from using accelerated depreciation has had to be taken into account on this type of conversion. Now, however, only straight-line depreciation taken over a 31½ year life is allowed for nonresidential real estate, so recapture is no longer a threat.

Business property investments in regional shopping centers can be profitable. The largest of these can encompass one million square feet or more of store area and serve a customer base of about 250,000 people. They usually have a magnet store or two to act as the main drawing card. Smaller community-type shopping centers may cluster around a supermarket and a drugstore. Reasonably priced land close to rapidly expanding outlying areas can offer the speculator a good opportunity.

The shopping-center owner attempts to build a long list of good-quality tenants with long-term leases. His compensation is generally in the form of a minimum rent plus a certain percentage of gross sales above minimum volumes. Because of the specialized nature of this field, shopping centers are best left to professional developers, though smaller investors can frequently invest through participation in joint ventures and limited partnerships (more on them below). A bad experience with a particular key tenant, such as when King's Department Stores and First National Stores closed many of their outlets, can seriously cut into profits.

Investment in shopping centers is also possible through common stock ownership. A handful of companies specialize in the field, but Rouse Company is the best known.

Real Estate Investment Trusts

Real estate investment trusts (REITs) are one form of indirect participation in real estate that allows investors to escape management headaches. Like mutual funds, REITs sell shares to the public to raise their capital; but, instead of investing in a portfolio of stocks and bonds, as do mutual funds, they invest in real estate and mortgages. REITs, like publicly traded investment companies, do not redeem their shares; rather, the shares are bought and sold over the counter or on the stock exchanges.

REITs come in two basic forms—equity trusts and mortgage investment trusts—or a combination of both forms, commonly known as a hybrid trust. Equity trusts own property outright and seek their profits from rental income and capital gains. Mortgage investment trusts make long-term mortgage loans to large real estate buyers and intermediate and short-term construction loans to builders and developers. It was within this latter segment that the excessive proliferation and subsequent shakeout occurred during the mid-1970s.

The main attraction of REITs is that they are able to pass on all the tax advantages of real estate ownership to their investors. By law, a REIT must distribute 95 percent of its taxable income to shareholders each year. Since the trusts are not allowed to reinvest their earnings, they rely heavily on borrowed funds to provide growth. Typically a REIT's capitalization will consist of 20 percent stockholders' equity, 40 percent in long-term debt, and 40 percent in bank loans and commercial paper.

The popularity of mortgage trusts reached faddish proportions during the late 1960s and early 1970s. Promoters, eager to cash in, put together projects of dubious merit that were snapped up by equally eager investors. As long as the economy remained robust, they could survive. But between 1973 and 1975 they collapsed like so many houses of cards. Indeed, even the strongest of the REITs took some hard knocks under the barrage of shifting long- and short-term interest-rate relationships, rising unemployment, soaring operating costs, and rent control. Rapidly rising short-term interest rates played havoc with financing arrangements and spelled doom for many of the highly leveraged REITs. Overbuilding during the early part of the decade also fueled the bust. Bankruptcies hit the industry, share prices plummeted, dividends dried up, and investors were left hanging.

As a result of this drubbing, REITs got a bad name in the investment community. It wasn't until 1980 that they staged a comeback. Then investors saw REITs as bargains, since they were trading below their breakup value. By then the real estate markets had moved from an overbuilt to an underbuilt condition, a situation that had begun to reverse in some segments and locations by 1986.

As you can see, there is more to investing in REITs than merely picking one off the shelf. You have to evaluate the merits of individual trusts by a careful study of a number of factors, including examination of past performance, capital structure, investment objectives, and management. You should realize that although REITs have a potential for high return, they have a similar potential for risk. However, considering REITs' management and that investors are more wary now than in the mid-1970s, a repeat of the previous excesses is not very likely.

Taxation of REITs did not change materially under the Tax Reform Act of 1986. Because Congress determined that REITs were portfolio investments rather than limited partnerships, passive loss limitations do not apply to them. Therefore, if an investor sustains a trading loss on a REIT, it can be used to offset up to $3,000 of ordinary income.

Real Estate Syndicates

The syndicate, or group participation form of real estate investment, usually is organized as a partnership, occasionally as a corporation. Syndicates raise capital by selling participations or shares. This capital is then used to pay off debts and even to pay tax-free dividends. In the past, accelerated depreciation has helped these syndications reduce investors' taxes. When property held by the partnership is fully depreciated, it is sold and the investors realize a profit. With the elimination of the capital gains rate, this profit is taxable as ordinary income. Real estate syndicates are also used as vehicles for property development and land speculation.

Most of them take the legal form of limited partnerships rather than general partnerships. Under a general partnership, all partners bear equally in the risks and rewards of the venture. This means all partners can be held liable for losses in excess of their actual stake in the project. Under a limited partnership, on the other hand, the limited partners are liable only to the extent that they are invested in the project. A general partner puts the deal together and manages it for a consideration, which he is paid regardless of how well or how poorly the venture goes. However, a well-conceived and properly managed project can bring highly expert management to bear, with rewarding results for the limited partners.

The 1986 revision of the Tax Code virtually did away with the tax-sheltering effects of these limited partnerships. This was accomplished by eliminating the capital gains rate, replacing accelerated with straight-line depreciation, and stretching out the depreciable life of a building to 31½ years. Moreover, a previous tax change limited the amount of loss that partnership investors could claim to the amount they are at risk. The '86 tax law defines income and losses from limited partnerships as passive. Passive losses can be used only to offset passive gains, not investment or wage income. For individuals whose limited partnership investments were held on the date the law was enacted (October 22, 1986) the passive loss limitation is being phased in over five years. In 1987 only 35 percent of excess losses will be disallowed; in

1988, 60 percent; in 1989, 80 percent; in 1990, 90 percent; in 1991, 100 percent. Unused losses are "suspended" and may be carried forward to be used in subsequent years to offset passive income. Alternatively, suspended losses can be used in full to reduce taxes when your entire interest in the partnership is sold.

Real Estate Investments and Taxes

Real property has intrinsic investment value, as we discussed earlier. It has had, in addition, special tax benefits which have made it especially attractive to high-income taxpayers. But Congress has a penchant for restructuring our tax laws on a fairly regular basis. So an investment made solely for tax reasons may turn sour when those tax benefits disappear. The Tax Reform Act of 1986 laid a heavy hand on the real estate industry. It took back some tax benefits that had been handed out only a few years earlier and others that had been on the books for decades.

Some of the tax benefits of real estate ownership have been retained. Homeowners who itemize may deduct mortgage interest and real estate taxes from their federal income tax. This also holds true for a second, or vacation, home. When a second home is rented as well as being used by the owner, tax treatment is a bit more complex. If two or more vacation homes are owned and used by the owner more than 14 days a year (or 10 percent of the time the property is rented at a fair rate), then the home on which the deductions are greater should be claimed as the second home. Rental income does not have to be reported on a vacation home that is rented two weeks or less annually.

A home that is rented and used less than two weeks a year by the owner qualifies as rental property. Because rental income and losses are classified as passive by the 1986 tax act, they are subject to the same rules and limitations as income and losses from limited partnerships. However, when the owner actively manages the property and his or her adjusted gross income is less than $100,000, then $25,000 of losses may be used to reduce income. For those with AGI over $100,000, losses are reduced by $1 for each $2 of added AGI.

When AGI reaches $150,000, the rental loss exception is exhausted. If your financial and tax situation is such that you are able to claim rental losses against other income, then all expenses associated with the property—taxes, mortgage interest, utilities, depreciation, etc.—are included. These "expenses" must first be used to offset rental income, then any excess can be used to offset other income.

When a principal residence is sold, the gain on that sale can be rolled over and added to the cost basis of the replacement home, so that the tax on the gain is deferred. This nonrecognition of the gain can go on for years, through two or two dozen home sales. Once the homeowner reaches fifty-five, a residence can be sold and up to $125,000 of the gain excluded from income. Conceivably, a taxpayer could parlay $10,000 into $125,000 tax-free using these two tax strategies.

What Can and Has Gone Wrong

A tremendous leap in interest rates is a perfect example of what can go wrong. If you owed a large real estate loan at 1 percent over prime when that rate was 5 or 6 percent, or even 10 percent, imagine your horror when the prime rate escalates to 20 percent, as it did in 1980. That jump could wipe out many a real estate investor.

Another example of what might go wrong was the sharp rise in California real estate values. This was accompanied by escalating property taxes. California homeowners on fixed incomes were often forced to sell or to take out second mortgages. When the upward spiral in home prices broke in the early '80s, a lot of people suffered, including banks and mortgage companies that had written mortgages based on inflated values.

Changing and deteriorating neighborhoods, demographic shifts, and rezoning can affect real estate investments. The revamping of tax laws, as discussed above, is another factor that can go wrong. An investment that makes sense under existing tax laws may prove to be a loser when those rules change. While present investors are sometimes protected by grandfather clauses, new investors are not. Thus, the value of real estate can be adversely affected.

PART III

How to Make Your Choices

CHAPTER 19

Forecasting with the Cyclical Indicators

FORECASTING IS A complicated process. Even the most expert forecasters are sometimes quite wrong, and ordinarily they are only partially accurate. Yet, like eating, forecasting is something that has to be done. Every action that each of us undertakes implies a forecast. Buying the week's groceries involves forecasting family needs and implies certain expectations about price behavior during the week. The actions of buying, selling, or even holding stocks all imply certain forecasts about stock prices.

The decision, then, is not between forecasting and not forecasting. Investors must forecast, and in so doing they must rely heavily on the work of others, at least for the needed data, and ordinarily for interpretations of those data.

Newspapers and business publications frequently carry reports of forecasts, with the fall of the year usually the most popular time for such reports. Investment advisory services, in most cases, carry forecasts, at least in summary form, throughout the year.

A forecast that appears each month is the one implied in the government's *composite index of leading indicators*. This forecast results from the efforts of a few economists to find a group of economic indicators that tend to move up or down in advance of the movements of general business. The reports of the current behavior of this index are widely watched, and the individual investor can advantageously pay some attention to these reports. However, the index is far from infallible, and most professional economists consider it to be only one of several forecasting tools available to them.

The index of leading indicators now being used by the U.S. Department of Commerce turned down four months before the 1953–54 recession, twenty-three months before the 1957–58 recession, eleven months before the 1960–61 recession, eight months before the 1970 recession, eight months before the 1973–75 recession, ten months before the 1980 recession, and three months before the 1981–82 recession. The index also turned down in 1950–51, 1962, 1966, and 1984. None of these downturns was followed by a full-fledged recession, although the 1966 economy is often described as one that experienced a mini-recession. The declines in the leading indicator index mentioned here were all drops lasting several months. A chart of the index also displays other, meaningless, short-term movements.

Actually, the particular index now in use wasn't even in existence on most of the dates cited above. The present index, introduced in 1975, is an improved version which, when computed historically, produced the above-mentioned results. The index used earlier failed to foreshadow the 1973 downturn, largely because several of its components were expressed in current dollars and were still pointing upward, reflecting the influence of inflation, when business actually was softening.

Leading Indicators: A Dozen Precursors

The revised index of leading indicators has twelve components, all tested for historical reliability in moving ahead of periods of general business expansion and contraction. The data for the components are gathered monthly and assembled into a combined index. The combined index measures departures from the base-year (1967) value of 100. However, when the combined index is first published, data for all twelve components are not available. For example, in any given year the index for May, published in June, is based on only ten components and is subsequently redone in July, when the other two components become available. Also, revisions in some of the individual components are made over a period of several months, leading to revisions of the combined index on those occasions.

The Twelve Leaders

Average weekly hours of production or nonsupervisory workers in manufacturing

Average weekly initial claims, state unemployment insurance

Manufacturers' new orders for consumer goods and materials, in 1972 dollars

Net business formation, 1967 = 100

Standard and Poor's index of 500 common stock prices, 1941–43 = 10

Contracts and orders for plant and equipment, in 1972 dollars

New private housing units authorized by local building permits, 1967 = 100

Vendor performance; percentage of companies receiving slower deliveries

Change in manufacturing and trade inventories on hand and on order, in 1972 dollars

Change in sensitive materials prices

Money supply, M2, in 1972 dollars

Change in business and consumer credit outstanding

SOURCE: *Business Conditions Digest,* monthly publication of the U.S. Department of Commerce.

The leading indicators are statistical measures that tend to foreshadow movements in the coincident group discussed later in this chapter. This is quite apparent in the indicators that report on new orders for consumer goods, on contracts and orders for plant and equipment, and in the index of housing permits. Movements in these indicators may be expected to be followed by movements in employment, production, incomes, and sales.

Other leading indicators generally have a rationale for their particular place in the timing sequence of economic measures. The stock market, for example, is sensitive to changes in the state of confidence concerning future busi-ness activity and future profits. Improved confidence about the future often leads to higher stock prices, and deteriorat-ing confidence brings stock prices down.

Changes in sensitive prices of crude materials—excluding foods, feeds, and fibers—reflect variations in demand-and-supply pressures for particular raw commodities. Thus a rise in this index could reflect rising levels of demand and, hence, expectations of increased business activity, while a drop in the index could signal the reverse.

The money supply, measuring the total of currency plus demand deposits and expressed in 1972 dollars, is another measure that often can be expected to precede, in its ups and downs, changes in the general level of business. Expansion of money tends to fuel expansion of business activity, while contraction of money tends to have a dampening effect on levels of such activity.

In recent years, investors, and especially stock market trad-ers, have devoted a good deal of attention to short-term movements in the money supply (without adjustments for price level changes). The weekly money-supply reports come out late in the afternoon every Thursday. Some observ-ers interpret increases in money as signs that the Federal Reserve Board is likely to restrict monetary growth and thereby tighten credit. Thus stocks often drop on Friday when the Thursday report shows a sharp rise in the money supply. If the report shows no gain or even a reduction in the money supply, the expectation sometimes develops that the Fed will ease the money supply and credit, and, accordingly, stocks may rise on Friday. This interpretation of money-supply movements is short term. The role of the money sup-ply in the leading indicator index depends on the actual movements of money rather than expectations of how money is going to move.

It is not generally a good idea to pay much attention to the movements of the leading indicator index for any single month. One reason for this caution is that movements of the index over short periods sometimes reflect the influence of random events, such as strikes or unusual weather patterns. For example, the initial reading for March 1985 showed a small decline in the indicator; this was later revised to show a slight increase. In this case initial data were temporarily distorted by serious delays in the mailing of income tax refunds by the IRS. Also, a general problem with the index is that it is oriented toward production and doesn't give proper weight to the larger role now played by the service indus‑ tries.

The leading indicators are actually part of a family of economic indicators. The two other branches of the family tree are the *coincident indicators,* which are generally the economic measures being led by the leading indicators, and the *lagging indicators,* which tend to bring up the rear, but which also have an importance of their own.

Coincident Indicators: Four-Track Broad-Based Activities

The coincident indicators are those that move with general business conditions, that is, those that move up and down with the swings that pervade most sectors of the economy. In general, one would expect the coincident indicators to encompass measures of employment, production, incomes, and sales, on the basis that these activities reflect the broad movements of the economy. As it turns out, these four aspects of economic activity are exactly the components of the index of coincident indicators.

The particular measure of employment used in this indicator is the monthly report on the number of employees on nonagricultural payrolls. This tests out better than other possible employment (or unemployment) measures as a reporter of the general ups and downs of business. One reason for this is that the payroll reports upon which this number is based reflect a markedly larger sample than does the household survey upon which the monthly labor force, total employment, and unemployment data are based.

The second coincident indicator is the monthly index of industrial production prepared by the Federal Reserve Board. This index measures activity in manufacturing, mining, and electric and gas utilities. Manufacturing activity tends to be cyclical and represents a declining share of the gross national product. However, the industrial production index reflects important activities and is still worthy of inclusion in the index of coincident indicators.

The income measure included is the monthly report on personal income. It is expressed in constant 1982 dollars and with transfer payments (Social Security benefits and other nonwage government "transfers" of funds into the hands of individuals) deducted. These adjustments improve upon the performance of the personal income figure as a measure of

CYCLICAL INDICATORS

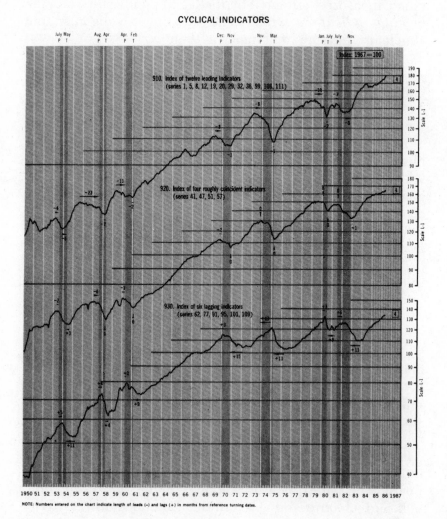

cyclical behavior, which is what is desired of a coincident indicator.

The final component in this index is a combined figure for manufacturing sales and wholesale and retail trade sales, expressed in constant 1972 dollars. This figure provides a comprehensive report on distribution and consumption activities and, like the personal income measure, is one from which the inflation influence has been removed.

A notable exclusion from the list of coincident indicators is the most comprehensive of all measures. This is the gross national product, the total dollar volume of the nation's output of goods and services. It is not included because it is available only on a quarterly basis rather than monthly and is subject to rather frequent revision.

The four coincident indicators are combined in a single index of coincident indicators, again using the year 1967 value of 100. The combined index tends to follow movements of general business quite closely, a result that is not surprising, given its broad composition. Although the combined index has a slight tendency to lead general downturns by a couple of months, its upward movements tend to coincide in timing with upswings in business.

The Coincident Four

Employees on nonagricultural payrolls
Industrial production, 1977 = 100
Personal income less transfer payments, in 1982 dollars
Manufacturing and trade sales, in 1972 dollars

SOURCE: *Business Conditions Digest*, U.S. Department of
  Commerce.

Lagging Indicators: Six Tend to Trail Behind

The third member of the indicator triad is the group of lagging indicators, those that rise or fall after the general upward or downward movements of the economy have appeared. For example, in the period from 1950 to 1985, the index of lagging indicators turned down, on average, five and a half months *after the peaks* in general business and turned upward, on average, ten months *after the low points.*

The lagging indicators, however, are more than faithful followers. A sequence exists among the three groups of indicators, so that the lagging indicators turn down before the leading, and later the coincident, indicators turn up.

The Six Laggards

Labor cost per unit of output in manufacturing, actual data as a percent of total

Ratio of manufacturing and trade inventories to sales, in 1972 dollars

Average duration of unemployment in weeks, inverted

Ratio of consumer installment credit outstanding to personal income

Commercial and industrial loans outstanding, in 1972 dollars

Average prime rate charged by banks

SOURCE: *Business Conditions Digest*, U.S. Department of Commerce.

Since the lagging indicators tend to make their moves before the leading indicators make theirs (in the reverse direction), the former have a place in the forecasting scheme. One would not expect the leading indicators to signal an upward or downward move until the lagging indicators had made a downward or upward move.

The family of leading, coincident, and lagging indicators forms a useful tool in the forecaster's kit. It is important, however, not to draw conclusions from observations pertaining to just one or two months. Unfortunately, the indicators don't foretell much about the severity or duration of business movements. Nor do they purport to forecast stock prices. But since the monthly reports on the leading indicators are widely published, it is easy for the general reader to follow them and thereby get some clues concerning the direction in which the economy is headed.

CHAPTER 20

Measuring the Market's Ups and Downs

THE MARKET IS "up." The market is "down." The market is in a sustained "rally." It is moving "sideways." The daily stock market reports make it sound as if all 2,000 issues that trade regularly on the New York Stock Exchange, plus the 800 or so on the American Stock Exchange, the 4,000 on NASDAQ, and the 15,000 others that trade on regional exchanges, Autex, and over the counter, are all moving in lockstep up, down, and sideways.

Obviously that's not the case. Just as obviously it would be an impossible task to provide a daily analysis of the aggregate price movements of all stocks. Yet investors, corporate money managers, stockbrokers, economic forecasters, government policymakers, and others concerned with the pulse of investment and business must have some way of keeping a running check on the investment climate.

So they have devised various averages to keep tabs on both the general trend and the present status of the market. Since the "market" is such a huge and diverse agglomeration, even the averages frequently have difficulty in agreeing on precisely what the trend and status of the market are at any given moment. Furthermore, just as the presence of a television news team can sometimes affect the outcome of the event it is covering, the averages themselves can have an impact on the extent and duration of a market movement. If the averages, particularly the more widely followed averages, say the market is "rising," investors perk up and start buying. If the averages say the market is "declining," they start selling to nail down profits or to trim losses. Other elements play their parts, of course: the general strength or weakness of business, the availability of credit, the cost of borrowing money, the needs of corporate finance. The factors affecting stock market movement and the movement of individual stocks are virtually limitless, and many of them defy analysis or rationality. Measurement of the stock market thus is an imprecise undertaking.

How to "Build" an Index

There are many ways to go about constructing an index of stock market activity. You could take a relatively small sampling of tried-and-true blue-chip companies and compute a simple, arithmetic average of their stock price activity on a day-to-day basis. You would have something like the Dow Jones Industrial Average. You could take a larger group of what you consider to be representative stocks and apply the same simple arithmetic averaging. You'd have something like the Associated Press and *New York Times* averages.

If you decided that such a simple price-weighted arithmetic average would not provide sufficient accuracy because it did not measure the impact of the stock's price on the total market volume, you could construct a so-called value-weighted average. You would factor in the differences in size of the components of your index by multiplying the price of each by the number of shares outstanding in each case. You would then average these resulting market-value figures and express them as a percentage of some base figure. You would then have something like the Standard & Poor's, the New York Stock Exchange, American Exchange, and the National Association of Securities Dealers Automated Quotation (NASDAQ) indexes.

This approach might not satisfy you either, because the largest components exert much more influence on the total than the smallest. You might regard this as a situation that unduly distorts the bottom line. So you would take still another tack. You would apply equal dollar investments to a fairly large group of stocks. The resultant index would be called an unweighted or equal-weighted average. You would need a firm grasp of mathematics, for you would then apply some rather complex geometric calculations to the daily price changes in order to come up with a result. Your index would resemble the composite index published by Value Line, an investment advisory company. It would also bear a resemblance to two indexes developed by Indicator Digest, Inc., another investment advisory publisher—the IDA, which covers all stocks traded on the New York Stock Exchange, and the AIDA, for those traded on the American Stock Exchange.

Different Indexes Yield Different Results

As you might suspect, these different approaches yield different results. For the most part, the differences are not so much in direction as in extent and occasionally in timing. The point is best demonstrated with a chart of three diverse averages—the 30-stock Dow Industrials, the S&P 500, and the 1,665-stock Value Line Average. For our chart, 1973 equals 100, making 1973 the base year for all three indexes. Value Line, the broadest based of the three, includes many secondary stocks, which makes it very volatile. In bull markets its rises are usually higher and last longer, while its bear market declines are more precipitous than those for the Dow and S&P 500. During the bull markets of 1980–81 and 1982–83, VL far outperformed the other two indicators, reflecting its representation in the high-technology industry.

Whereas by 1980 the VL and S&P averages had moved above their 1973 highs, the Dow took until 1983 to reattain its high of a decade before. This sluggish performance reflected the heavy concentration of cyclical industrial issues in the average. However, in the last few years the composition of the average has changed. Several consumer and/or service companies have been added to the list and a number of companies already on the list have shifted industry emphasis through acquisition, diversification, or divestiture. As a result, 47 percent of the average's value comes from companies which operate primarily in the service and/or consumer sectors. Thus, the Dow Industrials and the S&P 500 now track one another very closely.

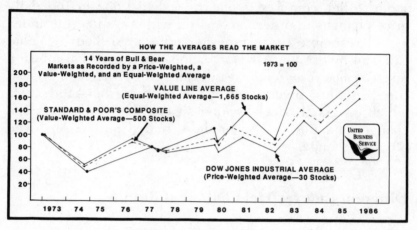

HOW THE AVERAGES READ THE MARKET

14 Years of Bull & Bear Markets as Recorded by a Price-Weighted, a Value-Weighted, and an Equal-Weighted Average

1973 = 100

VALUE LINE AVERAGE
(Equal-Weighted Average—1,665 Stocks)

STANDARD & POOR'S COMPOSITE
(Value-Weighted Average—500 Stocks)

DOW JONES INDUSTRIAL AVERAGE
(Price-Weighted Average—30 Stocks)

UNITED BUSINESS SERVICE

The "Dow"

The Dow Jones Industrial Average is the granddaddy of today's stock market measures. It's also probably the best-known and most widely quoted. The "Dow" dates back to 1896, when it contained an even dozen stocks, none of which remained on the list continuously. In 1916, another eight were added, bringing the total to twenty. It was not until 1928 that the average assumed its present shape. Not only were ten stocks added, but a new method of computation was adopted. It is still in use.

Before 1928, stocks which were split were adjusted by multiplying the split price by two or three, or whatever the split was, to make the price consistent with the presplit value. Adjustments made since 1928 take into account stock dividends, rights, and mergers, as well as splits.

Here are the thirty stocks that made up the Dow Jones Industrial Average in 1987. Dates in parentheses indicate the company's first appearance in the average. Only General

Electric was in the original average, though it has been in and out several times since.

Allied-Signal (1925)
Aluminum Co. of America
 (1959)
American Express (1982)
American Telephone &
 Telegraph (1916)
Bethlehem Steel (1928)
Boeing Corp. (1987)
Chevron Corp. (1924)
Coca-Cola (1987)
DuPont (EI) de Nemours
 (1924)
Eastman Kodak (1928)
Exxon Corp. (1928)
General Electric (1897)
General Motors (1915)
Goodyear Tire & Rubber
 (1930)

Int'l. Business Machines
 (1979)
Int'l. Paper (1901)
McDonald's Corp. (1985)
Merck & Company (1979)
Minnesota Mining & Mfg.
 (1976)
Navistar Int'l. (1925)
Philip Morris Cos. (1985)
Primerica Corp. (1916)
Procter & Gamble (1932)
Sears, Roebuck (1924)
Texaco Inc. (1916)
Union Carbide (1928)
United Technologies (1933)
USX Corp. (1914)
Westinghouse Electric (1916)
Woolworth, F.W. (1924)

What is now known as the Dow Jones Transportation Average boasts an equally long history. Until 1970, it was known as the "Railroad" Average; the name was changed when other types of transportation companies were added to the list that year. The twenty stocks that were originally used were all rails, some with names that are still familiar. But many others have succumbed to mergers and bankruptcies. The Dow Jones Utility Average made its debut in 1929. The initial list of twenty utilities included both electric and gas companies, as well as American Telephone & Telegraph, International Telephone, and Western Union. Today the list has been whittled to fifteen electric and gas utilities. The Dow Jones Composite Average was begun in 1933 as a compilation of the stocks used in the three individual averages. All of these are computed essentially the same way as the industrial average.

For several reasons, the historical significance of the Dow industrial average is subject to question. Until 1928, no adjustments were made for stock splits of less than 100 percent.

Furthermore, when the new issues were added, the continuity of the average was disrupted. Substitutions in the names of companies in the list were frequent in the early days; through 1939, more than sixty were made. While this probably made the list more representative of the current market, it also produced a historical bias.

Another complaint frequently lodged against the Dow, and one that has some justification, is that it is an elitist sampling of the market. Only 1.5 percent of the stocks listed on the New York Stock Exchange appear in it. Even when you consider that these issues constitute 25 percent of the total market value of Big Board issues, they are still an extremely narrow representation of all the issues regularly traded on all the exchanges and over the counter.

Critics of the Dow note that it is heavily loaded with cyclical stocks and includes few solid growth issues. However, the last seven additions to that average—American Express, Boeing, Coca-Cola, IBM, McDonald's, Merck, and Philip Morris—represent some of the fastest-growing sectors of the economy. Since price action of basic industry stocks is usually skewed by the ups and downs of the business cycle, these stocks are not necessarily representative of the market as a whole. Then, too, this venerable average completely ignores some of the most dynamic growth areas of today's market.

The S&P 500

Aside from the Dow, the most familiar average is the Standard & Poor's 500. This broad average is widely used by institutional investors and mutual fund managers as a yardstick against which to compare their own performance. In fact, some funds and institutions have adopted investment policies that restrict their holdings to those in the S&P 500 list, thereby giving up any attempt at outperforming this index.

Standard & Poor's also publishes separately the various component averages that make up the 500-stock composite. These are the 400 industrials, 40 utilities, 20 transportation companies, and 40 financial stocks. These new indexes were begun in 1957 to replace the original series started in the 1920s. As we noted above, the S&P averages are weighted. They are also expressed as a percentage of the base market value in 1941–43.

Other Indexes

The New York Stock Exchange Composite Stock Index uses as its base December 31, 1965 = 50, which approximates the average price of a share on the Big Board then. Thus, if the index stands at 60, it indicates that the market has advanced 20 percent above its value on December 31, 1965. The NYSE Index should not be confused with the figure cited daily by newscasters, the average price of a share on the New York Stock Exchange. The latter is simply the average price for all the stocks that traded on a particular day on the Big Board. There is no day-to-day continuity in this figure, for not all issues trade every session; neither is any attempt made to adjust for splits or other changes.

The American Stock Exchange Index is based on equal dollar investments in a list of 1,665 stocks—1,475 industrials, 19 rails, and 171 utilities. It uses June 30, 1961, as its base. The Indicator Digest indexes use 1964 as a starting point.

Indexes Are Useful—to a Point

Are market indexes useful tools for the average investor? Yes, up to a point. Certainly the person who plunges in and buys a stock with a high price-earnings ratio after the averages have recorded a steep and prolonged advance is asking for trouble. The investor who gets discouraged and sells stocks he has been holding through a protracted decline in the market is equally unwise. In other words, the averages are valuable as rough guidelines for timing your transactions.

Using the market averages as forecasting devices, although a favorite pastime of the technicians, can be tricky and unreliable. Complex formulas, involving virtually every conceivable variable, have been devised by serious students of the market, mathematical wizards, and charlatans. While some may prove accurate from time to time, no one has ever come up with a forecasting device of any kind that is always correct. If such an infallible formula exists, it is surely being kept under wraps by its originator, who is busy reaping his own fortune.

In trying to gauge market timing by consulting one of the market averages, you should use an average that represents the type of stocks you own or plan to purchase. The Dow industrials will be of little help if you are interested in utilities, glamour stocks, or rails. Junior growth stocks would more closely parallel the action tracked by the Value Line, IDA, or AMEX indexes.

By keeping in touch with the general trend of the stock market averages, you should develop a better understanding of the action of your own portfolio. Many investors operate in a vacuum. Their holdings are down and they grow panicky, overlooking the fact that the entire market is in the doldrums. Then, too, keeping an eye on the market rather than on a few individual stocks helps you keep things in proper perspective. If one of your stocks diverges suddenly from the norm, you are more likely to spot this countermovement, investigate, and take the indicated action. Use the averages, by all means, but use them judiciously.

CHAPTER 21

Getting the Picture from Charts

CHARTS, QUITE SIMPLY, are devices which can be valuable aids to investors. They translate into graphic form—with bars or lines—information which could also be presented in tabular form. The basic usefulness of a chart is the picture presented, its conciseness, and the ability to portray relationships that would not be visible in a table.

Here is a tabulation of information showing the daily high, low, and close of the Dow Jones Industrial Average over a two-month period:

		High	Low	Close			High	Low	Close
April	1	930.27	919.55	927.36	May	2	934.02	923.00	931.22
	4	926.70	913.48	915.56		3	939.70	929.27	934.19
	5	920.88	909.74	916.14		4	944.96	929.44	940.72
	6	922.12	910.07	914.73		5	949.46	934.53	943.44
	7	921.21	910.57	918.88		6	943.27	932.24	936.74
	11	928.85	916.47	924.10		9	938.52	928.77	933.09
	12	940.98	924.69	937.16		10	941.40	930.55	936.14
	13	942.76	927.49	938.18		11	937.84	923.85	926.90
	14	956.07	943.69	947.00		12	930.04	917.74	925.54
	15	953.10	941.74	947.76		13	932.58	923.17	928.34
	18	951.32	939.28	942.76		16	938.43	926.73	932.50
	19	944.28	934.79	938.77		17	939.45	925.20	936.48
	20	948.69	933.43	942.59		18	947.34	935.46	941.91
	21	949.37	933.43	935.80		19	945.13	933.34	936.48
	22	935.13	923.59	927.07		20	937.16	925.71	930.46
	25	924.02	910.45	914.60		23	928.17	915.03	917.06
	26	922.74	910.36	915.62		24	917.83	906.55	912.40
	27	928.34	913.08	923.76		25	916.72	901.46	903.24
	28	931.14	919.78	927.32		26	910.45	899.17	908.07
	29	931.99	922.32	926.90		27	909.60	896.29	898.83
						31	904.77	892.55	898.66

Just about any set of data can be depicted graphically, and the result is a "picture" that can be quickly comprehended. The chart opposite, top, shows the same information contained in the table, plotted on a simple arithmetic scale. This particular chart is a "bar chart," and its purpose is to show a range. In this case, the top of each bar represents the high price for the day, the bottom represents the low, and the cross line represents the close.

If the data to be plotted do not involve a range, the result would be a line connecting each of the points. Such a chart is called a "line chart," as depicted at the bottom of the opposite page. As will be noted throughout this book, many charts combine bars and lines, the better to portray the data, or picture, desired.

BAR CHART

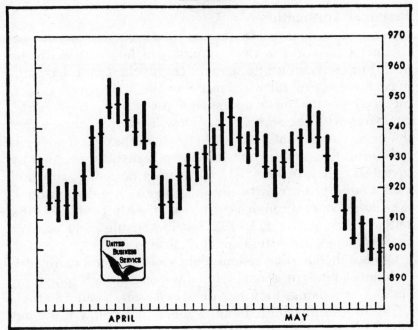

LINE CHART

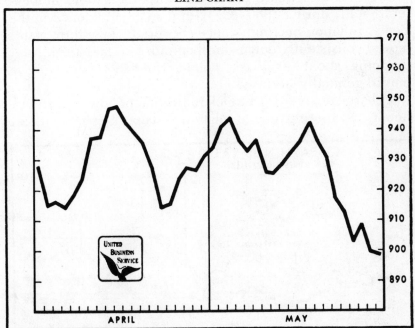

Practical Application

Here are some practical examples of how charts can be useful in conveying information. In the chart on price-earnings ratio you can tell at a glance how the price-earnings ratio for the stocks that make up the Dow Jones Industrial Average compares with the status of the Dow itself. You can see that the price-earning ratio stayed below 10X for over five years, indicating that stocks were not being realistically valued by investors. Then in late 1982 the market rallied sharply and P/Es soared to unrealistically high levels. Reason returned, the market went through a correction in early 1984, and P/Es settled back to the 11X–13X level. A rising stock market since then has lifted the Dow P/E close to 17X.

Or take the chart on federal debt yields, a good barometer of interest rates in general. It shows that though long-term yields were rising, they remained relatively stable through 1978. Short-term yields bounce above and below the long-term line in a fairly typical pattern. Mixed signals from the Federal Reserve Board generated sharp fluctuations in long-term yields during 1980–82. With market confidence in the Fed's inflation-beating stance restored, long-term rates moved consistently downward beginning in mid-1984. After dropping about 300 basis points, short-term yields have moved generally sideways.

A chart can give you a quick indication of how a particular item is performing now in relation to its performance in past

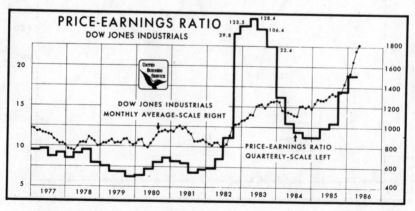

periods. From that picture you can frequently draw some conclusions about the future. Take the next chart, on private housing starts. It shows the long-range picture, with housing starts declining from 2 million in 1978, a healthy rate, to about half that amount in 1981 and 1982. Housing starts recovered in 1983 and moved sideways in 1984 and 1985 at the 1.75–1.8 level. Bolstered by lower mortgage interest rates, early 1986 starts were above 2 million, in line with industry expectations of a good year in 1986.

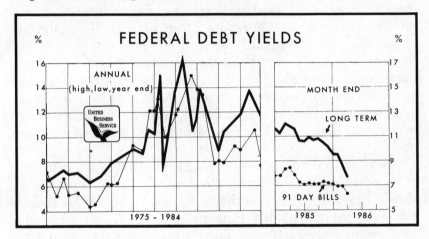

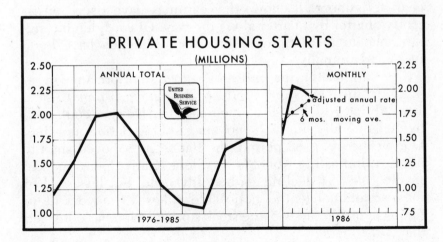

Charts and Your Investments

In the quarterly *SRC Blue Book of 5-Trend Cycli-Graphs*, published by Securities Research Company (a division of Babson-United Investment Advisors, Inc.), there are 1,105 stock charts and 73 industry charts, as well as various business and market-average charts. The stock charts contain plottings of monthly price ranges, volumes, relative performance line (Ratio-Cator), plus earnings and dividends over a twelve-year period. There are close to *1 million* plotting points in one book of 272 pages. Much of the book may be scanned in a fairly short time, though a real study would take much longer. Imagine how many volumes would be required to show this information in tabular form, how long it would take to comprehend the material, and the difficulty that would be encountered in comparing one company with another.

You don't have to possess a lot of investment expertise to draw some conclusions from the typical *Cycli-Graphs* chart shown here. It shows you that the stock of Abbott Laboratories rose almost steadily from its low in 1974 to a high in 1986, with only moderate downturns along the way. The chart tells more. It shows that earnings have risen consistently quarter by quarter along the way. Of considerable significance to the long-term investor, dividends have been increased annually.

The Ratio-Cator line indicates a stock's performance in relation to the Dow Jones Industrial Average. From 1974 to 1977 Abbott rose but did not outpace the Dow, as confirmed by the generally sideways movement of the Ratio-Cator line. During the 1977–82 period, the Ratio-Cator moved sharply upward, indicating Abbott's excellent relative performance. In the 1982–84 decline, Abbott advanced, but less so than the market, hence the noticeable sideways movement in Ratio-Cator. From 1985, the stock's price action has outpaced that of the market.

In confirmation of Abbott's excellent relative performance one need only compare its 2,400 percent price rise from a 1⅞ low in 1974 to a 47½ high in 1986 to that of the Dow. Its gain was 230 percent, from 570 in 1974 to 1,886 in 1986.

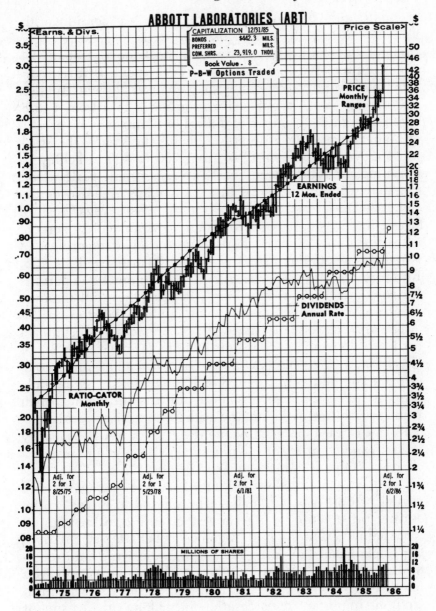

ABBOTT LABORATORIES (ABT)

Plotting the Percentages

You have probably noticed that the *Cycli-Graphs* chart looks somewhat "different" in that the vertical scale figures are not evenly spaced. That is because it is a "semi-logarithmic" or "ratio-scale" chart. Its purpose is to present everything on the chart in proportion. If a stock moves from 2 to 4, it has appreciated two points, or 100 percent. If it rises another two points, from 4 to 6, the gain is 50 percent. Another 100 percent move would have required a gain from 4 to 8. Even though the number of dollars or points may be greater at higher levels, the principle remains the same—the stock must move from 20 to 40 or from 200 to 400 to achieve a doubling, or 100 percent rise. The logarithmic scale is formulated so that any move of a particular percent uses the same vertical linear distance on the chart, regardless of where it may occur. Thus, for example, a move of 10 percent takes the same amount of space on the chart regardless of whether it occurs in a stock selling at 60 or one selling at 6. Furthermore, the use of a standard logarithmic scale permits the comparison of any one chart with any other so that movements may be perfectly related without fear of distortion.

The arithmetic-scale chart with which most people are acquainted does not work in this manner. A move from 2 to 4 looks exactly the same on such a chart as a jump from 4 to 6, or even an edging up from 98 to 100. Obviously, two points have greater significance when a stock is selling at 2 than when it is selling at 98, but the arithmetic scale conceals this. The extent of a price movement, large or small, is easily hidden, and comparisons of one stock with another on such a chart are difficult to make and can be deceptive.

Charts can also be something of an eye-opener. Over a period of time you might have become accustomed to the current price action of a certain stock, while losing sight of what happened in the past. A glance at a chart, particularly if the stock used to be a highflier, can be edifying and, sometimes, sobering. Similarly, when a stock is rising sharply, you might easily forget the base from which the rise was initiated, an important consideration in making an investment decision. A chart will furnish the relationship.

A good example of this sort of illumination might come from the chart in Chapter 20 which shows the performance of three market averages. The Standard & Poor's 500 is a value-weighted average. The Dow Jones Industrial Average, a simple price average of 30 different stocks, is somewhat biased by industrial giants. The Value Line Composite Average, with its 1,665 issues, is equal weighted. As explained in Chapter 20, a value-weighted average gives particular importance to heavily capitalized companies, and while this may reflect total market *value,* it does not tell us what the total market of all *stocks* may be doing. That is what the equal-weighted averages try to correct. In effect, they give one unit of value to a stock, regardless of whether it is a General Motors or a small company which is a fraction of the size of that giant.

Not Only for Technicians

Charts are basically a tool, one of many, which the investor may use to determine his investment action. There are myriad charts available, showing not just a stock's price action but market details, business statistics, interest rates, money supply—you name it. What a chart does is show the quantitative factors involved in the study of the market, a company, or an industry. It does not show the various qualitative considerations involved. In a manufacturing company, for example, these might concern management, product line, plant efficiency, labor relations, and many other items impossible to quantify, although they may be reflected to a certain extent in specific or general price action.

Many people tend to think that if someone uses stock charts in his investment decisions, he is a technician. Actually, the fundamentalist has just as much use for charts. The pictures they show and the amount of information they provide help to make the task of investment selection much easier for the busy person.

CHAPTER 22

Technical Analysis

Definitions

FUNDAMENTALIST. One who bases his investment analysis and decisions primarily on basic factors such as economic conditions, supply and demand, labor, products, earnings, and dividends.

TECHNICIAN. One who bases his investment actions and decisions upon a reading and interpretation of chart formations or compilations of statistics.

The discussions in this book are principally oriented toward the fundamentalist. This chapter is intended to furnish an introduction to the technician and some of his methods of analysis and must be very general in nature. To some, technical analysis is not a valid investment approach, perhaps because some of the technical theories seem too "far-out." Yet technicians will argue that their record certainly is no worse than that of the fundamentalists, and, in view of the number of those attracted to technical analysis, it may possibly be better.

There is no one method of technical analysis. In fact, there are so many methods and interpretations and there is such a wide variety of data and relationships developed that it is doubtful if any one person could become well versed in all. Certain methods utilize common data, but others are individual and unique. Some technicians base their market and investment decisions wholly or partly on the study of chart formations. Others may depend wholly or partly on statistical compilations and work relating one series of data to one or more other series. Using models of behavior based on prior study and experience, the technician derives from chart patterns and relationships and from statistics the material he needs to make his decisions.

Once the technician has created his models and his chart or statistical relationships, he must stick to them. He may refine them, but he cannot allow emotional considerations to influence his decisions. That is where many technicians go wrong. They allow their technical findings to be swayed by other factors. Perhaps this is because they are not completely convinced of the validity of their method, or perhaps their signal has been received far ahead of others. Thus, the technician may be alone and exposed with his findings. And that solitary position makes him wonder whether he has made a correct interpretation of his charts and data. He cannot entertain such doubts. While his method may not always work out —none is infallible, after all—it faces a greater risk of failure if he is influenced by exceptions, emotions, and outside considerations.

More Than Charts and Figures

People tend to think of technical analysis as meaning chart formations such as flags, pennants, channels, heads and shoulders, etc., but it involves much more. With the advent of computers, the technician may now tear apart stacks of statistics to obtain relationships, actions, and reactions over long periods of time—material which previously might have been too difficult to obtain. These studies permit the technician to determine a series of likelihoods and probabilities— of rises, declines, and side movements. They do not necessarily project the magnitude of the moves, only that a move will take place. Like any other analyst or investor, the technician is attempting to ascertain the optimum time to make his buys and sells.

The advantage of chart analysis over the fundamental approach is in calling a turn. Often the basics of a situation may look good, but for some unperceived reason the technical picture turns weak. It is at this point that technical analysis does better than fundamental. The lines often tell something more than the fundamentals may indicate, and it is this failure of the latter on many occasions which has led more people into technical analysis, not just of stocks but of all sorts of economic factors. Actually, fundamental and technical analysis seem to be coming closer together in investment decision-making. However, if the technical approach shows weakness in a situation and the fundamental does not, the former should be followed, because the fundamental will confirm too late. For example, look at the chart of Redken Laboratories.

Despite rising earnings, the stock developed weakness after achieving its all-time high in February 1985. Earnings continued in a generally rising pattern through August 1985 and the stock turned upward for the next six months, challenging but not breaking through its previous all-time high. The relative performance line moved sideways in this period, demonstrating Redken's weakness in relation to the Dow. The fundamentalist might have said the outlook remained favorable and the stock should be held. The technician, however, seeing weakness developing in the earnings and relative action, would have suspected that something was amiss and recommended sale of the shares.

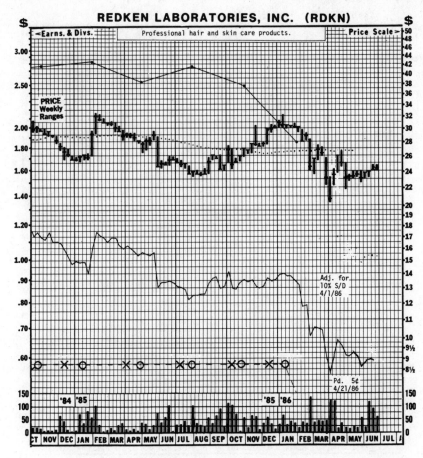

REDKEN LABORATORIES, INC. (RDKN)

Professional hair and skin care products.

The chart for H.J. Heinz gives an example of a rising price trend. Here we have a picture of declines which are accompanied by reduced volume and where rallies occur with increased volume. In addition, the stock's performance indicates relative strength at important highs. Accompanying this are the rising earnings trend and dividend increases.

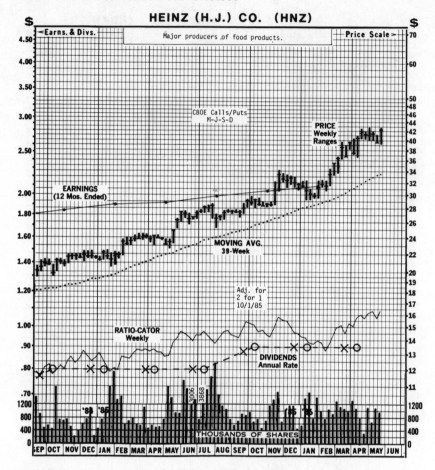

Some Technical Indicators

There are various popular indicators used in attempting to determine market direction. Some, which are best shown by charts, include (not necessarily in order of importance):

MARKET AVERAGES. The chart patterns of averages such as the Dow industrials, the Standard & Poor's 500, the New York Stock Exchange Composite, the Value Line Composite, etc. are studied for clues to future action.

TRADING VOLUME. This information, in figures or as plottings on charts, is important to determine whether strength or weakness accompanies various price movements.

SPECULATIVE INDEX. This is the relationship of American Stock Exchange volume to New York Stock Exchange volume and is expressed as a percentage. The theory here is that since most of the issues listed on the AMEX tend to be of lower or more speculative quality than those on the NYSE, they will be slow to participate in the earlier stages of a bull market and will be very active in the later and declining phases. Thus, the lower the figure, the closer the market presumably is to a bottom, and, conversely, the higher the figure, the closer it is to a top. In the past, this indicator has fluctuated within a 20 to 60 percent range. In more recent times, it has dropped to as low as 10 percent. The rising volume of options trading is blamed for the decline in AMEX volume and the value of this indicator.

ADVANCE-DECLINE INDEX. This index may be started at any point in time and is the net result of all the advances and declines which have occurred on the New York Stock Exchange since that starting point. The significance of this line is its comparison with the Dow industrials or other market averages to detect any divergence which may occur. Thus, in a bull market this line will often start down while the averages are still rising and, conversely, in a bear market will start to rise while the averages are still declining. It can be an early signal of a change in general market direction.

A ratio derived from relating advances to declines provides an overbought-oversold index, which, when substantially above or below 1.00, indicates one of those conditions.

UPSIDE-DOWNSIDE VOLUME. This is a tabulation of the shares traded on the NYSE at prices higher or lower than the previous day's close. The trend of either line may be used to confirm the movement of a market average, and the crossing of the lines is interpreted as possibly indicating a change in market direction.

NEW HIGHS-NEW LOWS. This is another indicator of market strength or weakness. In a strong market, the new highs should greatly exceed the lows and follow the market averages. The opposite is true in a weak market. It is when either line diverges from the averages and when the lines cross that an indication is given of a change in direction. A line representing the differential between these figures will perform similarly to the advance-decline index in peaking while the market averages continue to rise and in bottoming when the averages are continuing to decline.

ODD-LOT TRADING. This is the buying and selling activity of the small investor who deals in units of less than a round lot (100 shares). The extent to which this investor buys or sells has been used to indicate turning points for "informed" selling or buying. To greatly simplify the theory, the small investor is said to buy or sell at the wrong time, and the extent to which he does so provides a signal to the smart investor to do the opposite. Thus, odd-lot selling may peak around the bottom of the market, and odd-lot buying may reach its maximum around the top. The odd-lot index is the relationship of sales to purchases, and the higher the percentage, the more bullish the indicator. Thus goes the general theory.

A more recent study claims the odd-lotter has been maligned and has been more attuned to market action than generally believed. Thus, at major bottoms he is seen to have been a buyer and at major tops he is often a seller.

To further refine odd-lot indicators, odd-lot *short* sales are related to odd-lot sales. The resultant figure is considered a significant indicator, since the small investor does not usually sell short, and when he does so it is under rather extreme conditions. Once again, he purportedly picks the wrong time. While there may be some difference of opinion concerning these figures, when the odd-lot short-sales figure is up around 10,000 and the ratio is in the 4 to 6 percent area, a major bottom may be signaled; on the other hand, when short selling is low and the ratio is around 0.5 to 1 percent, a top may be indicated. But the whole theory, or its importance, has been diminished by growth in options trading.

SHORT INTEREST. This is the total number of shares sold short. The higher this figure, the more bearish are investors (frequently at the wrong time). But since the stock which has been sold must be bought back, it provides a good cushion of buying power when the short sellers seek to cover their short contracts. When the market is at its top, short selling has usually diminished to a fairly low figure, reflecting the general optimism. Member and specialist short selling are also looked at for sensitive market signals.

SHORT INTEREST RATIO. This figure is obtained by relating the monthly short interest to the average daily trading volume in the period concerned. When the ratio moves up to 2 or more, it is generally considered a bullish sign, and when it declines to 1 or lower, the signal is bearish.

BARRON'S CONFIDENCE INDEX. This is a relationship between the yields of high-grade and intermediate-grade bonds on the theory that informed investors will put their money into the former during periods of market uncertainty and into the latter during better times. A decline in this index indicates that more investors are seeking refuge in high-grade issues, and a rise indicates a more optimistic attitude. The value of this index is that presumably the stock market will follow the same pattern, but usually at a somewhat later date.

An indication of how some of these data look when plotted and related to each other is shown in the charts that follow.

TECHNICAL INDICATORS

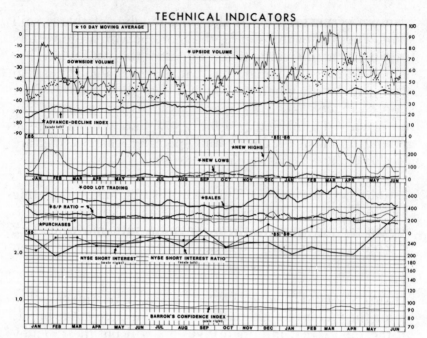

Irregular Forecasting Methods

There are many other methods of predicting market action. They are not especially technical but they are far from fundamental. Here are a few:

Years ending in 7 tend to have an upward trend.
National election years have certain patterns.
The first year of a new presidential administration is likely to be down or to be the worst of the four years of that administration.
An up or a down January sets the tone for the month and the year.
The first ten days of January set the tone for the month and the year.
There is usually a summer rally.
A poor July-August market is usually followed by a rally in September.
The direction of the market is indicated by whether General

Motors makes a new high or new low within four months of a previous high or low.

Strength or weakness of sunspots will affect the market.

A strong indication of bearishness or bullishness by investment advisory services is a sign that the market will move in the opposite direction.

It is obvious there are nearly as many ways to "forecast" the market as there are those willing to express an opinion, and the variety seems limitless.

Interpreting Chart Patterns

When it comes to technical analysis of individual stocks, you will find a variety of formations and interpretations. While some of these formations are rather easy to identify, others tend to be more obscure. Sometimes the technician must strain to identify the pattern that makes his point. Also, formations vary with the type of chart used—daily, weekly, or monthly, arithmetic or logarithmic—so that what shows up on one chart will not necessarily appear on another for the same stock. The technician then must decide which charts make him most comfortable and confident, and proceed accordingly.

The discussion of formations which follows is intended only as a brief explanation of the most common terms.

SUPPORT LEVEL. A price area in which the demand for a stock is sufficient to keep the price from dropping below it on repeated occasions. Once there is a breakout below the area, a new support level is created.

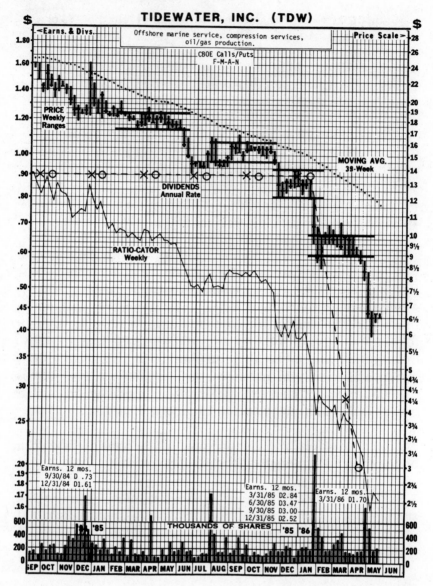

TIDEWATER, INC. (TDW)

Offshore marine service, compression services, oil/gas production.

RESISTANCE LEVEL. A price area which attracts selling sufficient to keep the price of a stock from rising above it on repeated occasions. However, once it has been broken through on the upside, the old resistance area becomes a new support level.

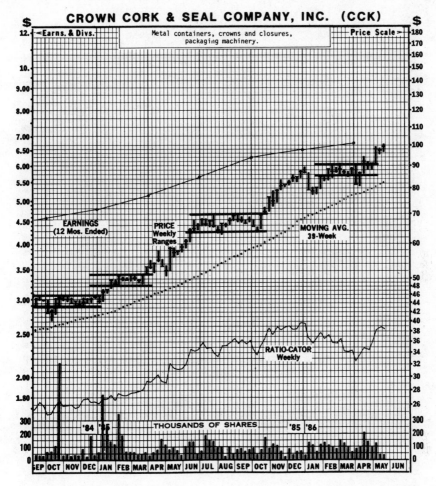

CROWN CORK & SEAL COMPANY, INC. (CCK)

Metal containers, crowns and closures, packaging machinery.

CHANNELS. These are drawn by connecting a series of highs and a series of lows to make parallel lines. Characteristically, the stock will trade within the ascending and descending channels, indicating a sell at the top of the channel and a buy at the bottom. A confirmed breakout in either direction would mean a buy on the upside and a sell on the down.

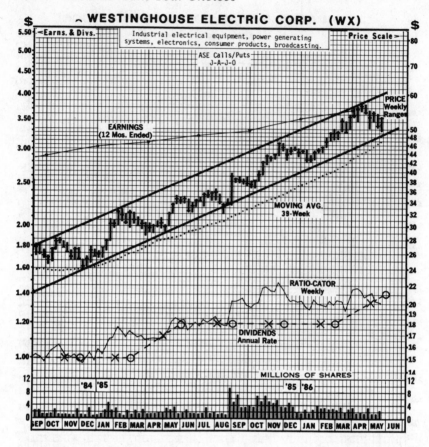

WESTINGHOUSE ELECTRIC CORP. (WX)

Industrial electrical equipment, power generating systems, electronics, consumer products, broadcasting.

ROWAN COMPANIES, INC. (RDC)

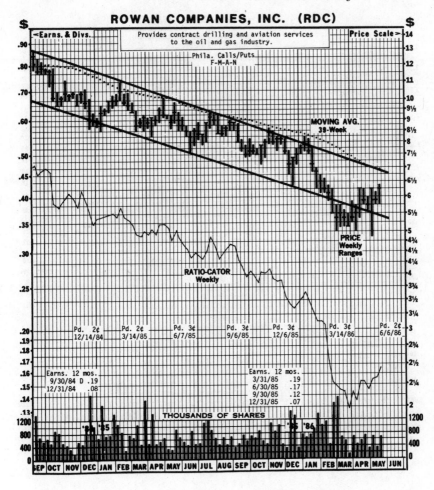

$**   **$

<Earns. & Divs.

Provides contract drilling and aviation services to the oil and gas industry.

Price Scale>

Phila. Calls/Puts
F-M-A-N

MOVING AVG.
39-Week

PRICE
Weekly
Ranges

RATIO-CATOR
Weekly

Pd. 2¢
12/14/84

Pd. 2¢
3/14/85

Pd. 3¢
6/7/85

Pd. 3¢
9/6/85

Pd. 3¢
12/6/85

Pd. 3¢
3/14/86

Pd. 2¢
6/6/86

Earns. 12 mos.
9/30/84 D .19
12/31/84   .08

Earns. 12 mos.
3/31/85   .19
6/30/85   .17
9/30/85   .12
12/31/85   .07

THOUSANDS OF SHARES

'84 '85   '85 '86

SEP OCT NOV DEC JAN FEB MAR APR MAY JUN JUL AUG SEP OCT NOV DEC JAN FEB MAR APR MAY JUN

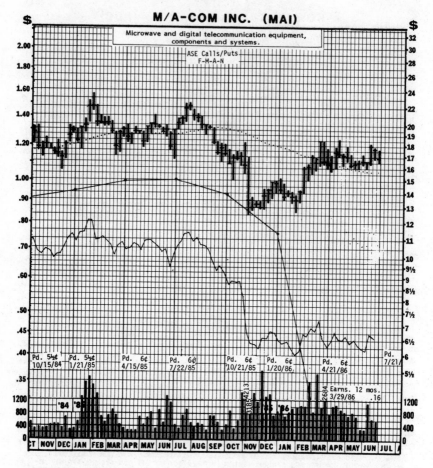

DOUBLE TOPS AND BOTTOMS (M AND W FORMATIONS). These are formations in which the stock fluctuates, hitting the same top or bottom on two, and sometimes three or four, successive occasions. The breakout from such a pattern is the clue to the action to be taken. The chart of M/A-Com Inc. is an example of an attempted upside breakout from the W formation, followed by a clear violation of the three successive bottoms. The chart for First Chicago Corp. is an example of an indecisive triple top which might have been in the process of making a fourth top or breaking through to create an entirely different type of formation.

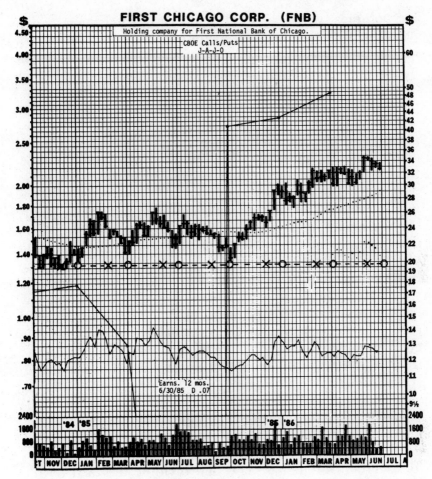

FIRST CHICAGO CORP. (FNB)

Holding company for First National Bank of Chicago.

CBOE Calls/Puts
J-A-J-O

Earns. 12 mos.
6/30/85 D .07

HEAD AND SHOULDERS. This formation's name is derived from the appearance given by the pattern of a head and right and left shoulders. The important thing here, if one has not previously sold on the higher head level, is to take advantage of the rally which forms the right shoulder, because price deterioration on reduced volume can set in very quickly.

Other patterns which may be drawn by connecting a series of highs and lows, usually during short time spans, include flags, pennants, triangles, wedges, and rectangles, all of which may give a message to the technician. And then there are bowls and saucers, and variations thereof, as well as trading volumes, which also tell a story. You must remember, however, that none of these patterns is exact and perfection is impossible. However, the astute and perceptive student may achieve a high percentage of successful interpretation.

RELATIVE STRENGTH. This is the relationship of the price of a stock to the price of the Dow Jones Industrial Average or perhaps to one of the other major market averages. The resulting percentage, multiplied by a factor to bring the plotting closer to the price bars on the chart, shows by the direction of the curve whether the stock is performing better, worse, or the same as the market average used. The line is studied for trends as well as for variations of direction from that indicated by the price ranges. For example, the price of a stock may reach a new high but the relative performance line may not, a possible indication of weakness. Similarly, strength may be observed when the price drops to a new low but the relative strength line does not. The charts printed earlier in this chapter of Redken and H.J. Heinz provide good examples of how effective the relative performance line (Ratio-Cator) may be on the downside and the upside, respectively.

MOVING AVERAGES. One of the popular indicators for determining market and individual stock strength or weakness is the moving average. This is obtained by adding up the prices for a certain number of days and dividing the total by the days involved to obtain an average. For the next figure, the price for the earliest day or week is dropped and the current one is added. A moving average rounds out the ups and downs, and the investor is then able to derive buying and selling signals from the action of the price in relation to the moving average curve. These figures are easily plotted, or they may be conveniently used in tabular form. The chart on page 238 plots moving averages for three different time periods and can be referred to for an indication of short- and long-term market direction.

The most popular time period for individual stocks appears to be 200 days, or roughly 40 weeks, although some investors prefer a much shorter span to achieve a greater degree of

SAVIN CORP. (SVB)

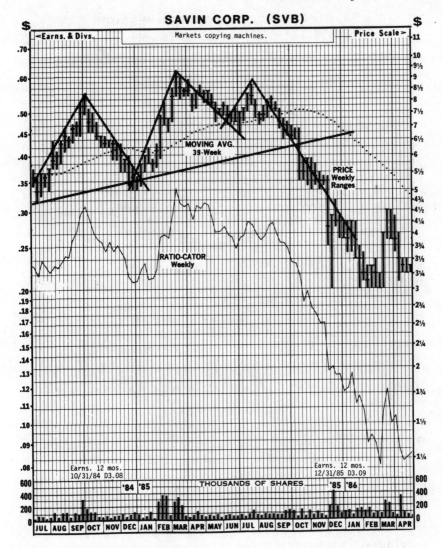

$ ◄Earns. & Divs.

Markets copying machines.

Price Scale► $

MOVING AVG.
39-Week

PRICE
Weekly
Ranges

RATIO-CATOR
Weekly

Earns. 12 mos.
10/31/84 D3.08

Earns. 12 mos.
12/31/85 D3.09

'84 '85

THOUSANDS OF SHARES

'85 '86

JUL AUG SEP OCT NOV DEC JAN FEB MAR APR MAY JUN JUL AUG SEP OCT NOV DEC JAN FEB MAR APR

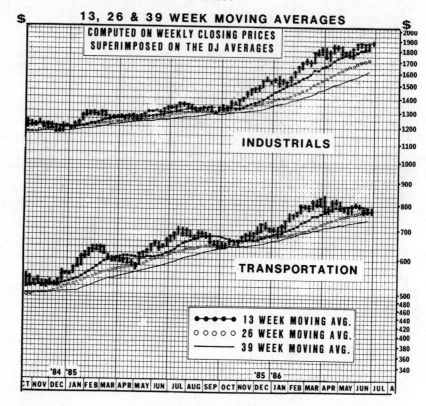

13, 26 & 39 WEEK MOVING AVERAGES

COMPUTED ON WEEKLY CLOSING PRICES
SUPERIMPOSED ON THE DJ AVERAGES

INDUSTRIALS

TRANSPORTATION

●●●●● 13 WEEK MOVING AVG.
○○○○○ 26 WEEK MOVING AVG.
——— 39 WEEK MOVING AVG.

'84 '85   '85 '86

CT NOV DEC JAN FEB MAR APR MAY JUN JUL AUG SEP OCT NOV DEC JAN FEB MAR APR MAY JUN JUL A

sensitivity. The moving average gives a quick indication of where strength or weakness may lie, but, as with all other formations, the user must follow certain rules to avoid false moves.

While all the charts used in this chapter include a moving average, the chart of Dart & Kraft is a specific example of the moving average–price range relationship. It portrays one of the interpretations of a moving average which holds that a buy signal is indicated when the stock price is above the moving average, declines toward it but fails to penetrate, and starts to move up again.

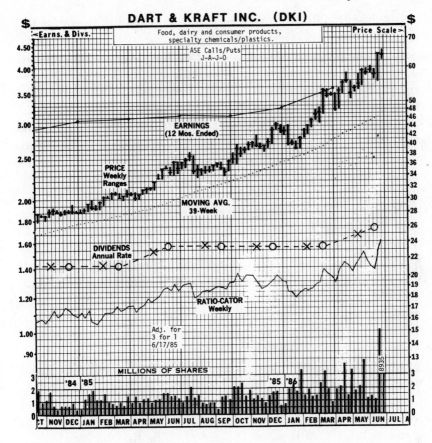

DART & KRAFT INC. (DKI)

Food, dairy and consumer products, specialty chemicals/plastics.

POINT AND FIGURE ANALYSIS. This method of interpretation of price movement has its own dedicated devotees. Basically, these charts are designed to show strength of price movement and to emphasize changes in direction. Just as with bar charts, formations are created by the plottings, and these form the basis for interpretation and analysis.

The Dow Theory

Most of the foregoing approaches to technical analysis involve the use of charts. One that does not, and one that certainly should be included in any compendium of technical analysis, if for no reason other than its wide following, is the Dow Theory.

The Dow Theory was developed around the turn of this century by the editors of *The Wall Street Journal.* It was never clearly stated in its original form, and it has been bent, twisted, distorted, and elaborated on for most of its existence by those who seek to apply it in their own fashion. But its basic tenet is that a trend should be expected to continue until a reversal is definitely signaled. For investors, this means that profits will be made by taking advantage of the primary trend, not by resisting it.

The Dow Theory assumes a bull market trend is in progress as long as each successive market advance continues to a higher peak than the one preceding it, and each successive secondary reaction stops at a higher bottom than the last. Conversely, a bear market trend is defined when each successive decline carries to a new low and each interim rally ends at a point below the previous one.

The Dow Theory also holds that these moves must be confirmed by similar action in different averages within a short period. The averages most frequently used as reference and confirmation points are the Dow Jones industrial and transportation averages. If the Dow industrials signal the start of a bull market, the faithful wait for the transportation index to move similarly, and when it does, they begin buying stocks.

On paper, the Dow Theory allows profits to continue indefinitely, while it restricts the extent of losses. In practice, it has been successful only some of the time. One reason is the wide divergence in interpretations of the same signals by different Dow theorists. Another reason is the great difficulty in pinpointing the moves that are indeed the true turning points of the market. Finally, the effectiveness of the Dow Theory has been diminished somewhat by its wide following.

In Conclusion

The analysis of the stock market as a whole or of individual stocks, whether by the technician or the fundamentalist, is not an easy task. You must endure a good deal of trial and error as you build up your own background and experience and as you develop the methods that make you most comfortable. It is often a slow and painstaking process. Except for the very lucky or those who are highly intuitive, success can come in no other way.

CHAPTER 23

How to Read an Annual Report

SHAREHOLDERS AND PROSPECTIVE shareholders can increase their knowledge of companies if they know how to read and analyze an annual report. In recent years these reports have become much more informative than they used to be, thanks to pressure from the Securities and Exchange Commission, the Financial Accounting Standards Board, auditors, and securities analysts.

Annual reports are easy to obtain. A company listed on the New York Stock Exchange, for example, is required to send one to each shareholder every year. In addition, many companies will send them to anyone who asks; address your request to "Investor Relations."

An even more detailed and comprehensive document is the 10-K statement that large, publicly owned companies are required to submit each year to the SEC. Some companies will send copies of the 10-K to shareholders and others on request. The 10-Ks are also available either in print or on microfilm at many large public and business school libraries.

But most annual reports contain sufficient information to give you a good basis for analyzing a company. You'll have to devote considerable time and thought to the task at hand to understand an annual report. It will help if you have some knowledge of the basics of accounting and financial statement analysis. But even if you don't, you should still be able to draw several valuable insights out of such a document, with a little coaching and guidance—the kind we're about to give you in this chapter.

What Is in an Annual Report

Since the annual report is not an official SEC filing, companies have considerable leeway in determining what the report will contain. Some give it to you in a straightforward, simple form, the figures juxtaposed with workaday text. But the trend in recent years has been toward typographical extravaganzas heavy on graphics, full-color photography, and artwork.

Whether the report is the former, the latter, or, as is more likely the case, falls somewhere between, it will typically begin with a letter to shareholders. This epistle is generally written by one or more of the company's top executives. It will usually summarize the highlights of the year and, possibly, offer some commentary on the business outlook for the firm. We caution you to regard this letter with some skepticism. It is not subjected to the auditing process, and in a good many cases its authors have succumbed to the temptation to tout. Still, it can give you some insight into what concerns top management. And, if you read the letters from several reports, you have a basis for comparing managements' views.

The letter is usually followed by a more detailed description of the company's various products or services, the recent performance of its operations, and perhaps the outlook for each sector. Here again you must keep in mind that the company is talking about itself, and a certain amount of puffery is likely to be present.

As your eyes pass by the list of company officers, pay particular attention to the names and affiliations of outside directors. Their stature, experience, and fields of interest can yield clues to the company's ultimate success and possibly even the directions it is likely to take.

But the real meat of the annual report will come out of the figures. Here again, the pattern is basically the same for all annual reports within an industry. And the information presented will be "consistent with generally accepted accounting principles," as the trade jargon puts it.

An annual report for a manufacturing or merchandising company must include a balance sheet, an income statement, a statement of accumulated retained earnings, a source and application of funds statement, an analysis of changes in working capital, and footnotes. We will discuss each of these areas in some detail. For illustrative purposes, we will use a mythical manufacturing company, which we will call TCA Industries.

The Balance Sheet

The balance sheet shows the financial condition of the company on the last day of its fiscal year. Normally, the figures for the previous year are also included to facilitate comparisons. Note that in the balance sheet for TCA Industries, our manufacturing company, the assets of the company are listed on the left-hand side and the liabilities and stockholders' equity, or capital of the corporation, are listed on the right-hand side. Note also that the totals for each side are in balance—that total assets equal total liabilities plus stockholders' equity. Another way to look at it is to subtract liabilities from assets, the difference being the stockholders' equity or ownership interest. More about that later.

The balance sheet will also yield the company's *book value*. Book value merely represents common stockholders' equity less goodwill, all other intangible assets, and preferred stock. In effect, then, book value is the amount of money stockholders originally invested in the company, plus profits the company has retained from year to year, subsequent equity offerings, and acquisitions.

Now let's go over the various categories of the balance sheet. *Current assets* are items that normally can be converted into cash within a year. *Cash* itself would include petty cash, checking accounts, and other demand or short-term bank deposits. *Marketable securities,* which are usually listed at cost, would be principally confined to short-term

U.S. Treasury securities or commercial paper. If the company held *other investments*—e.g., unconsolidated, partially owned subsidiaries or purchase mortgages on properties sold —these would be listed after current assets but before fixed assets. *Accounts receivable* are amounts owed by customers for goods delivered or services rendered. Presumably, these are collectible within a year. But note that the figure is net after an allowance for bad debts. *Inventories* consist of raw materials, partially finished goods, and finished products. The method of evaluating inventories is usually described in the footnotes of the balance sheet.

Fixed assets are items needed for carrying out the company's business and might include factory buildings, machinery, offices, and land. Traditionally, these items have been shown on the balance sheet at their original acquisition cost. Now some of the largest companies are required to show in their 10-K statements the estimated replacement cost of these assets.

Accumulated Depreciation is deducted from *gross plant and equipment* to reflect the fact that these assets have been declining in their useful value each year. Land, though, is never depreciated. Its balance sheet value doesn't change. Several depreciation methods for plant and equipment are available, and the footnotes will indicate which one has been used.

Intangibles usually refer to patents, franchises, or goodwill. While these assets may have a very real value, some companies follow conservative accounting practices and assign them only a nominal value. A *goodwill* value results when one company acquires another for a price exceeding its book value. The difference (goodwill) becomes an intangible asset which must be written off within forty years.

Prepaid Expenses refer to items that have been paid for but have a useful life beyond the next twelve months. *Deferred charges* refer to items the company has chosen to add to the balance sheet (capitalize) rather than treat as expenses that are shown only on the income statement. Some questions might arise if the deferred charge account has been increasing rapidly and is now shown as a substantial asset. Under

BALANCE SHEET

Assets

	Year Ending Dec. 31	
	(000 Omitted)	
Assets	1986	1985
Current Assets:		
Cash	$ 11,000	$ 8,000
Marketable Securities at Cost (market value: 1986, 6,000; 1985, 5,400)	7,000	6,000
Accounts Receivable (less allowance for bad debts: 1986, 200; 1985, 150)	114,000	90,000
Inventories	163,000	145,000
Total Current Assets	$295,000	$249,000
Fixed Assets		
Land, Plant & Equipment	$195,000	$168,000
(less accumulated depreciation)	68,000	65,000
Net Land, Plant & Equipment	$127,000	$103,000
Intangibles	24,000	13,000
Prepaid Expenses & Deferred Charges	6,000	5,000
Total Fixed Assets	$157,000	$121,000
Total Assets	$452,000	$370,000

Liabilities

	Year Ending Dec. 31	
	(000 Omitted)	
Liabilities	1986	1985
Current Liabilities		
Accounts Payable	$101,000	$ 77,000
Notes, Loans, etc. Payable	25,000	14,000
Long-Term Debt Due within One Year	5,000	4,000
Accrued Income Taxes	13,000	17,000
Total Current Liabilities	$144,000	$112,000
Long-Term Debt	98,000	80,000
Stockholders' Equity		
Preferred Stock, $2.50 cum. $50 Par Value (authorized and outstanding shares, 60,000)	$ 3,000	$ 3,000
Common Stock $10 Par Value (authorized 10,000,000 shares; outstanding 1986 and 1985, 5,000,000)	50,000	50,000
Capital in Excess of Par Value	7,000	7,000
Retained Earnings	150,000	118,000
Total Stockholders' Equity	$210,000	$178,000
Total Liabilities and Stockholders' Equity	$452,000	$370,000

new accounting procedures, research and development costs must now be expensed annually against income. Formerly, they could be capitalized and written off over a period of years.

Current Liabilities are items payable within a year. *Accounts payable* are sums owed to the company's regular vendors and suppliers. *Accrued expenses* refer to unpaid wages, insurance premiums, etc. *Notes* and *loans payable* refer to short-term money owed to banks and other creditors. *Long-term debt due within one year* is self-explanatory.

Accrued Income Taxes are federal, state, local, and foreign income taxes, also due within one year. Sometimes a deferred tax account is set up as a short-term, long-term, or other liability that may be due in future years. These deferred taxes arise from the fact that companies can employ different accounting procedures for shareholder and for Internal Revenue Service purposes. Thus they may report and pay less tax to the government than is reflected in the income statement for shareholders. There is nothing illegal about this, and the company, in fact, may never actually have to pay these additional taxes. But the quality of *earnings* would be diminished for a company with a large tax deferral account.

What is referred to as the capital structure or capitalization of a company will include such different securities as straight and convertible bonds, straight and convertible preferred stocks, common stocks, and warrants. *Long-term debt* usually consists of bonds and bank debt due more than one year from the date on the balance sheet. The interest rates and payment schedules for debt securities can be found in the footnotes.

Stockholders' Equity includes preferred stock, so to compute book value or earnings on shareholders' equity the preferred stock and dividends payable on it must be subtracted. The principal categories under common stockholders' equity are *common stock, capital surplus,* and *retained earnings.* These three items in total show the amount of equity or ownership that the common stockholder has in a corporation. *Common stock* is shown on the balance sheet at *par value.* But this is an arbitrary figure having no relation to market or liquidation value. *Capital in excess of par value* is what it says—the amount in excess of par value that shareholders have paid for their stock. This account would be set up when shares were initially sold. It would be increased after any subsequent new issues of stock. *Retained earnings,* also sometimes referred to as *earned surplus,* is the accumulation of profits remaining after payment of dividends on all outstanding securities.

Analyzing a Balance Sheet

Many investment analysts maintain that the balance sheet is more important than the income statement in assessing a company's prospects. Yearly increases in certain balance sheet items are good indicators of the company's growth potential.

There are a number of rather simple calculations you can make to help determine the financial strength of a company. Let's first consider the ability of a company to liquidate its debts and other obligations. This would logically come from current assets. Hence, to relate these two items, we employ the *current* (or *working capital*) *ratio.* This is computed by dividing current assets by current liabilities. A ratio showing current assets in excess of current liabilities by two to one is generally considered quite acceptable for the typical manufacturing company. But for certain other industries it might be either unnecessarily high or unacceptably low. Businesses require different amounts of working capital and liquidity. But where a company does have current assets in excess of current liabilities, that difference is available to reduce long-term debt or help finance growth.

It is also worth noting if working capital is expanding from year to year. A growing corporation probably needs expanding working capital.

A more exacting test for liquidity is the *quick ratio,* which is also called the *liquidity ratio* or *acid test.* This is figured the same way as the current ratio, omitting the inventory from the asset side. The rationale for this is that inventories may not be easily liquidated except at a discount. Cash on hand and that collected from receivables is used by a company to pay bills. If these sources are inadequate, operations may have to be slowed or bank loans floated in order to buy supplies or even to meet payrolls. A one-to-one liquidity ratio is reasonable.

To further test financial strength, long-term debt and preferred stock outstanding should be related to stockholders' equity. Creditors' and preferred stockholders' claims on assets in liquidation and on earnings for interest and preferred dividend payments have priority to those of common shareholders. Then, too, a relatively large amount of long-term debt or preferred stock may mean the company is burdened by these fixed-interest and dividend charges. This may help to leverage the company's earnings upward in years when there is rapid growth, but it works on the downside, too.

Capital structure varies from industry to industry. Utilities usually carry larger amounts of debt than manufacturing companies because of the stability of the former's operations. But generally speaking, shareholders' capital should total substantially more than long-term debt and preferred stock combined.

To help measure these relationships, you could compute a *common stock ratio* or a *debt to equity ratio*. The common stock ratio is derived by totaling all items in shareholders' equity except preferred stock and dividing by the total capitalization. The *debt to equity ratio* merely relates long-term and other liabilities to the common shareholders' equity.

Some analysts in making these same calculations deduct intangibles from stockholders' equity because of what may be their "uncertain" worth. Also, in computing the preferred stock's worth, the liquidation value of the preferred is sometimes substituted for the generally lower par value figure that is shown on the balance sheet.

The Income Statement

The *income statement,* sometimes called the *profit and loss statement,* is intended to describe the performance of the company's operations during the year. Again, the figures for the two most recent fiscal years are generally given. We will now discuss each of the categories in the income statement shown here.

INCOME STATEMENT (OR STATEMENT OF PROFIT AND LOSS)

	Year Ending Dec. 31	
	(000 Omitted)	
	1986	*1985*
Net Sales	$554,000	$478,000
Less:		
Cost of Goods Sold	(390,000)	(346,000)
Selling, General, and Administrative Expenses	(71,000)	(57,000)
Depreciation	(11,000)	(10,000)
Interest Expense	(5,000)	(7,000)
Income Before Taxes	$ 77,000	$ 58,000
Income Taxes	(35,000)	(27,000)
Net Income	$ 42,000	$ 31,000
Net Income Per Common Share	$ 8.40	$ 6.20

Net sales, in the case of our model firm, TCA Industries, represent money received by the company from the sale of its goods, minus any allowance for sales discounts or returned goods. *Cost of goods sold* includes raw materials, plant wages and salaries, utilities, maintenance, and other factory overhead costs. These expenses are directly related to the company's manufacturing operations. *Depreciation,* you will remember, was included on the balance sheet. Each year, a certain amount of depreciation is charged as an expense, and this figure is added to the accumulated depreciation figure on the balance sheet. Please note that while this is shown as an expense on the income statement, it is a non-cash expense because no cash actually leaves the company. Here again, companies have considerable leeway in choosing the rate at which they will depreciate their assets, and this can have a substantial impact on earnings. In our section on footnotes, we'll comment specifically on permissible depreciation methods.

Selling, general, and administrative expenses cover certain costs not involved directly in production and thus not shown under cost of goods sold. The expenses in this account would include such things as executive salaries, rent, miscellaneous office expenses, advertising, and travel. *Interest expense* is the amount paid in the latest fiscal year to bondholders and other creditors. Unlike dividends on preferred and common stocks, interest is a deductible expense and, therefore, is shown before income taxes.

We can now determine pretax income by subtracting these various expenses from net sales. We then subtract income taxes, which are all U.S., foreign, state, and local taxes. What remains is the *net income* or *net operating income* figure. Some companies set up a net operating income figure and below that an account to cover income and expense items which are essentially nonrecurring. These are items that would not be part of the company's normal business operations, such as profit or loss on the sale of a plant, the discontinuance of certain operations, the collection of insurance proceeds, and foreign expropriations.

The calculation for *net income per common share* involves subtracting from the net income figure any dividends paid on preferred stock during the year and dividing the result by either the number of shares outstanding at the end of the year or a weighted average of the number of shares outstanding during the year. If companies have sufficient convertible bonds, convertible preferred stocks, warrants, or options outstanding to dilute per-share earnings by more than 3 percent, they must also show *primary earnings per share* and *fully diluted earnings per share*. The primary earnings per share figure is arrived at by dividing net income after preferred dividends by common shares outstanding plus dilutive common share equivalents. The latter are those securities whose dividend or coupon rate at the time of issue was less than two-thirds the prime rate at that time. Since options and warrants have no payment, they are regarded as common stock equivalents at all times. The fully diluted earnings per share figure assumes the conversion of all outstanding securities that would reduce earnings per share.

Analyzing the Income Statement

There are a number of ratios you can use to derive information from the income statement. Some of these involve determining profitability, such as the amount of each dollar of sales the company is able to bring down to net or pretax income, or how much the company is able to earn on stockholders' equity.

In establishing the return on sales, you could calculate a *pretax profit margin,* a *net income profit margin,* an *operating profit margin,* and a *gross profit margin.* The pretax profit margin is computed by dividing pretax income by net sales. This may be a more significant number than the net income profit margin, because the latter can be distorted by sharp changes in the tax rate. The operating profit margin would be operating profit before interest expenses and, sometimes, depreciation, divided by net sales. The gross profit margin is the income that remains after only cost of goods sold is deducted from net sales, and again this figure is divided by net sales.

There is likely to be a sharp increase in profit margins in the years when sales have risen markedly. Also, industry leaders tend to have higher profit margins than their smaller competitors. A deterioration in profit margins might reflect more severe price competition or certain expenses temporarily running out of control. Some industries or businesses are inherently more profitable than others, so the ratios you calculate for the company you are examining should be compared with those of firms in similar fields.

A common stockholder also should be concerned about how much money the company is able to earn on his investment. The return should be much better than that which he could obtain from a bank savings account, for example. So the *return on equity* is an important ratio. This figure is calculated by dividing net income for the common stockholder (what's left after preferred dividends have been paid) by the previous year's common stockholders' equity. You use that figure to see what the company was able to earn on the stockholders' equity available to it at the beginning of the year.

If return on equity seems high it might mean that the company was using substantial amounts of borrowed funds (so-called leverage) and preferred stock instead of common stock. So check back in your analysis of the balance sheet to see what the common stock or debt to equity ratio was.

Some other items worth checking are the *tax rate* and the *inventory turnover* and *accounts receivable turnover*. The tax rate is taxes paid as a percentage of pretax income. As part of the Tax Reform Act of 1986, corporate tax brackets were reduced from five to three, and the maximum corporate rate was lowered from 46 percent to 34 percent, effective July 1, 1987. Most U.S. corporations are taxed at the maximum rate. Earnings from foreign operations are usually subject to a much lower tax rate, and the company might have substantial overseas business. The investment tax credit, by which corporations could temporarily reduce taxes in a year of heavy buying of equipment, is no longer available. Also, a much lower tax rate might reflect the presence in a particular year of tax-loss carry-forwards stemming from some earlier deficit years. That credit may not be available in subsequent years, either.

The *inventory* and *accounts receivable turnover* ratios are meant to show how liquid the company's inventory and accounts receivables are. The inventory turnover ratio is usually derived by dividing net sales (or, to be more exact, cost of goods sold) by the year-end inventory figure shown on the balance sheet. A high ratio would suggest strong demand for the company's products. A low ratio might indicate either severe competition or inventory obsolescence. These ratios, though, will depend on the business. A food chain is likely to have a much faster inventory turnover rate than a heavy-machinery company. The accounts receivable turnover ratio is net sales divided by receivables. A low ratio might indicate that the company has poor collection procedures.

Other Lodes to Mine

After you have gained an understanding of a balance sheet and an income statement, you would do well to examine three other related financial statements in the annual report.

The first of these is the *statement of retained earnings*. An example is shown below. The purpose, quite obviously, is to show changes in retained earnings from one year to the next. Net income is normally the principal contributor to retained earnings. But this account could also be affected by an acquisition or merger. The growth of retained earnings is important. It affects book value and the company's ability to pay dividends on the common stock.

Another statement that is closely related to both the balance sheet and the income statement is the *source and application of funds statement*. It shows the sources of a company's money or working capital and where it goes. Depreciation is an addition to working capital because, you will remember, this is treated as an expense on the income statement when it is really a noncash charge. In addition to dividends and capital expenditures, debt repayments would be an example of the uses of working capital. For a company in healthy circumstances, the bottom line figure will usually show a year-to-year increase in working capital, and not just because of a heavy reliance on long-term borrowings.

STATEMENT OF RETAINED EARNINGS

	Year Ending Dec. 31	
	(000 Omitted)	
	1986	*1985*
Retained Earnings at Beginning of Year	$118,000	$ 95,000
Net Income for the Year	42,000	31,000
Less Dividends Paid	(10,000)	(8,000)
Retained Earnings at End of Year	$150,000	$118,000

The third document is the *analysis of changes in working capital*. Its purpose is to disclose how the various changes in working capital actually showed up in the balance sheet in terms of current assets and current liabilities. A substantial increase in working capital might not seem quite as appealing if it resulted from an increase in inventories or receivables rather than an increase in cash or marketable securities.

Let us now turn to some of the other sections of the annual report that are mandated by the SEC. One of these is *management's analysis of operating results*. The SEC requires that material developments during the last two fiscal years,

SOURCE AND APPLICATION OF FUNDS STATEMENT

	Year Ending Dec. 31	
	(000 Omitted)	
	1986	1985
Working Capital Provided by:		
Net Income	$ 42,000	$31,000
Depreciation	11,000	10,000
Proceeds from Long-Term Borrowings	48,000	12,000
Sales of Plant & Equipment, Deferred Income Taxes, etc.	11,000	19,000
	$112,000	$72,000
Working Capital Used for:		
Dividends	$ 10,000	$8,000
Additions to Plant & Equipment	14,000	18,000
Reductions of Long-Term Debt	35,000	4,000
Acquisitions	34,000	—
Other	3,000	13,000
	$ 96,000	$43,000
Increase in Working Capital	$ 16,000	$29,000

ANALYSIS OF CHANGES IN WORKING CAPITAL

	Year Ending Dec. 31	
	(000 Omitted)	
	1986	1985
Increase (Decrease) in Current Assets		
Cash	$ 3,000	$ 2,000
Marketable Securities	1,000	2,000
Accounts Receivable	24,000	15,000
Inventories	18,000	25,000
Other	2,000	1,000
	$ 48,000	$ 45,000
(Increase) Decrease in Current Liabilities		
Accounts Payable	$(24,000)	$(14,000)
Accrued Income Taxes	4,000	(10,000)
Notes, Loans Payable	(11,000)	9,000
Long-Term Debt Due within One Year	(1,000)	(1,000)
	(32,000)	(16,000)
Increase in Working Capital	$ 16,000	$ 29,000

particularly those relating to the income statement, be discussed in considerable detail. Some corporations might extend the discussion back over the past five years. The SEC expects companies to be more factual and objective in this section than they might typically be in their letter to shareholders. However, this section likewise is unaudited, so it, too, should be read with some degree of skepticism.

The SEC also requires an unaudited five-year *statistical summary*. The summary normally will carry key items from the income statement and balance sheet, as well as some of the important ratios we have already discussed. Many companies expand this table to cover a ten-year span, which shows how the firm has responded to more than one economic cycle. This helps to establish significant trends in the company's fortunes. But, as an actual or potential investor, you're primarily interested in trying to predict the company's future.

Let us suggest here some of the trends you might look for. Have sales shown a sharp increase over the past five (or ten) years? If so, have the sales gains been consistent or erratic? Have earnings generally moved in line with sales? If not, can you find the reason in various expense items or the tax rate? Do the sales and earnings trends seem consistent with the general business picture and industry performance in that same time period?

You might also look to see if earnings per share have matched the improvement in net income. If not, it may mean the company has been "buying" earnings (through acquisitions) for stock and the effect has been dilutive. Have dividends ever been omitted or reduced? Have there been increases in the total dividend payments every year?

As far as the balance sheet items are concerned, we have already noted the importance of increases in working capital. But has long-term debt also increased substantially? Has long-term debt risen more than shareholders' equity? Has book value risen markedly? Other items worth looking at are changes in the number of employees and capital-spending trends.

The push by the SEC and the Financial Accounting Standards Board for fuller corporate disclosure in annual reports has resulted in companies being required to include (1) a breakdown of sales and earnings for at least five different product lines, if there are that many; (2) a price range of securities; (3) dividends, if any, paid during each quarter of the two most recent fiscal years. The product line breakdown can be helpful in revealing that some operations are considerably more important to earnings than they are to sales, or vice versa, than one might expect after reading the earlier textual material.

Analyzing a Common Stock

There are still other ratios with which you should be familiar. The *price-earnings ratio* is the market price of the common stock divided by earnings per share for that stock. You are likely to find some variation in price-earnings ratios for the same company's stock, because newspapers tend to use the latest twelve-month earnings figures that are available, whereas investment analysts generally prefer estimated current-year results. Also remember that price-earnings ratios will fluctuate over time, with the general psychology of the market, anticipated earnings growth, dividend yield, marketability, volatility, and the quality of the earnings per share.

The *dividend yield* is the indicated annual dividend rate divided by the current market price. By relating this return to a bank savings rate or the yield on AA or AAA corporate bonds, you can get some indication of the stock's appeal for income purposes. On the other hand, too high a yield may indicate that the dividend is shaky.

The *dividend payout ratio* is arrived at by dividing indicated dividends per share by the latest available annual earnings per share. This shows what percent of earnings is paid out in dividends. The *earnings retention rate* is found by subtracting the dividend payout ratio from 100 percent. If the payout ratio is 40 percent, the retention rate would be about 60 percent. That is, the company is reinvesting about 60 percent of its earnings. Some analysts suggest that if you multiply the retention rate by the percentage amount that the company returns on stockholders' equity, you get a good indicator of the future earnings growth for the company. What they are saying is that the company's growth will be determined by what it is able to earn on the new money it is retaining. So if the rate of return on stockholders' equity is 10 percent and the retention rate is 60 percent, future income growth might be about 6 percent. While some companies obviously are interested in pleasing their stockholders by boosting dividends, many do wish to retain as much of their earnings as they can in order to facilitate the corporation's growth.

The Footnotes Are Important

The footnotes undoubtedly constitute the most yawn-inspiring reading in the annual report. But they shouldn't be skipped. Fortunately, SEC rules require their type size to be at least as large as the numbers in the financial statement. The footnotes are important for several reasons. For one thing, they often explain the accounting methods used. There are a number of methods available that would meet an auditor's approval, each of which produces a different bottom line result. Furthermore, most companies employ one accounting procedure for stockholders and another for Internal Revenue Service purposes. This point is generally elaborated upon in the footnotes.

Here are some of the other items frequently covered in the footnotes:

Inventories, as computed for cost of goods sold and carried in the asset section of the balance sheet, can be assigned widely different values. Many analysts believe that in a period of rising prices the most conservative accounting treatment for inventories is LIFO (last in, first out) as opposed to FIFO (first in, first out). In figuring the cost of goods sold, LIFO assumes that the latest items added to inventory, which should be the most expensive in a period of inflation, are sold first. That means assigning a higher value to inventories in cost of goods sold. The effect is to increase expenses and reduce income. Lower income means lower taxes. It also means, though, that in expensing the latest inventory figures, the corporation will be carrying a lower inventory value on the balance sheet than the real figure.

Various acceptable methods are also available to compute depreciation, depending on when the asset was placed in service. Some of these allow writing off more of an asset's worth in its earlier years than in later years. Most companies use straight-line depreciation for stockholder purposes because it tends to reduce income less, and accelerated depreciation for tax purposes in order to reduce the amount of income subject to a tax bite. If corporations use the two different methods, they are subject to the alternative minimum tax on half the difference in earnings. A more conservative accounting practice is to use accelerated depreciation for both stockholder purposes and tax purposes.

Companies are now required to state in the annual report their pension accounting and funding policy, as well as the pension charge for the preceding year and the unfunded vested liabilities. For some corporations, these numbers are already large, and for others they are increasing rapidly. Some companies even have unfunded pension liabilities that represent a substantial percentage of stockholders' equity— or may even exceed stockholders' equity. As a result of strong investment performances and employee attrition, many company pension plans are *overfunded*. Finding this information in annual reports and other published reports is not easy. However, overfunded pension plans are a "hidden asset" and often a factor in takeover or leveraged buyout bids.

The annual report also must disclose any potential legal problems. You should be somewhat wary of these even though the company might indicate that in its opinion a suit against the corporation is "without merit." Adverse settlements in an era of growing "consumerism" have proved expensive for many companies.

As a rule, the footnotes contain a detailed breakdown of long-term debt by type of security and schedule of maturity.

Many companies lease rather than own equipment, and these leases can then become a substitute for longer-term debt incurred to purchase that equipment. Use of leases is sometimes referred to as *off balance sheet financing*. But under new regulations of the Financial Accounting Standards Board, these leases must be capitalized and shown as a liability on the lessee's balance sheet, albeit on a phase-in basis. FASB rules prohibit a company from capitalizing research and development outlays on the balance sheet and writing them off gradually against income over a period of years. Instead they must be expensed in the year incurred.

Some annual reports reveal in the footnotes stock options granted officers and other employees, plus intercompany transactions. Whether the company takes all of its available investment tax credit directly into earnings each year or amortizes it over a period of years may be revealed. Also detailed in the reports of multinational companies is the impact of certain currency changes.

Companies are also now required to carry in their annual reports a statement reconciling any differences between a tax rate for stockholder purposes and the statutory U.S. tax rate. Foreign taxes, state and local taxes, and the investment tax credit are some of the items that might account for such a difference.

The SEC now requires more than a thousand of the largest nonfinancial corporations to include in their 10-K statements the cost at current prices of replacing their inventory and productive capacity (plant and equipment). The 10-K also must show how depreciation and the cost of goods sold would be affected if the balance sheet were recalculated on a replacement cost basis. In doing this, however, companies are permitted to show cost savings that might result from replacing old equipment with more modern technology.

The Accountants' Report

Every public company must have its accounting records reviewed and audited by a firm of certified public accountants. That firm will also issue an opinion regarding the veracity of the financial statements in the annual report. The accountants' report is definitely worth reading, if only to see whether the auditors include some qualifications or exceptions or note changes in accounting procedures that are material. The investor should be concerned about any, departures from what is normally a routinely worded statement. The corporate examination by the auditors will generally include a review of bank statements, a physical counting of the inventory and an estimate as to its salability, and a confirmation of receivables.

As you can see, if you've only been looking at an annual report's photographs you haven't been getting half the picture. The text, the financial tables, and the footnotes can tell you a lot about the companies you own or contemplate owning—if you take the time to read them right.

CHAPTER 24

Analyzing Specific Industries

UNTIL NOW, WE have been discussing in general terms how to go about analyzing a company as a potential investment. Obviously, certain tests will be more important for companies in one industry than for those in another. Some industries are by nature cyclical. The ebbs and flows of their fortunes are tied closely to the ups and downs of the economy. Others are more stable. They follow the same path regardless of what business in general is doing. Still others are mature. They have grown just about as much as they ever will and, in fact, may even be declining. Others are emerging. New technology and changing life-styles are bringing them into prominence.

How do you know what tests to apply to which industries? Common sense is a good starting point. It is often easy to surmise which industries will be affected by rises and falls of the economy and which will not be. Then there is performance. There's a good chance that patterns occurring in the past will be repeated in the future. Finally, there is awareness. Careful study depends on keeping up with events and trends that might affect an industry. These broad categories, of course, embrace the many finer points of the financial analyst's art and science.

Financial analysts, in fact, spend most of their time poring over figures, reading extensively in the various industries they cover, and talking with key executives in those industries. Because of the vast amount of material which they must keep under surveillance, most analysts confine their efforts to a limited number of industries. Indeed, some devote their entire careers to a single industry, becoming as knowledgeable as many leaders in the industry itself.

To give you an idea of what you should be looking for in the industries that interest most investors, the analysts on our staff at Babson-United Investment Advisors have provided the commentary that appears in this chapter and the next. They won't get into the fine details, but they'll tell you the important things they themselves look for as they analyze their industries and the companies in them.

The Basic Industries

Automotive, chemical, coal, construction, machinery, metals, oil and gas, paper, textiles. These are the basic industries —"smokestack America," as it were. Without these industries, our way of life would be primitive indeed. For all the abuse that is heaped upon the steelmakers, the oil moguls, and the auto producers, theirs is no bed of roses. Between the demands of labor, the restrictions of government, the protests of environmentalists, foreign competition, and the exigencies of business, they do well to keep their heads above water, let alone turn a profit for their shareholders.

All these industries suffer to some extent from the cyclical nature of their markets. Some lead the economy, others follow it, and the rest move in close conjunction with the ups and downs in the business cycle. The ability to fine-tune capacity and output to demand is an important aspect of a company's profit record. These are capital-intensive companies, but some groups have less trouble generating sufficient cash flow to meet their capital needs than others.

While the investor can reap long-range profits from investments in basic industries, he must be willing to sit through the dry spells or be able to jump in and out with facility.

AUTOMOBILES AND TRUCKS. This industry, which includes manufacturers of parts and components, is one of the most pervasive influences in our lives. Not only is it the nation's single largest employer after the federal government, but it affects the prosperity of such giant industries as steel, nonferrous metals, chemicals, tires, and glass. When consumers are in a car-buying mood, the economy prospers; when demand for new cars ebbs, the entire economy suffers. Because the automobile has become such a necessity in the lives of most of us, it would be easy to conclude that demand is always high. The truth is, this is a highly cyclical industry, studded with peaks and riven with valleys. Personal income trends, the jobless rate, and consumer sentiment in general play major roles in the strength or weakness of auto sales.

Because theirs is, in the final analysis, a consumer industry, auto manufacturers must be able to anticipate taste trends, buying fads, and domestic and foreign competition. Then they must market products that will fulfill the fantasies and needs of their customers. Poor judgment or a misreading of the public's tastes can spell disaster, since model changes are not easily made. A manufacturer also must be able to gauge accurately the level of sales for a model year. Overproduction can be nearly as disastrous as misjudging style preferences. So can underproduction, for that matter.

Major factors affecting auto sales today include credit availability and cost, consumer confidence, used-car trends, foreign demand, and scrappage levels. Tied closely to sales is the cost of production. Is a union contract about to come up for renegotiation? Are costs of raw materials rising? When rising costs are coupled with sluggish sales, the industry is heading for hard times.

The greatest fundamental change in the domestic auto industry is the increasing penetration by foreign auto makers. Market shares for these manufacturers have been rising steadily. The domestics are now making moves to be more competitive by diversifying, improving productivity, and manufacturing overseas. The auto maker best able to accommodate the public's ever-changing demands will be of most interest to investors.

CHEMICALS. This industry is more truly an aggregation of many subindustries—organic and inorganic commodity chemicals, intermediates, functional specialties, and various product groups not strictly classified as chemicals, such as plastics, fertilizers, industrial gases, synthetic fibers, minerals, carbon black, etc. Within each of these subgroups, different forces are at work. The supply-demand balance, competition, price-cost differentials, geographic advantages, and alternative processes vary from one product area to another. Thus, the product mix of an individual company must be studied before assessing other information bearing on its prospects for the future. The subindustries vary widely in cyclicality, from the sustained growth of specialty chemicals or industrial gases to the feast-or-famine swings of fertilizers.

Once the analyst has determined a company's product mix, he can see what portion of the business is in mature product lines and what portion is concentrated in expanding fields. While a company should have a sizable stake in growth areas, its more mature business areas are likely to produce a substantial cash flow, not only for current income but also for investment in the growth ventures. However, a company must be willing to recognize and phase out those weaker lines which are no longer generating sufficient cash flow. A key consideration is the company's market share in each subgroup, since market leadership is the prime determinant of profitability and growth for a chemical company.

A highly important factor for many firms today is the status of their fuel supplies and raw-material feedstocks. How a company handles long-term supply contracts, process changes, and conservation requirements is a clue to the ability of its management. How well it manages captive resources and moves to alternative resources is also vital. Other considerations include environmental legislation, research, technical services, pricing strategy, foreign currency devaluations, cash flow versus capital requirements, and the upgrading of returns on investment.

Chemical stocks can be profitable investments if caught at the low end of a cycle. Yields are reasonable and price-earnings ratios usually below average.

COAL. Approximately 80 percent of the coal produced in this country annually is consumed by steelmakers and electric utilities; another 10 percent is exported. The needs of all other manufacturers, households, etc. are satisfied with the remaining 10 percent. This underutilized fuel constitutes 88 percent of our energy reserves but only 20 percent of actual fuel consumption. There are stumbling blocks which must be surmounted before this nation begins to fully use this abundant energy resource. They include labor problems, environmental concerns, reduced worker productivity, government regulation, transportation, and achieving more efficient and widespread use of automation.

Of the two major consumers of coal, utilities are the larger users, accounting for about two-thirds of production. Coal is used to produce nearly 60 percent of all electric power generated each year. This proportion is expected to increase very gradually over the balance of the 1980s. In addition to the growth inherent in this larger share of the market, demand for electricity is expected to grow by 2 or 3 percent a year. New coal production will come primarily from the western states, where the bulk of coal is stripped from surface mines.

The steel industry uses metallurgical coal, which has the ability to coke when burned in the absence of oxygen. Most of the reserves of premium low-volatile coking coal are located in West Virginia, with Virginia and Kentucky accounting for less than 40 percent of medium- and high-volatile coking coal reserves. Growth prospects in this end of the coal business are less robust than for steam coal, reflecting the reduced demand forecast for steel.

Among the 35 largest coal producers, only six derive 40 percent or more of their earnings from this product. The others are divisions of companies whose main thrust is in other industries. A number are "captive" coal producers, owned by steel or utility companies intent on assuring a dependable and less costly source of fuel. Those few companies which derive the bulk of their earnings from coal mine either steam coal or a mix of both types.

In looking at individual companies, you should determine whether steam or high- or low-sulfur metallurgical coal is mined. If the company mines metallurgical coal, the bulk of it is probably exported, and the company's record of earnings will likely be spotty. Another important factor is the type of contracts that have been negotiated with consumers. If most are long term, do they provide adequate escalation clauses? Labor relations are a vital factor in this industry, which has been beset by wildcat strikes and showdowns with militant and unpredictable unions.

For investors, there are only a few companies from which to choose. Some of these have long-term potential for growth, both from the increasing value of their reserves and from such areas as coal gasification. Investment timing is important, since the coal industry reflects fluctuations in the business cycle.

CONSTRUCTION. Although this is a cyclical field, many of the industry groups that comprise it have tended to move prior to the swings in the economy in general. The classic pattern has been that when the economy is running full steam—when interest rates are high, savings are depleted, mortgage money is tight—then housing begins to suffer. Conversely, toward the end of a downturn, interest rates decline, savings rise, the money supply increases, and building loans are easier to obtain. Building activity turns the corner as a result and signals a turn in the economy.

Some 10 percent of the gross national product is derived from construction spending, making the industries involved one of the economy's most important sectors. Because stimulation from Washington may create artificial swings in the housing-start figures, the analyst must be aware of any pump priming from this source. Shifts in housing trends—from single-unit to multiple-dwelling housing, from suburban to urban, etc.—must be watched.

These trends can have a significant impact on the types of building materials that are in demand. Population shifts, such as the rush to the Sunbelt, also can make or break regional suppliers.

In the mid-1980s, conditions in the building industry are favorable. Housing starts have been above average for several years, although still shy of the baby-boomer- and inflation-driven peaks of the late 1970s. With the widespread acceptance of variable-rate mortgages and an active secondary mortgage market, even a rise in interest rates may not have the unfavorable impact of years past.

Though pushed and pulled by lower interest rates and curbs on public spending, commercial and public construction has remained fairly stable, while industrial construction expenditures have lagged since the 1980–82 recession. These trends have impeded producers of construction equipment. However, continued weakness in the dollar will make domestic construction-equipment makers more competitive with foreign manufacturers.

Remodeling and renovation of existing homes is a key segment of the building industry. It is from this sector that the industry derives a stable and continuing revenue base. Those firms which supply the commercial as well as do-it-yourself remodeling market have generally better records for consistent growth than the volatile home-building companies.

MACHINERY AND MACHINE TOOLS. While these two allied industries are cyclical, their cycles are dissimilar. Machine tool orders are often used as a bellwether of business upswings. Conversely, orders for the machinery industry lag behind in an upturn, sometimes by as much as six months. The key to this dichotomous behavior lies in the nature of their respective markets. Hard-goods manufacturers in anticipation of better times must tool up to meet the expected increase in demand; hence machine tool orders rise even though business in general may still be in the doldrums. Machinery makers serve the heavy industries—auto and truck, oil, coal, construction, utility. The huge outlays required for this type of equipment can be postponed until a recovery is well under way, creating a lag in orders for machinery.

Prosperity for tool and machinery manufacturers is dependent on real growth in gross national product, a good level of capital spending, and customer confidence in the direction in which the government is steering the country. Order levels can swing by 50 percent or more in one year. Within the industry itself, capital spending plans hinge on long-range economic forecasts. If these prove too optimistic, machinery and tool makers are left with excess capacity, which can play havoc with profits.

In analyzing an individual company, you should determine whether it is a market leader in its specialized line, if its research program has been productive, its sales and marketing efforts effective, its service organization strong, and its markets expanding. A company should be geographically diversified, with worldwide sales, and it should be vertically integrated. In looking at order backlog figures, you should note, if possible, whether order levels are up across the board or only in certain segments of the company's operations.

METALS. This is another lagging industry; it picks up steam only after the economy is well on its way to recovery. But unless economic conditions are sufficiently robust to support the industry at near-peak capacity, these companies get caught in a squeeze between rising costs and falling prices for their products. As a whole, the industry sells in large volumes and operates on razor-thin margins. Thus, recent trends toward disinflation have hurt profitability by restricting these companies' ability to gain even slight price increases.

Since early in the 1970s, steel demand has not kept pace with the overall growth of gross national product. Increases in steel imports have prompted protectionist measures, although it remains to be seen whether these steps will prove helpful. Within the steel industry, the specialty producers have managed to counter the trend by carving out individual niches. For the foreseeable future the primary focus of major steelmakers will be cost cutting and capacity rationalization.

In terms of price and demand, copper companies have had the most volatile record. Historically, domestic producers have raised capacity in response to demand increases and rising prices only to see demand dry up—creating an inventory excess and sagging prices. Here, too, imports have become increasingly troublesome for domestic producers, who are being pitted against lower-cost producers in developing nations. Some of the latter are government owned and not always operated with profit as a primary motive.

Demand for aluminum has picked up steadily from the December 1981 low, but pricing, particularly for primary ingot, has been troublesome. While the value of aluminum is influenced by currency fluctuations, demand is sensitive to interest rates, as more than 40 percent of the industry's shipments go to the construction and automotive industries. The trend toward lighter, more fuel-efficient cars bodes well for the white metal. In fact, each year auto manufacturers use more aluminum to fabricate their products, to the detriment of the steel industry. Other areas where the use of aluminum is on the rise include building, containers, and electrical products.

Throughout the metals industry there has been a wave of cost cutting to compete with foreign producers. When the dollar is strong, foreign companies compete in the U.S. market, but with the slide in the value of the dollar the competitive situation has eased. In addition, major wage concessions granted by labor unions, plant modernization efforts, and the closing of obsolete and inefficient production facilities have enabled domestic producers to reduce costs and operate more efficiently. However, it is still wise for investors to keep close tabs on when labor contracts are due for renegotiation, not only for the obvious reason—to assess the possibility of a strike or a major concession from management—but also to gauge whether or not demand reflects true market conditions or prestrike stockpiling.

Over the long run, metal stocks tend to sell at a discount to the market, due to below-average demand growth and vulnerability to cyclical swings in economic activity. Market share leaders, low-cost producers, and broadly diversified companies usually represent the best opportunities for investors seeking cyclical stock market profits.

OIL AND NATURAL GAS. Getting oil and natural gas from deep inside the earth into our homes, cars, and factories requires the efforts of many companies. Some of these are major integrated corporations involved in every aspect of the business from wellhead to gas pump. An even greater number concentrate in one area such as contract drilling, oil-field equipment and services, or oil/gas exploration and development.

The fact that four of the nation's ten largest corporations are oil companies is not surprising in view of their global operations and enormous capital needs. Estimates of annual industry capital requirements to develop oil productive capacity exceed $50 billion. Despite technological advances, finding oil is not an easy task, as evidenced by the fact that roughly one-third of all wells drilled are dry holes. Moreover, the upgrading and maintenance of refineries require huge infusions of cash. Thus, outside of selling off assets to raise sufficient capital, the ability to finance these processes is critical.

Historically, internally generated cash flow has funded the bulk of the industry's operations. A glance at a few balance sheets, however, will show that the group has taken on a considerable amount of debt—largely as a result of industry consolidation that has led to several big mergers among the major oil companies: Mobil/Superior and Chevron/Gulf, for example. Typically, most oil firms can accommodate up to 50 percent of their capitalization in the form of long-term debt. For investors interested in following the industry, a key figure to monitor is a firm's operating cash flow. This can provide a clue to the safety of dividends as well as to the company's ability to finance growth.

Investors should also ascertain the size of the company's reserves base, its finding costs, location and amount of developed and undeveloped acreage, and past record of increasing reserves. The accounting method chosen for reporting the valuation of oil/gas reserves—successful efforts or full-cost accounting—can also have a bearing on a firm's profits. The former method is considered more conservative since it results in a higher level of expensing and a lower level of reported earnings.

PAPER AND FOREST PRODUCTS. This is a relatively concentrated industry, in which the top dozen or so producers now account for more than half of industry output. A few of the companies produce paper only, buying pulp and selling in bulk, whether the output is newsprint, kraft, or bleached white printing or writing papers. But most companies in the industry are vertically integrated in varying degrees. They may grow their own pulpwood, which they convert into corrugated cartons, paper bags, computer output forms, disposable diapers, food packaging, and/or specialized coated papers to be used in making such things as this book's cover and papers for electrical condensers. In addition, many produce lumber and plywood for the building trades.

The entire industry is highly capital intensive, requiring huge expenditures for new plant capacity and upgrading papermaking machines. The expense of air- and water-pollution control equipment has burdened the industry in the last decade, but this was mitigated somewhat by the availability of low-cost, tax-exempt industrial revenue bonds for financing this equipment. Analysts must assess closely the unfilled spending requirements of individual firms, as well as their financing ability.

Probably the most consistent and profitable sector of the paper industry has been the tissue market—facial and toilet tissue and paper napkins and towels. Along with production efficiency, marketing and consumer brand awareness are important to these companies. Although domestic market growth in recent years has only slightly exceeded population growth, industry leaders have shown strong and consistent profit trends based on market share gains, broadened product lines, and increasing penetration of largely untapped foreign markets.

For general producers of stock for the packaging and printing markets, capacity utilization of plant and equipment is watched closely as a clue to the industry's pricing flexibility. In the past, as output rose to 90 to 92 percent of capacity, paper companies were generally able to raise prices by more than their relatively fixed capital and operating costs, leading to substantial profit leverage. This was usually reflected in good relative performances for the companies' shares. Because modern equipment and controls can be operated for longer periods without maintenance shutdowns, capacity utilization has become a less reliable indicator in recent years. Currency exchange rates, which bear heavily on the success of foreign competition, are another factor in the fortunes of domestic firms.

The forest products industry represents an important sector of the economy, one that should remain strong as population and economic growth put increasing pressures on resources generally. Because of the cyclical nature of many of the industry's products, investors should look for companies with well-diversified positions, sizable market shares in several product lines, creative management, and aggressive marketing strategies.

TEXTILES. While this industry remains fairly fragmented, a considerable amount of consolidation has taken place. Of the approximately 5,500 textile companies, the five largest concerns capture about 25 percent of total industry sales. Serving such cyclically sensitive markets as apparel, home furnishings, and industrial fabrics, the textile industry tends to be pretty much feast or famine. To help reduce this inherent vulnerability to overall economic conditions, the industry has undergone a considerable technological, managerial, and marketing face-lifting in recent years.

Along with the trend toward consolidation, textile manufacturers have been placing increasing emphasis on cost control, with particular attention being given to all-important inventory controls. When heavy inventory accumulation occurs along with sluggish business activity, the result is product markdowns and reduced profits. Research and development has also become a top priority as companies search for new technologies to increase productivity, reduce costs, and meet constantly changing fashion trends.

Raw-material costs account for more than 50 percent of the value of all textile shipments. Synthetics are a good deal more stable in price than cottons and wools and have gained good consumer acceptance for their durability and easy care. Manufacturers are diversifying both inside and outside the textile area. So, when choosing a textile issue, the analyst must be particularly alert to such items as cost control, use of advanced technology, product mix, and diversification. Some of the major difficulties facing the textile industry include import competition, labor costs, and the growing need for capital to modernize facilities. It is most important to keep these in mind when analyzing individual companies.

The textile group historically has moved in line with the

industrial averages. Growing in importance is the individual company's dividend policy. Since the textile group's profits can be volatile (owing to its cyclicality), the analyst should look closely at the company's record of consistency of dividend payments. Stability of cash flow should also be examined as ongoing modernization depends oftentimes on the amounts of such internally generated funds.

Science and Technology

Aerospace, data processing, electronics, and health care. The industries in this segment have several characteristics in common. Their shares usually trade at a premium over the market; dividend payouts tend to be modest, research and development expenditures large, and earnings growth rates well above average. New-product development costs are huge, yet necessary, as product obsolescence is a constant threat. However, the rewards for technological breakthroughs are sufficiently large to offset these risks.

The long arm of the federal government reaches into almost every facet of operations, in the form of product, price, and advertising regulation, safety and environmental standards, and funding. Cyclical influences are less apparent in technology companies than in the basic industry group. In some areas, in fact, members may move in a countercyclical pattern.

Investors willing to take on a degree of risk with these stocks are often rewarded by an above-average return. At the same time, more than the usual degree of selectivity is essential when investing in this premium-priced group of industries.

AEROSPACE. The aerospace industry frequently moves counter to the prevailing business cycle, a phenomenon that has its roots in government funding. As an employer of 5 percent of all manufacturing workers and as the source of equipment vital to the nation's defense, the aerospace industry encounters little resistance from Congress in obtaining huge fund allocations, particularly in bad times. In recent years, sales of military equipment to foreign nations, most notably the Arab bloc, also have been a significant factor in supporting the industry through economic downturns.

Military spending accounts for 60 percent of total aerospace revenues. Six major companies control the bulk of this business. Defense spending began to accelerate in the mid-1960s and picked up momentum in the mid-1970s only to slow again in the late 1970s and early 1980s. However, the $1.7 trillion the government allocated for defense spending in the 1982–87 period has provided a cushion for the industry. Meanwhile, commercial sales are revving up again and should remain strong though the early 1990s, somewhat offsetting an expected slowing in defense spending. A repeat of earlier buying binges by the airlines of new equipment seems likely for the next several years.

In looking at individual companies in the industry, the analyst must always keep in mind the possibility of a major new military contract award or cancellation. Product diversification, as well as the military-commercial balance, are areas he should study. Also important in this industry are the amount of aggressiveness a company displays in pursuing new contracts, its research program, and its ability to finance new products.

DATA PROCESSING. As an industry, data processing is a virtual infant compared with such graybeards as shipbuilding and railroading. Mushrooming growth in the 1960s saw one technological breakthrough after another as applications and utilization expanded hand in hand with declining product prices. Computer usage has become so prevalent today that even home computers have moved from the realm of science fiction to the shopping-center shelf.

The industry is divided into four major segments, but there is considerable overlapping from one area to another. The mainframe market is dominated by a few large companies, with International Business Machines doing two-thirds of the business. Software is marketed by all the majors, by publicly owned smaller companies, as well as myriad privately and individually owned enterprises. Add-ons, or peripheral equipment, are packaged and sold by the mainframe manufacturers and also by numerous others, large and small, some concentrating in this one area and others offering it as part of a widely diversified product line. However, the number of players in the fields of software and peripherals has been substantially reduced in the last few years by takeovers, mergers, and bankruptcies.

Microcomputers, the newest segment of the business, were made possible by developments in microminiaturization. Again, some of the majors have reached down to expand the bottom end of their lines into the fast-growing mini and micro fields. Although a few specialists control this end of the business, competition from the other entrants is intense and has squeezed out some of the weaker, undercapitalized companies.

Cyclical influences such as capital spending have the biggest impact at the heavy end of the business—large mainframes. Manufacturers operating in this area spend heavily for product development; IBM alone expends $1 billion annually on research and development. Foreign operations also bulk large, often accounting for nearly half of a company's sales. However, currency fluctuations, governmental restrictions, and labor relations can affect profits from overseas operations, while competition from foreign manfacturers has adversely affected profits in domestic operations.

In line with other high-technology stocks, computer issues have long commanded premium price-earnings multiples. Similarly, the bulk of earnings have been plowed back rather than being distributed to shareholders. But market conditions and industry maturity have wrought changes so that price-earnings ratios have worked down significantly in recent years. Selected issues in this area are attractive for long-term growth.

ELECTRONICS AND ELECTRICAL EQUIPMENT. In discussing this industry, it is difficult to generalize, since it covers manufacturers of such diverse products as citizens' band radios, television sets, massive generating equipment, semiconductors, and highly sophisticated scientific instruments. While one segment may be seriously hurt by a business downturn, another may not be. Some areas may require large infusions of capital to stay afloat; others are characterized by the ease of entry for new companies. Those companies that primarily produce household appliances and home entertainment equipment will be subject to the same influences as other consumer product companies, while those fabricating expensive capital equipment will move in line with the cyclical basic industries. Of course the larger companies have a stake in both ends.

The future health of these producers is assured by the massive sums that will have to be spent by industry and government to reduce the nation's dependence on oil, to improve mass transportation, to develop alternative energy sources, to automate manufacturing, to explore the universe, and to advance our technological applications. The government is also pouring billions into electronic warfare devices, intelligence and surveillance equipment, and improvement of the nation's retaliation capabilities.

In analyzing individual companies, you should look at the competitive position, marketing expertise, patent position, product diversification, government-commercial product mix, and research leadership. Many of the larger firms in this industry are multinational and subject to the usual considerations of currency stability, regulation, and political climate. As a whole, these issues are attractive investments.

HEALTH CARE. Key factors in the appraisal of health care securities include federal regulation, research, and marketing strength. For some companies, especially the major drug firms, international business also involves significant considerations. Actually, more than half of the health care dollar goes to nonprofit hospitals and to doctors. But investor-owned businesses also bulk large; here is a partial listing: ethical pharmaceuticals (with promotion directed toward the medical profession), proprietary drugs (consumer advertised), medical supplies and equipment, wholesale distribution, diagnostic products, and health care services (investor-owned hospitals, nursing homes, and health maintenance organizations being notable areas). Diversification is another aspect of investment appraisal, since many companies cover a broad range of health care fields.

A common denominator for appraising companies in this industry is federal regulation. Even the merest rumor of Congressional committee hearings can have a marked impact on the price of their stocks. Although the government underwrites a sizable chunk of our medical bills, soaring costs to some extent have been fostered by Washington's efforts to improve the quality of health care and the safety and efficacy of health care products. These costly standards are forcing smaller companies out of business and concentrating activities into fewer, stronger companies. At the same time, ironically, the Federal Trade Commission (FTC) periodically engages in antitrust litigation aimed at preventing such concentration.

The key regulatory agency is the Food and Drug Administration (FDA), which has unusually strict standards for new drug clearance. Several years and millions of dollars must be expended to bring a new drug from its initial research stage, through animal and human testing, to final FDA clearance. The clearance of new medical devices has been somewhat less difficult, but still more costly than small companies can generally afford. Hence, an analyst is essentially concerned with tracking the research progress of the larger companies, including the cost-effectiveness of the research approach and the progress of products through the various test stages. Moreover, he must keep abreast of the technological competition among the companies in every major health care field.

Marketing strength is another important facet. In ethical drugs, a company's basic marketing force is its detail staff, people who keep physicians and pharmacists informed on products and their usage. In proprietary drugs, the marketing effort is centered in advertising and promotion directed to the consumer. Another government watchdog, the Federal Trade Commission, steps in here to see that advertising doesn't get out of bounds.

International business plays an important role in the operations of health care companies, particularly for the major drug manufacturers. Because Japan is second to the United States in total health care expenditures, it is an especially significant market. Other international aspects include the handling of currency fluctuations and tax shelters.

Thus far, we have touched on a few of the general considerations which apply to the appraisal of several segments of the health care industry. In weighing the specifics of a given company within that industry, the analyst must start by knowing how the business is divided. What are the company's major products? What services does it provide? Where are its geographical markets?

Then each of these factors is appraised with regard to competitive strengths, basic earning power, and potential for future growth. Yesterday's success may become a company's Achilles' heel due to intensified competition or harmful side effects. A new product may well bring new life to a sleeping giant almost overnight.

As in other industries, ultimate considerations include the quality of earnings, the overall growth trend in terms of profits and dividends, and the relative price-earnings ratio of each individual stock of the companies within that industry.

For the investor, health care stocks have above-average long-term potential.

Transportation Industries

Airlines, railroads, and trucking. The movement of goods and people is big business, but it also is a business which has been, and will continue to be, in a state of flux. The trucking industry has significantly increased its share of the freight hauling market, to the detriment of the rails. The airlines have made major inroads into the passenger hauling market, once dominated by the railroads. In recent years, another contender for freight revenues has come into its own, intermodal shipping or container leasing.

In general, the transportation industries are cyclical, reflecting changes in the level of freight being moved and in the amounts being spent for travel. All are capital intensive, while most are also labor intensive. The public outcry for less government in the private sector has had a significant impact on the transportation industries as the airlines, rails, and truckers have witnessed reductions in federal regulatory constraints.

AIRLINES. This capital-intensive industry's sensitivity to economic conditions has produced a boom-and-bust earnings pattern over the years. Scheduled air carriers dominate intercity public transportation, holding at least 85 percent of that market. That dominance is not likely to be challenged in the foreseeable future.

Potential investors should seek information on a carrier's overall financial strength, as debt ratios vary widely. Planned equipment purchases and options to buy new planes are also valuable indicators of future financing needs. Equipment utilization rates, load factors, passenger yields, and degree of exposure to business and tourist markets are also important tools in the investment selection process.

Passage of deregulation legislation in 1978 gave airlines greater rate-setting flexibility while also easing entry requirements on new and existing routes. The Civil Aeronautics Board's authority over domestic rates, mergers, and acquisitions terminated in 1981, while the CAB was abolished in 1985. Deregulation brought on considerable changes in the operating environment, including intensified competition on lucrative routes, rampant fare discounting, and abandonment of marginal short-haul service by many of the trunk lines. Meanwhile, regional carriers are expanding into interstate markets and gaining market share. Another result of deregulation is the recent trend toward consolidation. This should prove beneficial to both the industry and consumers, as fare structures and operating profits should stabilize. It seems probable that those airlines which can capture the largest market share while staying financially healthy will be the winners.

Perhaps the most important long-term impact of deregulation on the investment decision regards the emerging importance of management. In a free-market environment the stakes are likely to be far greater than under a regulatory umbrella. Also, success or failure will increasingly stem from managerial decisions.

Historically, airline stocks begin to outperform the market prior to the trough of a recession, in anticipation of renewed traffic growth. Investors are cautioned that stock action, like profits, tends to be volatile, with fast-paced movements on both the upside and the downside.

RAILROADS. Few industries are as closely linked to business cycles as the railroads. Fluctuations in such basic industries as autos, steel, mining, coal, and capital goods have a decided impact on carloadings. As the revenue ton-mile (movement of one ton of freight one mile) performance is the analyst's basic tool for measuring traffic growth, these variations are crucial. In one major business cycle of perhaps two years' duration, these figures can vary by 100 billion tons. Fixed costs are high, so operating profits are hard to come by in recessions. Thus, when reviewing this industry, current and projected economic trends are important factors.

Rails are among the most labor-intensive of industries, with wages accounting for more than 48 percent of revenues in the mid-1980s. Therefore, it is important to keep tabs on the timing and content of union contracts. Other major costs include maintenance of way, structures, and equipment, and transportation accounts (fuel, loss, and damage). By measuring a carrier's transportation expenses against revenues, the analyst can compare the efficiency of one road with another. A similar comparison can be made with maintenance costs and revenues to get information on the condition of fleet and property.

Another important consideration is the railroad's geographical operating area. The industry is generally reviewed in three segments, Eastern, Western, and Southern. Operators in each area have many similarities, but they have important and distinct differences in weather conditions, types of freight hauled, and their areas' growth prospects.

Deregulation has also been in the cards for the nation's rails, while the Interstate Commerce Commission is already moving to loosen the regulatory noose around the industry. The Railroad Revitalization and Regulatory Reform Act of 1976 provided the initial catalyst to the ICC's increasingly constructive stance on questions of track abandonment, rate setting, and mergers.

The latter point has, in recent years, resulted in a flurry of proposed combinations, which adds a unique shading to rail investment decisions. Here one must determine the outlook for the combined systems, resulting in individual stock valuations on the basis of the proposed entity and in accordance with announced merger terms. Dividend restrictions also appear in formal agreements and must be weighed. Since consummation of a proposed merger can take up to three years, the possibility of the merger never reaching fruition, mainly because of monopoly worries, must also be considered. In such instances, sharp stock price corrections can occur as investors reappraise the value of each firm.

TRUCKING. More than half of all the freight moved within the country is carried by truck. In view of the prominence of the trucking industry in transporting raw materials to manufacturers and manufactured products to the market, it is not surprising that the industry tends to be an economic bellwether. Changes in the weekly intercity truck tonnage figures, whether they are changes in direction or velocity, often signal a shift in the business climate. For this reason, the group is important to the analyst trying to ferret out clues to business trends.

The industry is labor intensive, with personnel costs taking almost two-thirds of every sales dollar. This is strong testimony to the effectiveness of the International Brotherhood of Teamsters in dealing with a fragmented industry to negotiate ever-escalating labor contracts. Equipment and terminal maintenance have risen sharply in recent years and are significant expense items for the motor carriers.

The Motor Carrier Act of 1980 provided for significant changes in trucking regulations, including relaxed entry requirements, reduced operating restrictions, greater pricing flexibility, and a phaseout of single-line collective ratemaking. That legislation, combined with the dynamic changes already taking place in other transportation sectors, suggests that realignment of the nation's transportation industries will continue in response to demands for maximum energy efficiency.

When the dust from deregulation finally settles, many transportation specialists expect large intermodal companies —with important trucking components—to emerge as the most viable competitors in coming years. An investor considering trucking firms should therefore keep in mind the sweeping changes affecting the nation's transportation system and the likelihood of an acceleration of merger and acquisition activity within the trucking group in particular. Financial strength, professional management, and access to capital are the key elements to success in this industry for the next decade.

For the investor, this industry can provide some exciting rides. The shares generally are volatile and, caught at the bottom of a cyclical swing, can be rewarding investments.

CHAPTER 25

More on Specific Industries

THE INDUSTRIES REVIEWED in the previous chapter were largely those that make the things we use and those that transport the goods to market. In this chapter, we shall look at the industries that most closely touch our own everyday lives—the consumer-oriented segment of the economy. It's a large segment; personal consumption expenditures make up nearly two-thirds of our gross national product.

Consumer Products and Leisure Time

Food processing, lodging, the media, motion pictures, personal care, recreation equipment, and retailing. How each of us chooses to spend his disposable income has a strong influence on these industries. Thus, competition is intense and top profits go to those companies with the greatest marketing skill and highest advertising budgets.

A constant parade of new products designed to dazzle and bewitch the consumer into parting with his cash is a necessity for survival in these industry areas. To some of these companies, the energy shortage poses a major threat, and to others product obsolescence is a continuing specter. Shifting demographic patterns can have a pervasive influence on the entire group.

284

FOOD PROCESSING. Because of their relatively stable earnings growth and high dividend yields, food processing stocks historically have been attractive as both defensive and growth investments. Since food is literally the world's most basic need, it stands to reason that this industry would enjoy rising demand for its products. Since the United States is the largest producer of foodstuffs, the long-range potential for domestic food processing companies is impressive.

While the overall industry outlook is undeniably favorable, the rate of growth of any individual company hinges on several important factors. One of the most important considerations when analyzing a food stock is the company's vulnerability to and ability in dealing with the volatile commodities markets. Since ingredients are a major consideration, knowledge of present and future commodities price projections and supply-demand prospects is important.

Profit margins can narrow if demand weakens in the face of growing supplies. The same is true when the supply is low, since higher prices often lead to consumer resistance. So a company's ability to keep tight control on ingredient costs is of the utmost importance in determining its earnings potential. A diversified product line helps protect a company from the risk of oversupply or undersupply of any one ingredient. Many of the larger companies have expanded into nonfood areas to further reduce their commodity-related risks. When inflation rates ease, commodity prices tend to stabilize or even decline, allowing the food processing company to increase margins and profitability.

Other major operational costs include energy, labor, packaging, research and development, and advertising and promotion. The energy situation bears close watching, as for the most part the industry is heavily dependent on natural gas in its processing operations. Research and development, marketing, and advertising and promotional capability are vitally important contributors to the success of companies operating in this highly competitive environment. A successful food processor is one that is able to identify growing markets, has the research and development skill to come up with products that will meet these new demands, and has the advertising and promotional expertise to gain an adequate market share.

Because of the stability of the group, the stocks of the top-quality multiproduct diversified companies tend to be very attractive to conservative investors. On the whole, food company issues have limited downside risk even under adverse economic conditions and are appropriate defensive investments.

LODGING. The hotel and motel industry has undergone a metamorphosis in the last two decades. A field once controlled by the independent owner-operator is now dominated by a handful of large motel-hotel chains. Increased mobility, rising construction and real estate costs, and widespread acceptance of expensive computerized reservation systems and other equipment have placed demands on the industry that could only be met by large, well-financed companies. Gone to seed by the roadside are most of the "Bide-a-Wee" and "Dew Drop Inn" cabins. Today's motorist bypasses these anachronisms on his way to a well-equipped, up-to-date motel featuring two pools, four restaurants, and a sauna.

Economic cycles play a role in the fortunes of the innkeepers. The business traveler long has been their bread and butter. As corporate profits decline, business travel shifts from luxury class to economy. But helping to smooth out these ups and downs is the pleasure traveler. As disposable incomes have risen, pleasure travel has increased. Although individuals also feel the pinch in a recession, they give up their pleasures as a last resort and resume them at the first signs of an upturn.

The two most important factors affecting the profitability of an individual chain are occupancy levels and room rates. The analyst is concerned with any major trend changes in these figures. Room rates must adequately cover the cost of the building. However, competitive or other conditions can cause temporary reductions in rates.

Individual companies differ in the kinds of services they provide, i.e., restaurants, large convention quarters, extensive recreation facilities, etc. The percentage of overall income which is derived from these facilities and the profitability of each should be determined. Some innkeepers have diversified into such areas as bus transportation, catering, cruise ships, and casino gambling. These nonlodging functions should be reviewed as separate entities. If an operator has significant foreign exposure, it should be studied in relation to the possible impact it could have on future profits.

The industry faces several uncertainties, not the least of which is overcapacity. GNP growth is a good measure of the industry's health, since 75 percent of revenues are derived from business travel. Occupancy rates have been only mediocre since 1984. Furthermore, room rate increases, which are expected to be in the 3 to 4 percent area, will provide little relief. The increase in domestic travel as a result of growing terrorism abroad will have only a minimal effect on profits because of room overcapacity, and this has been discounted in stock prices.

THE MEDIA. Although the industry is made up of somewhat diverse segments—broadcasting and publishing—it has an underlying similarity of purpose—the dissemination of information and communication of ideas. But broadcasters and newspaper publishers depend more on their advertisers than on the public for their bread and butter. Readership and audience figures are vital to their marketing success, but revenues are derived largely from advertisers.

Both broadcasters and newspaper publishers enjoy high operating margins, leverage, and profits; small volume gains can generate significant profit increases. For publishers, the increasing use of automation and photocomposition equipment has reduced labor costs. Because broadcasting time is limited, advertisers are reluctant to cut back on their TV and radio commercial messages even during recessions. Thus the broadcasters are not as subject to cyclical influences as are the large metropolitan newspapers. In good times, there is a mad scramble among advertisers to secure time slots on the highest-rated network programs. Quite the opposite is the case for newspaper ad linage, which is highly sensitive to business cycles.

A discussion of the media industry is incomplete without mention of the new developments taking place in television. Viewer choice is no longer limited to the fare of the three major networks. Satellites, cable television and pay cable, as well as videocassette recorders and videodisk players, are ushering in an era of "narrowcasting"—programming geared to the special interest of select audiences. Also, several major newspapers are experimenting with placing their publications on computer or television screens. Down the road, television will gain increasing interactive possibilities, permitting such activities as shopping from your TV, using a home computer. Many media companies (particularly newspaper publishers) are now diversified, so that representation in more than one area can be obtained in one stock.

This industry is generally an attractive one for the investor. There are companies appropriate for the speculator and others more suited to conservative tastes.

MOTION PICTURES. Though the motion picture industry bears little resemblance to its former self, it is likely to be around for many years, despite continuing prophecies of doom. There will still be a demand for the type of entertainment that only the movies can provide. We suspect, too, that many people will continue to prefer seeing movies on a theater screen. Even with rising ticket prices, movies will probably be less expensive than many other forms of entertainment. The increased popularity and affordability of the videocassette recorder (VCR) has cut into moviemakers' profits somewhat, but most of the companies are capitalizing on this trend by preselling video rights in order to finance movies. Also, movie companies with huge libraries of old, popular films have found that they are now sitting on gold mines. Cash generated by the eventual release of these films will be substantial.

The movie stocks, however, almost defy analysis. In fact, there are few if any "pure" movie stocks. Gone are the days of the big studios and their stables of stars—their properties, as it were. Many of the major film companies are now divisions of conglomerates with far-flung interests ranging from airlines to zinc. Others have evolved into vast entertainment complexes with important stakes in recorded music, publishing, and cable television, and are now supplying the industry's old archenemy, television, with most of its prime-time product. Those remaining few movie companies with the least diversification seem eager to explore other growth avenues.

Even for the most diversified companies, individual motion pictures can have an enormous impact on earnings. With one major box office smash, a company's earnings can mushroom, its cash position improve significantly, and its stock price rise dramatically.

For every hit there are usually many misses, though the industry is trying to elevate its batting average by releasing fewer but bigger movies. In addition, the hefty guarantees that are demanded from exhibitors actually assure a profit for some films. The industry must anticipate what its public will want to see many months in the future. This is dangerous business—for the movie moguls themselves, for the analyst, and for the investor.

PERSONAL CARE. The personal care industry is highly competitive, with a score of large firms vying for 75 percent of the total dollar volume. A company's success or failure is largely determined by its marketing and merchandising ability. Huge amounts are spent annually trying to capture consumers' dollars and product loyalty. Advertising, packaging, new-product development, and promotion are major expense items. Spending for personal care products has been on the rise in recent years, reflecting the increase in the number of women working outside the home, a bulge in the number of persons in the 25–35 age bracket (a prime age for this type of spending), and the rise in disposable income. These favorable demographic factors and market trends are expected to continue.

There is a wide difference between the world of cosmetics and that of toiletries. Each has its own distinctive characteristics. Channels of distribution, advertising methods, packaging, promotional expenses, and competitive climates are different, and the analyst must approach them separately. Sales and earnings should be studied on a division-by-division level so these differences can be taken into account. Cosmetics are at the top end of the industry with medium- to premium-priced products, high profit margins, and fashion-related product lines. The more mundane toiletry business includes such pedestrian products as shampoos, deodorants, toothpaste, shaving products, and hair coloring.

While the industry as a whole is fairly recession-resistant, inflation does have a stifling effect on growth. Periods of high inflation necessitate increased consumer spending for food and shelter and reduce the demand for personal care items. At the same time, manufacturers are forced to pay higher prices for raw materials and supplies. The combination can seriously squeeze profit margins. Alternatively, a dramatic decline in the inflation rate can be quite beneficial. Then companies enjoy rising profits as a result of a leveling off and possibly a decline in raw materials costs. Because so many of these companies are multinational, it is imperative to determine how much of a company's business comes from overseas.

New products are the lifeblood of this group's growth. A company's record of developing and marketing new products may be a clue to its future potential. A strong and creative management which recognizes new consumer trends and is willing to make the changes necessary to accommodate these new ideas is one key to success in this highly competitive industry. Diversification efforts have further enhanced the outlook for many personal care firms as maturation of the domestic market looms late in the 1980s. Health care firms have been favorite targets for acquisition, given the compatibility of their operating requirements and marketing channels with the personal care sector.

RECREATION EQUIPMENT. This fragmented group includes manufacturers of boats, bowling equipment, sporting goods, video games, snowmobiles, and camping equipment. Thus, conditions which might hurt one company might not hurt another. However, the industry as a whole is sensitive to changes in the economy and in the level of disposable income. In line with some other leisure-time groups, recreation product manufacturers are among the last to be hit in a recession and the first to recover as business heats up.

Demographic conditions favor this group for the next few decades. The 35–54 age group—where most of the big-ticket recreation equipment purchases originate—is expected to increase by more than 60 percent through the year 2000. Americans are enjoying rising discretionary incomes, longer vacations, shorter workweeks, a high level of employment, and excellent retirement benefits, all of which are spurs to recreational activities.

Important to the success—or failure—of a company are its product research and development, its ability as a marketer, its skill in keeping costs down in an inflationary climate, and its product reputation. Because recreation equipment often tends to be seasonal, oriented to a particular population segment, easily duplicated, and short-lived in popularity, a broadly diversified product line is vital to a company's stability.

These stocks, bought in an up cycle, can be highly rewarding. Leisure is big business, and the choices for investments are varied. However, those companies with strong managements, broad product diversification, and products which can be used near the home seem to have the most attractive prospects.

RETAILING. An overview of retailing involves considering the business cycle, inflation, unemployment, consumer disposable income, installment debt, and savings. This industry is affected by seasonal factors, regional weather conditions, fashion trends, the promotional environment, and consumer buying habits.

Retailing covers a wide range of merchandising which is generally separated into food and nonfood groups. In the latter group, general merchandisers are studied separately from the specialty stores. But even within these broad categories, there is considerable overlapping. Food supermarkets are adding more and more shelf space for nonfood items, and specialty stores are dealing in health and beauty aids. These two types of stores are not only competing with each other, but are encroaching on the business of the general merchandisers.

Central to all retailing is the competitive position of the individual company in its given segment. The food supermarket seeks to balance low prices with quality and convenience. The convenience chains stress their round-the-clock neighborhood shopping convenience and underplay their higher prices. A specialty store may appeal to a shopper's desire for service, high fashion, and top quality. Some retailers play both ends of the mass-class market, with boutiques and bargain basements. Important in a retailer's success is the competitive force of the company's image. Site selection is often the key to the store's ability to achieve this success.

In appraising managements, you must consider how well central control and local autonomy are balanced. Chain stores do their buying from a central location on information fed from decentralized outlets. Many of the major department store enterprises are known as "ownership groups," since each division has a high degree of autonomy. However, staff support functions—computer systems, strategic planning, and real estate development—are centralized. Whatever the organizational structure, management's effectiveness in monitoring information, measuring results, and taking corrective action is what counts.

One measure of a company's progress is sales growth, which may come through adding new stores, replacing outdated units, or through acquisitions. The yardstick here is the annual figure for square feet of retail floor space. Growth of space is somewhat meaningless by itself; productivity of that space should be examined by comparing annual changes in volume of sales per square foot.

In appraising retailers' earnings, look at gross margins. This figure is derived by subtracting the cost of goods sold from total sales volume. Inventory control is an important factor in maintaining a favorable level of gross margins. Frequently there is considerable shrinkage between the initial markup and gross margin, reflecting pilferage, errors, and markdowns. Food supermarkets and other self-service operations have limited personnel expenses and rapid inventory turnover, and therefore low expense ratios and low gross margins. Effective expense control is also an important contributor to company profits.

Though retailing for the most part is a mature and intensely competitive field, the group offers some excellent growth selections for the judicious investor.

Financial Services

Banks, insurance companies, and savings and loan associations. For those companies that provide financial services, interest-rate trends are an all-important key to their fortunes. The spread beteween short-term and long-term rates, or between the rate of interest earned and rate paid, can make the difference between a profit or a loss.

Investments made by these financial companies turn the wheels of American industry, fund most of the housing, and keep the various levels of government operating. They tend to make stable, consistent investments with modest yield and good growth potentials.

BANKING. An understanding of the banking industry requires an in-depth study of balances—balances between loans and deposits, between interest rates paid and interest rates earned, between deposit inflows and disintermediation, between short-term loans and long-term loans, and so on. The prosperity of the industry can often swing in either direction on no more than a quarter-point change in the prime lending rate. Thus it is important for the analyst to understand the subtle nuances of these balance and ratio relationships.

To facilitate study, banks generally can be segregated into two groups—money-market-center banks and regional banks. Within these categories are banks whose focus is wholesale, retail, domestic, or international—or any combination thereof. Money-center banks react more rapidly and dramatically to changes in the business climate. Regional banks, with their longer-term portfolios, more stable deposit bases, and better-balanced customer mixes, are in a more advantageous position to withstand economic cycles. Not surprisingly, their stocks display a similar pattern, offering the investor stability, modest yield, and good appreciation potential.

Money-center banks, which are heavily dependent on commercial and industrial loans, can be hard pressed when the demand for such loans dries up, reflecting customers' increased use of cheaper money from commercial paper, notes, and other sources. Banks in need of loan customers often accept less attractive risks. An example of this is the surge in high-risk loans to underdeveloped countries, loans which have resulted in large losses for some international money-center banks.

When analyzing individual bank stocks, important items to examine include loan volume and quality, the health of the regional economy, operating expenses, and noninterest income. The latter, generated by account service charges and credit card, data processing, and trust fees, has become an increasingly important component of bank earnings in recent years.

Banking is one of the few industries in which book value or net worth per share has any substantive meaning. Unlike a manufacturer with large amounts of capital tied up in inventory, a bank has assets that are usually of a type that can be easily turned into cash.

Banks report earnings on two different bases: net operating income, which includes profits from operations only, and net income, which includes operating income as well as gains or losses from portfolio transactions. The first figure is the one generally used in comparing statistics on banks.

Stocks in the larger banks can provide you with an equity position to cash in on favorable interest-rate swings. But, because these bank stocks tend to be more volatile than those of the regionals, you'll have to keep a closer eye on them. Regional banks provide an opportunity to include some close-to-home investments in your portfolio.

INSURANCE. Until the late 1970s, life insurance companies were able to generate steadily rising annual income streams. However, the deregulation of interest rates and high rates of inflation permanently altered profit trends for this segment of the insurance industry. Traditional whole-life premiums, which provided low rates of return to policyholders, failed to appeal to consumers. Through policy loans and terminations, funds flowed out of policies into financial products paying substantially higher rates of return. Slow to adapt to the change, life insurers eventually developed competitive products. However, the new policies don't produce the level of profits that whole life did. Furthermore, policy lapses continue to run at a high rate.

Today, the life insurance industry is highly competitive. When analyzing these companies, look at premium growth, mortality experience, lapse rate, reserve position, and operating expenses. The policy mix—ordinary, term, and group —is important, since each type has its own characteristics. Nonlife revenues generated from annuities and accident and health insurance are also important sources of profits.

The earnings trend of property-casualty insurers has always been characterized as cyclical. When companies are experiencing strong profit growth, there is a tendency to cut premiums to garner greater market share. At present, the industry is just beginning to recover from the longest and steepest slump in its history. When interest rates were soaring, companies were eager to invest premiums—so much so that policies were substantially underpriced and high risks were assumed. When interest rates plummeted and claims soared, losses swelled.

It appears that the industry has learned a tough lesson and will be more cautious in pricing policies. The key to evaluating a company's underwriting profitability is its combined ratio. This statistic is made up of a company's loss ratio (losses to earned premiums) plus its expense ratio (expenses to premiums written). Other items to examine are investment income, incurred losses, and loss reserves. The latter figure represents funds set aside to cover unpaid losses, estimated future claims, and costs related to these payments. Reserves should be larger than necessary to avoid unpleasant surprises on future earnings.

While intense competition has contributed to the woes of the property-casualty industry, jury awards have also impacted profits. Both Congress and state legislatures are now taking steps to correct this problem. Federal tort legislation is expected to be enacted; some states have passed bills, and several are considering tort reform measures. Government reform will be welcomed by property-casualty insurers, as long as insurance premiums aren't capped.

SAVINGS AND LOAN ASSOCIATIONS. S&Ls are a major source of home mortgage capital, supplying more than half the credit for housing in this country. Mortgage funding is generated primarily from the deposits of savers, but advances from the Federal Home Loan Bank are a secondary source. Earnings are derived from the spread between the interest costs on deposits and the return from mortgages outstanding. Origination fees on new mortgages are also a source of income. New funds are also raised by the sale of mortgages and participations in existing mortgage portfolios.

Because mortgages tend to be written for the long term, and deposits are frequently short term, S&Ls can be in the unenviable position, under high interest-rate conditions, of having to pay as much or more for borrowings as they are earning on portions of their loan portfolios.

As a result of financial deregulation, savings and loans can now offer money-market accounts. This allows them to compete with mutual funds for a larger part of the nation's deposits. The diversification of their income stream through product innovations also should make their earnings less susceptible to the rise and fall in interest rates. Therefore, S&L shares should be less cyclical and more growth oriented. As deregulation progresses, evolution in financial services and S&Ls will continue.

Public Utilities

Electric power, natural gas pipelines, telephone companies. The tie that binds these three public utility groups together is regulation, at both federal and state levels. Indeed, the only growth some companies can expect will come from rate increases granted by the regulating agencies that control them. This is particularly true for some of the more poorly situated electric power companies and for those pipeline companies that have failed to diversify. Of the three industry areas, the telephone companies have suffered the least from regulatory manipulation, only because they require rate boosts less frequently.

In general, investors turn to these groups for generous yields, gradual growth, and better-than-average stability. The electric utilities are particularly liberal in their dividend payments; the integrated natural gas distributors are the least generous.

ELECTRIC UTILITIES. As one of the most capital-intensive of industries, electric utility companies are vulnerable to interest-rate swings, shifts in the money supply, and inflation. The industry has to combat such problems as fuel availability, rate regulations, and pressure from consumer and environmental groups. Because electric power companies all face these difficulties, there is a tendency to view them as a homogeneous unit. There is, however, a wide variation in the investment opportunities represented within the group.

One of the most important criteria in evaluating the group is the regulatory climate under which the company must operate. Is the regulatory agency sympathetic to the needs of the company, with decisions rendered promptly and a reasonable return on equity allowed? (A 15 percent return on equity is a workable figure.) If construction work in progress is included in the rate base, so much the better.

In comparing company earnings, an analyst must pay close attention to the quality of those figures. If a large percentage of profit comes from allowance for funds used during construction, the quality of these profits is questionable.

A utility's financial position is particularly important, since the company's future depends heavily on its ability to raise new capital economically. Two important ratios are *fixed charges coverage* and *debt to equity*. A fixed charges ratio of two times is desirable—that is, earnings that are twice as great as total bond interest and preferred dividends. In the debt to equity ratio, when debt moves up to account for more than 60 percent of capitalization, the balance begins to get unhealthy and equity financing becomes the obvious alternative. If, however, the stock is selling below book value, equity financing will result in heavy earnings dilution. The greater the percentage of capital requirements that can be generated internally from cash flow, the healthier the utility.

The fuel used by an electric utility has an important bearing on its attractiveness. Hydropower, coal, and nuclear energy have been the preferred generating fuels in this era of more costly oil and less abundant natural gas. However, the near-disastrous malfunction at the Three Mile Island nuclear plant in Pennsylvania in 1979 precipitated a controversy which cast a cloud over the future of nuclear power. Stringent safety guidelines have since been imposed on utilities with nuclear exposure. Thus, fuel risk has evolved as a significant criterion in evaluating securities within the utility group. A final measuring stick to apply to these companies is their comparative earnings and dividend growth rates.

As long as inflation remains within bounds and interest rates stable, electric utilities offer above-average current yield, reasonable dividend growth, and moderate price appreciation.

NATURAL GAS PIPELINES AND DISTRIBUTORS. For the domestic natural gas industry, the mid-eighties have been a time of confusion. Major changes in federal rules and regulations have been implemented at a time when many in the industry already had their hands full with the problems of oversupply and increased competition. The industry is also faced with domestic consumption that has virtually stagnated at a level of around 18 tcf (trillion cubic feet) a year, some 20 percent below the peak in 1973. As a result, transmission (pipeline) companies have found themselves in the difficult position of having to renegotiate long-term take-or-pay contracts originally signed with producers in the late 1970s and early 1980s, when natual gas was in short supply and prices were higher.

Exacerbating the situation is Order 436, issued by the Federal Energy Regulatory Commission late in 1985. The order is designed to promote competition among pipelines while reducing discriminatory practices. It requires that pipelines choose between providing "open access" transportation services for all customers and maintaining traditional practices of carrying mainly gas they have contracted to purchase and resell. While a dilemma for most piplines, Order 436 should benefit selected distributors by allowing them access to plentiful, low-cost supplies.

Although the gas industry is likely to remain unsettled over the near term, the longer-term outlook remains quite positive. Demand is expected to gradually recover, which should alleviate the gas "bubble" situation that has plagued the industry since 1983. Furthermore, the Federal Energy Regulatory Commission has lifted the ceiling on most price-controlled natural gas (discovered before 1978) and is expected to implement comprehensive deregulation of industry pricing before long.

Natural gas issues appeal to the conservative investor seeking a reasonably high yield and rising dividend income. Typically, gas utilities, or distributors, fit this description. Past dividend growth should be examined as a possible clue to future growth in payments. Pipeline companies tend to offer not only above-average income but also the potential for appreciation.

The size and location of a transmission company's pipeline system is worth noting, as these can provide some indication of the firm's market growth prospects. Also, several of the smaller firms are often mentioned as potential takeover candidates owing to their attractive supply arrangements, diversification moves, stability of earnings, etc.

TELEPHONE COMPANIES. These utilities are in a better position than most of their regulated colleagues. Although they are not completely immune to inflationary cost pressures, future capital needs are manageable. Costly pollution controls, customer conservation measures, and soaring fuel prices have not affected the communication companies. Earnings quality is generally high, reflecting conservative accounting practices and limited allowance for funds used during construction.

Although telephone companies are dependent on favorable treatment on rates, improved industry fundamentals should lessen the amount of rate assistance needed in the future. In general, costs have been well controlled in the industry, while direct distance dialing and electronic switching equipment have provided more efficient operations and lower maintenance costs. Revenue growth has been accelerated by the increase in household formations and the installation of second phones, which have outpaced population growth.

The seven regional holding companies created during the

breakup of the old American Telephone & Telegraph system dominate the industry, servicing 80 percent of U.S. telephones. Servicing of the remaining 20 percent, or one out of five telephones, is parceled out among numerous independents. However, the five largest—GTE Corp., United Telecommunications, Continental Telecom, Southern New England Telephone, and Centel Corp.—serve well over three-quarters of all non-Bell telephone users.

While the Bell regionals are located in the more densely populated areas, the independents generally cover the smaller but more rapidly growing rural and suburban sections, where phones are being added and toll usage is rising at a fast clip. Thus, the threat of bypass is not nearly as prevalent for the independents as it is for the Bell regionals. The Bell companies are restrained from entering certain businesses under terms of the Modified Final Judgment handed down at the time of the divestiture. However, the Bell regionals are slowly chipping away at these restrictions. Most of the independents offer broad diversification beyond the area of basic telephone service.

As a general rule of thumb, the more diversified a telephone company becomes, the percent of earnings that are paid out annually in the form of common dividends decreases. This is due to the nature of the businesses into which telcos diversify—telecommunications-equipment manufacturing and sales, financial services, and software development and marketing are a few. The nature of these industries requires that earnings be plowed back into operations to fuel future growth. Therefore, within the industry, there are a variety of choices for the right combination of current income and growth potential.

Regulation for telephone companies has generally been less of a problem than for electric utility companies, and there is little to suggest that this is likely to change. However, investors should be aware of changes in the regulatory climate that could affect future earnings.

CHAPTER 26

Cashing In on the Future

A MODERN INDUSTRIAL economy, free-world style, is a constantly changing body. New industries emerge, and old industries disappear. Some regions advance, while others fall behind. Cities decline, and suburbs grow. The crucial industries that provide power and transportation undergo transformations.

Some sources of change in the economy are the result of legislation. Others may reflect influences like wars or weather changes. Many major changes, however, are generated within the system itself.

Many years ago, the Austrian-born economist Joseph A. Schumpeter identified the process of innovation as the primary source of internally generated change. In furthering understanding of the complexities of a modern economic society, the work of Professor Schumpeter, probably the most neglected of the great twentieth-century economists, has major contributions to make.

Dr. Schumpeter's first writing on the subject of innovation was published in 1911 in Germany. This work was not translated into English until 1934. In 1939, while at Harvard, Dr. Schumpeter expanded upon and further developed the ideas of his youth in a two-volume work called *Business Cycles*.

Innovation, in Dr. Schumpeter's system, takes four forms:

the introduction of a new product, the utilization of new methods of production, the opening up of new sources of supply, and the development of new forms of business organization. Examples abound.

New-product innovation may be illustrated by such diverse examples as the automobile, the introduction of antibiotics, the microwave oven, and the videocassette.

New methods of production may be illustrated by developments in the steel industry, from the Bessemer process through the open-hearth furnace to the modern basic oxygen process. The jet engine powers airplanes by means superior to the internal combustion engine.

Food processors have found new methods for preserving foods by spraying and freeze-drying them. Dry packaging, which is cheaper than glass and metal containers, has been developed for liquid food products.

Innovative new sources of supply are illustrated by Alaskan oil, iron ore from Labrador, electronics from the Far East, and fresh produce from South America and Europe.

Finally, new forms of business organization have evolved, such as the limited-liability corporation and the one-bank holding company, the "full-service" bank, and the fast-food emporium.

Innovation Versus Invention

The business innovator or entrepreneur should be distinguished from the inventor. First, many innovations, such as the supermarket or the medical clinic, have little or nothing to do with invention. The inventor's skills are likely to be of a mechanical or scientific nature, while the innovator's strengths lie in the ability to conceive better production methods, products, and business organizational forms. The innovator may start a new business, select a site, obtain the capital, hire the people, provide the raw materials, and sell the product. Like many inventions, a particular innovation may come to nothing, but the hallmark of successful innovation is the earning of profits.

The profits of innovation will attract new entrants into the field. Sometimes the competitors have to circumvent patents or copyrights, or attempt to offer a superior product. In other cases, entry may be possible by duplicating the activity elsewhere, say, in some other location. The entry of competitors will stimulate plant and equipment spending and increase output and employment. The increase in output will bring down prices and reduce profits. Eventually the innovating industry becomes mature. Firms in the industry may attempt to sustain themselves by superior management, by consolidation, and by making minor innovative adaptations of the basic product.

The Effects of "Future Shock"

Superimposed on Dr. Schumpeter's ideas is the acceleration of change that has now reached such proportions that there is hardly anyone in our midst who can escape its effects. "Future shock," Alvin Toffler called it in his 1970 book by the same name. Mr. Toffler's claims are hardly an exaggeration. Think of all that has been discovered, invented, produced, and experienced in the brief span of years we have been around. Today's twenty-five-year-old will see more changes by his fiftieth birthday than today's fifty-year-old has experienced since he was twenty-five.

While all this is apparent and interesting, what is more to the point is how we can profit by this acceleration of change. Perhaps those among us with the imagination of Jules Verne find it easy to envision a world a quarter-century into the future. But most of us are not such visionaries. Our feet and minds are firmly planted in the here and now; we think we're doing well if we can anticipate a week, a month, or a year ahead.

Given the limitations of our prophetic powers, perhaps we should turn to the past for some clues. What were the conditions that fostered the growth of such an industrial giant as International Business Machines? From its humble beginnings as a manufacturer of scales and cash registers in St. Louis, Missouri, in 1911, who could have foreseen its rise to a behemoth grossing over $50 billion a year?

By 1954, when IBM marketed its first large-scale stored-program computer, it already had achieved a commendable growth record, with annual sales well over $400 million and net income approaching $50 million. To some analysts, who failed to comprehend what the future held for the computer, IBM was already a maturing company. Anyone venturing to buy ten shares of stock at that time—which would have cost less than $3,000—would have owned 363 shares worth almost $100,000 at the close of 1977. Even made as late as 1977, an investment in IBM would have produced a 10 percent compound annual return over the next nine years. Ten shares of the stock costing $2,500 in 1977 would have grown to forty shares (reflecting a 300 percent stock dividend in 1979) worth $6,100 by mid-1986.

This success story has less to do with technical leadership —Sperry Rand, now merged into Burroughs Corp. to form Unisys, beat IBM to the market with a large-scale computer —than with recognizing the product potential and creatively moving to capitalize on it. The leadership of Thomas J. Watson, the development of an outstanding marketing organization, and access to adequate financing were also major factors in the company's growth.

Why Some Companies Succeed

A study of IBM's modus operandi reveals a number of factors that contributed to the company's success. Early on, it established a strong position in the computer industry; by 1964, it had sold 75 percent of all computers in place at the time. It worked hard to build a solid customer relationship, providing programs, hardware, peripheral equipment, installation, and services. It nurtured strong customer loyalty, effectively disarming the competition. It built up a large base of future revenue by renting as well as selling its equipment. It worked to make its customers "dependent" by generating a steady stream of new products and supplies to operate, expand, and upgrade the old.

Xerox and Polaroid are other examples of companies that were able to capitalize on the "captive customer" situation by coming up with new products that consumed company-produced supplies. American Telephone & Telegraph was another past master of this technique, supplying first the apparatus required to use the service, then providing the service, and finally creating broader and broader applications of that service. Had it been less successful in its integration, it might not have been broken into its component parts by the government. The lesson, then, is that you must not only find companies capable of producing goods and services for the next new era, but you must find companies with the imagination to provide for and capture the markets for those goods and services.

Watch for Trends

In any search for future profit opportunities, then, you must give thought to the changing trends of our society. For example, there has been a shift toward later marriage, fewer babies, and single-parent households. The increase in demand for energy-saving devices and supplies has created new areas of opportunity. People are working fewer hours. Women are working away from their homes. Which are the industries that will benefit from these shifts and which will be hurt?

A classic example of a company that felt the pinch of later marriages and the declining birth rate is Gerber: "Babies are our business—our only business." In a series of defensive maneuvers, Gerber branched out into other areas—life insurance, day-care centers, and a broad line of products for infants—then quietly retired its long-standing slogan. Conversely, delayed marriages and more single-parent homes have tended to increase the demand for apartments, furnishings, and other consumer products. The upsurge of women in the work force has had a noticeable impact on the sale of convenience foods and on the growth of the fast-food business. As a result, old-line food packagers have been among the most sought-after merger candidates in recent years.

Another demographic change that is being felt in sundry

ways is the increase in the number of people among us aged sixty and older. The Sunbelt states were the first to feel the effects of the older people in their midst. The population explosion in these areas has far outpaced growth in the more northern states as retirees flocked there to escape the cold. Longer life spans have benefited the life insurance companies, the leisure industry, travel-related companies, and consumer products firms. Increasing at an even greater rate is the population segment made up of persons eighty and older. This trend benefits the broad spectrum of health care services and extended-care nursing facility companies.

Profits in "Cleaning Up"

While there has been a "graying of America," there has also been a "greening of America." We as a nation have become aware of the finiteness of our environment and are bent on preserving it. Hazardous-waste cleanup has provided profits for some companies while creating expenses for those who have been judged guilty of fouling the environment. Investors who assess these situations accurately stand to do well with their portfolios.

Consumerism will have its effects on business and investments. Some companies will falter as the market for their products dries up. Other companies will be formed to provide newly demanded consumer services. Some companies will meet the new challenges with creativity and will wax; others will ignore the trends and will wane.

We've already alluded to the prospects for health services in an aging society. But the area should be singled out for some special consideration, for it represents a field containing a potentially bountiful harvest for the canny investor. Not only must products and services be made available for a population that is growing older, but they must be provided for one that is bent on remaining as young, fit, and healthy as possible for as long as possible. Ethical drugs, hospital supplies, medical appliances, physical fitness equipment, and electronic diagnostic equipment all provide potential avenues for profitable investment.

Cashing In on "Getting There"

Vancouver's Expo '86 had as its theme transportation and communication. Which of its futuristic visions of people movers and word transmitters will actually come to pass? Will a space shuttle become a reality? Will picturephones replace telephones? Will electronic equipment make commuting to an office a thing of the past? Will a computer do most of your driving for you? These are concepts that have gone to the drawing board and beyond. Picturephones are available, at a price. Computer chips control an increasing number of the functions on cars and allow a growing number of persons to work from home.

These areas could provide major investment opportunities as demand for such products increases. Someone has to supply the chips, the phones, the electronics, the computers, and the training for the users. Someone has to provide the capital and, in turn, reap the rewards for undertaking the risks.

Making Money on Money

Financial services are emerging as an area of increasing investment opportunity. Many of the traditional barriers between banks, insurers, and brokers have been lowered by deregulation. Cross-industry mergers have created one-stop financial supermarkets. It's now possible for consumers to buy stocks, insurance, and socks at one retail outlet.

Technological changes may have a greater impact on the future of the financial services industry than on most other groups. Automated teller machines (ATMs) have gained widespread consumer acceptance and have replaced their human counterparts in many locations. Electronic funds transfer (EFT) and direct deposit have also wrought significant changes in the banking industry. So-called debit cards, powered by semiconductor brains (implanted chips), may eventually replace cash, checks, and credit cards. And home computers may make it possible to perform any type of financial transaction from the comfort of your own living room.

How can you profit from these trends? The companies that will benefit most will have to be more forward-looking and innovative than their competitors. But they will need substantial capital support. Individuals willing to invest in the industry's future delivery systems should be well rewarded over time.

Some Guidelines

So now we get down to the real nub of this chapter. How do you break out of the rush of today's events so you can cash in on tomorrow's investment winners? From the foregoing brew, let's distill a few guidelines.

First, look for companies in the process of developing new products or new ways of doing things. Look for companies on the ascendancy in their fields, not those that have matured or passed into a declining phase or those entrenched in a mature industry.

Second, look for companies that have the managerial expertise necessary to capitalize on their innovations.

Third, examine the basic trends in our society. Look for the real changes in direction that are already occurring and that are likely to occur in the years ahead, based on what is happening today. Then, look for companies already positioned to take advantage of the trend.

Fourth, don't confuse a fad with a trend. We've already cautioned you to exercise diligence in distinguishing between a substantive change in cultural or economic direction and a passing fancy. Sometimes it's not easy to tell the difference, particularly at the outset. Once you have discerned a bona fide trend and invested accordingly, keep an eye on your investment to be sure that conditions do not develop to jeopardize the trend or the position you have staked out in it.

CHAPTER 27

Where to Get Advice

"WHERE DO I get investment advice?" That's a difficult question to answer, because the answer depends on what kind of advice you expect to get. If you want panaceas, secrets to surefire success, or that one key that unlocks all the mysteries of the stock market, you'll find them aplenty; they litter the road of broken investment dreams. You need but ask— friends, relatives, passersby in the street—and you will be deluged with all manner of theories, explanations, and "wisdom." It is no wonder that a new investor so often finds himself reeling under the barrage of information and opinion available. The intelligent and experienced investor who has delineated his investment objectives stands a better chance of obtaining usable advice. He has been around long enough to know the superficial, appreciate the possible, and recognize the charlatan. For the novice, this chapter attempts to highlight the major categories and sources of investment information.

Some investment sources present facts only and leave interpretation to the reader, while others provide an interpretation of the facts and specific advice. Most investors, without substantial time to devote to the formulation of their portfolios, prefer the latter. No matter what sources you choose, the most important prerequisite for successful investing is the formulation of a specific goal. The retiree, dependent on his dividends for "eating money," should think twice before acting on a speculative recommendation, no matter how reliable he perceives the source to be.

Your Broker and the Bank

Your broker can provide good information if he has a large research department to back him up. Many sizable houses publish market letters as well as company and industry studies for which they charge. Other investment houses put out literature that is available to clients free of charge. Some will analyze a portfolio and make suggestions in line with a given investment objective. An important caveat to keep in mind, however, is that brokers survive on commissions and thus are under pressure to advise change. If you are not an aggressive trader, watch out for excessive switch recommendations.

Many banks also offer a number of services. The simplest is a custodial arrangement under which the bank maintains physical care of the securities, keeps accounting records, and executes transactions at the owner's request. No advice is included. Some banks offer more extensive services, ranging from periodic portfolio reviews and recommendations to continuous supervision. Most banks tend to be conservative in their recommendations and thus are not really appropriate advisors for the aggressive speculator.

Standard & Poor's and Moody's

Two financial publishing firms, Standard & Poor's and Moody's, are in a class by themselves. Both offer a wide range of services. Standard & Poor's provides more than a dozen—from *Corporation Records*, which includes factual descriptions of all important corporate and many public issuers of both listed and unlisted securities, to *The Outlook*, a weekly advisory letter. Especially valuable for the individual investor are S&P's monthly paperback publications, *Stock Guide* and *Bond Guide*. The *Stock Guide* shows earnings, dividends, yield, capital structure, working capital, and market price data. The *Bond Guide* gives ratings, interest dates, form (bearer or registered), redemption provisions, earnings, prices, and both current yields and yields to maturity. Occasionally brokers and dealers distribute these to active customers free of charge.

Moody's publishes large reference volumes on listed industrials, over-the-counter industrials, utilities, Governments, and financial companies. It also offers numerous other services, including a weekly *Bond Survey*. Moody's and S&P are the major rating agencies for corporate and municipal debt offerings. Most of their publications are relatively expensive but are available in major university and public libraries.

Advisory Services

Advisory services vary widely in their scope and slant. Some rely on technical factors and try to gauge the likely short-term movement of the market as a whole and of individual securities. Others recommend fundamentally strong companies with only secondary emphasis on the near-term outlook for the market. Some seem consistently to presage doom; others tend to look mainly on the bright side.

The *Value Line Investment Survey,* one of the larger and better-known advisory services, covers more than 1,700 stocks. Each stock in the list is reviewed comprehensively every three months, and each week the service covers four to six industries, on a rotating basis. Stocks are rated for safety and expected performance. The service each week also covers the outlook for the stock market and the economy, and highlights certain individual stocks. Sometimes other special studies are included. The service is relatively expensive but is available in many libraries.

The weekly *United & Babson Investment Report* is among the oldest and largest of these services. It presents a concise summary of economic and business news, and includes coverage of commodity price trends, as well as industry or topical studies and specific buying and selling advice on individual securities. In the first issue of each month, it publishes a supervised list of common stocks, divided by investment objective. It is generally upbeat and steers its clients toward quality and investment for the longer term.

Standard & Poor's *Outlook*, which we mentioned earlier, is another of the larger and better-known investment letters. It plots an investment course similar to United's, though its content is more fully devoted to securities investment rather than including broader commentary on economic, business, and financial affairs, as does United's.

Countless other advisory publications are available, many of which are general in nature, such as *Indicator Digest* and *The Predictor & Tillman Survey*. Still others embrace particular investment philosophies. These include *Dow Letters* and *Dow Theory Forecasts*, which use the Dow Theory as their springboards; *The Dines Letter*, which follows gold and gold-related securities; *The Speculator*, which advises on stocks selling for $20 or less; and the *Professional Tape Reader* and *Zweig Forecast*, which recommend stocks on the basis of strict technical models. Another technically based newsletter, which covers more general information than the latter two, is *The Astute Investor*, written by Robert Nurock.

Many of the services on the market are one-person, one-typewriter affairs. The Investment Advisors Act of 1940 requires all such advisors to be registered with the Securities and Exchange Commission. However, the registration is designed to guard against fraud; it does not indicate any particular expertise or guarantee favorable results.

We should mention here another type of service available: chart books. Although their publishers generally do not provide specific investment advisories, their products can be useful in showing you past performances and price, earnings, and dividend trends of various stocks. Such charts are particularly helpful in discerning technical market trends. Securities Research Company, a division of Babson-United Investment Advisors, Inc., publishes monthly security charts and quarterly *Cycli-Graphs*, as well as quarterly wall charts of market averages and an annually issued thirty-five-year stock chart book. Daily Graphs, R.W. Mansfield Company, and Trendline provide similar services.

Before leaving the realm of advisory services, some mention of the sources of information available to the mutual fund investor is in order. *The Wiesenberger Investment Company Service,* published by Warren, Gorham & Lamont, provides an annual compendium of information about mutual funds and investment companies, and an explanation of their functions and various uses to the investor. Data are included on the background, management policy, and salient features of all leading companies, including income and dividend records, price ranges, and comparative operating details. A similar but newer publication is the *Mutual Fund Source Book.* The quarterly softcover is put out by Morningstar, Inc. Again, these relatively expensive publications are available in many libraries.

A valuable statistical source on the fund industry as a whole is the *Mutual Fund Fact Book*, published and updated annually by the Investment Company Institute, 1775 K Street, N.W. Washington, D.C. 20006.

The *United Mutual Fund Selector* provides a wealth of information on mutual funds. Published twice monthly by the Babson-United Investment Advisors, Inc., the *Selector* in one issue provides comparative tables that track the recent and longer-term performance of more than 700 funds. The other issue includes a supervised list of mutual funds and provides specific recommendations in line with different objectives. Every issue contains general features about the industry, detailed discussions of certain funds, and answers to investors' questions.

The Financial Press

The financial press is brimming with valuable information. Most daily newspapers provide some sort of financial section, which generally includes price quotations as well as business highlights and sometimes commentary. *The Wall Street Journal,* the only national daily business and financial newspaper, provides much more extensive coverage of financial news, including, in addition to comprehensive price quotations, news about companies, industries, commodities, financial affairs, taxes, labor, and public policy. *The New York Times* publishes a comprehensive business and financial section daily. *The Journal of Commerce* is an excellent resource for the commodity investor and also includes extensive business news, with emphasis on national and international economic developments.

The Media General Financial Weekly is a compendium of financial facts and statistics providing coverage of stocks, bonds, mutual funds, options, and commodities. Also included is a digest of major money-market instruments. The stock and bond tables are especially helpful. The stock tables provide at-a-glance data on individual companies' price trends relative to the market, five-year compound-earnings-per-share growth, profit margins, price relative to industry, dividend data, the composition of shareholders, and pertinent data on the company's financial position. The bond tables provide S&P ratings, conversion terms (if applicable), current yields, and yields to maturity.

Barron's, published weekly by Dow Jones & Company, provides a good wrap-up of the preceding week's economic and stock market happenings. It includes an extensive section on stock and bond quotations, economic and market statistics, timely articles on various companies and current economic events, and a section on commodities. Editorial commentary is liberally interjected.

Magazines

Numerous magazines available on the newsstand or by subscription can provide up-to-date information. *Business Week, Financial World, Forbes, Fortune, Money Magazine,* and *U.S. News & World Report* are examples. *Financial World* and *Forbes* are more heavily weighted with investment news; *Money Magazine* is oriented toward financial planning for individuals; the others deal more with general business topics. For investors with a strong interest in a particular industry, there are trade journals such as *Supermarket News* and *Women's Wear Daily*.

Government Publications

U.S. government publications can yield clues to economic trends that might affect the investment climate. *Business Conditions Digest* provides data on the cyclical indicators— leading, coincident, and lagging (see Chapter 19). *Economic Indicators* is a monthly compendium of statistics on gross national product, employment, production, prices, money and credit, federal finance, and international trade. The *Survey of Current Business* is another comprehensive statistical source that includes detailed commentary on various economic subjects. The Federal Reserve Bank of St. Louis publishes *Monetary Trends* and other excellent bulletins on the money supply and interest rates, available at no cost. For labor and employment trends and developments, there is the *Monthly Labor Review,* published by the Department of Labor. Many of these publications may be available at your local library.

Investment Counselors

For the well-to-do investor who wishes to leave the research and decision-making to someone else, there are investment-counseling firms. Their annual fees, as a rule of thumb, will run at least 0.5 percent of the value of the portfolio being managed. Most firms handle large accounts only, those valued at $300,000 and up. They provide in-depth investment advice, watch clients' portfolios continually, and notify them when changes appear warranted. Major companies in this category include David L. Babson; Loomis Sayles; Scudder, Stevens & Clark; and United Investment Counsel, a subsidiary of Babson-United Investment Advisors, Inc.

A number of small investment-counseling companies do handle accounts of less than $100,000, but they generally either pool funds or restrict portfolios to stocks on a master list. Thus, technically, their counsel is not individualized. The annual fee is usually 0.5 percent on the managed assets, with a minimum in the vicinity of $100 to $200. Danforth Associates is an example of a company providing such services.

There you have it: a sampling of the wide spectrum of investment advice and information available to you. With experience, you'll be able to tell how much digging you want to do on your own, how much you're willing to pay others to dig for you, and whose advice best suits your own investment needs and philosophy.

PART IV

Mastering the Strategies and Tactics

CHAPTER 28

Five Rules for Investors

UNTIL NOW, THE focus of this book has largely been on the definition and analysis of various savings and investment vehicles. Now it's time to start applying this body of information to the construction and maintenance of your own program. As with any other undertaking, you will be better served if you set down some rules ahead of time.

We have five that tend to crystallize the investment philosophy we at Babson-United Investment Advisors have pursued for more than half a century. We believe they will serve you well, too. After reading our earlier chapters, you should find none of them surprising.

The thoughts have all been expressed at least once before in this book; some will be expressed again. By bringing them together here, we provide a yardstick against which you can measure future investment decisions. Read them carefully. Commit them to memory. Recite them whenever you have an investment decision to make. If you are a compulsive investor, tempted by every hot tip that comes your way, tattoo them to the back of your hand. Ignore them at your peril.

The five: Set your goals. Buy the best-known companies. Invest for the long term. Avoid fads. Diversify.

Set Your Goals

RULE NUMBER ONE. Set your goals. Decide what you want your savings to do for you. You wouldn't buy long underwear for a trip to the Bahamas, nor would you travel by way of the Yukon when you finally set out. But you'd be surprised at how many investors pack their portfolios with inappropriate garb and travel needlessly circuitous routes to their investment destinations.

Before you plunge into your savings and investment program, sit down and list your objectives on paper. College education for the children? How long before they'll need it? How much will they need? Retirement fund for yourself? When will you want to start drawing on it? Next year? Three years from now? Trip to Europe? New car? Emergency fund?

The answers to these questions are important, for they will determine whether you should invest for capital growth or current income. Most of the time you will have to accept one or the other. Rare indeed is the investment that offers a generous helping of both. The answers, too, will tell you how much risk you can reasonably assume—and which type of risk.

Suppose you're a mid-career salaried individual who can divert regular amounts of income from your family's spending stream to savings. Your aim is a retirement fund to supplement your company's pension. As with most of us who labor in the corporate vineyard, the Internal Revenue Service enjoys a generous share of your income. Since you're already earning enough so you can set some aside, and since your objective is relatively long term, there's no reason for you to shoot for investment income now. It would only have to be shared with Uncle Sam. What you want is capital growth and little or no current income.

Furthermore, since you have a secure job and considerable time before retirement, you're in a position to assume some market risk in the chance of making better-than-average capital gains. That's because if you should lose, you would still be in a good position to replace those lost dollars from regular earned income. So you concentrate your investment efforts on building a portfolio of growth stocks.

Now, suppose you have a maiden aunt in her middle years whose pay just barely covers her needs. Let's further suppose that she inherits or otherwise comes into a $25,000 windfall. Not only is this a sum larger than anything she had ever known before, but it is a bit of fortune that is not likely to be repeated.

What should she do? Her first objective would be to preserve that capital, since her ability to replace it is negligible. So she chooses investments that will provide the highest posssible current return and the greatest possible "safety." Savings certificates and bonds, both corporate and government, spring immediately to mind. But there are common stocks that fit the description, too, that would provide some chance for dividend growth and capital appreciation at minimal risk to her nest egg, all the while giving her a substantial current return, which, of course, she immediately reinvests.

Your uncle the doctor, his children through college, his retirement approaching, would take still another tack. He would have to reevaluate his investment program, gradually shifting it from the growth orientation of earlier years to an income orientation to provide his "eating money" in retirement. Again, because his working years are drawing to a close, he would have to concentrate on preservation of principal, since his opportunities for replacing it are fast closing.

The doctor's case illustrates another point you should keep firmly in mind. Your investment goals can—and usually do —change as you proceed through life. Therefore, you should subject your program to periodic review to see that its objectives remain consistent with your needs.

Buy the Best-Known Companies

RULE NUMBER TWO. Buy the best-known companies. Stick with the tried and true. There is far too much risk in trying to unearth tomorrow's Xeroxes. The mortality rate of these ventures is staggering, and you'd do best to leave this kind of financial wildcatting to someone else.

There are plenty of firmly established companies around that offer attractive investment possibilities. Abbott Laboratories, IBM, and PepsiCo still can add zip to a portfolio despite their maturity.

There are promising lesser lights like Genuine Parts, SYSCO, and Wallace Computer Services with good survival records despite the vagaries of the economy and the stock market. They have been in business for a long time, their products are well known, their markets firmly established, and their financial condition solid. They're not necessarily blue chips. Some, in fact, have a clearly speculative tint. But because they have demonstrated an ability to survive, they should not be overlooked.

Equally important, their stock prices are reasonable in relation to such fundamentals as assets, earnings, and dividends. In short, there are plenty of attractive, reasonable investments that offer the promise of real and substantial profit someday for the investor who can take the risk.

Invest for the Long Term

RULE NUMBER THREE. Invest for the long term. Patience with the stock market is more than a virtue. It is a must. Things rarely work out overnight on Wall Street, and when they do, almost everyone is taken by surprise. So, when you buy a good stock, buy it for the long pull. Consider yourself a part owner of the business. You have become one because you believe the business is fundamentally sound and the prospects excellent. Therefore, you don't have to watch the daily gyrations in your stock's price with fear in your throat when it is down and exultation in your soul when it is up.

Take Anheuser-Busch, for example. The investors who bought this stock in late 1976 probably were motivated by the company's still-premier position in the brewing industry and, perhaps more important, the fact that the shares were selling at only about a third of their old high. However, earnings had been battered earlier that year by a strike, and

Philip Morris's Miller Brewing was becoming an ever more formidable competitor. The value was there, to be sure, but so were the risks.

Over the next three years, the stock essentially went nowhere despite a surge in earnings and further gains in industry market share. Those investors not liberally endowed with patience undoubtedly bailed out. But in early 1980 the stock began to move. And move it did, more than tripling by 1983. Following a ten-month breather during which the shares lost less than ten points, the stock took off, tripling again by early 1987. Investors were impressed by Anheuser's ability to increase its market share, despite a no-growth period for the beer industry generally.

The key was patience. Those who waited prospered. Those who wanted instant rewards lost out, as they usually do in the stock market.

It might help you to develop patience if you think of your commitment in a stock as you do your investment in your own home. You bought your house to fill a specific need after applying certain qualifying tests. As long as your living requirements remain the same and nothing seriously wrong develops with the structure or the neighborhood, you stay put.

You don't regularly check with your real estate broker for the current value of your home, and you shouldn't need to be constantly concerned with the day-to-day price fluctuations of your stocks. Even if you read in the real estate section of the Sunday newspaper that "Home Values Slump as Mortgage Money Tightens," you don't rush out and sell. You realize any such slippage in price will be temporary. Think long term with your stocks just as you do with your home.

Avoid Fads

RULE NUMBER FOUR. Avoid fads. Stay clear of the crowd, even when it looks right. This is one of the most important rules of successful investing—and one of the most frequently violated, to the ultimate chagrin of legions of hapless violators. If everyone seems to be rushing out to buy stocks in a particular industry group or company, let them. But don't do it yourself. If a particular stock seems to be the darling of the day, don't compete. Let the others have it.

Fads come and go on Wall Street just as they do on Madison Avenue or Seventh Avenue or Main Street U.S.A. One big trouble with fads is that it's sometimes hard to tell when something is just that—a passing fancy—or if it's truly a technological or sociological breakthrough and represents something that will become a fixture in our everyday lives. The distinction is particularly difficult to make in the early stages, when the temptation is greatest to "get in on the ground floor."

Who could have foretold, for instance, back in the 1950s that a photocopying device being toyed with by a little firm known as the Haloid Company out of Rochester, New York, would change the lives of nearly all of us and in the process firmly affix the word "Xerox" in our lexicon? The spectacular success of that xerographic photocopier made fortunes for its supporters, who, corporate legend tells us, included cabdrivers and bartenders.

Or who could have known that an instant-picture camera developed by Dr. Edward Land would catapult a manufacturer of polarized-lens sunglasses to the forefront of American industry in the days following World War II? Investors in Polaroid in those days were surely involved in a gamble. They won, and some of them won big.

But for each of those two legendary corporate successes, how many "hot ideas" have failed, leaving their gamble-oriented investors holding the bag? More to the point, how can you—or anyone—separate the Xeroxes and Polaroids from the failures? The plain fact is that few can. And since your chances of riding a loser are tens or hundreds of times greater than climbing aboard a winner, you'd do best to let the out-and-out gamblers play those odds. There will be ample opportunity for reaping substantial returns from the winners once they have become established, as thousands of investors in Xerox and Polaroid have learned over the years.

Consider those who perceived a great new day as digital timepieces began to replace the world's conventional wristwatches, and invested accordingly. The watches caught on all right, but electronics companies thronged to that market-place in such numbers that many fell helplessly aside and were trampled in the stampede, their backers with them. The industry is more stable now that the shakeout has occurred, and investors have a better chance to see which ones will provide the best long-term prospects. The same thing happened with pocket calculators, double knits, and citizens' band radios. It will happen again with something else. And again. And again.

It sometimes happens with the stock of an established company. A new product or new process is announced, and before its true market worth has been established, eager investors are beating a path to their brokers' offices to grab a piece of the action. Remember when Bausch & Lomb announced the soft plastic contact lens back in the early 1970s? The stock shot up in anticipation of a surge in sales. Complications set in and the "surge" was disappointing. The stock settled back into its previous mundane pattern.

When such a situation develops, the stock's price eventually rises above its intrinsic value and the "greater fool" theory takes over. Those who play that game purchase shares in the hope of eventually selling at a profit to a "greater fool." Pity the "greatest fool"—the one finally left holding the bag. That is not a risk with which you need burden yourself.

Diversify

RULE NUMBER FIVE. Diversify. Spread your risks, for few "sure things" prove to be such. Someone once said that the way to make money is to put all your eggs in one basket and then watch that basket like a hawk. That's fine, as long as the stock you choose soars; as it does, so will your fortunes. The corollary, of course, is that if the stock plummets instead, your fortunes vanish. Even if you know a company intimately and its industry inside out, you still stand to lose, for luck is very much a part of the game. Too many things can happen that no amount of research will foretell.

Take microcomputer maker Commodore International. Its prospects in the much touted home computer field appeared bright in the late 1970s. Investors were eager to share in the bonanza, and Commodore looked like a good choice. Rapidly rising earnings propelled the shares from one high to the next, with the stock splitting five times in four years. A softer-than-predicted demand for computers for home use and competition from the proliferation of small manufacturers took some of the euphoria from the home computer market during 1983, and Commodore shares began their decline. From a June 1983 high of 60, the stock had dropped to about 6 three years later.

One young acquaintance of ours, in his enthusiasm for his own PC, put his entire $25,000 inheritance in Commodore early in 1983. The stock was then trading at 42; when it hit 60 he was elated. He had made $10,000 in just a few short months. When the stock started to drop, in spite of continuing earnings increases, he remained confident. The 1984 December quarter report released early in 1985 showed a sharp earnings decline; then our friend sold. The stock was selling at 13, and his inheritance was worth less than $8,000.

The lesson is clear. Even if you have only a little to invest, spread it around. Diversify your holdings to reduce the overall risk. If one element in your portfolio goes sour, the others should hold it up.

There are several ways to do it. One, of course, is to buy securities of a variety of companies. By choosing well-diversified firms you can spread the risk even further. Or you can buy mutual funds. Even here, you should diversify, buying several different funds.

Besides diversifying as to companies and funds, be sure to spread your investments over a number of different industries as well. Look for promising industries, though; don't buy into a dead-end field just for the sake of diversifying.

Your diversification will likely restrict your portfolio to an "average" or even "mediocre" performance. You will miss the thrill of instant riches. So also will you avoid sudden financial disaster. But you will sleep better at night.

So there you have the five key rules for successful investing. Here they are again, all in one place for your quick review:

1. Set your goals.
2. Buy the best-known companies.
3. Invest for the long term.
4. Avoid fads.
5. Diversify.

CHAPTER 29

How the Stock Market Works

ONCE YOU HAVE set your investment objectives and promised yourself to stick with the best companies, be patient, avoid fads, and diversify your holdings—that is, to abide by the five rules outlined in the preceding chapter—you're ready to start polishing your investment techniques. An understanding of the basic workings of the stock market and of your buying and selling choices within that framework is essential to your mastery of successful investing.

To provide that background, we shall discuss briefly in this chapter the various securities markets, the major stock exchanges, the types of orders you can use in executing your buys and sells, and, finally, some important considerations regarding the timing of your buying and selling.

The Role of Investment Bankers

When a company originally offers new securities for sale, it does so through the *primary markets*. In recent times, the primary market has been largely a bond market, with relatively few new common stock issues being offered. Securities are sold in the primary market either through private placement or public offering. In either case, the details are usually handled by investment bankers. Private placement is a choice made by the company for a variety of reasons; privacy, economy, and circumvention of certain registration requirements are the most common. Since there is no public participation in private placement, nothing more need be said about it here.

On public issues, investment bankers use three basic methods of bringing the securities to market: standby agreements, agency marketings, and purchasing-distributions. *Standby agreements* are usually employed when companies seek to sell more stock or bonds to their own security holders by way of a "rights" offering. Since most of the rights will be exercised, there is little market risk to the investment banker handling the details. But since the company wants all of the capital from the issue as soon as possible, it arranges with the banker to buy up any rights that are not exercised. The investment banker, in turn, will market those securities to the public.

The *agency marketing* procedure is used when the investment bankers perceive some difficulty in marketing an issue, either because of its size or because of its doubtful reception by the public. Or it might be employed because the issuing company is confident that the issue will sell and there is little marketing risk involved. In this instance, the investment banker may take an issue on a "best effort" basis. The bank will receive a commission on that portion of the issue which it makes its "best effort" to sell, but it does not actually buy the issue itself for resale. In effect, the investment banker merely serves as the "broker," seeking to match buyer and seller.

However, most of an investment banker's business comes from *purchasing-distribution,* where the banker buys the entire issue outright and resells it to the public. The banker then assumes the marketing risk associated with the underwriting. Sometimes a syndicate of underwriters is formed so that no single firm assumes full risk on the issue.

When you as an individual investor buy original-issue securities, you pay no commission on them; the fee has already been worked into the selling price. However, you are more likely to be buying "previously owned" securities than new issues. In that case, and likewise when you yourself sell any securities you hold, you'll be dealing in the *secondary market*. Trading in existing securities occurs in the organized exchanges and the over-the-counter markets.

The organized exchanges are actually auctions where traders and investors negotiate by setting "asking" prices and making "bids" on thousands of different securities. The New York Stock Exchange (NYSE) is by far the most important of these trading centers. It is followed in order of importance by the American Stock Exchange (AMEX), the Midwest Stock Exchange (MW), the Pacific Stock Exchange (P), and the Philadelphia Stock Exchange (Ph).

The New York Stock Exchange

The New York Stock Exchange was formally established in 1792, though it was not known by its present name until 1863. Often called the "Big Board," it is a corporation with more than 1,200 members, each of whom has purchased a "seat" (membership) on the exchange. This membership gives its holder the privilege of trading on the floor of the exchange; no one else is allowed to do so. Members of the NYSE include member-firm corporations, specialists, floor brokers, and registered traders. Each type of membership is designed and regulated to assure the continuation of an efficient, liquid market.

Member firms are the various brokerage houses that do commission business with the public. Their seats are usually filled by general partners or holders of substantial amounts of common stock in the firm.

Specialists are the exchange members responsible for maintaining orderly markets in the stocks of specific companies. Each of the more than 2,300 stocks listed on the NYSE is assigned to a specialist. Each specialist rides herd on a number of these assigned stocks, making sure to avoid excessive spread in the bid and asked prices in the auctioning process. In maintaining an orderly market for their assigned securities, the specialists may buy and sell for their own accounts. Their operations are governed by the statutes and regulations of the Securities and Exchange Commission (SEC) and the exchange itself. In addition, specialists execute orders which other exchange members have left with them. In this capacity, they are acting as brokers or agents.

Floor brokers help commission brokers when they become swamped with orders to execute. In this way, they protect the customer against the possibility of missing a market because of an overburdened stockbroker.

Registered traders buy and sell stocks strictly for their own personal accounts. The activities of these traders are monitored by the exchange, which requires that their transactions contribute to the market's liquidity.

In order for a stock to be listed on the New York Stock Exchange, certain criteria must be met and maintained. Among them: a demonstrated earning power of at least $2.5 million annually before taxes for the most recent year and $2 million for each of the two preceding years under competitive conditions; net tangible assets of $16 million, though greater emphasis will be placed upon the aggregate market value of the common stock; at least $18 million in market value of publicly held common stock; at least 1.1 million common shares publicly held; at least two thousand holders of 100 shares or more.

The listing agreement between the New York Stock Exchange and the company is designed to assure timely disclosure to the public of earnings statements, dividend notices, and other data which can affect security values and hence investment decisions. A company is not guaranteed continued listing on the exchange.

AMEX and the Regional Exchanges

The American Stock Exchange had its start in the 1850s, though it was not known by its present name until 1953. Before that, its name was the New York Curb Exchange, reflecting its earlier history, when trading was done outdoors at a number of New York City street corners. The Curb Market moved indoors at Trinity Place in 1921.

The AMEX follows procedures much like those of the New

York Stock Exchange, although listing requirements are not as stringent as those of the NYSE. As a general statement, it can be said that companies traded on the AMEX are less mature and seasoned than those on the NYSE.

The principal regional exchanges are the Midwest Stock Exchange, the Pacific Stock Exchange, and the Philadelphia Stock Exchange. Altogether, there are eight domestic stock exchanges outside of New York City. In addition to the three already noted, there are exchanges in Boston, Cincinnati, Chicago (Board of Options Exchange), Salt Lake City (Intermountain), and Spokane. Besides these, five Canadian exchanges actively trade mining, uranium, and oil stocks, as well as industrial issues.

In addition to these organized exchanges, there is a huge and active over-the-counter market. It consists of various brokers and dealers who make markets in securities not listed on the exchanges. In recent times a growing number of securities listed on the organized exchanges have been trading in the over-the-counter markets as well. This development has come to be known as the "Third Market." When securities trade in the over-the-counter market, they are bought and sold on a negotiated price basis rather than in an auction market.

A Central Securities Market

Since the early 1970s, the Securities and Exchange Commission has been moving toward the formation of a central marketplace. In 1975, Congress, by amending the securities laws, provided the SEC with the power to take the necessary steps to implement such a market. Congress's objective in ordering the changes was to increase competition among the NYSE, regional exchanges, and over-the-counter traders and to ensure that investors get the best possible price for their transactions.

In 1978 a pilot program was initiated. This Intermarket Trading System (ITS) linked the New York and Philadelphia Stock Exchanges for trading eleven issues. More securities were added to the ITS roster, and other exchanges joined the electronic network. In 1982, the National Association of Security Dealers (NASD) automated dealer trader system (CAES) was linked to ITS. There are now eight exchanges on the system trading more than 1,100 issues.

Types of Orders

Investors have at their disposal several types of orders they can use in executing their purchases and sales of securities. A full understanding of the uses and advantages of these various orders can help you become a more successful investor.

The most frequently used orders are the market order and the limit order. When you place a *market order,* you are instructing your broker to execute the desired transaction at the prevailing market price. He is obliged to consummate the trade at the most advantageous price to you. This means that in the case of a buy order he seeks the lowest price, while in the case of a sell order he seeks the highest price.

Market orders are particularly valuable in that they are executed rapidly at a price close to the last sale price. This characteristic is particularly desirable in a rising or declining market. In effect, this order protects you against the possibility of missing a market. The obvious disadvantage of a market order is that you cannot be certain of the exact price at which your order will be executed. This factor can be crucial in an erratic market, because you cannot be certain that your order will be executed anywhere near the most recent sale price.

Limit orders are used when you indicate to your broker the price at which you wish the order executed. These orders are placed "away from the market," in that the broker leaves the order with the specialist assigned to the particular stock. The specialist enters your limit order in his books, according to the time he receives it, along with others left with him. If the stock reaches the limit price, the specialist will execute the order according to when it was received. Obviously, some limit orders are never executed. If and when the limit order is executed, the specialist informs your broker, who in turn relays that information to you.

A limit order is useful because you can specify the price "or better" at which you wish the transaction to occur. Issues with limited markets and wide price spreads are the most appropriate candidates for limit orders. Over-the-counter stocks frequently display these characteristics.

The principal disadvantage of a limit order is that you can miss a market completely over a fraction of a point. For instance, an investor buys a cyclical stock such as Ford Motor Company at $100 a share and simultaneously places a limit order to sell at $120. That order might never be executed, although the stock could sell at 119½ or 119¾. On the other hand, the stock could reach the $120 limit price, but there could be insufficient buyers to cover all the limit orders on the books at that price.

A limit on the buy side is always placed at a price below the current market. A sell limit is above the current price. When buying a stock that is moving down, you place the limit in hopes of a better price. If the stock is moving up, you use a market order.

When selling a stock that is declining rapidly, you would sell at the market. But in selling a stock that is rising, a limit order might get you a better price.

Several other types of orders are available, too. Although they are more valuable to those who trade frequently or tend to tinker with their portfolios than to those who choose good stocks and hold them for the long term, you should have some passing acquaintance with them.

Stop orders, or *stop loss orders,* specify a particular price at which a stock should be bought or sold. A buy stop is always above the current market and a sell stop is below. The buy stop—at a price above current market—limits the loss or protects a gain on a short sale. The sell stop—below market—protects a gain or limits a loss on a long position. When the issue reaches the specified price, the stop order automatically becomes a market order and is executed. But, as we said earlier, a market order is executed at the most favorable price near the last sale price, and there is a chance that when execution occurs, there will be a substantial spread between the execution price and the last sale price. A large backlog of stop sell orders can touch off a price break sharp enough for trading to be suspended.

Stop Limit Orders are a hybrid form of stop and limit orders. A specified limit is indicated that the buyer or seller will accept, should the stock reach the stop price. For instance, an investor wishes to sell 100 shares of Ford Motor at 90 stop, limit 89½. In other words, if the price of Ford Motor falls to $90 per share, his stop order becomes a market order to sell. But if the order is not executed by the time the stock reaches $89.50, the limit order takes effect and no transaction occurs.

Day Orders are orders which are only good for one day. Hence, if it has not been executed, the order expires at the end of the day on which it was placed. All market orders, obviously, are day orders. Limit orders are also day orders unless the customer places them as open orders, which is usually the case.

Fill or Kill (FOK) orders are price- as well as time-limited; if they cannot be filled immediately at the set price, they are killed and the current price level of the stock is reported to the buyer for reconsideration.

Open Orders can be placed for a specified period or can remain effective until executed or canceled.

GTC Orders (Good Till Canceled) run indefinitely. However, the NYSE requires that all GTC orders be confirmed with the floor specialist on a semiannual basis. GTC orders pose certain risks, in that an investor could forget that he has them outstanding or they could be executed at a time the investor finds unsatisfactory.

Finally, an investor can place a *discretionary order*. In this case, the broker determines the timing for buying and selling as well as the selections and number of shares to be bought and sold. Under these circumstances, the investor is utilizing a complete discretionary order. This order must be given in writing to the broker and then must be approved by an officer of the broker's firm. A limited discretionary order allows the broker to decide only the price and timing. In using discretionary orders, it is absolutely essential that the investor have an established and trusting relationship with his broker.

Special Timing Situations

There are times when the price of a stock is affected by the impending distribution of a dividend or stock right. Buying or selling at these times requires the consideration of information an investor does not usually have to evaluate. Take *ex-dividend,* a term we discussed in Chapter 5. As we explained, the declaration is the date a company's directors vote on the dividend. The date the checks will be mailed to shareholders is the payment date. The date a shareholder's name must be on the corporation's record books to receive a dividend is the record date. Finally, the ex-dividend date is the date that determines whether the buyer or the seller receives the dividend.

The exchanges and the over-the-counter markets have determined that investors must purchase a stock five business days before the record date to be eligible for the dividend payment. In other words, a purchaser of stock must buy before the stock trades ex-dividend in order to receive the dividend payment. Otherwise, the previous owner will receive the dividend.

When a stock sells ex-dividend, the market price will drop by an amount approximating the dividend. Hence a buyer will pay less for the stock but will not receive the dividend. Once the stock comes out of ex-dividend, the market price will rise to its prior level, other things being equal.

Should the investor buy or sell during ex-dividend trading? As an overall rule, it is best to execute purchases before ex-dividend trading begins. That way, you are entitled to the dividend payment. While the price will decline during ex-dividend trading, it will probably return to its former level shortly after ex-dividend trading stops. An exception is the investor in a high tax bracket. The lower price level of the stock trading ex-dividend is preferable to receiving the dividend, on which a high income tax will have to be paid.

Sales are best executed after ex-dividend trading, since the stock probably will recover the amount it declined during ex-dividend, and in addition you will receive the dividend payment.

When a company decides to issue new securities through a rights offering to its shareholders, it issues *stock rights,* also known as *preemptive rights.* These are short-term options granted to shareholders to purchase new stock issues, generally at reduced price levels. Stock rights are distributed to shareholders in certificate form. The shareholder can either exercise the rights and purchase the stock at the designated price or he can sell the rights in the open market. Rights are issued for common stock and debentures (especially convertibles). You can determine the market value of the rights with this formula:

$$\frac{\text{Stock Market Price–Subscription Price}}{\text{Number of shares required to buy one}}$$
$$\text{share at subscription price} + 1.$$

Hence, a stock selling at $30 per share, with rights to purchase one share at $20 for every three shares owned, means that the rights themselves are worth $2.50 each, or:

$$\frac{\$30 - \$20}{3 + 1} = \frac{10}{4} = \$2.50$$

An investor should exercise rights to purchase stocks solely on the basis of the prospects for the stock generally. The attitude that rights should be exercised because they offer a "bargain" is not valid, since the rights themselves can be sold.

The term *ex-rights* denotes when a stock is selling without rights, the rights having been retained or exercised by the seller. As with dividends, you must own the common stock before it trades "ex-rights" to be entitled to the rights. The price of a stock will also decline by the value of the rights on the day the stock trades ex-rights. Once a stock trades ex-rights, the amount of the decline is determined by the following formula:

$$\frac{\text{Stock Market Price–Subscription Price}}{\text{Number of shares required to buy one}}$$
$$\text{share at subscription price.}$$

Hence, in the situation already described, the stocks decline by a value of $3.33 when ex-rights trading begins. According to the formula:

$$\frac{\$30 - \$20}{3} = \frac{10}{3} = 3\tfrac{1}{3} = \$3.33$$

A stock might sell at depressed levels throughout a rights offering, but normally it will recover after expiration of the rights. This period can be regarded as an attractive purchasing opportunity, providing overall prospects are sound.

Buying Low and "Taking Profits"

Fortuitous investment timing is probably an even more difficult endeavor than deciding what securities to buy. The most naive investor recognizes that the fastest route to stock market success is to "buy low and sell high." But even the most seasoned professional is hard pressed to pick market tops and bottoms with any degree of consistency. Experienced hands don't even try; they leave that game to novices driven more by greed than common sense.

They also know that when the market in general is down, even the bluest of the blue chips will likely go down, too. But because the decline is the result of a general market drop and not due to any fundamental changes in the individual company's stock, experienced investors recognize this as a buying opportunity, and they add to their portfolios accordingly. They know that once the market starts back up, the quality issues will probably bounce back faster than others.

So much for buying "low." What about selling "high"? If it is considered advantageous to put money into a good stock when it is down, then shouldn't it be sold when the market is up? Generally, we would say no. In stock market parlance, this is called "taking profits." Presumably, the reason you want to do so is to allow you to reinvest the proceeds in another stock, which you hope you'll be able to run up into a similar profit. How will you do this? If the market is "high," so then are most quality stocks. Putting the money into anything less would be like gambling. Putting the money into the bank while you wait for the market to go down again into a "buying range" would foreclose the opportunity for further capital gains should the market continue to rise. Not only that, in your profit taking you would incur a capital gains tax liability, thus eroding the real size of the gain.

If you want to sell a stock, do so because you question its long-term prospects, not simply because you have a profit. Or because you have an overconcentration in a certain area and wish to diversify your holdings. Or because you have some capital losses against which you can offset these gains and thus upgrade your portfolio.

Dollar Cost Averaging

You don't have to wait for the market to hit its low before adding to your investments. There is an investment strategy that will give you good results over a long period of time. It is called dollar cost averaging and it is a simple technique that sidesteps altogether the issue of market timing. All it requires is that at regular intervals you make investments of a constant dollar amount in a stock or a variety of stocks that have generally favorable long-term prospects. Your dollars purchase fewer shares when the market is up, but they buy more when it is down. Because the market is fluctuating a certain amount even during a period of relatively flat price movement, this technique can bring a profit. For instance, if you had put $1,000 each into shares of Abbott Labs and General Cinema in January of every year from 1975 to 1986, your equity position would have been about $136,486 ahead after making your 1986 investment. You'd have had dividends to reinvest on top of that, of course.

ABBOTT LABORATORIES

	Amount	Price (Adjusted)	No. Shares Bought
January 1975	$ 1,000	3	333.33
January 1976	1,000	6	166.67
January 1977	1,000	6	166.67
January 1978	1,000	7	142.86
January 1979	1,000	9	111.11
January 1980	1,000	10	100.00
January 1981	1,000	14	71.43
January 1982	1,000	14	71.43
January 1983	1,000	19	52.63
January 1984	1,000	22	45.45
January 1985	1,000	21	47.62
January 1986	1,000	33	30.30
	$12,000		1,339.50

1,339.50 shares times 33 (1/2/86 price) = $44,203

GENERAL CINEMA

	Amount	Price (Adjusted)	No. Shares Bought
January 1975	$ 1,000	1	1,000.00
January 1976	1,000	2	500.00
January 1977	1,000	3	333.33
January 1978	1,000	3½	285.70
January 1979	1,000	4	250.00
January 1980	1,000	6	166.67
January 1981	1,000	6½	153.85
January 1982	1,000	9	111.11
January 1983	1,000	14	71.43
January 1984	1,000	22	45.45
January 1985	1,000	26	38.46
January 1986	1,000	39	25.64
	$12,000		2,981.62

2,981.62 shares times 39 (1/2/86 price) = $116,283

In Conclusion

Proper timing of your buys and sells can get to be a complicated matter if you let yourself become preoccupied with it. Obviously, you should give it some thought as you adjust your portfolio, but in general you should place greater emphasis on sound values. When you do that, it is almost impossible to lose over the long term. Good stocks go down with everything else in bear markets, but they tend to bounce back faster. We don't believe you will profit in the long run by jumping from stocks to cash and back to stocks again with the ups and downs of the market. The experience of mutual funds and major banking trust departments confirms the assertion that investors with the most money and experience tend to remain fully invested in the best stocks most of the time.

While you might be advised to lighten up your portfolio at critical junctures in the stock market, you'll find that if you stick with the best stocks they will rise more often than they will fall. This, over the long pull, is where your brightest profit opportunities lie.

CHAPTER 30

Capitalizing on Special Situations

BACK IN THE freewheeling days before erection of the federal regulatory superstructure, fortunes were made by taking advantage of "inside information." Deals were struck, stock prices manipulated, mergers consummated, securities bought in advance of public knowledge of favorable developments, or sold in advance of adverse publicity. The trouble was, those fortunes were made at the expense of investors not privy to the information. That meant the investing public was often left holding the bag after the execution of such schemes.

It's much harder to do such things today, and those who tread into this forbidden territory can pay mightily. A recent example is Dennis B. Levine, a young (and for a time highly successful) merger banker. He was accused by the SEC of pocketing about $12.6 million in stock-trading profits—thanks to advance knowledge of some fifty-four corporate takeovers during the 1980–85 period. This was by far the largest insider trading case in history, and it rocked Wall Street. When Mr. Levine pleaded guilty and agreed to cooperate with the government, it seemed certain that other shoes would drop. But whose? Would the public's belief in the integrity of the financial markets be damaged? Meanwhile, the Street received another jolt in the spring of 1986 when five young people (including two analysts) were accused of trading on inside information. It is a foregone conclusion that enforcement of existing laws pertaining to insider trading will be more strictly enforced as a result of these and subsequent scandals. That tougher legislation will be enacted also seems highly probable.

Corporate officers and directors are required to make "full disclosure" of anything that might affect the price of their company's securities. This includes filing intentions of their personal sale or purchase of large blocks of the company's stocks or bonds. It also includes making known more basic information regarding the company, such as an impending legal judgment, merger possibilities, major diversification intentions, the advent of new products, and the like.

You might wonder, then, whether any "special situations" can yet exist. The fact is, they do, and they often can reap handsome rewards for the alert investor. The major point is that you have as much chance as the company's key officers to share in these developments. What, then, is a special situation?

It is any unusual opportunity for profit which the market as a whole has failed to recognize. It might be a merger or acquisition or the introduction of a new product, as we mentioned above. It might be a hidden asset value. It might be a new management policy. Or new management. Although companies are required to make full disclosure of their intentions, they are not required to broadcast them. Ferreting out a special situation frequently takes a good deal of detective work that goes above and beyond routine analysis of a company.

Mergers, Acquisitions, and Takeovers

Mergers, acquisitions, and takeovers are among the more common forms of special situations. Many companies today are seeking capital expansion not only through internal growth but also externally. They can achieve this by acquiring companies that complement their existing operations. It is often less expensive to acquire another company's existing assets than to build new assets from scratch—especially if the other company can be acquired by purchasing stock that is selling cheap in relation to these assets.

A special situation exists for shareholders of both the acquiring company and the company that is a candidate for takeover. Almost always, once it sets its sights on acquiring a company, a corporation will offer a premium price for outstanding shares to entice shareholders to sell. In other words, it will make a tender offer to buy stock of another company at a stated price for a stated period. The holder of such shares must then decide whether his best long-term interests lie in selling or in holding out for a better deal later. That deal might come in yet another tender offer by another acquisition-minded company seeking to outbid the first. Or it might come with an attractive conversion arrangement of his stock for that in the parent company once the acquisition is completed.

It's one thing to be the holder of stock in a company that is being taken over. It's another to be able to "discover" such companies, then buy their stock before such tender offers are made. This is where the real profits lie in such a special situation—finding takeover candidates, buying their stock, and waiting. Of course, this won't work for every company whose stock is selling below book value. Some of them will be bridesmaids but never brides; others will be perennial wallflowers.

Perceptive investors may also profit by buying stock in companies that are doing the acquiring. Such opportunities abounded in the late 1960s and early 1970s, when the investment community witnessed the epidemic of acquisitions that spawned the conglomerates. The fever ran so high in those days that companies were stumbling all over each other to outbid on available takeover candidates. The bidding became so fierce and the pace of takeover so pell-mell that many conglomerates found after their buying spree was over that they had not purchased good value. Indeed, many had purchased major headaches and had dashed into industries they knew little about. There was a substantial shakeout during the market declines and straitened business climate of the mid-1970s, and this tended to break the fever. In fact, many of the original conglomerates, such as Gulf & Western and Textron, have streamlined their operations in recent years by shedding disappointing business divisions and, in some cases, using the proceeds to buy in more of their own stock. Textron, on the other hand, decided to make one more major acquisition, that of Avco. So far, at least, it has been a highly profitable deal for shareholders of both concerns.

This is not to say, though, that we have seen the last of the big takeovers. There were some real blockbusters in 1985— Philip Morris gathering in General Foods, for example, and Procter & Gamble acquiring Richardson-Vick's. Not long after those mega-unions, U.S. Steel hooked up with Texas Oil & Gas to form USX Corp., and General Electric unveiled plans to merge with RCA in a $6 billion-plus deal.

Companies can also move to boost their market share by acquiring other firms in the same industry. In early 1986 PepsiCo agreed to purchase Seven-Up from Philip Morris— a move targeted to boost its share of the total soft drink market to 35 to 38 percent, or just a whisker below Coca-Cola's 39 percent. No sooner had the ink dried, than Coke made a bid for Dr. Pepper and increased its market share to 47 percent. But intra-industry mergers often run into opposition from the government on the grounds that these combinations reduce competition. Thus, it came as no surprise when the Federal Trade Commission objected to both Pepsi's and Coke's takeover plans. Philip Morris decided to look for another buyer for Seven-Up, while Coca-Cola chose to fight the FTC's decision.

Spin-Offs and Turnarounds

Sometimes, instead of adding to its whole, a company will subtract. It will "spin off" a certain segment of its operations into a separate company. This, too, presents special-situation opportunities for investors.

For example, Engelhard Minerals & Chemicals spun off its Philipp Brothers commodity trading unit in May 1981, retaining its metal manufacturing and mining divisions. Phibro, as the spin-off was called, then steered its own course, joining with Salomon Brothers (to form Phibro-Salomon, now known as Salomon Inc.) in October of the same year. The latter's shares rose about 150 percent between May 1981 and May 1986, thus easily outperforming the general market, though Engelhard actually lost some ground during the same period. In early 1984, Time Inc. decided to spin off 90 percent of the stock of Temple-Inland Inc., which held the company's forest products operations. The Temple-Inland shares rattled around in the low 30s for much of the next year, but subsequently surged past 50.

Another special situation is the turnaround. A company in decline suddenly springs back to life—and those investors who sense the change, or those who were patient enough to hold their shares, convinced of their inherent value, will be rewarded. Sometimes a change in management will alert the market to the new potential in the situation. Other times a new strategy that capitalizes on social changes will suffice to tip off investors. More often than not, however, the shares bounce back when no one is looking. Take Sears Roebuck, for example. From a low of about 16 at the end of 1981, the shares gradually eased higher, contrary to the market as a whole, to over 20 by May 1982. Obviously some investors had recognized Sears' greater emphasis on the financial service area. Two acquisitions in 1981, Coldwell-Banker, the nation's largest real estate brokerage firm, and Dean Witter, a securities dealer, were added to the well-established and profitable Allstate Group, Sears' insurance and mutual fund division.

The results of a turnaround are not always dramatic, but solid improvements in a seemingly hopeless situation can and do frequently occur when strong and creative management is brought in to mount a rescue operation.

New Products

Special situations may also originate through introduction of new products. A notable case was SmithKline, when it introduced a new ulcer therapy drug, Tagamet, in 1977. Tagamet quickly became number one on the list of prescription drugs sold worldwide. Indeed, the drug firms are good places to look for such special situations, since they have a serious commitment to research.

Companies in other industries that spend heavily on research and development bear exploration, too, especially where a good record already has been established in the creation of new products. Aerospace, chemicals, and electronics have provided their share of special situations via new products.

And that commitment to research will occasionally produce some totally unexpected results. Upjohn, for example, came up with a hypertension-reducing drug a few years ago, which, it was later discovered, helped overcome male baldness as well. While U.S. commercialization of the resulting new product, *Regaine*, began in 1987, the stock benefited in both 1985 and 1986 from the anticipation of big future earnings—which may or may not develop. Often, with new product introductions, it is the anticipation of how well they will do that sends the company's stock soaring, rather than the realization of those hopes.

But the laboratory is not the only place where new products are born. The marketing department can spawn its share. Gillette has done surprisingly well in marketing personal care items. And consumer product giants such as American Home Products and Procter & Gamble always seem to be a step ahead of the competition.

Entertainment certainly has profited from new "products." In the case of Twentieth Century-Fox (now privately owned), that "product" was a film called *Star Wars*. For MCA, it was *Jaws*. For Warner Communications, the "product" is home entertainment in all its forms. The Atari electronic and video games division, for instance, started as a dubious, small acquisition in 1976 but had become the most important profit contributor to the company by 1981. Investors would have to have been nimble in taking profits. The stock dropped sharply in 1982–83 on large losses from this same division. These special situations have reaped good rewards for investors, but they are not easy to capitalize on, because of the virtual impossibility of predetermining what will capture the moviegoing public's fancy.

Investing "At Home"

Beyond these special-situation profit opportunities are those afforded by companies in your own geographical region. They are special situations in the sense that you as a "neighbor" often have a unique opportunity to understand their problems and their possibilities.

You should remember, though, that investment decisions should always be made on the basis of objective facts rather than on subjective or emotional interpretations of facts. The latter, whether applied to investing "at home" or anywhere else, will only multiply your potential for making sour investments. Keeping a logical mind regarding your investment decisions does not mean that regional or local investment vehicles should be avoided. It only means that these opportunities should be examined with a more careful eye, lest your regional chauvinism be allowed undue weight in the final decision.

The first step in considering local investment is to determine what kind of investment is available. Utilities and banks spring immediately to mind. However, you should not buy stock in them at random, any more than you would with any other kind of investment. You have to examine their individual strengths and weaknesses and evaluate their long-term prospects. You have to look at the effectiveness of their management, their pattern of earnings and dividend growth, and the regulatory and economic climate in which they will be operating in the future.

Obviously, you need not confine your search for home-grown investments to banks and utilities. Perhaps your area is noted for some particular product or industry. You would be in a good position to judge the leading companies in it. Perhaps you work for a local investor-owned company, or you have friends or relatives who do. Even lower-echelon employees frequently can sense what is happening in the company and are in a position to say whether it is expanding, contracting, or holding its own.

If you're employed by a company that offers an employee stock purchase plan, you are eligible for one of the most assured special situations—the opportunity to buy stock that is in some way subsidized by the company, either through a share-price discount or a matching funds program. These are opportunities that should not be allowed to pass by.

Besides homegrown equity investment possibilities, you should not overlook the opportunities presented by bonds issued by your own state or its municipalities, particularly if you are in an income tax bracket that would make their tax-free status attractive. Besides being exempt from federal income taxes, their income generally is also exempt from state and local taxation, another special situation that can mean additional profits for you.

CHAPTER 31

How to Use Options in Trading

REGARDLESS OF WHAT may be written to the contrary, options trading is not an exact science. No amount of studying, charting, planning, or figuring will guarantee favorable results. By planning a carefully programmed strategy and observing a few rules, you can reduce your losses and increase your chances for gains. Options trading is less costly but more risky than investing in the underlying equities. The mathematically inclined may derive much comfort from setting up elaborate systems of charting and calculating options trades. For others, a more simplified approach should produce satisfactory results.

A few rules which apply to all types of options trades should be adhered to. First, diversify. Start out by limiting yourself to only one option on any one expiration date. Second, before making any commitment, set upper and lower limits at which you will cover. This will limit gains but, more important, will limit losses. Third, if you are a buy-'em-and-forget-'em type, go no further—options are not for you. Fourth, buy calls or sell puts only after several days of down markets. Conversely, buy puts and sell calls only after several rising trading sessions.

Buying Calls

The simplest option transaction to understand is the purchase of a call. Say, for one reason or another, you expect "ABX Corp." to rise in price. Your capital is limited, but you still want a piece of the action, so you decide to buy a call. This is the classic motivation for call buyers—leveraging their capital. The stock is trading at 65, but there are calls available at premiums of 6¢ a share ($\frac{1}{16}$) up to $15. Striking prices range from 50 to 90, and expiration dates are October, January, and April. (For a review of the mechanics of options, see Chapter 14.)

CALL OPTIONS ON "ABX" SELLING AT 65

Striking Price	Premiums on Options Expiring in:			
	October	January	April	
50	14⅞	15⅜	—	In the money
55	10⅜	11⅛	—	In the money
60	6¼	7⅜	8	In the money
65	3¼	4½	5⅜	At the money
70	1½	2½	3½	Out of the money
75	⅜	—	—	Out of the money

This set of quotations presents a wide range of choices. How should you decide where to put your money? There are rules which help narrow the choices. First, don't buy a call that is far "out of the money" (striking price above trading price). In the example, the price of ABX stock would have to rise 15 percent to reach the 75 striking price. Second, let time improve your odds by choosing an expiration date two to five months away. In our example, the January call series qualifies for this. Third, limit your risk by buying an option with a striking price not more than 10 to 12 percent above the stock price. In the example, the selection rules narrow the choice to the January 65 or 70 options. In the case of the January 65 call, the premium of 4½ represents time and is a pretty steep price to pay. The January 70 call will participate in any rise in ABX shares at a lower premium cost, and because of the leverage factor should produce a larger percentage gain.

By reducing the premium to a cost-per-week basis, you will have a better idea of the time value. Rather than reaching for the moon, you should decide beforehand that you will sell once you have a reasonable profit on the call. On the loss side, you should also make a decision to close out the trade when the premium drops below a preset level. In any case, it is always good policy to be out of the position at least a month prior to expiration. Remember that 70 percent of options expire worthless, so buying calls in expectation of a short-term profit is risky business.

Selling Calls

Why do investors sell calls? To maximize their return. In addition to obtaining dividend income, the seller pockets the call premium. Unlike the buyer, who usually buys calls on high-volatility issues, the seller chooses low-volatility, high-yield stocks. He is willing to settle for the smaller premium this type of stock commands in order to increase his return.

Since your objective as a writer is to increase income while retaining your stock, you will choose to write the option with the highest striking price if you expect your stock to rise in price. Your premium may be only $100 on 100 shares of $30 stock, but on an annual basis your income has been increased by $400, for a 13.3 percent return. Should you anticipate a drop in the stock price, you would get greater protection by writing the in-the-money option with the highest premium. A price reversal would mean you would lose your stock yet still make a profit.

An investor who does not actually own the underlying stock may sell what is known as a "naked call." This strategy takes courage, for the downside risk is potentially unlimited. The speculator in naked calls sells an option on stock he doesn't own but which he may have to deliver at a price well below the market. For example, a speculator sells a call at 50 on a stock trading at 48 and receives a $300 premium in return. The stock rises sharply to 58 and he is called on to deliver. He must purchase shares for $5,800 to deliver at $5,000. His loss is $800, minus the $300 premium, or $500. To prevent this type of squeeze, a simultaneous GTC (good till canceled) order is placed to cover the option if the premium rises to $600, limiting his loss to $300, the amount of the premium received when the call was sold.

Another means of reducing risk is to sell only calls that are out of the money, where the stock is trading below the striking price. Since only 3 percent of all stocks rise or fall as much as 20 percent in a year, the odds favor the seller of calls with far-out-of-the-money striking prices.

Trading Puts

The put buyer expects to profit by a drop in the trading price of the underlying stock. He may make his profit by delivering his shares at a price above market or by covering the put. And he may be either long or short the shares, since the choice of whether or not to exercise is his. If he is short the shares, he will probably elect to cover, as it is generally more profitable. The long buyer is protecting his shares against a drop in price. If the market moves up, the put buyer's loss is limited to the premium paid for the option. This loss may be reduced by selling a covering put prior to expiration.

The put buyer has effectively locked in a profit—or limited a loss—at the exercise price. Unlike with a stop loss order, which may be executed at a price lower than specified on the order, a put buyer is guaranteed receipt of the striking price at exercise.

The put seller agrees to accept delivery of shares at the striking price and receives the option premium in return. For an investor interested in acquiring a particular stock which he considers too high priced, selling a below-market put may accomplish his purpose. Suppose you like the long-term prospects of XYZ Industries but at 48½ think it is currently overpriced. You can write a put at 45, receive $200 in premium income, and if the option is exercised your shares will have cost you $4,300, plus commission. The shares will have been acquired at 10 percent below current market. Should the stock fail to drop below the striking price, you would not acquire them but would be ahead by the $200 premium income.

As a put seller, you should observe some very basic rules. First, be sure the stock is one you wish to own—and at that striking price. Second, be certain you have the cash or the buying power in your account to take delivery on the shares. Third, remember that if the stock drops in price and you have only the minimum collateral required, you could be faced with a margin call for additional capital.

Hedging with Options

One of the most frequently employed strategies is the "straddle," the purchase of a put and a call on the same underlying stock having identical striking prices and expiration dates. In an uncertain market, this tactic allows the trader greater latitude for error. If the stock rises or drops substantially, he will be a winner. Sideways price action, of course, would mean a loss on both options. For example, you would buy a November 30 call on Volatile Manufacturing (market price 33) at 5 and a November 30 put at 1¼, spending $625 plus transaction costs. A rise in the stock's trading price to above 36¼ or a decline to below 23¾ would produce profit. In either case, one option would expire worthless, while the other would generate the profit. Obviously, in actual practice the losing side (leg) could be cut short by the sale of a covering option.

In trading straddles, you should choose stocks with a high "beta" coefficient—that is, those whose prices tend to be volatile. These issues have a greater probability of moving far enough and fast enough to make a straddle profitable. Choose options with striking prices close to the trading price of the underlying issue. Also select higher-priced issues, since the premiums on these usually represent a smaller percentage of the stock's trading price. You will also add to your chance for success if you place your straddle on an issue that has an established price range. For example, on a stock trading in a channel between 80 and 100, the options would be at a 90 striking price. An issue with a clearly defined resistance and support level gives you better odds for success.

Because stocks fluctuate, the straddler will generally have ample opportunity to cover both options at small profits before expiration date, particularly if the underlying security has a high beta. As a trader in straddles, you must keep on top of your investment at all times, making new moves as indicated by market conditions. At the point where the premium on either the put or the call leg is sufficient to make the entire straddle profitable, that leg should be sold out and the proceeds reinvested. This procedure is known as "leg lifting."

On the opposite side is a straddle seller, an investor who anticipates only a narrow movement in the chosen stock over the life of the straddle. As a straddle seller, you wish to enlarge on the premium you would receive by selling only a call or a put. Concurrently, you subject yourself to the risks of both positions. Should the stock break out of its trading channel on the upside, you will be forced to deliver your shares at the lower-than-market exercise price. However, since you retain premiums from both the call and the put (which has expired worthless), you have a greater margin for profit than with either option alone. If the stock drops, the call expires unexercised. But you will have to take delivery on stock put to you at the above-market strike price. Again, downside protection from a straddle is greater than from the put alone, reflecting the premiums from both options.

The further a stock moves in either direction from the striking price, the greater the amount of equity required in the margin account. A substantial cash backlog is a must for dabblers in straddles.

Spreads—Bullish and Bearish

Spreads may be accomplished using either put or call options. As a spreader, you would buy a call (or a put) and simultaneously sell a call (or a put) on the same stock, using options with the same exercise date and different striking prices to transact a price spread. For a calendar spread, you buy and sell options with the same striking price but different exercise dates. A bullish spread using calls might entail buying an at-the-money call (strike and trading price similar) and simultaneously selling a call that is out of the money. Should the stock advance as anticipated, a profit is made on the buy side, and the call which was sold is covered, leaving a limited profit. If the market drops, the call which was sold expires worthless, and the call which was bought may be covered to limit the loss, for a smaller loss on balance.

A bullish put spread requires buying a put with a striking price below trading price while selling one with a higher strike price and the same expiration date. When the premium on the long put (the one purchased) exceeds the proceeds from the one sold (short), the spread is termed a "credit"; the reverse situation results in a debit spread.

Price spreads which use options bought and sold with the same expiration dates and different striking prices are also referred to as "vertical" or "perpendicular" spreads. When the expiration dates differ, the spread is a "calendar," "horizontal," or "time" spread.

Bearish investors wishing to spread may do so with either puts or calls. Using calls, the trader inverts the technique used by the bull, by buying an out-of-the-money call and selling an in-the-money call. Should the stock drop as expected, the call which was bought expires worthless and its cost is deducted from the proceeds of the call which was sold. While this limits the profit when the market price of the stock moves as anticipated, it also limits the loss if the stock rises counter to expectations. A bearish put spread involves selling a put with a lower striking price than the one on the put which is purchased.

Since margin rules relating to puts and put spreads are complex, you should become well versed in them before using these strategies. A long put (one which is purchased) must be paid for in full and has no loan value in a margin account. Furthermore, to qualify for put-spread margin treatment, the long side must not expire before the short side of a spread. These and other special margin rules are explained in the prospectus of the Options Clearing Corporation, a document which your broker will furnish. One of the main advantages in using options is the additional leverage they provide the trader, so understanding the margin rules is a must.

Still another technique, called "ratio writing" or "variable hedging," involves selling calls on more shares than are actually owned. A ratio writer holding 100 shares of Cyclical Steel trading at 65 would sell one covered and two naked calls to gain greater income as well as greater downside protection. For example, he could sell three January 70 calls on his Cyclical Steel to receive a premium of $750 ($250 per call). This gives him downside protection to 57½ rather than to 62½ with one call. But a rise in the stock to above 70 leaves him vulnerable to three exercise notices and the need to satisfy them with 200 shares bought at the market. Even though his break-even point is 77½ on the Cyclical Steel, he would still face having to raise the capital to deliver the shares. The trader, of course, would cover before getting into this situation.

Risk Versus Reward

The use of any combination strategy such as straddles, spreads, variable hedges, or the like increases the cost of the transaction, thereby reducing profits. Furthermore, there are possible tax implications that should be taken into account before plunging. For example, buying a put in a stock you already own might change the long-term status of that issue. If the stock has not been owned long enough to qualify as a long-term holding, the purchase of a put would wipe out the time previously accrued toward that qualification. Until the put is liquidated, a new holding period will not begin. Conversely, calls may be used to turn a short position into a long position.

It is possible to provide considerable protection against investment risks through the informed use of options. But this is possible only if you have a complete understanding of the subject or have an investment advisor willing and able to guide you through the intricacies of the various maneuvers.

CHAPTER **32**

Investing in Commodity Futures

THE SEARCH FOR profits in the commodity futures markets is not one that is generally pursued by the conservative investor. If he considers "playing the commodities markets" at all, his thoughts are just that—entertainment, a divertissement from more conventional investment avenues. More adventuresome investors pursue futures with greater seriousness, their eyes always on that chance to maneuver their stake into a killing.

That's fine if you're psychologically up to it, and if you fully understand the rules of the game. In this chapter, we'll introduce you to some of the basics needed for trading in futures contracts. However, because it is impossible to cover all of the topics adequately in a single chapter—or, indeed, in a single book—we strongly recommend that if you are serious in your intent to participate in this investment area you expand your knowledge before starting to trade.

You'll recall from Chapter 15 that the clearing house always breaks even. Everything it takes in it pays out, less commissions and fees. The same concept is a fair description of commodities futures trading in general. It is a zero-sum game, with the participants swapping money among themselves, the only attrition coming from those clearing house expenses. That being the case, in order to win you must take money from another player, who, in turn, is attempting to take money from you. Theoretically, your odds of winning should be fifty-fifty, and they are—on a single trade. In the aggregate, however, the odds are much less favorable that you will win; indeed, some observers claim they are nonexistent. Unfortunately, there is no reliable body of information on the success rate of commodity traders. The consensus among people in the business, though, is that most speculators lose, and the lion's share of profits goes to a relatively few professional traders. You can make money in the futures markets, but the competition is keen and success does not come easily or without cost.

Should You Speculate?

Whether participation in the futures markets constitutes out-and-out gambling or is a valuable and necessary part of our economic structure has been vigorously debated by moralists. We will not proffer a judgment on the question here. However, we will make this assertion: Successful commodity speculation demands the acquisition of price forecasting skills and the mental discipline to manage money in high-risk situations. The latter is the more difficult to master and probably is the principal reason the average trader loses over the long run. But price forecasting is only a little less demanding.

Choosing a Broker and Account Executive

As a beginning trader, your first decision would come in the choice of a brokerage house and an account executive within that firm to handle your orders. Basically, three types of brokerage houses are available to you. The most familiar is the wire or commission house that deals in almost any type of investment medium. The primary business of such firms is usually stocks and bonds, but many maintain separate commodity departments. The second type is the specialty brokerage house that restricts itself to transactions in commodities. These firms are offshoots of cash or trade houses. In the past, the latter would have provided the better service, but in recent years, many of the wire houses have built their commodity departments to the point where they are equally capable of providing efficient handling of orders. Lastly, there are discount brokers. Their main function is to fill your order as rapidly as possible. Generally, they do not provide any other support service and will not give you trading advice. Essentially, they are the self-service gas stations of the industry. Their commission charges will be substantially below those of a full-line or specialty brokerage house.

As for your choice of an account executive, if you feel you need specific trading advice, you probably will be more comfortable with someone who has experience in trading and is knowledgeable about the kinds of things important to your trading system. Conversely, if you like to plan your own trades, you may not like having someone fill your ear with advice. Whomever you choose, you should remember that all account executives are salesmen first and traders second. They make their living from commissions, not from successful trading of their own accounts. It is to their benefit, of course, if you win, and they will make every effort to assist you in that regard.

Opening a commodity trading account is a fairly simple procedure. The account executive will send a form called a margin or customer's agreement. It details the obligations you share with the brokerage firm when trading. The National Futures Association (NFA) also requires that customers provide personal and credit information such as current estimated annual income and net worth, age, and an indication of previous investment and futures trading experience. You will have to sign a statement of risk as well. This is primarily for the protection of the salesman and the firm. It is their proof that you were informed and presumably understood that commodity trading is more risky than placing your money in a savings bank.

You will have to deposit some cash when opening the account. The amount will vary from firm to firm, but it generally runs from $2,000 to $5,000. On the whole, specialty and discount commodity firms will require less up-front money, but all firms will expect you to meet the margin requirement in whatever commodity you have chosen.

Keeping Things Straight

Once the account is open, you will receive a variety of forms to alert you to what entries are being made in the broker's computer. Thus, if errors are detected, they should be called to the account executive's attention and corrected. The following list represents the basic correspondence nearly every commission house or specialty firm sends out.

STATEMENT OF ACCOUNT. When the account is opened and a margin deposit made, a statement of account showing the balance is sent to you. Thereafter you will receive one at the end of each monthly trading period, listing the credits (winning trades, new money added, or favorable adjustments), the debits (losses, cash withdrawals, and unfavorable adjustments), and the end-of-month balance.

TRADE CONFIRMATION. This is a record of a sale or purchase of a commodity futures position for the stated price and number of contracts. You'll have two confirmations for each completed trade, one for the entry price and one for the exit price.

PURCHASE AND SALE. When a trade is completed, that is, when a purchase is offset with a sale or a sale offset with a purchase, the broker will tally up the results, subtract the commission, and debit or credit the account accordingly. All the details of the trade appear on the purchase-and-sales slip, plus the *closed out* account balance. The latter figure does not include any gains or losses you might have outstanding in open or uncompleted trades. The net debit or credit for each trade is what appears on the monthly statement of account.

OPEN TRADES. When a new trade is entered but not offset, you will receive along with the confirmation slip a statement of open trades. This form shows a listing of all your open positions (including the new trade), their respective gains or losses, and the total account equity balance as of the close on the day the new positions were taken.

Because of the high leverage and rapid equity changes that can occur in a commodity account, a trader must be aware of his cash position on a daily basis. The statement of open trades does serve this purpose, but since it is sent only when a trade is actually made or offset, its usefulness is limited. To augment the statement of account, you should maintain a record of your daily account equity. This can be made as comprehensive as you like, but it should include at a minimum the daily profit and loss position on all open trades, the commission costs, and the net account balance. The net account balance is the amount of money that would be left in your account if all open positions were closed out at the day's settlement prices, and all commissions paid. That figure is your account's real net worth at any one time.

The Kinds of Orders

With the account open and margin money posted, getting into the battle requires only a call to your account executive, plus a little knowledge of orders. The following list covers the basic information you will need in order to properly convey your order to the salesman.

AT THE MARKET. Buying or selling a commodity "at the market" is the quickest and surest way to enter or exit a commodity market. A floor broker who receives this order will immediately execute it at the most favorable prices available at that moment. This is a "must fill" type of order.

LIMIT ORDER. If you issue the instruction "Buy at 45 or better" (the "or better" is understood and need not be given), you have posted a limit order. The floor broker will buy at your specified price or lower, but not higher. Unlike market orders, limits are not "must fill" orders, and a broker will not guarantee completion even if the market should go through your limit price. All you are assured is that if the broker can fill the order, he will do so at your price or better.

STOPS OR STOP LOSS ORDERS. Stop loss or stops are orders placed above or below the current market prices to protect a profit or limit a loss in an open position. When the stop price is reached, the order is executed "at the market."

Stops can also be used to enter a new position. If your price analysis indicates that a commodity must advance to a certain level before it is a good buy, you could use a buy stop; until it reaches that price no execution will take place.

Buy stops are always written at prices above the prevailing market, while sell stops are always below the market. When entering a market using stops, you must remember that stops become market orders when reached. Fills, therefore, can become unpredictable. However, by using stop limit orders, you can control, or at least limit, the price which you are willing to pay for the new position. You would not want to use a stop loss limit for a position that is being protected, because, like any limit order, there is no guarantee the broker can fill the order even if the market trades at your price. Assume you want to buy a commodity at 45 but do not want to pay more than 45¼. Your instruction would be: "Buy at 45, stop limit 45¼."

ON CLOSE OR ON OPEN ORDERS. These are executed, as the terms imply, during the commodity's opening or closing range, or not at all. Both of these orders are attached to either a market or a stop instruction.

ONE CANCELS THE OTHER (OCO). Like the preceding instruction, an OCO order is a contingency order. Something else has to occur before the floor broker can execute. In this case, you have placed two conflicting orders on the same contract (it can be used on different commodities as well) but want only one filled. You might do this if a commodity is in a trading range and you want to go with the breakout, but you aren't sure which way that will be. The solution is to use an OCO order. The instruction is to buy at 46 stop or sell at 44 stop, OCO. Whichever side is reached first will be filled; the other end will be canceled.

GOOD TILL CANCELED (GTC). Ordinarily, if an order is not filled during a day's trading, it is considered canceled automatically. It is possible, however, to instruct the broker to keep the order open by adding a GTC notation. The floor broker will keep this order in his deck of resting orders and will execute it at the first opportunity. The danger with this type of order lies in the ease with which it can be forgotten.

This catalogue of orders is by no means complete. It represents the most commonly given trading instructions, and the ones most likely to be accepted on an exchange. But even in this modest list will be found a few orders not accepted on some exchanges. Any type of contingency order is particularly vulnerable to being turned down by a floor broker. The market often moves so quickly that instructions weighted down with many options are too difficult to handle. As a rule, the more complicated you make the order, the less likely is the floor broker to accept it. It is usually best to keep your instructions as simple as possible.

Buying, Selling, and Delivery

There are two methods of selling commodity contracts. Either you make or accept delivery of the actual commodity, or you offset the contract by taking an equal but opposite position in the same commodity. Offsetting is a fairly straightforward and simple process. Most futures contracts are settled in this manner, and for individuals not actually involved in the cash commodity, offsetting is the most practical way to meet a contract obligation. But delivery is an alternative, and one with which the speculator should be familiar. Ordinarily, it is the speculator who has bought a contract who is the most concerned with delivery. Short sellers must notify the clearing house when and where delivery is to be made, and this notice of delivery is passed along to the buyers. As a result, the seller has control of the delivery process. Since speculators do not usually have the product, speculative sellers are rarely concerned with making delivery. On the other hand, the long holder stands a good chance of receiving a seller's "notice to deliver" if he keeps the contract into the delivery month.

Some clearing house operations pass delivery notices to

the buyers with the oldest position; others send delivery notices to the brokerage house with the oldest net positions. In most commodities, however, the exchanges allow the long holder receiving a delivery notice the option of redelivering, for a fee, the notice back to the clearing house or brokerage firm for delivery to the next-oldest long. The rules and procedures of delivery and redelivery vary with each commodity exchange, and the speculator should be aware of the specifics in the market in which he is trading. This is doubly important if the particular commodity has no redelivery provision or if the provisions are exceedingly difficult to meet. Your broker should be able to provide you with the details, but if he does not have the information, you can write or call the exchange. Your best bet, of course, is to be out of the contract well before delivery time.

Other considerations relating to commodity contracts include margin requirements, daily price range limits, and commissions. We have not included margin requirements here, because they frequently differ from firm to firm and because the exchanges themselves routinely raise or lower margins to counteract changes in volatility.

Each commodity has a specific maximum amount by which it is allowed to move either up or down from the previous day's settlement price. This is known as the daily limit. The limits are intended to prevent unusual circumstances from causing extreme one-day price changes. If the price does go up or down "the limit," trading is not necessarily stopped. It means no orders will be filled beyond the limit prices. Trading often continues to take place at the limit, but usually those traders wanting to take up the disadvantaged side disappear, and trading dries up.

There are some exceptions to the limit rule. Some commodities don't have a daily limit when they reach their delivery month, since these markets merge with their respective cash prices during the delivery month. However, this is not a universal situation, so you should check with your broker if in doubt. Index futures, for example, do not have a daily limit. (See Chapter 16.)

If a commodity has risen or fallen the daily permissible limit for two consecutive days, the following day's limit will be increased by a specific amount, which may vary from one exchange to another. If the commodity continues to trade to the limit, the size of the daily limit will also expand until the first nonlimit day occurs, and then it reverts back to its original level.

Three Classes of Commissions

There are three classes of commissions: regular, day, and spread. A *regular commission* is what a brokerage firm charges for a commodity transaction that takes more than one day to complete. The *day rate* is for a position entered and exited within a single day. A *spread commission* refers to a type of trading in commodities called "spreading." It is similar to hedging except that the cash position is replaced with another futures position. In effect, with spreading you get two positions for slightly more than the price of one.

When you pay a commodity commission, you pay your in-and-out charges at once—the equivalent of a "round trade" in stock market parlance. You don't pay for each leg of the trade separately as you do in a stock. Furthermore, you don't pay the commission until you terminate your position in the contract. Each commodity has its own commission structure, and commissions on each type of commodity contract will vary from broker to broker.

Market Quotes and Price Forecasting

To follow what is happening in a commodity and to determine your financial health at any given moment, you must be familiar with commodity quotes. Where do the quotes come from? In each exchange, market observers are posted on the outskirts of the pit, their function to report price changes to the various ticker services. The services, in turn, send the information to brokerage-house clients.

Your account executive will have access to these quotes and can keep you informed of intraday changes. A more complete record of overall commodity trading will appear in the following day's newspapers. If you live in a sizable city, it is possible that your daily newspaper will carry a fairly complete listing of commodity quotes on its financial pages. If not, you might want to subscribe to *The Journal of Commerce, The Wall Street Journal,* or *The New York Times,* all of which carry extensive listings.

Keeping tabs on these price changes after the fact is one thing. The real key to success is in being able to judge the movements beforehand. This is one of the most complicated and diverse aspects of trading, because there is no *best way* to forecast prices. There is even some argument that prices are random and cannot be forecast at all. However, short of darts, coin flipping, or moon phases, two general approaches to forecasting do lie at the foundation of nearly every commodity trading method you will likely encounter. They are, as in stock market analysis, *fundamental* and *technical.*

Traders generally have strong opinions on whether the fundamental or technical approach is the better. There really is no clear-cut answer, because what works well for one individual may not work at all for another. But you should become familiar with both methods of analysis, for they are the tools of the trade. In theory, the fundamental approach seems to appeal to most beginning traders because they feel better about basing buying and selling decisions on supply and demand factors than they do on a series of lines drawn on a piece of paper. The majority of traders, though they may lean heavily toward one discipline or the other, use both methods to some degree.

A fundamentalist operates on the principle that prices will rise if supply is short relative to demand and will fall if it is abundant. Fundamental analysis is an attempt by the trader to figure out what the supply and demand balance will be for a given commodity over a given period of time. Once this set of figures is divined, the fundamentalist then must decide what they mean in relation to current prices and whether the market has erred in interpreting the facts.

For the fundamentalist to trade, the market forces setting the futures prices must be in error, or there would be no reason to trade. For example, if the market price today for a hog contract deliverable six months in the future is quoted at

46¢ a pound, that is what the market, based on all the current trading and statistical input, believes hogs will be selling for six months from now. Through statistical analysis, the fundamentalist seeks to justify or disprove the market's judgment. If, in his opinion, the market forces are wrong, he will buy or sell accordingly.

While the fundamentalist is submerging himself in myriad statistical data relevant to supply and demand, the technician is content to view price, volume, and open interest as the true measures of the market. To him, fundamentals are irrelevant. He is interested in market action as it is reflected in changing prices, not external data that are difficult to determine, overwhelming in volume, and more often than not inaccurate or old.

The technician assumes that price changes are not without pattern, and that by studying past action it is possible to predict the direction of future market movement. Moreover, he believes markets act irrationally at times as the result of unpredictable changes in the mood of the trading public. A fundamentally strong market, for example, can easily collapse for no more apparent economic reason than a hard-to-measure change in public confidence. A technician feels he is better able to detect psychological or irrational shifts and act on them than the fundamentalist, who needs statistical input to justify a position change. Two of the more popular technical methods traders use are price charts and moving averages.

Your Trading Plan

A trader can devote a considerable amount of time and money to the development of a trading system. With the aid of a personal computer, he can develop some highly sophisticated trading methods. But no matter how meticulously he constructs his system, it will not be perfect, and he would be foolish indeed to proceed as if it were. Even the professionals expect to lose on a large percentage of their trades. At best, the trader hopes his plan will succeed more often than it fails, and that it will return him a profit over the long term.

As you devise your own plan, keep these thoughts in mind. Also heed our earlier comments on the importance of devising some sort of price forecasting system. Without one, you will be at a serious disadvantage. Then you should draft a realistic trading plan—and develop the discipline to exercise that plan properly. The need for discipline cannot be overemphasized. Fear and greed are the commodity trader's worst enemies, and they can cause even the best traders, using superior price forecasting systems, to make costly errors. Indeed, one of the lures of a mechanical trading system is that buying and selling signals are given mathematically, thereby eliminating much of the human element. For a more detailed study on the psychological aspects of trading in stocks and commodities, see *The Investor's Quotient* by Jacob Berstein (New York: John Wiley & Sons, 1980).

In its simplest form, a trading plan defines the criteria for entering a trade and specifies the point at which the position should be terminated. The latter is the more difficult, and where the greatest discipline is needed. A market can do one of three things: It can go with your position, it can go against your position, or it can do nothing. A trading plan must consider, *in advance,* the alternatives, and provide a course of action for each of the three possibilities. Failure to do this leaves the speculator at the mercy of his emotions and makes commodity trading far more difficult—and more risky—than it need be.

Another important part of your trading plan is money management. Unfortunately, there is no single formula that can be set forth to tell you how you should manage an account's capital resources. Trading and financial conditions are different for each individual, and money matters must be handled on a personal basis. But keep in mind that capital protection is the key segment in any money-managing effort. How well you succeed at this effort, in fact, is probably the single most important element in whether you win or lose in the long run, since the game ends immediately when the chips are gone. That suggests, at the very least, that overtrading in all its forms should be studiously avoided. If there is a mistake in judgment to be made—and all traders make plenty—let it be on the conservative side.

PART V

Taking Care of the Housekeeping

CHAPTER 33

Choosing a Broker

BACK IN THE good old days, the broker you started with would probably still be handling your investments on the day you died. It was a lifetime decision, like choosing a family doctor, and one that could have considerable impact on your financial health. Today this decision is not likely to be so final. With the advent of discount brokers and brokerage-company mergers, lifetime associations with one firm and one representative are now a rarity. As a result, the criteria for selecting a broker have changed.

If you are starting your investment career from scratch, having never invested or had a brokerage account, you would probably like some guidance in developing a personal investment portfolio. In this case, an old-line, full-service company would be best. However, if you are planning to do your own research and require only efficient and economical execution of your orders, a discount brokerage firm would best fit your needs. It should be noted that these rules are not ironclad; today more and more discounters are offering expanded services, while full-service firms are extending discounted commissions to their clients. Therefore the best advice is to shop around, not only to get rate discounts, but also to fulfill your individual service needs.

Full-Service Houses

Obviously there are still legions of investors who are looking for service, the staple of the conventional brokerage firm. If you are looking for a company that will safeguard your certificates, forward dividend checks, execute specialized transactions, and service financial products such as tax shelters, IRAs, Keogh plans, insurance programs, and money-market funds, then a full-service firm is just the ticket.

A full-service firm will offer you all the above-mentioned services and will contact you from time to time to offer investment "suggestions." More stocks are "sold" to investors than are "bought" by them. Before acting on any of your broker's recommendations, you should be sure the stock he suggests fits your investment goals. Don't be sidetracked from your particular financial needs by the tempting visions of a quick profit, for these are few and far between and are seldom shared.

Speculation is no substitute for investment, and you should view with suspicion any broker who tries too hard or too often to get you to accept his profferings. Always keep firmly in mind that his motivation in persuading you to buy is not his desire to be a nice guy, but a piece of the commission you'd pay. On the other hand, a smart account executive is one who realizes he'll do best in the long run by giving his clients good advice and the kind of service they want.

Discount Brokers

Keep in mind that there may come a time when you no longer require all the services you are paying for. At this point you may want to switch from a full-service broker to a discount broker.

Discount brokers came along when the Securities and Exchange Commission began putting on the pressure for negotiated commission rates. Until the mid-1970s, all brokers used a fixed schedule of rates, a situation the SEC regarded as a hindrance to free enterprise. It reasoned that if rates were unplugged from the schedule, competition among brokers would result in lower commissions. Despite its actual and philosophical proximity to the center of the free-enterprise system, the brokerage industry objected strenuously. The SEC proceeded in spite of the protests. Its first step was to rule that the commission on the portion of all trades above $500,000 could be negotiated. The limit was later dropped to $300,000. This did not help small investors, whose flight from the stock market had been a major factor in the financial straits that had beset many brokerage houses. So on April 1, 1974, the SEC started freeing up the other end. Trades of $2,000 or less were taken off the fixed schedule. Finally, as of May 1, 1975, the vast bulk of trades between these limits was included, and the move to fully negotiated rates was completed.

Did it help? Not much. In fact, in many instances investors found themselves paying more in commissions, as a percentage of the transaction, than they had under the fixed rates. Here is where the discounters emerged. By cutting out all extra services and by running tight, no-frills offices, they were able to offer substantial savings to investors seeking straight no-nonsense transactions. Eventually the full-service houses, which had been scorning small individual accounts as unprofitable, began to see that there was indeed a dollar to be made in that area. They started challenging the discounters. Free enterprise at last was beginning to work in the brokerage industry.

Today, discounters control 20 percent of the retail share volume, according to the Securities Industry Association. This figure is up from the 18.4 percent share captured by discounters in 1984, 13 percent in 1982, and the meager 1 percent controlled in 1975. This growth, which forced full-service firms to lower overhead and enter the discount market, has narrowed the distinction between "genuine" discounters and full-service brokerage houses. Moreover, while full-service firms have begun offering "no frills" order placement and lower commission rates, discounters have *expanded* their lines of service to include the same products that once set them apart from full-service outlets.

How Much Should I Pay?

The developments outlined above are good news for you, for they place you in a better bargaining position. Full-service houses base their commission rates on the dollar value of the transaction. Their fees also reflect the overhead incurred by the firm in providing you with plenty of research material on specific stocks and industries. Even so, you still may be able to negotiate discounts with your account representative. Discounts at full-service firms will range anywhere from 10 to 40 percent depending upon how much and how often you trade. Also, the firm may offer a low minimum commission for trades of less than, say, $2,000. These fees are comparable to the price floors at discounters. The key to obtaining any type of discount or minimum rate is simply to ask for it.

Much like their full-service competitors, most discount brokers base their fees on the dollar amount of the transaction. However, some discounters base their rates on the number of shares of stock handled in a single transaction. If you buy and sell large numbers of high-priced shares, the difference between the two pricing methods can be substantial. The traditional dollar amount fee structure may be better for those trading in low-priced (under $40) shares. Oftentimes it is difficult to tell which pricing scheme a particular broker is using, especially since advertisements tend to focus on the most attractive schedules and rates. What you will want to do is study a number of brokers' commission schedules. Then choose the firm that offers the fee structure that best suits your kind of trading. Obviously you should shop around before deciding which broker to use.

Special Programs Available

Many brokers, especially the conventional firms, offer reduced commissions through specialized investment plans. Perhaps the best-known of the brokers' specialized plans is the Merrill Lynch "Sharebuilder Program." This plan features discounts of 15 to 35 percent for purchases from a selected list of stocks in transactions of $5,000 or less. Dividends may be reinvested automatically as well. Some companies have reductions on commissions for "round-trip" trades; that is, on a stock bought and sold within forty-five days, the fee for the sell side is cut in half. For an active trader, this type of account offers big savings, but for the long-term investor it is useless.

Some full-service brokerage firms and banks, which were allowed to establish or acquire discount brokerage operations beginning in 1982, have expanded their service lines to include overall money management. This smorgasbord of offerings includes free checking, low-interest loans, credit and debit cards, free travelers' checks, and consolidated monthly (and yearly) statements listing all financial transactions. Some cash management accounts require an initial deposit of cash and/or securities of $20,000 or more, others much less.

The National Association of Investment Clubs (NAIC) is an institution that helps individuals to organize investment clubs and promote the principles of conservative investing. Investment clubs are usually comprised of a group of ten to fifteen people who meet monthly to invest money regularly; they are not unlike a small mutual fund. The NAIC charges groups a nominal annual fee ($30 plus a $7 per member charge). It provides members with regular publications as well as low-cost investment plans which take advantage of dividend reinvestment plans offered by many corporations. In sum, an NAIC affiliation is an excellent introduction to the field of investments.

An organization geared to the individual shareholder is the American Association of Individual Investors. The AAII was formed for the purpose of "assisting individuals in becoming effective managers of their own assets through programs of education, information, and research." The AAII, an independent, nonprofit corporation, publishes a monthly investment magazine. The annual membership dues of $48 include the price of a one-year subscription to their investment periodical.

Making the Choice

If you live in or near a large urban area, you probably have access to offices of several of the major firms, plus some local firms. In deciding upon one, you can canvass friends and business associates who have had dealings with them. Your lawyer and banker might be able to help, too, particularly in providing insights as to the quality and extent of services offered.

It is not imperative that you live close to your broker's office; toll-free telephone numbers have eliminated that need. If you are a long-term investor, some distance might be advantageous, since it will tend to reduce the number of hot tips you receive. One advantage of a local broker is your ability to settle in person any problems that might arise.

Extensive comparison shopping is not necessary if you decide to go with a full-service firm. Their commissions vary little since they incur similar overhead costs. What will differ at each of these firms is the breadth of their product lines. Similarly, investors whose transactions are modest will find little variance in the commission rates of the major discounters. However, the more active investors, especially those with big-ticket trades, can reduce fees by dealing with more than one discount firm.

Whether you decide to choose a full-service or a discount firm, the broker should be a member of the New York Stock Exchange. You should select one that provides not only the $500,000 ($100,000 for cash) account protection insurance required by law through the Securities Investor Protection Corporation (SIPC), but also additional coverage.

Once you have made the choice of a brokerage firm and an account representative, you should take time to acquaint him with your investment goals. It is the only way he has of knowing your needs and how he can help you implement them. Don't hesitate to let him know exactly what you expect —and don't expect—of him.

Your next step will be to open an account. This involves filling out some forms, and there is not a great deal of difference from one firm to the next as to what type of questions you'll be asked. But it's a simple process; opening a charge account at a department store is probably more complicated.

Besides supplying basic information such as full name and address, you will be required to give your Social Security or tax identification number. You will also need to instruct the broker as to how you wish him to handle your dividends and certificates and what type of account you are opening—joint, margin, etc. You'll have to provide the name of your bank and employer, too. For a margin account, you will have to complete and sign a customer's agreement and loan consent.

While you are completing the account forms, you may want to ask the broker about the bank from which dividends and other checks are drawn. Many brokerage firms draw checks on distant banks to take advantage of "the float." Until the check clears, which sometimes takes as long as a week, your money is providing the broker, the issuing banks, or both with an interest-free loan. Ask your broker to have your checks drawn on a local bank. Most firms are willing to do this. Once these forms have been completed, you will be ready to start on a new adventure in investing.

CHAPTER 34

Safeguarding Your Securities

IMPORTANT AS IT is to select the right investments to meet your financial needs, the protection of these assets once they have been acquired is equally vital. The safeguarding process should begin even earlier, before any money has ever been invested. Your choice of brokerage firm, how you elect to have your securities held, and what records you keep are all factors crucial to the safety of your investments. These are also matters which can and should be attended to before embarking on an investment program.

Holding Your Securities

There are four basic ways you can hold your securities. You can obtain and safeguard the certificates yourself. You can have them registered in your own name and have them held by a bank, a lawyer, or someone else as custodian. You can register them in your own name and keep them on deposit with your broker in a custodian account. Or you can keep them in street name—this means leaving your certificates in your broker's name and in his possession.

Which way is best? The answer depends on your own psychological makeup and the way you plan to operate your brokerage account. If you prefer to keep a firm grip on your possessions, you'll probably want to take delivery of the certificates and see to their safekeeping yourself. This means you will have immediate access if you need them for such things as loan collateral. It also means some inconvenience, for you must be sure to keep them safe, preferably in a safe-deposit box at the bank. It means you must go down to the bank and remove them when you sell, then be sure they are safely delivered to the broker for transfer.

If you do a good bit of traveling or are away from home much of the time, you might wish to place them in your own name but have your bank or lawyer hold them for you. You might make such an arrangement temporarily if you go away on an extended trip. While you are away, you may effect a transfer merely by signing a stock power and sending it to the custodian. Or you may sign a power of appointment beforehand.

Alternatively, you can have them registered in your own name but held by your broker. That way a sale can be executed by sending him a signed stock power. But in recent years, some brokers have experienced back-office logjams that have resulted in delays in obtaining certificates and even in lost certificates. Even though shares held by your broker in your name eventually would be returned to you in a brokerage house bankruptcy, there inevitably would be a delay. This could result in a loss of capital if the stock began dropping in price and you were unable to sell.

Street name accounts are popular with investors who trade their securities frequently. Shares held this way can change hands without being endorsed by the owner. However, besides running the risk of lost or mislaid certificates or bookkeeping mixups, in some cases you have no direct control over your securities. You would lose this control if you signed a hypothecation agreement, a document that gives the broker the right to pledge his customers' securities as collateral for loans the broker himself takes out. You need not sign such an agreement if you have a strictly cash account, but you must do so in order to open a margin account. Normally, such an arrangement would not cause any problems, but it could in a brokerage house bankruptcy. Thus, even with insurance against brokerage house failures, your street name investments could be tied up for a long time if something went wrong.

How SIPC Protects You

Creation of the Securities Investor Protection Corporation (SIPC) by Congress in 1970 was a boon to investors. Until then, when a broker went bankrupt it was catch as catch can for the investor whose securities were held in street name at that house. Under SIPC, brokerage accounts are insured for up to $500,000, of which $100,000 can be cash. SIPC does not protect customers against market losses from price declines.

An individual having several accounts with the same brokerage firm may or may not be covered separately for each account. For example, if you had an account in your own name, another as a trustee, and a third held jointly with your spouse, you would be covered to $500,000 in each. But if you merely had three different types of account in your own name only—cash, margin, bond, etc.—coverage would be limited to a total of $500,000.

With the exception of those firms engaged solely in the distribution of mutual funds, variable annuities, insurance, or investment advice, all broker-dealers registered with the Securities and Exchange Commission must be members of SIPC. Funding for SIPC comes from assessments on member firms. The agency does have access to additional funds in emergencies; it may borrow up to $1 billion from the U.S. Treasury through the SEC. Once the insurance corporation determines that a brokerage firm should be liquidated, application is made to the federal district court for appointment of a trustee. The trustee, in turn, notifies all customers of the firm. Claims against the broker should be submitted directly and promptly to the trustee.

How well has SIPC worked? It was created at a time when a major shakeout was occurring in the brokerage industry. In the first five years, it handled thousands of liquidations, most of them relatively smoothly, most of them involving small regional firms. Experience shows that in segregated accounts, where the shares are fully paid and held in the customer's own name, restitution has been prompt. In margin accounts, the experience has not been as favorable. Margined shares are held in street name and may be held by a bank against a broker's loan. Thus, they might be sold off during a market decline to maintain the required collateral to cover the loan. This means that in a brokerage house liquidation, customers with margin accounts could be paid off in cash rather than securities. This, in turn, means they might have to accept a sizable loss. In addition, it sometimes takes considerable time to sort out the failing firm's affairs, and in a liquidation that occurs during a down or falling market— when most of them do occur—this can mean even deeper losses for the holder of a margin account.

Besides carrying the required basic protection, some brokerage houses carry supplementary insurance protection. This would be a point to check out during your selection of a broker, if the size of your account warrants it.

Good Records Are Important

Whether you hold your own certificates or they are held for you by your broker, it is important that you keep accurate records of what securities you own and where they are located. For each transaction you make you receive a confirmation slip, which carries all the information needed for your records and for filing your income tax return. The confirmation slip shows the number of shares bought or sold, the trade and settlement dates, price per share, total amount of the transaction, and the net amount. Because confirmation slips may get misplaced over the years, you should keep a chronological record of all your transactions. Certainly this record should list the number and cost of the shares held, the trade date, and the net received in a sale or the gross paid on a buy. If you hold your own securities, you should be sure to record the certificate number in case of loss.

Your broker will send you monthly or quarterly statements indicating the status of your account. These statements should be retained for a reasonable period of time, because they provide good records of your transactions. Another reason you should keep them is to provide you with corroborating evidence of a claim against the firm, either in a bookkeeping slipup or in the event of the firm's bankruptcy. Some firms include on the year-end statement the total margin interest charged to the account during the year.

If you have taken possession of your own stock or bond certificates, you have the problem of delivering them to the broker when you make a sale. But you can safely do this by mail, using certain precautions. One way is to execute a power of substitution—a stock or bond power. Your broker, bank, or stationery store should be able to provide the necessary form. The power should be endorsed with your name appearing exactly as it appears on the face of the stock or bond certificates. No other information need be filled in on the power; your broker will complete it. After signing it, you will mail the power and the unendorsed certificate to the broker in *separate* envelopes. Another way is to endorse the certificate itself. You do this by affixing your signature and the brokerage firm's name in the appropriate places on the back of the certificate. An endorsed certificate should be sent only by *registered mail*. This is also true of bearer bonds— those that can be cashed in by anyone bearing them.

Although bonds now must be issued in registered form, previously issued bearer bonds are still outstanding. The cartoon of the rich old man sitting in a bank vault clipping his coupons is all but an anachronism these days. There are several advantages of registered bonds. For one thing, the bond-holder's name is registered on the company's books, so interest checks are mailed directly to him. Notifications of calls, redemptions, and the like also are mailed directly to the holder. On the other hand, with coupon bonds he must watch for notices of such events in the financial press, since the issuing company has no other way of notifying him. However, if a bank or other institution is acting as trustee, custodian, or investment manager for him, they are responsible for keeping abreast of such developments. Registered bonds are not transferrable to another party unless they are endorsed. Bearer bonds, because they are so readily turned into cash, require special care in safekeeping.

If Certificates Are Lost or Destroyed

Replacing lost bond or stock certificates is a costly and time-consuming process, so a thorough and determined search should be made before initiating replacement proceedings. If certificates are destroyed in a fire or are stolen, it is possible that your insurance carrier may be responsible for underwriting some of the costs involved in getting them reissued. Be sure to check into this if you ever lose any this way.

Once you have ascertained that the certificates really are missing, you should notify either the bond trustee or the stock transfer agent. The trustee or agent will place a stop on the security to prevent its sale. If you have been assiduous in your record keeping, you will have noted the certificate numbers, which you should pass along to the trustee or agent. Then you will be required to furnish a perpetual indemnity bond to protect the company from any losses it might incur should the lost securities turn up later. Such surety bonds are expensive—they typically cost around 4 percent of the certificate's current value. Then you will have to meet certain conditions established by the company, and they vary in strictness from firm to firm. No corporation likes to reissue, and some do their best to discourage replacement until absolutely sure the certificate is lost. If the original should turn up within a year of buying the surety bond, you can get back only part of the premium; after a year, you will get nothing back.

There are times when you must reregister a certificate. Again, it is the bond trustee or stock transfer agent who will make the change. The agent generally is a bank, but in some cases the issuing company acts as its own agent. The bond trustee will always be someone other than the company. In any case, the name and address of the agent appears in the company's annual report, and this would be another useful piece of information to add to your record book.

If your shares are held jointly as joint tenants with rights of survivorship, the survivor receives full title on death of the co-owner. Shares held as tenants in common have no such survivorship rights; the decedent's share goes into his estate.

When the securities are held with survivorship rights, the survivor can have them reissued in his own name merely by forwarding a certified copy of the death certificate to the transfer agent. In some cases the transfer agent may require a residence certificate for tax purposes. It makes no difference whether the conjunction "and" or "or" is used between the joint owners' names, as long as the shares are held as joint tenants with rights of survivorship.

Are Old Certificates Valuable?

According to those who keep track of such things, five out of every hundred old stock certificates traced have some value. In 2 percent of the cases, the obsolete certificates have a worth of $1,000 or more. With odds like these, time spent doing some digging on your own or money spent on experts to do the digging for you can prove well invested. There are at least three firms that specialize in tracing old certificates: R. M. Smythe & Company, 24 Broadway, New York, NY 10004; B.S. Lichtenstein & Company, 101 Maiden Lane, New York, NY 10038; and Tracers Company of America, 39 Broadway, New York, NY 10006. If the shares turn out to have any value, you will receive information on how to collect. These companies are also useful if you should need to establish the date a security became worthless for tax-loss purposes. In the past, the Internal Revenue Service has considered them sufficiently authoritative to accept their information without challenge.

If you want to pursue the investigation on your own, your local library may be an invaluable source of information. Not all small libraries have an extensive business and financial section, but they might have arrangements with state libraries that can obtain books for you. Here are some books to look for: *Robert D. Fisher Manual of Valuable and Worthless Securities*, *Directory of Obsolete Securities*, and *Capital Changes Reporter*. An older volume might also be in stock— *Valuable Extinct Securities*, published by R.M. Smythe in 1934.

Determining the value of old stock certificates is only the

first step in receiving such windfalls. Not infrequently, they turn up in Great-Aunt Bessie's trunk, made out in her first husband's name. Before you can collect, you will have to establish your right to them. Of course, if they were issued in bearer form, it's finders keepers.

Should your old certificates turn out to be among the other statistical 95 percent—that is, they are worthless shares of a defunct corporation—don't be discouraged. Your search was probably worth the satisfaction gained in knowing for certain that you did *not* toss Great-Aunt Bessie's fortune out with the trash, and for the authoritative information you have collected for estate tax purposes. What's more, you may be surprised to learn that some antique certificates have value as collector's items—particularly if they are dated pre-1900, have decorated details and vignettes, or bear famous signatures. "Scripophily" is a growing specialty of the antiques and collectibles market. R.M. Smythe & Company is an expert in this area as well as in the tracing of a certificate's historical worth, and holds regular auctions in New York and London for scrip collectors. For the $20-per-stock research fee, Smythe provides a written appraisal of both the market and the antique value of the certificate.

Minority Shareholder Rights

Normally, a shareholder has the right to vote, to receive a portion of the profits, to inspect company books, to share corporate property, and to subscribe to subsequent stock issues. When a company goes private by buying up a majority of its outstanding shares, or merges with another company in an exchange of its stock for that of the acquiring company, usually 3 percent or less of its common stock remains outstanding. Owners of this remaining portion are known as minority shareholders and have forfeited virtually all of their rights. Numbers alone have silenced their voices. The best way to protect yourself and your investment against this problem is to avoid getting boxed into the position in the first place.

The most frequently given reason for getting into the position is that the tender price of the stock was unfair. Yet the alternative to accepting the offer is equally unattractive—ownership of a batch of unmarketable shares. Attempts to obtain judicial redress are almost always unsuccessful. The usual court response to aggrieved shareholders is that they go through the appraisal system in effect in their state. This is frequently a complex procedure that yields varying results.

Just plain ignorance is another factor contributing to a shareholder's finding himself in a minority position. He received the tender offer but did not know what to do with it, so he ignored it. Most corporations make a concerted effort to buy back small batches of stock in such cases, so several offers are made before they close the books on such conversions. Once the major part of the stock has been tendered, the minority shareholder might as well face the facts—he is not going to get any more for his shares than the tendering holders received. If he continues to hold out, he might as well forget about dividends, too.

Shareholders occasionally have an opportunity to join in a settlement on a class action suit. If they held the stock during the critical time period, they should receive an application to participate in the settlement. However, this is not always the case, and unless they return the application by the stated date, with the required documents of proof, they will not share in the settlement.

Unless your investments are in a trusteed account or otherwise supervised, it is your responsibility to safeguard them, physically and otherwise. Although most publicly owned corporations will extend themselves within reason to protect and inform shareholders, it is up to you as an individual investor to read all company communications and take action when required. The small amount of time, care, and intelligence you must spend on your investments will pay off in the long run.

CHAPTER 35

Running Your Investment Program

NOT EVERYONE IS financially able to invest a few thousand dollars at a time to buy securities in round lots. Fortunately, that isn't the only way they can be purchased. Several alternatives are available for the periodic investment of smaller amounts of money. Among the choices are monthly investment plans offered by brokerage houses, dividend reinvestment plans operated by individual companies, and mutual fund accumulation plans.

Besides these rather formally structured programs, you can, of course, design your own plan for making regular additions to your savings and investment program. You can have funds deducted from your salary and set aside for periodic investment. The bond-a-month payroll savings plan has proved a boon to millions in building a financial reserve of U.S. Savings Bonds. You can pick stocks in three or four—or a half-dozen—different well-diversified companies and by investing a predetermined monthly amount on a rotating basis build yourself a mini-mutual fund of respectable size in fairly short order.

The possibilities are endless, bounded only by your own imagination and desire to accumulate a savings and investment portfolio. We will discuss several alternatives in this chapter. One of these is the monthly investment plan offered by many brokerage houses. These plans vary from one firm to another, but the concept is the same—to provide a systematic periodic method of building a stock portfolio. Generally, you're allowed to invest a regular monthly or quarterly amount in one or more stocks chosen from a list of thirty or forty Big Board issues. Although there may be a discount of up to 25 percent from standard commission rates on these trades, the expenses can prove costly on small transactions. In addition, a small service fee may be charged. Usually a minimum of $20 can be invested.

Dividend Reinvestment Plans

Well over a thousand companies offer their shareholders the choice of having dividends automatically reinvested in stock instead of being paid directly to them. In addition, the plans allow cash to be added to the dividend to purchase more shares and to build the pot faster. Many of the companies with such plans pay all or part of the commissions and bank fees involved. A goodly number will reinvest the dividends in shares at a 5 percent discount from the market price. Several companies have extended this discount to apply to shares purchased with shareholders' additional cash contributions. With a small initial investment to acquire a few shares through the customary channels, you can then enroll in the company's dividend reinvestment plan, add small cash infusions, and acquire additional shares at a reasonable fee or perhaps with no fee at all.

Here's how the plans work. Enclosed with your first dividend check should be application forms and information about the company's plan. Once you're enrolled, your dividends will be reinvested automatically in shares and fractions of shares (computed to three decimal places). Cash additions are generally limited to $20,000 or less a year, with a minimum addition of $10. If a pro rata commission is charged, your share probably will not amount to more than 1 percent of the amount invested. The bank fee is charged at a rate of 4 to 5 percent of the invested amount, but only to a maximum of $2.50 to $3 per transaction. If you plan to make small cash additions, it would save on the bank fee to lump these annually or quarterly. Even after paying the bank fee and commission, your cost will be only about $4 per $100 invested, compared with the $7 or so it would cost by going through a broker.

To find out which companies offer such plans, you can ask your broker or check the Standard & Poor's *Stock Reports,* if your local library subscribes. Once you've zeroed in on a few companies that offer the plans, you can get the full details about each by writing the corporate secretary for a booklet. Your broker or the *Stock Reports* will provide the address.

Aside from being a painless and economical way to build a portfolio, dividend reinvestment plans offer the additional advantage of growth through compounding. From the initial investment forward, the reinvested dividends themselves are earning more dividends. This means that even if you do not add any more cash as you go along, your investment works harder for you with each passing quarter.

Participants in dividend reinvestment plans receive a detailed statement of their account after each investment is made. If you decide to make voluntary cash additions, you should send them shortly before the dividend payment date. Most companies accumulate participants' cash additions until collectively there is enough to purchase a round lot. That means your cash could sit around for a month or more without earning any interest.

Bank service charges are deductible for tax purposes if you itemize. Commission costs are handled in the usual manner by adding them to your cost basis. Even though the dividends are reinvested, they are taxable as income in the year received. In plans which reinvest dividends and/or cash at a discount from market price, the amount of that discount is taxable as income in the year received.

Mutual Fund Programs

Most mutual funds offer some kind of systematic investing program. In general, these fall into two types—contractual and voluntary. Contractual plans have earned a bad name with their front-end load. But some of the worst aspects were reduced with the 1970 revisions in the Investment Company Act. The plans work by committing an investor to pay a pre-determined amount into the fund over a period of ten to fifteen years. Before the reforms were instituted, the unwary investor found that the lion's share of the load fee for the entire life of the plan was skimmed off in the first year's investment. While this was wonderful for the salesman, it did little for the investor. Even with the 1970 revisions, the front-end load remains fairly heavy—as much as 20 percent of the first year's contribution can be allocated to sales charges, as long as the load fee is 9 percent or less of the total investment. In a 150-payment plan, more than half the total load is collected in the first 36 payments.

Operators of the plans point out that the penalty serves to encourage people to complete the programs. Furthermore, because a contractual plan is, in effect, "a letter of intent," the load fee could be at a lower rate than on a voluntary plan, if the total investment was large enough. The contractual plan offers the person who has trouble disciplining himself a form of forced investment program. Of course, there is nothing in the contract that requires completion of the plan, except the threat of forfeiting the large sales fee collected in the plan's early years.

Voluntary or systematic investing programs are looser. Often they are without any specified number of payments or amount to be paid. A simple notice is sent as a reminder at the appointed time. Terms and conditions of the various programs offered by a particular fund are set out in that fund's prospectus.

Stock Dividends and Rights

Another way to build your portfolio is to invest in companies that regularly pay stock dividends. By limiting your choices to such issues you could build a sizable portfolio in just a decade. For example, Georgia-Pacific paid one or more small stock dividends annually for many years. Had an investor purchased 100 shares of this stock in January 1967, he would have had 404 shares ten years later—plus 122 shares of Louisiana-Pacific obtained in a spin-off. His cash would have doubled. By the simple expedient of putting up the $20 or so required to round out the fractional share at each distribution, he would have held 458 shares of Georgia-Pacific and 135 shares of Louisiana-Pacific at the end of the decade.

Adding the small amount of cash required to exercise rights is another means of increasing your holdings. Rights offerings are a common method of raising capital in the utility industry. In the last few years, American Electric Power has offered shareholders rights on a one-for-ten, one-for-nine, one-for-eleven, and one-for-fifteen basis. Shares acquired through rights are free of commissions, and prices are under the market. In a six-year period, the owner of 100 shares of American Electric Power would have added close to 60 more shares if all rights had been exercised.

U.S. Savings Bonds

Until now, this chapter has discussed alternative methods of acquiring and building assets with marketable securities. However, as a supplement to stocks, bonds, and mutual funds, well-rounded financial plans often include nonmarketable investments such as U.S. Savings Bonds, savings time deposits (time certificates), and/or annuities (which we discuss in detail in Chapter 43). While it is not always possible to adhere to a program of regular investment, serial purchase has the advantage of producing income on a monthly or quarterly basis at retirement. We provide an example, using Savings Bonds, in Chapter 45.

U.S. Savings Bonds, in fact, should not be overlooked as you consider investment alternatives. Though snubbed by "sophisticated" investors, more than $82 billion worth of E or EE bonds were outstanding in mid-1986. Their popularity lies in their safety, convenience, low denominations, fair rate of return, and ease of purchase and redemption. More than two-thirds of Savings Bond sales come in the form of payroll deductions, with close to 10 million workers enrolled in this periodic savings plan.

Series EE bonds replaced Series Es, which were no longer marketed after 1979. EEs are priced at 50 percent of their face value. In the past, the term to maturity varied according to what interest rate the government wished to pay. In 1982, Congress authorized the Treasury to periodically change the interest rates on EE Bonds. Although the rate can be changed, on bonds held five years it cannot be reduced below the rate which was guaranteed when the bonds were first sold. Prior to 1982's Tax Equity and Fiscal Responsibility Act, Savings Bond interest-rate changes were limited to 0.5 percent every six months. Terms of the plan are fairly complex; suffice it to say that EE bonds will pay a floating rate base of 85 percent of the average yield on five-year Treasury notes, but not less than 6 percent interest if held five years. Series EE bonds are issued in denominations from $50 to $10,000.

You need not redeem Series E or EE bonds at maturity; they shift automatically into an extension period. However, they reach final maturity after forty years. Those issued between 1941 and 1952 have reached or are reaching their final maturities. Even then, you don't have to redeem them, but they no longer accrue interest. A better plan is to cash them in or exchange them for Series HH bonds at their value at final maturity.

The stated return on Series E and EE bonds is an average return; in the early years it is well below the guaranteed rate, thus providing an incentive to hold them at least to maturity. The income generated by Savings Bonds is subject to federal income taxes, but not to state and local taxes. On Series E and EE bonds, interest is compounded semiannually but is not actually paid until the bonds are redeemed. Likewise, tax on that interest need not be paid until it is actually received. Hence, a Series E or EE bond is a means of deferring income taxes and qualifies as a "tax shelter." However, if you desire, you may pay the tax on the interest annually as it accrues.

The tax liability on accrued interest is an important factor in deciding what to do with bonds you have held for a number of years. By cashing them in, you could subject yourself to a large tax bite. If after retirement you expect your tax bracket will drop, waiting until then to cash your Savings

Bonds makes sense. There's another way to do it and continue to defer the tax on your stored-up interest. That is to exchange the E or EE bonds for HH bonds.

The main difference between EE bonds and HH bonds is that the latter pay interest currently, rather than compounding it. They don't necessarily pay the same amount of interest, either. As with Series EE bonds, interest on HH bonds is less than the stated rate when these bonds are redeemed in the first five years of their life. HH bonds, which are now available only in exchange for EEs, mature in ten years. Interest on them is paid by check semiannually and is taxable in the year paid. However, the tax on the accrued interest of any E-type bonds exchanged for HH bonds is not payable until the latter are sold, disposed of, or reach final maturity. Series HH bonds are available in minimum denominations of $500. Any shift of E or EE bonds to HH bonds must be in multiples of $500.

Since Savings Bonds are registered securities, no one but the actual owner may cash them. This also means they can be replaced if lost or destroyed. To replace bonds, write the Bureau of the Public Debt, 200 Third Street, Parkersburg, West Virginia 26101. Provide as much information as possible about the missing bonds—their registration numbers, date and place of purchase, names and addresses of owners, and the like.

Savings Bonds are not transferrable or acceptable as collateral on loans. Partial redemption of E bonds of over $25 face value, EE bonds of over $50, or H-type bonds of over $500 is allowed; the reissued portion will carry the original issue date. Smaller denominations may be exchanged for bonds of larger denominations only when you are making another change, such as a revision in ownership form or name. Again, the original issue date is applied to the reissued bonds.

Redeeming a bond you own is almost as easy as buying one. All you need is your signature and proper identification. On an E or EE bond, you will get your proceeds on the spot. H or HH bonds may be redeemed at a Federal Reserve Bank or branch office, or by the Treasury Department, Securities Transaction Branch, Washington, D.C. 20226.

When a more complicated transaction is involved, such as

changing the name of a beneficiary, adding the name of a co-owner, or changing the name on inherited bonds issued in a decedent's name, you will have to furnish certain documents. These changes cannot be made on the spot. Instead, the bond must be sent to a Federal Reserve Bank for payment or reissue.

Other U.S. Obligations

Other U.S. Treasury and agency securities are not as elaborately packaged for consumption by the general public. In fact, most members of that public rarely trade them, even though they often yield more than Savings Bonds. However, if you do decide that your program could use some "Governments," there are four ways you can buy them and three ways you can sell them.

For most investors, the most convenient channel for buying and selling is through a local bank. Bank fees vary but generally amount to a flat charge of $20 or $30, plus mailing expenses, per transaction for amounts up to $100,000, and an added fee of around $5 per $100,000 above that.

Alternatively, your broker can handle the business for you. Here again, the expenses vary widely, so it's best to inquire beforehand. Some brokers will fill the order on a net basis, that is, charge the asked price and derive the "commission" from the spread between the bid and asked price. Others charge a flat fee of, say, $25 plus another $25 if you want the bonds delivered to you rather than being kept by the broker.

For the investor who buys in round lots ($100,000 or more), a dealer in government bonds will charge the asked price and receive as his compensation the spread between the bid and asked price, just as is done by some brokers.

On new issues, you can buy directly from the Federal Reserve Bank in your district. Your order must be received by the stated deadline, accompanied by certified or cashier's check (or cash, if you go in person) to cover the amount of the offering price. There is no commission involved and the transaction can be handled entirely by mail. Contact your nearest Federal Reserve Bank for the necessary forms and information.

Thus, you can buy government securities from a bank, a broker, a bond dealer, and the Federal Reserve Bank. You can sell or redeem them through a bank, broker, or dealer, but not through the Federal Reserve Bank. However, you can "roll over" maturing Treasury securities into newly issued ones through the Federal Reserve Bank.

Deregulation and Savings

Just as savings institutions charge different rates of interest to different types of borrowers, so do they pay interest according to the type of account involved. They pay the highest interest rate on the largest deposits left longest on deposit. Forced by competition, consumerism, and deregulation, the industry now pays interest on checking accounts and escrow accounts where money is held for payment of taxes and insurance premiums on mortgaged property.

Deregulation, begun in 1980, was completed in April 1986, when the interest-rate ceiling and minimum balance requirements were removed from passbook savings accounts. Restrictions on NOW accounts, short-term deposits, and money-market accounts were lifted on the first of the year. With banks and savings and loans now operating in a competitive environment, the consumer should pay careful attention to details. Will you have to pay fees when the balance falls below certain levels, or for excess withdrawals, or for use of automated teller machines (ATMs)? Are there restrictions that would reduce your return from the account? Account structures vary from one savings institution to another, so shop around.

The single most important item to evaluate when comparing savings accounts is the effective annual yield. Before you switch your account to a higher-paying one, make sure the additional interest won't be offset by unexpected charges. Compare how the interest is compounded—annually, semi-annually, quarterly, monthly, weekly, daily, or continuously. The shorter the period the greater the interest accrual.

Although some new financial products have been marketed by savings institutions in the last several years, expect more innovations in the next few years. Consolidated statements, showing activity and balances for all your accounts held by the bank, are now fairly commonplace. Tiered accounts, favoring large deposits, are also gaining acceptance. Because credit cards are an especially lucrative product for banks, marketing in this area is fast-paced. If you are solicited, compare the card's annual fee and interest charge with those you pay on your present cards—the new offer may be a better buy. Deregulation has freed the industry to compete, so before you invest in a money-market account or a term certificate, investigate.

Self-discipline, in fact, is the real key to any successful savings and investment program. Another is regularity. Resolve to put something away on a regular basis, then see to it that you keep up the "payments." By using some combination of the methods outlined in this chapter, you should be able to draft a plan that suits your needs and objectives.

CHAPTER 36

Tax Pointers for Investors

WHEN IT COMES to tax laws, Congress is an inveterate tinkerer. It is constantly adjusting, dismantling, and reassembling; adding new gadgets, altering old ones, and "reforming" rules that are "unfair." Yet it rarely succeeds in simplifying, even when it deliberately sets out to do so, as it did with the Tax Reform Act (TRA) of 1986. The key words in selling yet another "reform" were *fair* and *simple*. Did the final product, more than two years in the making, turn out to be either? Your opinion depends on how the 1,700-page act treated you. It is certainly simpler for those who no longer have to file the long form. It is "fairer" for those whose tax bracket will shift downward to 15 percent. But for persons whose pet tax shelter was disrupted and for those who own rental property, run a business, are self-employed, have an IRA, have children with investment income, etc., the new rules are more complex than ever, and their fairness is questionable.

Once a new tax act is written, it goes through a year or so of settling, during which time its flaws become glaringly apparent. Congress then attempts to remedy the errors by passing a technical corrections act. In other words, there is seldom a time when tax law status quo is reached. As a result, investors are always making financial decisions on tax law that is either outmoded or soon to be so. For this reason, unless yours is the simplest of investment programs, you would be well served to seek the advice of a qualified professional to help you map tax strategies that mesh with and enhance your investment goals and personal financial plan. However, to get you started, here are five basic rules.

Don't Let the Tax Tail Wag the Investment Dog

The cardinal rule is to let the basic validity of the investment itself be the deciding factor in whether to acquire, hold, or sell. Thus, tax considerations should always play a secondary role in your decision. But once a decision has been made, you should examine its tax consequences. Although TRA's elimination of the special tax rate on long-term capital gains has wiped out most of the tax advantages that could be garnered from timing securities sales, a few remain. Both short- and long-term capital gains are taxed as ordinary income at a maximum 28 percent rate. Capital gains and losses are netted, and net losses (both short and long) can be used to offset up to $3,000 of ordinary income, dollar for dollar. Any excess losses may be carried forward to be used in a later year. The old adage about taking losses and letting gains run is now good investment advice as well as good tax advice.

Give Uncle Sam His Due

Don't cut off your nose to spite Uncle Sam's face. Many investors who have enjoyed substantial capital appreciation on well-chosen securities are reluctant to cash in on these profits because of the tax liability involved. A large profit— even one in which Uncle Sam shares—is better than a smaller profit later (he'd get a piece of that, too) and infinitely preferable to a loss. When it's time to sell, sell—and give Uncle Sam his due!

As noted previously, you can blunt the tax effects of a substantial capital gain. Any capital losses taken in the same tax year or carried over from a previous year can be used to offset the gain, dollar for dollar. Thus, you can use the gain as an

opportunity to weed out your portfolio by selling off investments in which you're showing losses and which should be
unloaded anyway.

Suppose you took a flier on a "sure thing" last year and it
has done so poorly you want to dump it. You also hold a blue
chip that has been growing steadily for years and you have
no intention of selling it. Why not use the loss as an opportunity to raise your cost basis in the blue chip? Sell the "sure
thing" and at the same time sell an equivalent dollar amount
of the blue chip. But while you're transacting that business,
instruct your broker to replace the shares of the blue chip
with an equivalent number. Not only does this strategy offset
the tax-deductible loss with a taxable gain, but also it lowers
the taxable gain on the blue chip shares when they are sold
by reducing their cost basis.

Don't Go to the Showers on a "Wash Sale"

Many investors play losses against gains by selling a position to establish a loss, then buying the shares back because
they believe in the long-term soundness of the investment.
That's fine, as long as you don't run afoul of the 30-day repurchase limitation, the so-called wash sale rule. That rule prohibits you from claiming a loss on any security that you've
replaced with a substantially identical security within 30 calendar days before or after the sale of your original holding.
The wash sale rule applies only to losses; you can repurchase
immediately before and after establishing a gain.

Remember, the wash sale rule applies on either side of a
loss sale. You may sell your holding first, then wait the 30
days to buy the replacement shares, or you may buy the re-
placements first, and then sell the original holding after the
appropriate period has passed. The date of the sale is the
date the loss is established. The wash sale rule applies even
if the maneuver spills over from one tax year to the next. This
has useful connotations, for it means that with proper forethought you can establish a loss toward the end of the year
or delay taking it until the start of the next, depending on
which would be more advantageous for tax purposes.

Another point that's important to remember about the

wash sale rule is that it may apply to more than the common stock itself. The rule says "substantially identical" securities, and this can mean the common stock, warrants, or options on the common. It can mean bond issues sold by the same company which have similar yields and maturities, even if the bonds are from a different issue. However, you probably would not run afoul of the wash sale rule if you sold common stock and bought bonds or preferred stock in the same company within the 30-day period, as long as these were not convertible into the common.

In fact, that is one way to avoid problems with the wash sale rule if you want to establish a loss yet retain a position in the company. Another way is to sell the securities to establish the loss, then buy a similar position in another company within the same industry group that possesses similar investment attributes as the stock you sold.

Don't Trip Over the Calendar

Much portfolio adjusting is done toward the end of the year as investors obtain a clearer picture of their gain-loss situation. If you do this, keep one eye on the calendar.

If you're a cash basis taxpayer, as most individuals are, you can sell a stock any time to the last day of the year to establish a loss. But to establish a gain, you have to sell at least five business days before the end of the year to allow the transaction time to clear. You have to watch the calendar, too, to avoid problems with the wash sale rule discussed above.

Don't Compare Stock Loss Apples with Tax Saving Oranges

Remember, a $1,000 loss does not mean a $1,000 saving on your income tax. If you're in the 28 percent tax bracket, it means a $280 savings; in the 15 percent bracket, a $150 savings.

Year-End Tactics

As the tax year draws to a close, you may be in the enviable position of owning shares that have appreciated substantially, but which you think are due for a correction. You would like to lock in the gain but defer the tax liability to the following tax year.

You can do this by "selling short against the box" in the current year, while delivering the shares in the following year. The holding period ends at the time of the sale, but the gain is not realized until the shares are delivered. For example, you sell 100 XYZ short on December 20 but don't deliver your shares (to close the short sale) until January 30 of the next year. Your tax liability is incurred on the latter date.

Buying a put on shares you hold at a profit is another means of locking in the gain while delaying the tax bill. As with a short sale, the holding period for the underlying stock ends with the purchase of the put. Your gain is reduced by the cost (premium) on the put, but should the stock go up in price, contrary to your expectations, you share in that gain. For example, you hold XYZ at a cost of $25, and it is trading at $50. In December, you buy a February 50 put for $3. If the stock drops to $45, you exercise your put and realize a gain of $22 ($50 − $25 − $3). If the stock rises to $60, your put expires worthless, giving you a $3-per-share short-term loss on the put. Your shares may then be sold for $60, giving you a $35-per-share gain.

Charitable Gifts Aid Donor and Donee

TRA 1986 has eliminated some, but not all, of the benefits from making gifts to charities. First, nonitemizers can no longer deduct charitable donations. Second, the rules covering gifts of appreciated property have been tightened. If you file the long form, you still can take tax deductions on gifts donated to public charities that meet criteria outlined by the IRS. In general, this includes churches, hospitals, and educational, medical, and research organizations.

Deductions for gifts to organized charities are generally restricted to 50 percent of adjusted gross income. In the case of appreciated intangible personal property such as securities, your deduction is limited to 30 percent of your adjusted gross income. Within that limit you may take a charitable deduction for your cost basis in the securities and avoid the tax on the capital gains. However, the untaxed appreciation becomes a preference item for those taxpayers who incur the alternative minimum tax.

If you hold property on which you have a loss, it is better to sell it, establish the loss, and donate the proceeds to charity than to give the property outright. Otherwise, no one would be able to claim the loss; it would be "lost" for tax purposes.

There are other vehicles for making charitable contributions, obtaining tax deductions, and meeting other financial goals as well. One example is the charitable remainder trust. Such a trust must be set up as a "guaranteed annuity trust," a "unitrust," or a "pooled income fund." In any of these forms, the trust gives you, or someone you designate, the lifetime use of the property. On the death of the beneficiary, be it you or an income beneficiary designated by you, the property goes to the charity. The advantage of charitable remainder trusts is that you get a large charitable deduction upon making the gift, yet continue to enjoy the property's use.

Since these and other less-than-routine charitable gifts can be complicated, they should be undertaken only with your total financial picture in mind. Furthermore, you should have the help of qualified legal and tax counsel in planning and implementing large charitable gifts.

PART VI

Investments and Your Financial Plan

CHAPTER 37

Are Your Affairs in Order?

WHEN WAS THE last time you gave your family's financial situation a thorough going-over? In the rush of everyday living, it's easy to let these things slip. Yet, when you stop to think about it, in the process of managing your income and outgo, you're running a sizable "business." How well or poorly you do it depends in large part on how thoroughly you have organized the job.

When you first started out, it was an easy task, and you could handle it efficiently on a week-to-week, month-to-month basis. Then came a house, with a mortgage running twenty years or so. And children. And the start of a nest egg for the future. The management task has become considerably greater as you have added more places for your money to go and have moved up the income scale.

Your acquisitions quite likely have come gradually—so gradually that you may not have recognized just how complex your affairs have become. No longer can the week-to-week, month-to-month approach suffice.

Then, too, there is the concern that your family might have to get along without you at some point. How well have you prepared for that possibility? If you were to duck out for good tomorrow, would you leave behind a jumble of records, some here, some there, for your survivors to try to find as best they might?

If you are the well-ordered type, you probably have things well in hand. Even so, you might profitably run through this chapter in the event you have overlooked some point worth reviewing or reworking. If you feel your family's financial program needs some organization, you can use what follows as a starting point.

Finding Your Net Worth

The first thing to do is to find out where you stand. How much are you worth? Take a stab at the answer before you write anything down. Chances are, when you do the arithmetic, you'll find that your guess was on the low side.

"Well, let's see," you say. "I have some life insurance, we're buying a house, the car's almost paid for, we have a few stocks and bonds. That's about all. Guess I'm not worth much, am I?"

Using the work sheet opposite, you can create your personal balance sheet, carefully listing all your assets and liabilities. Most of the information should be in your files, but some data will require additional digging. Rather than relying on instinct or guesses in valuing your home (most people's largest single asset), consult a broker or check your newspaper's real estate section for current market values of similar properties in your area. Once the balance sheet is completed, you will have an overall picture of your financial condition.

The reason you might mislead yourself into believing you don't have much material worth is the state of your wallet. It's pretty flat most of the time for a good many of us. But think of what you're buying with what comes out of it. Sure, there are the necessities—food, heat, clothing, contributions, a night out once in a while. You don't have much to show for the shelling out on these items.

But what about the mortgage payment? A portion of that goes each month toward paying off the principal and increasing your equity in the property. This is like a savings account. The same is true, though to a lesser degree, of your automobile. Your life insurance policy, too, might be build-

CASH RESERVE ASSETS

Cash on Hand .... $ _____
Checking Accounts .... _____
Savings Accounts .... _____
Money-Market Accounts .... _____
Credit Unions .... _____
CDs—1 Year or less .... _____

PROPERTY ASSETS

Residence .... _____
Vacation Home .... _____
Furnishings .... _____
Jewelry and Art .... _____
Automobiles .... _____
Other Property Assets .... _____

EQUITY ASSETS

Realty Investments .... _____
Stocks .... _____
Mutual Funds .... _____
Variable Annuities .... _____
Business Interests .... _____
Other Equity Assets .... _____

FIXED ASSETS

Bonds:
  Government .... _____
  Municipal .... _____
  Corporate .... _____
CDs—More Than 1 Year .... _____
Fixed Annuities .... _____
Other Fixed Assets .... _____

RETIREMENT ACCOUNTS

Vested Portion of Pension ..... $ _____
Other Co. Savings Plans .... _____
IRA .... _____
Keogh .... _____

Total Assets .... $ _____

LIABILITIES

Home Mortgage .... _____
Other Mortgage .... _____
Bank Loans .... _____
Auto Loans .... _____
Charge Accounts .... _____
Education Loans .... _____
Insurance Premiums .... _____
Taxes:
  Federal .... _____
  State .... _____
  Local .... _____
Other Debt .... _____

Total Liabilities .... $ _____

NET WORTH

Total Assets .... $ _____
Total Liabilities .... — $ _____

NET WORTH .... $ _____

409

ing some cash value each year—yet another form of "enforced" savings not immediately visible.

In fact, most of your net worth is "invisible." Or it's so visible that you don't really see it. Take your furniture. You probably don't think of that in terms of its material value. Yet, you laid out cash for it; it represents an investment. You'd have to lay out more cash to replace it if it were lost. Same thing for your home appliances. Add up their value— the refrigerator, dishwasher, clothes washer, dryer—just these major items represent a sizable sum in themselves. Of course, their value diminishes each year with their use, but as long as they are of use they have value. They are part of your assets.

Almost anything you own can be included among your assets. This includes sporting goods, jewelry, cameras, boats, home workshops, garden tools, snowblowers, bicycles, and art. Of course you wouldn't forget to include the value of your vacation home. As you work up an inventory of such things you can see just how much you have accumulated along the way.

Another "invisible" asset might be your interest in your company's pension or profit-sharing program. Some companies have group life insurance policies, and you might be contributing to one that will return these contributions when you leave the company or retire. You should check up on the status of your company benefits from time to time and add their value to your assets.

Don't forget to add in savings and checking accounts and the current worth of your stocks and bonds. Since your house has probably increased in value since you bought it, include the full current market value on the asset side of your ledger. Now add everything up.

Chances are, you owe money, too. Get this all together. The balance due on your mortgage. On your car loan. On any other loans outstanding. Insurance premiums. Current household bills.

Subtract the total of these liabilities from the total value of your assets and you'll have your net worth. Not bad, you might conclude. By making an accounting at about the same time each year, you'll get an idea of how well you're progressing. You'll also have an idea of what your goals should be, where you should be devoting more or less emphasis. This provides an excellent chart of the family's financial progress.

Where Does the Money Go?

Great. But where does all your money go each month and each year? Find out by drawing up an income statement. Your checkbook is probably as good a data source as you can get, particularly if you write checks for most of your bills. If you don't pay by check, by the way, you ought to consider doing it, because it serves as an excellent record, and it can provide proof of payment if you're ever challenged on that score. Taking your most recent full-year period, go through your records and write down all expenses, putting them into such general categories as mortgage or rent payments, auto loan, heat, lights, phone, food, clothing, entertainment, and so on.

Next, jot down your total income, making note on the expense side of the amount taken out for taxes and Social Security. Work your figures over until the "income" and "outgo" sides of the ledger balance. This income statement gives you an idea of how much you're paying for what. It makes a good starting point for drawing a budget.

Controlling the Outgo

A budget is needed to keep future spending under control. It need not be cast in concrete at the start of the year; in fact, it should not be so rigid that it allows no flexibility. Your budget shouldn't run your life, but instead it should serve as a map of your financial trip through the upcoming year and as a chart to keep you on course.

Once you have these three basic tools—a balance sheet, an income statement, and a budget—you're well on the way to getting your family finances under control. A couple of other things might be worth mentioning at this point.

One is a household inventory. The other is an insurance checkup.

As you probably discovered when you added up your possessions for your net worth tally, you own a lot more than you realized. Should you be hit with a burglary or fire, it might be difficult to remember the specifics in placing an insurance claim or filing a loss deduction on your income tax return. It would be a lot easier to have a list made ahead of time. It wouldn't be a bad idea to keep a copy of that list somewhere other than in the house, say, in your safe deposit box at the bank or perhaps in your insurance agent's file. You ought to update the list from time to time. Include specifics as to brand and style, your cost, date acquired, and estimated replacement cost.

In an inflationary period, you are at risk, too, with your homeowner's insurance coverage if you don't add to it from time to time. One reason is obvious: If you have a total loss, you wouldn't be fully covered on replacement costs. The other isn't so obvious: if you're not covered to within 80 percent of the value of the property, your coverage for any partial loss will be reduced to the extent that full coverage falls short. To make sure that your coverage is up to snuff, you should give it a yearly checkup. You can also ask your insurance agent to write an inflation escalator clause into your policy, and coverage will be automatically increased each year in line with the rise in prices. You should be certain your other casualty and liability coverage, such as that on your automobile, is periodically upgraded as well.

Providing for Illness, Disability, and Death

While you're thinking about insurance, you should give your health and life insurance programs a going-over. Since it is not the purpose of this book to educate you on that score, we'll only mention in passing the need to take a look at them from time to time to make sure they still meet your needs, both immediate and long term. With medical bills rising constantly, one hospital stay alone would put you behind unless you're adequately covered.

If your family insurance program doesn't include disability coverage for the principal breadwinner, you ought to consider taking some on to provide continuation of income in the event of his incapacitation. This protection, frequently overlooked because of its expense, in some ways is more important for younger families than life insurance, since disabling illness and accidents are more likely prospects than death.

That does not mean life insurance should be ignored, either. How much coverage you carry depends on how you regard such protection, how much you think the family will need to function comfortably in the absence of the principal wage earner, and how much you can afford to lay out for premiums.

Again, without getting into an involved discussion, we believe that, in general, term insurance buys you more protection for your dollar than whole life, which shunts a portion of the annual premium into a "savings" program that builds up cash value. We believe that by investing the difference yourself you can do much better over the long run—provided you discipline yourself to put that money aside each year. Your term policies should have a guarantee that they will be renewable at the end of each term regardless of your health at the time, and you might do well to pay a bit extra for a guarantee that the premiums will be paid if you become disabled.

A Record-Keeping Checklist

So, now that you have your income and outgo under control and your insurance coverage checked, what other records need to be assembled? Here's a list to get you started.

Will. Note where copies are filed, when it was last drawn, and when any changes were made.

Safe-deposit boxes. Note where they are located and list their contents as of a certain date. Note where keys are kept.

Insurance. List all policies and their numbers, and note where they are located and whom to contact if needed.

Bank accounts. Note account numbers, location of passbooks, and other pertinent information on all family accounts.

Securities. Provide a complete current listing, including costs, and note where certificates are located.

Real estate. Maintain a list of capital improvements with supporting invoices for tax purposes; note basic expenses such as property taxes, utilities, etc., as well as mortgage data.

Income taxes. Retain copies of final returns for past several years and keep complete data for the current year.

Professional advisors. List names of attorney, trustee, and executor of the estate, insurance agents, stockbrokers, tax counsel, physicians, etc.

Requests and recommendations. Provide notes on disposition of personal effects after death for sentimental or other reasons not specifically mentioned in the will; provide suggestions for survivors on how best to make sure of the resources and advisors; list obituary material.

Once these records have been assembled, don't keep them a secret. If you are married, go over them with your spouse, explaining each item and its significance.

But contemplation of death shouldn't be the only motivating force behind establishing a good record-keeping system. If you sell your house, it can help you establish costs so you can reduce capital gains tax liability on appreciated value. If the IRS challenges your tax return, you have your defense readily at hand. You can tell at a glance how your investment portfolio is performing. You can detect potential financial problems ahead of time and take remedial measures before they become expensive crises.

The earlier you start such a system, the more help it can be to you in preserving your hard-earned assets and making them work more efficiently for you. Now is the time to get on with it.

CHAPTER 38

Investing for a College Education

IF YOU HAVE children, chances are that one of your primary financial objectives is to provide college educations for them. If you haven't priced a college education lately, you're in for a shock. And if you have some years to go yet before the youngsters are ready for college, your shock will be compounded by inflation if you don't start setting something aside now.

The sooner you begin your college fund, the easier your task will be. It will be a twofold job: first, to provide the assets; second, to make sure these assets work as hard as they possibly can while they're waiting to pay the college bills.

If you have a chunk of cash you are able to salt away immediately, all to the good. A portfolio of good-quality growth stocks should appreciate sufficiently over the next decade to give you a solid start toward paying the bills.

Or you might have to set aside funds a little at a time. The secret to success is to do it on a regular basis. Such a program takes discipline, but it can pay off handsomely. For instance, if you had invested as little as $200 each birthday, since your child was one year old in 1964, in a growth stock like Abbott, and plowed back all dividends, the $3,600 cost would have been worth about $13,000 in 1982 when he or she was ready to go off to school. By increasing the yearly contribution as your earnings rose, you could have accumulated enough to pay the entire cost of college.

It is well to keep firmly in mind as you start planning for your children's educations the importance of protecting your fund from inflation, because college costs are rising faster than prices in general and the trend is likely to continue for the foreseeable future. That's why we have placed emphasis on common stocks. The earlier you begin your college investment program the greater will be the benefits from capital appreciation of good investments.

Keeping the Tax Man at Bay

Whether you invest in a portfolio of growth stocks or prefer the comfort of investments that provide greater "safety" of principal, you must consider the potential effect of taxes on the nest egg. With growth stocks, the big bite comes when they're sold. And with the elimination of the special capital gains rate they are taxed as ordinary income. With income securities the bite is more gradual, a year at a time as the income is earned. However, there are still some ways to reduce the impact of taxes. The most effective ways involve investments that allow income to be deferred or that pay income that is tax exempt.

U.S. SAVINGS BONDS. As noted in Chapter 35, one of the features of Series EE Bonds is that interest is not paid as it is accrued but is left in and compounded semiannually. Bond-holders do not have to pay income taxes on this accrued interest until they redeem or otherwise dispose of the bonds. If you buy bonds in your child's name, they will be taxable to the child. Since up to age fourteen a child's unearned income (in excess of $1,000) is taxed at his or her parents' highest rate, EE interest should be deferred. When the child reaches college age the bonds can be liquidated to help defray expenses. Although the accrued interest on them will be taxable, it will be at the child's tax rate, presumably lower than that of the parents.

CUSTODIAN ACCOUNTS. While custodian accounts generally allow assets to be removed from your estate, they have the same income tax drawbacks as EE bonds. Above $1,000, any income earned by transferred assets is taxable at the donor's top rate. No gift tax is incurred as long as the value of assets transferred is $10,000 or under. When a husband and wife make a joint gift the exclusion is $20,000 annually.

However, there are some other things you should know about using custodian accounts. The first is that assets automatically go to the child, no strings attached, when he or she reaches legal age. In some states, that is eighteen, and if that's the case in your state and you have any qualms about your ability to keep your child persuaded not to blow the wad on something other than college at that point, you might better consider another approach (see below).

Another important point is that you should name someone other than yourself as custodian. That's because if you are both the chief donor of assets and the custodian, and you should die while the account is still in force, the assets will be counted in your estate.

MUNICIPAL BONDS. One way of avoiding the "kiddie tax" is to buy tax-exempt bonds or their stripped version. Stripped municipal bonds are noncallable, and they are backed by Treasury and agency bonds. One advantage of strips is their low cost; they sell at deep discounts to their $100 face value. These are purchased under the Uniform Gift (or Transfer) to Minors Act and, as explained earlier, become the child's property.

SINGLE PREMIUM LIFE INSURANCE. Earnings from whole life (cash value) insurance grow tax-deferred until a policy is surrendered or lapses. These insurance earnings may be tapped by the insured at any age—by borrowing from the policy—without penalty or tax liabilities. A parent who buys a policy on his or her own life can, when the child reaches college age, take a policy loan to help fund educational expenses. Interest cost is low and up to 75 percent of the principal can be borrowed. When outstanding at the death, policy loans (and accrued interest) reduce death benefit. If a policy is allowed to lapse or is surrendered, then the earnings are taxable, but when paid to a beneficiary, proceeds are tax free.

Whole life insurance guarantees a minimum interest rate during the initial years, with annual adjustments thereafter. Buyers of variable life may invest in bonds, stocks, money markets, and other portfolios. If the insured chooses well and the account manager is skilled, policy earnings will prosper, but there is no guarantee. Either type of policy is suitable for meeting college expenses, but variable life, with its potential for gains and losses, is best used for long-term goals.

Doing It with Trusts

Grantor or reversionary trusts, such as the Clifford trust or the spousal remainder trust, have been virtually eliminated as family tax-planning tools. Income on these is taxable to the grantor, unless the grantor retains less than a 5 percent reversionary interest in the assets in the trust at its inception. Income from a grantor trust in existence on March 1, 1986, is not taxable to the grantor but to the beneficiary. However, if the beneficiary is under fourteen, trust income above $1,000 is taxable at the parents' top rate in any case. Capital gains taken within the trust are taxable to the grantor whether the trust is or is not grandfathered.

Countdown to Retiremen

RETIREMENT EVE IS no time to start wondering what you'l
have for "eating money" once you bid your fond adieus t
your job. Five to ten years ahead is not any too soon to begir
figuring. Probably you have a pension plan where you work
But do you really understand how it operates—and how
much you are likely to get out of it once you hang up you
tools? You're pretty sure to be eligible for Social Security
when you retire. But do you have any idea how large the
monthly checks will be?

If you're like the vast majority of workers, these two items
will provide the lion's share of your retirement income. To
make any kind of realistic projections about your financial
needs in retirement you'll have to have a rough idea of how
much they will give you. You'll also have to know early
enough so you can start laying away some savings to provide
extra income.

A ballpark figure is sufficient. It's impossible to get a precise fix anyway, because of the changes that will occur in
your income and in the Social Security rules during your
remaining years on the job.

The quickest way to estimate your potential retirement
income situation is to assume you're retiring right now and
compute your benefits on that basis. Ask your company what

the pension plan would pay someone who retires this year at your income level and with the number of years' service you'll have at retirement age. Then estimate the Social Security benefit you'd receive if you retired this year. Your nearest Social Security office can give you the figure.

Add the two together. In all probability, that's pretty close to what you'll get in dollars of equivalent buying power when you do retire. Could you live on that sum? Make a quick calculation of your living costs in today's dollars under circumstances approximating those that will exist when you do reach retirement age. Remember, in retirement your income needs will be more modest than they are while you're working. No more expensive business lunches, not as many new clothes, no commuting costs, etc. If your mortgage is paid off at retirement age, your housing costs will be lower. With the children grown and gone, there will be fewer mouths to feed, no more college tuition bills to pay. Do the projected expenses fall within the projected income?

If not, you'll have to get cracking and (a) build some savings and/or (b) develop some ways of earning money in retirement.

How Much to Save?

Because conditions may change drastically between now and the time you retire, particularly if you are relatively young, it is difficult to judge with any degree of accuracy how much you'll have to save to provide an adequate retirement nest egg. But remember, inflation will have to be figured both during your saving period and during the period you'll be drawing upon the account.

Just to give you an idea of what you're up against, let's assume that inflation continues at a 5 percent rate. At that rate, prices double in roughly fourteen years. (The consumer price index doubled in the ten years to 1985.) To provide, at a 5 percent inflation rate, the same buying power for $1,000, you'll have to have $1,276 if you retire in five years, $1,629 in ten, $2,079 in fifteen, and $2,653 in twenty. Remember, too, that during retirement that same process will continue;

think what the effects will be on a nest egg that has to last three decades or so. Or what will happen to your life-style over that period if you don't have such a reserve.

Obviously, the earlier you start saving, the easier the task will be. Suppose you decide you'll need $100,000 on which to retire comfortably at age sixty-five. If you're forty-five now and your assets grow at a 10 percent rate (including income and appreciation), you'll need to save $1,746 a year for the next twenty years, or $140 a month compounded. If you're fifty-five now, you'll have to sock away $501 a month to meet your goal. The moral is obvious.

Savings Alternatives

After you've estimated how much retirement income you'll need and how much you must save to get it, you have to draft a retirement program.

It's stating the obvious to say your aim in providing a retirement nest egg is to build your assets as large as possible within reasonable bounds of risk. It's something else again to come up with a program that meets this goal.

The list of alternatives is well known, and we won't belabor it here. Basically, your choices divide into three general categories: *savings* (bank accounts, cash value life insurance, annuities, bonds, etc.); *equities* (business ownership, real estate, and common stocks); *speculations* (oil-drilling participations, commodity trading, options trading, etc.).

Weighing the obvious risks, you can quickly trim the list substantially at the outset. Unless you have funds you can really afford to lose, we'd suggest you leave the speculations to wealthier investors. Unless you're ready and able to undertake management of a business or real estate, we suggest likewise for these. Most retirees aren't interested in spending the time necessary to manage a business or keep tabs on rental property. That leaves stocks, bonds, bank accounts, insurance, and annuities for most.

By limiting your choices to these, you have substantially reduced, but not eliminated, the risk factor. Let's review our earlier comments on risk. Most likely your first thought is of the risk that your assets will shrink in the face of a decline in the securities markets just when you need to liquidate. That's a valid concern, and it should not be overlooked.

But there are other kinds of risk, and they are as important to consider. We have just demonstrated the risk of lost buying power of your savings. Then there is the risk that you'll get yourself locked into some investment to the extent that you can't easily or economically shift into a more lucrative one should the opportunity arise. Finally, there is the risk that the investment to which you entrust your savings will turn sour and fail altogether.

Ideally, you'd like an investment that would keep your capital intact, that would grow sufficiently fast to overcome inflation, that would be flexible, and that would not go down the tubes. Unfortunately, no single investment or savings vehicle exists that can guarantee all these goals at once. There will always be some element of risk involved. The trick is to get that risk under reasonable control and to spread it out to minimize its effects on your total program.

How do you do this? First, you determine which risks you can most easily live with. If you're nervous about putting your capital on the line, you'll have to live with the risk of shrinking buying power as you indulge in the "safety" of fixed-income investments. If you're more aggressive, you'll have to face the risk that your capital might possibly vanish in equity investments.

Isn't there some happy medium? We believe there is, and we've been preaching it for a good many years. It's called diversification. Don't put all of your retirement nest egg savings into the same investment basket. Your "mix" will be largely determined by the length of time you have before retirement and the amount of risk you're willing to undertake in relation to your expected return.

What kind of mix do you need to yield the desired results? If you have ten to fifteen years before retirement, we'd suggest you go heavily on the side of common stocks, to minimize the risk of buying-power erosion. By choosing from only the strongest and best companies, you can select a portfolio of stocks that is highly resistant to market risk as well.

Don't make the list of stocks too long; keep it within manageable bounds. A half-dozen to a dozen companies should provide sufficient diversification.

How much of your savings should you devote to equities? We would say 70 percent and still feel conservative, dividing the remaining 30 percent among bonds and savings certificates.

To retain flexibility, select bonds with maturities five or six years out, rather than those of longer term. This will minimize market risk should you wish to shift investments along the way.

As you move to within five years or so of retirement, you could begin to tilt portfolio acquisitions more toward fixed-income securities. You shouldn't start any wholesale shifting of equities already in your portfolio, though; there might be tax consequences that could be reduced if action is delayed until after retirement, when your taxable income and possibly your tax bracket will be lower.

As you make the transition into retirement, you might have a portfolio consisting of 60 percent equities and 40 percent fixed-income assets. Because the inflation risk is likely to be present during all of your retirement years, you should think seriously about retaining a solid position in equities to help offset the constant rise in the cost of living.

Making Savings Grow

There's more to the creation of a nest egg than just putting funds aside. You must make them work as hard as possible while they wait for you to retire.

We've talked about determining how much savings you'll need for retirement and the various savings options open to you. Now let's look at some ways to make the retirement fund grow.

The first, and most obvious, way is to make regular additions to it. You've got to discipline yourself to do this, or your plan is doomed from the start. Play tricks on yourself, if you must. Have pay deducted from your salary so you never "see" it. Write yourself a check each month and deposit it to your retirement account. Start a regular investment program with your broker or with a mutual fund.

Another way to make savings grow is via compounding. Be sure all of your assets—including the income generated by them—are working for you all of the time. Keep dividends reinvested, rather than cashing and spending the checks; enrolling in dividend reinvestment plans will expedite this. Pay any taxes out of pocket rather than out of the fund. Choose savings accounts that offer the most attractive compounding.

A third way is to defer taxes wherever you can. By putting off tax obligations until you pass into a lower tax bracket, you'll obviously have a lower tax bill. Not only that, you'll have the advantage of compounding with the earnings that otherwise would have gone to pay current taxes.

There are several ways of deferring taxes. If you are self-employed, you can start a Keogh plan (see Chapter 41). Depending on your income level, you can also invest money in a tax-sheltered individual retirement account (IRA) (see Chapter 42). You can buy an annuity, where tax on the income generated by your contributions is deferred until you begin to draw benefits out. If you choose the right option on your ordinary life insurance policy, the dividends it earns may accumulate without any current tax liability.

You should take maximum advantage of any pension plans, savings programs, stock options plans, or salary deferral arrangements offered by your employer. While not all these plans will include a current tax benefit, they will provide you with a regular and disciplined savings program. For more on employee benefit plans, see Chapter 40.

Equities Have a Unique Advantage

But perhaps the greatest potential available to you for deferment of taxes lies with equities. The most convenient way to establish an equity position is through common stocks, and the best way to defer taxes via stocks is to choose those which emphasize capital growth. You pay taxes on dividends as received, but you don't have to pay any tax on appreciated value of the stocks until you sell them.

If you want to go whole hog and you're up to it, you can establish an equity position via outright ownership of a business or of rental real estate properties. If you possess the necessary know-how and talents, and if you do your homework properly, these could provide you not only with an appreciating asset but with a continuing source of income in retirement and a new "career" in the bargain. But it's risky, and not something that you should plunge into with all of your resources, for a loss could be disastrous and your time for recouping is severely limited.

Supplementing Retirement Income

If you think you'll need to generate extra cash to make ends meet in retirement, you should lay the groundwork before you get your gold watch. Whatever your motives for pursuing a postretirement career, the earlier you start preparing for it before you actually step down from your primary job the better are the chances for its success.

For one thing, you might have valuable contacts in your profession that will not be as readily available once you retire. For another, there might be some resources at hand; more and more companies are helping their older employees prepare for second careers. Sometimes these can constitute major incentives for stepping down early to clear the decks for younger managers on the way up. At any rate, an early start can give you the chance to work out a lot of the kinks before you actually have to start depending on the income from the new career. And you should count on plenty of kinks.

The first step, naturally, is to decide what you'll do. Explore the possibilities carefully. Check your potential market —be sure there's really one out there for whatever it is you consider, be it as modest as a garage fix-it shop or as ambitious as a globe-girdling consultant practice.

As you do your planning, don't forget to take the Social Security rules pertaining to taxes and earnings limitation into account. Remember that if you work and collect benefits, for every two dollars you earn above the limit you will lose one dollar of your benefit. At age seventy, you are no longer subject to the earnings limitations. However, if added earnings push your adjusted gross income above the $25,000 (single) or $32,000 (couple) base, half your Social Security or half the amount exceeding the base (whichever is lower) will be taxable as income.

Choose a business in which you have some demonstrated expertise—either professionally or via a well-developed avocation. Remember, the odds of failure of small businesses are very high. The more savvy and management skill you can bring to the job the better the chances of making a go of it.

Guard your resources. Zero in on something you can try in a small way first, so if it doesn't work you won't have lost all your savings. Remember, your ability to replace lost wealth after retirement will be severely limited, if not nonexistent.

If you don't like the idea of putting your savings on the line, you might consider working for someone else instead. You might find your expertise affordable to a small business on the less than full-time basis you'd be able to provide.

But remember, you'll be "retired." Unless it's really what you want, be careful not to replace one all-consuming career with another. By shaking things down before retirement, you can get an idea of how to pace yourself, what kind of time the new venture will take.

CHAPTER 40

Employee Benefit Plans

THANKS TO MAJOR legislation passed by Congress in 1974, most of the nation's workforce now qualifies for some type of retirement-oriented employee benefits. In fact, upward of 28 million workers currently participate in company-sponsored pension plans. If you are one of these workers, it's important that you be as familiar as possible with how your plan works. What type of plan are you enrolled in? How long do you have to work before your benefits are fully "vested"? What payment options do you have at retirement?

How important are employee benefit plans? If you did the retirement income calculations outlined in Chapter 39, you probably discovered that your projected pension income is larger than your estimated Social Security benefits. This should not have surprised you. Privately funded benefits probably will contribute a growing share of the average worker's retirement income in the years ahead.

The rapid growth of employee benefit plans since 1974 has not been without effect on the nation's businesses and financial markets. Not only do the plans provide ongoing employment for a bevy of lawyers and fund managers, but they also have become an important source of investment capital. Private pension fund portfolios now own about 25 percent of all outstanding corporate bonds and 12.5 percent of the nation's publicly traded stocks.

ERISA Sets New Standards

Why was 1974 such a watershed year for employee benefit plans? That was the year that Congress passed the Employee Retirement Income Security Act, more commonly referred to by the acronym ERISA. Although the act did not force employers to offer pension benefits to employees, for the first time it spelled out several regulations governing all employer pension plans.

What are ERISA's major provisions? Most of the act's regulations establish standards for a pension fund eligibility, contribution limits, vesting, and funding. For example, ERISA generally requires that if an employer sponsors a pension plan, all employees must be eligible to participate in the plan after reaching age twenty-five and serving one year with the company. The rules also prohibit plans from discriminating on behalf of any group of employees, such as owners or management.

While ERISA allowed companies to choose from one of four vesting schedules, the Tax Reform Act of 1986 mandated that companies adopt more rapid vesting schedules. The revised schedules, which become effective in 1989, require vesting at a 20 percent per year rate. Employers may start vesting with the first year the employee enrolls in the pension plan or delay it for two years. Thus, the employee's pension assets would be his property after five to seven years. The law also lowered the age at which employees must be covered by the company plan from twenty-five to twenty-one.

The funding requirements are designed to assure that adequate capital is available when an employee begins to draw benefits. How reliable is a pension when its sponsor has been negligent about the plan's funding? Employer contributions must adhere to a certain schedule. This prevents "backloading" of plans as employees approach retirement age.

Pension Benefits Insured

What happens to your pension if your employer goes bankrupt? In its infinite wisdom, Congress created the Pension Benefit Guaranty Corporation when it passed ERISA. The PBGC guarantees vested pension benefits in much the same manner as the FDIC insures bank deposits. In mid-1986, the PBGC had $1.7 billion in liabilities from terminated pension plans under its supervision. This insurance protection is funded by plan sponsors, each of whom must pay a set premium to the PBGC per plan employee.

From this brief overview of ERISA, you can see that the regulations are a problem for plan sponsors. For most companies, the cost of complying with the regulations has been tremendous. Since 1974, therefore, many corporations have either cut back on the scope of their pension plans or altered them to shift more of the costs onto workers.

What's What in Pension Plans

Sorting out the post-ERISA world of employee benefit plans is made more difficult by the lexicon peculiar to the field. For example, do you know what CODAs and ESOPs are? Or what distinguishes a thrift plan from a profit-sharing plan?

All employee benefit programs can be classified as either "defined-contribution" plans or "defined-benefit" plans. The latter term is just another name for ordinary employer pension plans. If you participate in such a plan, your retirement benefits will likely equal a fixed dollar amount or a set percentage of either your "career pay" or "final pay."

As noted previously, the ERISA regulations have become a major disincentive to funding pension plans. And a 1982 change in the law may further curtail the use of ordinary pension plans. The maximum annual defined benefit you can receive is now limited to the lesser of $90,000 or 100 percent of the average compensation during your three highest-paid years. But 1986 legislation reduced the maximum benefits that early retirees could receive. At age fifty-five the maximun benefit a retiree can receive is $40,000; at age sixty it is $60,000; and at sixty-two to sixty-five the limit is $72,000.

Defined-contribution plans, however, can take several shapes. And over time, such plans are usually a better source of retirement income. The three most common types are profit-sharing plans, stock-bonus plans, and thrift plans. A fourth, known as 401(k) or "cash or deferred arrangement" (CODA), has been very popular with employers and employees alike. However, the 1986 reform limited 401(k) contributions to $7,000 per year. Because defined-contribution plans are not subject to all of the ERISA regulations, they are less expensive to administer than pension plans.

Profit-sharing plans are a popular type of defined contribution among employers, particularly in small companies. Since annual contributions on behalf of employees are made from profits, in theory such a plan encourages employees to work harder. No profits, no profit sharing.

Stock-bonus plans are also known as "employee stock ownership plans" (ESOPs). Here, as in a profit-sharing plan, the company sets up a trust for the benefit of employees. And in both cases, the benefits put in trust for each participant must be in direct proportion to salary for the plan to be judged nondiscriminatory. But in contrast to a profit-sharing plan, employer contributions to ESOPs must be in the form of company stock and are based on a set formula rather than on profits.

A thrift plan usually has the features of either a profit-sharing plan or an ESOP. However, to participate you are required to contribute a given percentage of your salary to the plan. The employer then "matches" your contribution, either on a dollar-for-dollar basis or at a lesser rate such as 50¢ on the dollar.

What do all of these plans have in common? All three allow employers more flexibility than do pension plans. They also foster greater employee loyalty. Above all, defined-contribution plans—i.e., CODAs, profit-sharing plans, ESOPs, and thrifts—permit workers to accumulate substantial retirement nest eggs on which taxes are deferred until withdrawals begin.

Some Companies Provide Several Plans

It's possible to be covered by one or more of these defined-contribution plans at the same time. In fact, thrift plans are often used to supplement employer profit-sharing or ESOP benefits. Within limits, such an arrangement allows employees to make voluntary after-tax contributions to their accounts. But by law, the aggregate defined contributions that are made by your employer on your behalf each year cannot exceed the lesser of $30,000 or 25 percent of your salary.

What can you do if your employer's contributions fall short of this maximum? If you can afford it and if your salary qualifies you to do so, you can make a deductible IRA contribution. You should also contribute as much as possible—up to the $7,000 maximum—to your employer's 401(k) plan. Unlike thrift plans (employee savings plans) these deferral plans enable you to contribute pretax dollars.

Calculating Your Benefits

To avoid confusion, we have so far stayed away from going into too much detail on each type of plan. From a retirement-planning perspective, what is most important is that you make a yearly approximation of how much your accumulated benefits are worth. If you are covered by one or more of the defined-contribution plans discussed above, making such an estimate is fairly simple. That's because employers send out annual statements summarizing these accounts.

But making the same evaluation of your pension plan benefits is almost impossible. Employers are not always willing to divulge all of the information you need to make such a careful appraisal. However, they must supply you with answers to the following questions:

Who manages the plan? Depending on the fiscal health of your employer, it could be advantageous if a bank or insurance company manages your pension plan assets and administers the payment of benefits.

Is the plan contributory or noncontributory? If it is contributory, the company's only responsibility is to match your contributions to the plan. But if the plan is noncontributory, the employer is required to make contributions on your behalf at a level based on a percentage of your salary.

What formula is used to determine the size of your retirement pension? Your benefits might be based on your salary at retirement, the average of your highest-paid three years, or your average career earnings. This amount is then multiplied by your years of service to the company.

Are benefits integrated with Social Security? Employers can reduce the pension benefits paid to employees by 50 percent of the amount of Social Security primary benefits they receive at retirement.

How are benefits distributed? Many plans offer several options, including a lump-sum distribution, a payout in installments over a preset period, or a joint and survivor annuity. Most pensions are reduced if you retire early. Depending on the options you and your spouse choose, your benefits may or may not continue for your spouse. However, as a result of the Retirement Equity Act of 1984, unless a spouse signs a written statement requesting otherwise, a married retiree will automatically be put into a joint and survivor annuity.

The Tax Reform Act of 1986 and Pension Plans

This act may change many aspects of employee benefit plans in addition to those already cited in this chapter. Because the revisions were substantial, employers were given until the end of 1988 to revise their plans. The rules determining whether a plan is "top-heavy" (unfair to the rank and file) were tightened. The definition of "key employee" was broadened and clarified. It also placed a limit on the aggregate amount that an employee can collect from all plans. If the annual distribution exceeds $112,500, a 15 percent tax penalty is levied on the overage.

Reform also reduced the contribution limits and changed the taxation of distributions from 403(b) tax-sheltered annuities. These are the retirement plans that cover employees of nonprofit organizations. The contribution limit is the lesser of $7,000 or 25 percent of the employee's salary. Elective contributions may be made to 401(k) plans up to the same limit, but will reduce the 403(b) contribution. When the employee retires and annuity payments commence after 1986, he or she will no longer be able to receive a portion of the payment tax free indefinitely. Using the IRS tables, the exclusion ratio is calculated, and once the annuitant's cost is recovered, remaining payments are fully taxable. If the retiree dies prior to recovering his cost, then unrecovered costs are deductible on the final income tax.

Collecting Plan Benefits

Here, too, Congress busied itself to disallow previously bestowed tax breaks. The tax treatment of lump-sum distributions was significantly changed. Both ten-year averaging and capital gains elections will disappear eventually. Ten-year averaging was replaced with five-year averaging except for those persons who had reached age fifty by January 1, 1986. This age-qualified group can elect ten-year averaging, using 1986 tax rates, or five-year averaging, using 1987 or later tax rates. The election can be made prior to reaching age fifty-nine and a half, but if the ten-year method is chosen, it can be used only once.

Capital gains treatment of contributions made prior to 1974 is being phased out over six years. In 1987 all of those contributions are eligible for capital gains treatment; in 1988, 95 percent; in 1989, 75 percent; in 1990, 50 percent; and in 1991, 25 percent. However, no change was made in the rules allowing lump-sum distributions to be rolled over to an IRA.

What should you do now that you have all of this background information on pension and employee benefit plans? Keep two things in mind. First, remember that the pension tax laws are not set in stone but are subject to change at the whim of Congress. Second, know that few people can afford the luxury of choosing between employers based on the merits of their retirement plans. And fewer still are in a position to influence management's selection of plans. But by knowing the advantages and drawbacks of all your company's plans, you'll be in a better position to select those best suited to your present and future financial needs and through advance planning to offset any shortfalls. Investigate all of your options.

CHAPTER 41

Keogh Plans

UNTIL 1962, SELF-EMPLOYED individuals enjoyed none of the retirement savings tax breaks available to their corporate peers. As a result, corporate pension and retirement programs waxed into extremely lucrative fringe benefits with the blessings—and indeed the tax-subsidized dollars—of Uncle Sam. Meanwhile, the retirement savings of persons who worked for themselves waned, laboriously financed as they were with after-tax dollars.

Representative Eugene J. Keogh, Democrat of New York, took up the cudgel in Congress for the self-employed with his sponsorship and active support of legislation that would at least partially remedy the situation. His bill was assigned the number HR-10 in the 87th Congress, and it ultimately became the Self-Employed Individuals Tax Retirement Act of 1962. As with so many other pieces of legislation, its ponderously formal name has been obscured by history, and it is commonly known as the Keogh Act or, simply, HR-10. Retirement programs established by self-employed individuals under the act—and its subsequent amendments—are known as Keogh plans or HR-10 plans.

In its original form back in 1962, the Keogh Act did not provide much of a tax incentive. It allowed a self-employed person to set aside the lesser of $2,500 or 10 percent of his earned income each year, and to deduct from current taxes half that amount, or $1,250 on a maximum contribution. Furthermore, it provided penalties—stiff to the point of being confiscatory—for excess contributions and premature withdrawals. The stringency of the rules is a mark of the political price the opponents exacted before agreeing to let the legislation pass.

The benefits were liberalized in 1968, permitting the entire contribution to be sheltered. Then, in 1974, the contribution limit was given a significant boost to 15 percent of earned income, to a $7,500 annual maximum. The penalties for excess contributions and premature withdrawals were eased, and other liberalizations were provided. The maximum annual contribution that could be made to a defined benefit plan was doubled in 1982 and doubled again in 1984 to the lesser of $30,000 or 25 percent of earned income. Today a self-employed person has much the same retirement savings opportunities as do employees enrolled in qualified plans.

How Keogh Plans Work

So much for the evolution of Keogh plans. Suffice it to say that as a result of the Tax Equity and Fiscal Responsibility Act (TEFRA), for the years after 1983, contribution limits and benefits for Keogh, S corporation plans, and Simplified Employee Plans (SEPs) were brought into line with those of corporate qualified employee plans. But since Congress has a habit of changing laws every few years, as can be seen with the changes brought about by the 1986 Tax Reform Act, you should check the latest information before setting up a Keogh plan.

Who qualifies for a Keogh? Basically, if you pay a self-employment tax (Social Security), you qualify. But if you establish a plan for yourself you will also have to contribute for any full-time employee (one who works 1,000 hours or more per year) who is twenty-one years of age or older. These contributions must be in the same ratio as your own, unless the plan is integrated with Social Security. Contributions you make for employees (but not for yourself) are 100 percent tax deductible as a business expense.

As we said before, you can set aside up to 25 percent of your earned income (after the Keogh contribution) to a $30,000 limit annually. Both your contributions and all Keogh earnings are exempt from federal taxes as they accrue. Taxes on them are deferred until withdrawals start. Voluntary nondeductible contributions of up to 10 percent of your aggregate compensation for all years since you have been in the plan are also allowed.

Since 1976, self-employed individuals have been able to initiate defined-benefit plans that allow them to shelter more than the allowable limits under a defined-contribution Keogh. Under a formula based on earned income and age at entry in the defined-benefit plan, the maximum benefit that can be funded is the lesser of $90,000 annually or 100 percent of average compensation for the three highest consecutive years as a plan participant. Essentially, what these "Maxi Keoghs" do is allow a participant to make annual payments to a straight life annuity to the same extent he could if he were covered under a corporate defined-benefit plan with the maximum benefit level the same, $90,000 annually. While too complicated to detail here, these plans can benefit highly compensated professionals, and they should be discussed with a tax advisor.

As we indicated earlier, there are some penalties against which you must guard. You can be penalized for making early withdrawals. That penalty is 10 percent and is added to the ordinary income tax levied on the premature distribution. However, if you have made voluntary contributions to your plan, you may withdraw those assets at any time without incurring any penalty.

To make it easier and less expensive for you to begin a Keogh program, "master plans" and "prototype plans" have evolved. Under a master plan, several individual plans are grouped together, funded, and administered in common by a bank or insurance company. A prototype plan is individually administered under sponsorship of a professional association or a regulated investment company. A much more expensive alternative would be to have your advisors draft your own individual plan, which then would have to obtain Internal Revenue Service approval before your contributions could qualify for deduction.

Investment Alternatives

There are three basic investment alternatives available for Keogh plans. The first is to contribute to an insurance company's qualified annuity plan. The annuity contract might guarantee a fixed or a variable rate of return over the life of the Keogh. However, any portion of the Keogh funds used to purchase separate life insurance protection is not exempt from taxes.

The second alternative is to deposit Keogh funds with a bank or a trust company. Both act as custodians for the retirement funds and usually manage them as part of a professionally invested pool of pension funds. A third alternative is to invest in a mutual fund program through a custodian.

If you are so inclined, you may act as trustee for your own Keogh plan, saving red tape and costly trustee fees. If this is not permitted by your state, or you are not so inclined, you may use an institutional trustee or custodian and still make investment decisions for the plan by using a self-directed arrangement.

Banks have been the traditional repositories for self-directed plans, but insurance companies, savings and loan associations, and credit unions have a sizable share of this business. Some brokerage houses have custodial arrangements with banks, and you can set up a self-directed Keogh through them.

When considering a self-directed plan, weigh the advantages of control, flexibility, and modest cost against the disadvantages of having to do your homework in maintaining a solid portfolio. You should also remember that when the plan includes employees, you assume fiduciary responsibility for the entire Keogh plan if you manage it yourself.

Can you switch from one investment alternative to another? For the most part, yes. If you are in a mutual fund program, it's no problem to shift assets from one type of fund to another. You can also shift from a mutual fund to a trusteed account with a bank for investment in common stocks or other securities of your choosing. The greatest difficulty arises when you try to exit from an insurance annuity program. The best way to do this is to stop funding the annuity, i.e., freeze the assets, and divert future contributions elsewhere. Note that any "rollover" of Keogh assets from one type of plan to another must be completed within sixty days. Otherwise you immediately subject the account to taxes.

Collecting Your "Benefits"

When may benefits begin? Keogh assets cannot be withdrawn before age fifty-nine and a half without incurring penalties. An exception is made if you become severely disabled or die before that age. However, if your plan allows you to make voluntary contributions, you may withdraw them at any time without penalty. You must start withdrawing benefits when you are seventy and a half.

What is the tax status of the benefits you have built up over the years when the time comes to convert them into a retirement income program? Uncle Sam did not "excuse" the taxes you avoided during the contribution years, you can be sure of that. What he did was to allow you to defer them until you started using the assets you salted away. Besides the advantage of compounding we mentioned earlier, this also means that when you start drawing out the "benefits" you're generally in a lower tax bracket. Thus, the bite is not as great as it would have been had you had to pay during your earning years.

Withdrawal Options

Once you are eligible to begin withdrawing Keogh assets, you have several choices as to how you do it. You may take a lump-sum distribution or, under an annuity arrangement, you may choose to withdraw assets over your own lifetime, or over your lifetime and that of your spouse or other named beneficiary.

If you opt for a lump-sum distribution, you may roll it over to an IRA, use five-year averaging, and in some cases ten-year averaging or capital gains treatment. The 1986 Tax Reform Act eliminated ten-year averaging and phased out, over a six-year period, capital gain treatment for lump-sum distributions. To replace these favorable distribution methods, five-year forward averaging for lump-sum distributions received after age fifty-nine and a half has been adopted. This works the same way as ten-year averaging, only the lump-sum distribution is treated as if it had been received over a five-year period. Thus, the single filer rate is applied to 20 percent of the distribution and the result is multiplied by five.

Individuals who were age fifty by January 1, 1986, could elect to use special transitional rules allowing ten-year averaging once before age fifty-nine and a half. This precludes its use again after age fifty-nine and a half. Capital gains treatment, if used by these individuals, is at a flat 20 percent rate. Otherwise the phase-out rules on capital gains treatment of the pre-1974 portion of a lump-sum distribution allow the entire amount to be treated as a capital gain in 1987. The percent is reduced to 95 in 1988, 75 in 1989, 50 in 1990, 25 in 1991, and 0 thereafter.

When distributions are made under an annuity arrangement, part of each payment is treated as a tax-free recovery of voluntary contributions, if any were made. The balance is treated as ordinary income. If benefits cease prior to recovery of all voluntary contributions, the unrecovered portion may be taken as a deduction on the annuitant's final-year tax form.

Distributions After Death

If you die before distribution of plan assets has begun, then they must be distributed within five years of your death. But there are exceptions to this. The five-year distribution rule does not apply if plan assets are to be paid to a named beneficiary over his or her lifetime and will begin within one year of your death. The rule doesn't apply if assets are to be distributed to a surviving spouse over his or her lifetime. In this case the distribution must begin by the year you would have reached seventy and a half. If distributions had commenced before your death, then the assets must continue to be paid out to the named beneficiary at least as fast as previously.

There are tax implications for Keogh benefits received on the plan participant's death. In plans using retirement income, endowment, or other life insurance contracts, the entire cash value of the contract at the time of distribution must be included in the recipient's income, unless within sixty days of receipt it is irrevocably converted into an annuity. If conversion to an annuity is not elected, the cost basis of the insurance paid from voluntary contributions can be recovered. It is subject to the same tax treatment as other lump-sum distributions. When policy proceeds are ultimately paid they will not be taxed to the beneficiary. In addition the participant may transfer the policy so that proceeds will not be included in his or her estate. The first $5,000 of the distributions received from a plan may be excluded from the beneficiary's income as a death benefit.

Summing Up

There you have the basics of Keogh plans—how they originated, where they are now, and what you can and can't do with them. For self-employed persons, the advantages of contributing to a Keogh are greater than ever. But by the same token, the liberalization of these plans could prove expensive for self-employed individuals who must contribute to retirement plans for a number of employees.

CHAPTER 42

Individual Retirement Accounts

WHEN FIRST INTRODUCED in 1975, IRAs were an instant hit—more than 1.3 million taxpayers established accounts. Yet at that time these retirement savings accounts were only available for workers who were not covered by any other pension plan. Furthermore, contributions were limited to 15 percent of wages up to a limit of $1,500. In 1981, IRAs were opened to all workers and their nonworking spouses, regardless of participation in another qualified or government pension plan. The contribution formula was also enhanced, so that a worker could defer 100 percent of wages up to $2,000 in an IRA. In 1987 eligibility restrictions were placed on IRA plans once again.

How IRAs Work

Individuals who aren't active participants in tax-qualified pension, profit-sharing, or stock bonus plans, in 401(k), 403(a or b), Simplified Employee Plan (SEP), or government pension plans may contribute up to $2,000 tax deferred to an IRA. An active participant is defined as an individual who is covered by any tax-qualified plan for any part of the year. Furthermore, a worker who meets his or her company's plan eligibility requirements is considered an active participant whether he or she is enrolled in the plan or not.

Wage earners who are covered by one or more tax-qualified plans may still be eligible to make a *tax-deferred* IRA contribution if their adjusted gross income (AGI) is within prescribed limits. The limits are $25,000 for a single person and $40,000 for married couples. AGI for the purpose of determining IRA eligibility is the amount after passive losses and taxable Social Security benefits, but before IRA deductions.

Reduced IRA contributions are also allowed for singles with AGIs no greater than $35,000 and for couples whose AGIs don't exceed $50,000. The contribution is reduced ratably (to a floor of $200) according to the amount by which AGI exceeds the limits. However, when one spouse participates in an employer's retirement savings plan, the other spouse is not eligible for a *tax-deferred* IRA contribution even when his or her employer has no tax-qualified plan, if their AGI exceeds $50,000. For example, John Doe, who is covered under his employer's pension plan, earns $30,000. His wife, Jane, earns $15,000, so she can make a tax-deductible IRA contribution of $1,000. If her AGI were $20,000 she would not be eligible for a tax-deductible IRA contribution whether her employer had a pension plan or not.

An additional $250 may be contributed to a spousal IRA for a nonworking husband or wife. Prior to the passage of the 1986 Tax Reform Act, spousal IRAs were not allowed if the spouse had *any* earnings. The 1986 law allowed the $250 IRA contribution if earnings were $250 or less. However, when a couple's AGI exceeds $40,000, the spousal IRA contribution is reduced at the same rate as the wage earner's. Thus, if the couple's AGI was $42,000, the wage earner could add $1,600 to his or her IRA and the nonworking mate could contribute $200 to the spousal IRA.

A New Class of IRAs

Individuals who don't qualify for deductible IRAs may still make IRA contributions, but these must be designated as nondeductible. Deductible and nondeductible contributions together cannot exceed the $2,000 or $2,250 (spousal) annual maximum. Although these IRA contributions aren't tax sheltered, earnings on them accrue tax-deferred. If nondeductible contributions are made they must be designated as such on that year's income tax form. In addition, the total of all nondeductible contributions made to date that have yet to be distributed, the year-end value of all IRAs, and the amount of distributions in that year must be reported on the income tax form.

Because earnings on nondeductible IRAs accrue tax-deferred, these IRAs have merit, particularly for young wage earners. However, at a 33 percent maximum tax rate, a taxpayer must earn $2,985 to make a $2,000 nondeductible contribution to an IRA. Conversely, contributions which *are* deductible *save* taxes. The following table shows the comparative after-tax costs of contributing $2,000 to a deductible versus a nondeductible IRA.

Tax Rate	Deductible	Nondeductible
33%	$1,340	$2,985
28%	1,440	2,778
15%	1,700	2,353

A $2,000 investment which grows tax-deferred at 8 percent per year will be worth $9,300 in 20 years. But if that same $2,000 was invested in a fully taxable account it would be worth only $6,100 if its owner was in the 28 percent bracket.

Flexible Investment Options

How can you invest your IRA funds? There are three basic types of individual retirement savings programs—individual retirement accounts, individual retirement annuities, and trust accounts established by employers or employee associations.

An individual retirement account must be a domestic trust

or a custodial account created for the exclusive benefit of an individual or his beneficiaries. The trustee or custodian must be a bank, a savings and loan association, an insurance company, a federally insured credit union, a mutual fund, or any person who can demonstrate to the satisfaction of the Internal Revenue Service the ability to administer the account in accordance with the law.

To make it easier and more economical to establish an IRA, the Internal Revenue Service has created model trust and custodial agreements. By using Form 5305 (Individual Retirement Trust Account) or Form 5305A (Individual Retirement Custodial Account), you can establish an IRA almost as easily as a bank account.

Depending on whom you use as a trustee or custodian, you have a wide degree of flexibility in choosing the investments that fund your IRA. Most banks will set up an IRA using savings certificates. Most mutual funds will set one up using shares in the fund as assets. Stockbrokers, working with banks, can set up an account funded with stocks and bonds. These can be arranged so you can have an active hand in choosing the securities that fund the account.

Gold and silver coins minted in the U.S. were added to the approved IRA investment list beginning in 1987. The coins that qualify for IRAs are gold U.S. one-ounce, half-ounce, quarter-ounce and tenth-ounce pieces and U.S. one-ounce silver coins. The coins must be held by the plan trustee, not by the individual planholder.

No part of a trust or custodial IRA can be invested in life insurance. However, IRA moneys may be invested in annuities provided the death benefit, if the annuity has one, is not tied to mortality assumptions. Your interest in the account must be nonforfeitable, and the account's assets may not be commingled with other property except in a common trust fund or common investment fund.

An individual retirement annuity is a contract (either an annuity or an endowment policy) issued by a life insurance company in your name for your exclusive benefit or that of your beneficiaries. As with custodial or trust accounts, your interest must be nonforfeitable. Furthermore, to assure that payments will be used for your retirement, contract terms must provide that the annuity is not transferable and cannot be used as security for a loan. The annual premium cannot exceed the lesser of 100 percent of your earned income or $2,000, and any premium refund must be applied toward the payment of future premiums or the purchase of further benefits.

If you purchase an endowment contract, you can deduct only that portion of the premium allocable to retirement savings; any portion of the premium that pays for current life insurance is not deductible. However, if there is a difference between the cost of the retirement savings portion of the premium and your maximum allowable deduction, you may invest the balance in a separate IRA. The insurance company will provide you with an annual statement indicating the portion of the premium allocated to life insurance which is nondeductible.

Another possibility that might be available to you is participation in a group retirement annuity. The group annuity contract will be treated as an individual retirement annuity, provided it meets all the requirements of such an individual annuity.

Employer-Sponsored IRAs—SEPs

To encourage employers to sponsor IRAs for their employees, the Revenue Act of 1978 created Simplified Employee Pensions (SEPs) under the IRA umbrella. Using an SEP, an employer need not set up a special plan or draft a trust agreement as with other types of retirement programs. All the employer must do is prepare a written allocation formula—or use the prototype formula prepared by the Internal Revenue Service—and follow some simple administrative and disclosure procedures.

In fact, what the employer does is set up a separate IRA for each participating employee. The employer then may contribute up to 15 percent of compensation, but not exceeding $30,000, a year for each employee. Employer-sponsored plans may not discriminate against any class of employee. In fact, if the employer sponsors an SEP, every employee must participate—with three exceptions—and that participation can be a condition of employment. The exceptions: employees under age twenty-one, those with fewer than three years of service in the last five years, and employees who received less than $300 in compensation from the employer in the last year. Not included for determining SEP participation requirements are employees who are covered under collective bargaining agreements and nonresident aliens. In most other respects, the same rules that govern individual retirement accounts apply for SEPs.

Note the Penalties

There are penalties for making excess IRA contributions, for withdrawing funds from the account too early, and taking out too little or too much. You may not take a current income tax deduction on excess contributions. Furthermore, you are charged a 6 percent excise tax on them (this is not deductible on your income tax) for each year the excess remains in your account. You can avoid the penalty by removing the excess —and any earnings on it—from your IRA before the due date of that year's tax return. Excess contributions left in the account may be applied toward future years' contributions to reduce the impact of the 6 percent excise penalty.

The rules are equally explicit on premature distributions. If you receive a payment from your IRA before reaching age fifty-nine and a half, or becoming permanently disabled, it is considered a premature distribution. The amount withdrawn is included in your gross income for that year *and* you must pay an added 10 percent tax on the distribution.

You can be penalized for not taking enough out of your IRA, too. Once you reach age seventy and a half, you must withdraw either the entire balance in your account or start a schedule of regular withdrawals based on your life expectancy. If you fail to take out a sufficient amount you'll be hit with a 50 percent excise tax on the underdistribution. For example, if your minimum withdrawal at age seventy and a half is $1,000, but you only take out $600, you will have to pay a $200 penalty (50 percent of the $400 you failed to withdraw from your IRA). If you can show that the underpayment occurred because of a reasonable error, or that you are taking remedial action to correct the error, the IRS will waive the penalty.

Taking too much from an IRA aggregated with all other retirement savings plans can cause problems. Distributions from IRAs, qualified retirement plans, and tax-sheltered annuities which exceed $112,500 in any one year are subject to a 15 percent excise tax. Special higher limits apply for years when a lump-sum distribution is received. This penalty, which was new with the Tax Reform Act of 1986, became effective in 1987.

You'll Pay Taxes—Eventually

Uncle Sam's generosity has other limits, too. When he lets you set up an IRA, he does not forgive the taxes that you would otherwise have to pay—he merely allows you to defer payment of them. That deferral is operative until you start taking "benefits" out of your plan.

There are three ways in which you can take benefits from your IRA. The first option is to take all assets in a lump-sum distribution. If you choose this alternative, the total value of the account must be added to your taxable income for that year. However, now that income averaging has been eliminated, this election could trigger a prohibitive tax liability. A lump-sum payment can be taken any time after fifty-nine and a half, even after installment payments have commenced.

The second method is to use the assets which have accumulated in your IRA to purchase a single-premium individual retirement annuity. Payment options vary on annuities. Usually the contract guarantees a specified return on the annuity's value over your lifetime or the lifetimes of you and your spouse. But once annuity payments begin, you generally cannot change payment options. If you are uncertain about your future income needs, it would be unwise to lock yourself into an annuity contract.

The third, and most flexible, alternative is to arrange to receive distributions from the custodian in installments. The payments can be made as frequently as you see fit, perhaps monthly or quarterly, and are limited only by the total worth of your IRA. If your income requirements change, you may take the remaining assets in a lump-sum payment. Installment payments and annuity distributions are also taxable as ordinary income in the year they are received. If you elect to take installment payments remember that assets remaining in the account will continue to compound tax-free.

Nondeductible Contributions Complicate Distributions

The real confusion on nondeductible IRAs begins when distributions commence at or after age fifty-nine and a half. Since there is no tax due when nondeductible contributions are withdrawn (distributions of deductible IRA assets are taxable) it would be advantageous to deplete these assets first, or at least be able to determine from which account assets should be withdrawn. However, a foresighted Congress circumvented this potential tax advantage by writing complex distribution rules into the new law. These changes are especially disadvantageous to those who have large rollover IRAs.

When an individual has made both deductible and nondeductible IRA contributions, distributions will be counted for tax purposes as coming from both types of funds. The distribution will be taxable in the same ratio as nondeductible contributions bear to the value of the account, plus the distribution at the year end. All IRA and SEP accounts are aggregated to make these calculations, and withdrawals are totaled for each year.

Take, for example, a taxpayer who contributed $2,000 annually to an IRA for six years, the latest of which was a nondeductible contribution. Two years later, when the account is worth $16,000, he begins taking out $100 a month. At the end of that year the account's value, assuming 6 percent growth, is $15,724. To determine how much of the $1,200 in annual withdrawals is taxable, he adds $1,200 to the closing balance of $15,724 for an account value of $16,924. Next he finds the percentage of the total that his nondeductible contribution constitutes ($2,000 ÷ $16,924 = 11.8%). Therefore only $142 (11.8% of $1,200) of the $1,200 withdrawn from his IRA account is nontaxable.

As IRA assets are gradually depleted by distributions, the nontaxable portion of withdrawals increases. The following table, using the assumptions above (6 percent growth, $2,000 annual contributions, $1,200 in annual withdrawals, etc.) shows a dozen years of this progression. At the end of the twelfth year, $1,945 of the $2,000 in after-tax contributions has been recovered under the new formula. An increasing portion of distributions will be tax exempt in the ensuing years until the account is entirely exhausted.

Ending Value	Amount of Withdrawal	% Taxable	Withdrawal Amount Taxable	Untaxed
$15,724	$1,200	11.8	$1,058	$142
15,431	1,200	12.0	1,056	144
15,121	1,200	12.3	1,052	148
14,792	1,200	12.5	1,050	150
14,444	1,200	12.8	1,046	154
14,075	1,200	13.1	1,042	157
13,683	1,200	13.4	1,039	161
13,267	1,200	13.8	1,034	166
12,827	1,200	14.3	1,028	172
12,403	1,200	14.7	1,024	176
11,911	1,200	15.3	1,016	184
11,390	1,200	15.9	1,009	191

At age seventy and a half withdrawals *must* commence. Furthermore, you can no longer contribute to your account even though you may still be working. However, you can continue to contribute $250 to a spousal account for a younger, nonworking spouse. You have until April 1 of the calendar year following the year in which you attain age seventy and a half to begin taking distributions. Thus, if you are seventy and a half any time in 1987, then you must withdraw the minimum required amount by April 1, 1988.

The minimum distribution would be based on your account's value at the end of 1987. If an account holder is a male, then one-twelfth of the total value would have to be taken out by April 1, 1988; if a female, one-fifteenth of the

value would be required. These withdrawal fractions are from IRS Form 5329 (Return for Individual Retirement Arrangements Taxes). When withdrawals are made over two life expectancies, an IRS annuity table is used to determine required amounts.

IRA Is Soon Exhausted

Using the withdrawal timetables mentioned above, many retirees outlive their IRA assets. When the IRA is a rollover of a pension plan lump sum, outliving its assets could create a serious financial bind in old age. To correct this inequity, planholders are now allowed to take withdrawals based on a new life expectancy for each succeeding year after age seventy and a half. However, the IRS has not provided instructions for implementing this method. Using existing IRS tables for commercial annuities shows that for a male the account would not be totally exhausted until age one hundred eleven, and for a female, until age one hundred sixteen.

The following table shows the drawdown of an IRA using the old method compared with distributions made using a new life expectancy figure for each year of survival after age seventy. We assume the man's account has a $50,000 value

Age	Divisor		Amount Withdrawn		Year-End Balance	
	Old	New	Old	New	Old	New
70	12.1	12.1	$4,421	$4,421	$49,079	$49,079
71	11.1	11.6	4,731	4,527	47,783	47,987
72	10.1	11.0	5,062	4,668	46,066	46,678
73	9.1	10.5	5,416	4,757	43,875	45,188
74	8.1	10.1	5,796	4,787	41,150	43,564
75	7.1	9.6	6,201	4,856	37,830	41,757
76	6.1	9.1	6,636	4,910	33,842	39,770
77	5.1	8.7	7,100	4,891	29,111	37,663
78	4.1	8.3	7,597	4,855	23,552	35,444
79	3.1	7.8	8,129	4,862	17,072	33.063
80	2.1	7.5	8,699	4,717	9,568	30,660
81	1.1	7.1	9,307	4,621	931	28,185
82	.1	6.7	996	4,501	0	25,657

at the start of his seventieth year and a 7 percent annual growth rate.

If the minimum required distribution is taken annually, not only will assets outlast the account holder under the new method, but annual distributions (and their tax impact) will be more consistent from year to year. After taking the final distribution, the planholder will have received $80,091 using the old method for calculating withdrawals. By using a revised life expectancy annually, distributions will total $61,372 at age eighty-two, while remaining assets will equal $25,657. Of course, withdrawals can always be accelerated when and if the need arises.

Unisex Actuarial Table

A new table of life expectancies has been adopted by the IRS for calculating returns from commercial annuities. This table is based on actuarial experience more recent than the figures that have been previously used. If the unisex table is adopted for determining IRA minimum distributions, planholders will benefit greatly. The following table, which uses the same assumptions as above, clearly demonstrates how a planholder would benefit by using unisex life expectancies to draw down his or her IRA. In fact, after taking the age eighty-two distribution, this planholder would have collected $55,718 in distributions, yet still have $36,920 left in the account. At the end of the eighty-second year the IRA would have produced 16 percent greater total return than under the old IRS method.

Age	Divisor	Amount Withdrawn	Year-End Balance	Age	Divisor	Amount Withdrawn	Year-End Balance
70	16.0	$3,344	$50,156	77	11.2	$4,525	$46,158
71	15.3	3,508	50,159	78	10.6	4,659	44,730
72	14.6	3,676	49,994	79	10.0	4,786	43,075
73	13.9	3,848	49,645	80	9.5	4,852	41,238
74	13.2	4,024	49,096	81	8.9	4,958	39,167
75	12.5	4,203	48,330	82	8.4	4,989	36,920
76	11.9	4,346	47,367				

Using Tax-Free "Rollovers"

So far, we have discussed individual retirement accounts whose primary aim is to serve as repositories for regular annual contributions. But the law allows them to serve another —and, as it turns out, extremely popular—function. IRAs may be used to channel retirement funds from one qualified pension program to another, with no immediate tax consequences to the employee. This is what has come to be known as a tax-free rollover. There are several ways you can use a rollover. You can use one if you change jobs and want to take your built-up retirement benefits with you. You can use a rollover to shift funds into an individual retirement account and leave them there to continue building up under your direction and management. If you wish, and if your new employer has a plan that can accept them, you may place the assets in his plan, where they will be handled as if they had been there all along.

You can also use a tax-free rollover to change your IRA investment vehicle. Say you have an IRA with a mutual fund and you're not satisfied with the fund's performance. You can roll the assets over into another mutual fund or into a custodial or trusteed plan where they will be invested in something else. You can also use a rollover to shift benefits into an IRA if your employer terminates his qualified plan.

Some Rules on Rollovers

Whether you use a tax-free rollover to shift assets from one plan to another, to shift them into your control, or for some other reason, you must observe certain rules. Here they are. First, you must transfer the funds distributed from the old plan into the new one within sixty days of the distribution. Second, if property other than money is distributed, you must transfer that same property (usually stocks or bonds) or proceeds from the bona fide sale of that property to the new plan. Third, you may use the tax-free rollover provision only once in a twelve-month period.

If you reinvest your retirement assets in a rollover IRA from a qualified plan, you must have terminated employment with the company operating the qualified plan. In other words, while you may stop participating in a company plan where you work, you cannot shift any assets built up in the account into an IRA until you reach normal retirement age, which is the age at which the company plan regularly allows workers to retire and start drawing benefits. Furthermore, if you have made any after-tax contributions to the company plan, those amounts may not be rolled over into an IRA, although earnings on them can.

As you have perceived by now, the rules surrounding IRAs are far from simple. What's more, they tend to change with alarming frequency. So, when you're ready to think seriously about an individual retirement account, you should check with your nearest Internal Revenue Service office for the latest rules. Ask for the most recent edition of IRS publication #590, "Tax Information on Individual Retirement Savings Programs."

CHAPTER 43

Annuities as Retirement
Fund Vehicles

THE MAIN PURPOSE of an annuity program is to eliminate the gamble that your retirement funds and life span will come out even. A secondary purpose—particularly for those still some distance from retirement—is to provide a vehicle for creating these retirement funds and for protecting them as much as possible against the ravages of inflation and taxes.

Since annuities are tied closely to the concept of life insurance, they are sold primarily by insurance companies. In fact, insurance companies are the only ones legally permitted to vend commercial annuities. Mutual funds and stock brokerage houses that have begun in recent years to market annuities with special "investment" twists do so through tie-ins with life insurance companies.

You can purchase an annuity all at once with a relatively large chunk of cash (called a "single-premium annuity") or a little at a time through regular installment payments (called an "annual-premium annuity").

An immediate annuity is a single-premium annuity that starts to provide income at once. (Payments must begin within a year of inception.) A deferred annuity is one you purchase, either as a single-premium or annual-premium annuity, on which income distributions begin at some future date as specified in the contract. The period during which

455

you are paying into the annuity but are not drawing income is called the "deferral period" or "accumulation period."

Annuities as Savings Vehicles

Deferred annuities, whether single-premium or annual-premium, have long been popular repositories for savings that someday will be used to provide retirement income. One reason for this popularity is that an annuity program provides a discipline for regular savings. Another is that, in general, the assets thus set aside may be confidently regarded as "safe."

It's because of this safety that the government has encouraged the use of annuities in personal retirement savings programs. By law, annuity earnings are not subject to income taxes during the accumulation period. This makes annuities suitable for retirement savings either inside or outside Keogh and IRA plans. Since employees of charitable and educational organizations are allowed to contribute generous portions of their incomes to annuities, such contracts often form the backbone of these employees' retirement savings.

The tax features of annuities have become one of their greatest selling points. In fact, the increasing use of deferred annuities as tax shelters rather than as retirement savings plans has prompted Congress to rewrite the tax laws governing them several times, the most recently in 1986. Congress retained the tax deferral of annuity earnings, but revised the taxation of annuity payments.

During the accumulation period, your principal may be invested in a variety of ways, depending on the type of annuity selected. In a fixed annuity, the insurance company invests in bonds or debt instruments that return a fixed amount. The company can therefore guarantee you both the safety of principal and the rate of return. In the initial accumulation years the interest rate may be a few percentage points above the minimum rate guaranteed for the annuity's duration. However, the guaranteed rate frequently falls below the rate of inflation and even in the best of times barely keeps ahead of it.

To overcome this drawback, insurers introduced variable annuities, which allow the buyer to allocate his investment among portfolios of money-market funds, bonds, stocks, etc. Your investment may be reallocated a few times during the year. Your principal enjoys the benefits—and pays the consequences—of ups and downs in the stock market. Earnings on the account also reflect the skill of the portfolio managers and your wisdom in making allocations among portfolios. You're trading a guaranteed result for the chance to obtain a better inflation hedge.

How an Annuity "Pays" You

Historically—and annuities date back at least to the ancient Phoenicians—sellers of annuities agreed to pay buyers a predetermined amount periodically for life. No more, no less. But along the line, various payment options have been woven into the annuity fabric. These have evolved largely because of the quirk in human nature that resists giving away assets irrevocably, and out of the strong desire of one spouse to assure continued financial security for the surviving spouse as long as she (usually) should live.

Once the annuity begins making regular payments to you it becomes an income annuity. At the point where you shift from a deferred annuity to an income annuity, you must take care to choose the desired income option. Once income payments begin, you generally are not able to change options.

There are several options. A *straight life annuity* provides a predetermined amount of income for the life of the annuitant. Period. When he or she dies, all payments stop—even if they fall far short of the amount paid into the annuity.

A *joint and survivor annuity* is one that provides income for the lifetime of two persons, generally a husband and wife. It may continue income at the same level until the second one dies, or it may provide larger payments while both are alive and reduced payments after one dies.

A *life annuity with installments certain* provides income for the lifetime of the annuitant. In addition, it guarantees to make these regular payments for a specified number of years, paying them to a designated beneficiary if the annuitant should die within that period.

An *installment refund annuity* pays income for life to the annuitant. But if he should die before receiving as much money as he paid in, the payments will go to a beneficiary until that amount has been reached. A *cash refund annuity* does the same thing, except that instead of continuing regular payments to the beneficiary, it provides a lump sum equal to the amount of undistributed principal.

An important point to remember is that these various options do not provide the same amount of income. The more guarantees the annuity has, the lower the payments to you. Thus, in making the proper choice, your main task is to determine what your present and future needs are likely to be. Forethought is especially important, because, as we have said before, once you make a commitment on how you'll receive payments, the decision is generally binding.

How Much Will It Pay?

Your health plays no part in your ability to purchase an annuity—unless the annuity has some life insurance aspects tied to it. The amount of income an annuity provides is determined by your age at the time the income payments begin and by the type of annuity you choose.

The extent of the guarantees provided by the insurance company will also affect the payment level. The more guarantees, the lower the benefits. Thus, straight life annuities, which guarantee nothing beyond a steady income as long as you live, yield the highest return. But when you die, the payments stop, and your estate receives nothing, even if the payments fall far short of the amount you paid in. They go instead into the pool to provide benefits for those who live beyond the life expectancy of the age group. Simple enough logic.

A more common situation involves a husband and wife who desire to assure lifetime income for both. A joint and survivor annuity, which is simply a straight life annuity on two lives, answers this need for many.

Because of the multitude of individual variables involved, no one type of annuity is best for everyone. However, you should keep these considerations in mind as you pick your way to a decision:

Since an annuity's main purpose is to deliver the highest income possible, you should look for the one that does this best. A straight life annuity will usually win.

If you want to leave assets behind for your heirs, you can generally do it more profitably by means other than annuities. Divide your assets accordingly between annuity and estate.

Don't automatically assume a joint and survivor annuity would be best for you and your spouse. Where the wife is younger, which is usually the case, payments may be significantly reduced on a joint annuity, because it covers two lives. Even if she is two or three years older than her husband, the income level will probably be lower than that of a similar annuity for the husband alone. As you shop around, then, compare the income of a joint and survivor policy against the combined incomes of annuities purchased separately by husband and wife.

If you do choose a joint and survivor policy, consider taking one that reduces payments after the death of one spouse. Since living costs generally decline when one spouse dies, this arrangement would provide more income for both during their lifetime together.

Should You Use Annuities?

We've discussed the various options open to you as a potential annuity buyer. What should you do? If you are sold on the safety and dependability of annuities, you should probably allocate a portion of your retirement savings to them. If they are bought well in advance of retirement, their tax-deferral feature gives them a significant edge over investments that are taxable. But if you select a fixed annuity, it should be balanced by equity-type investments that will grow sufficiently to keep pace with inflation.

Another reason to be wary of becoming locked into an annuity program is that the very tax-deferral feature that attracts you to it could later work against you. That's because the only way you can escape a hefty tax on the accumulated earnings of the annuity is to take them out on an annuitized basis, that is, at a regular rate based on your life expectancy at the time you begin withdrawing them. As we noted earlier, this decision is an irrevocable one; once you've made it, you're stuck with it. You can no longer get your hands on the assets you've committed to this program, regardless of how desperately you may need them later.

What if you decide to redeem an annuity during the accumulation period? If you do, you'll have to pay a tax all at once on the accumulated income. And if such a withdrawal is made before age fifty-nine and a half, you will be liable for a 10 percent penalty as well. If you anticipate such a contingency, you would do better to ignore the tax advantage and put your cash in an investment that is accessible without penalty.

Consider a "Private Annuity"

When they think of annuities, most people think of the type purchased from an insurance company—commercial annuities, which we have just discussed. However, it is possible to enter into an annuity agreement quite independent of an insurance company contract. "Buying" one "privately" has much to commend it.

The provision of a lifetime income for the annuitant is only one of the motives for using private annuities. More often the use of these contracts is associated with estate planning. Because of their various advantages, private annuities might be put to good use in your financial planning program. However, there are certain disadvantages and potential pitfalls to avoid.

To create a private annuity, you (the annuitant) agree to "sell" certain assets to another party (the obligor) in return for a promise to pay you a fixed amount of money at regular intervals over your lifetime or for a set number of years. This payback must have a direct bearing on your life expectancy and it must be in accordance with the IRS table for annuity valuation. Currently these tables are based on a 10 percent interest rate. This means that when a person aged seventy transfers an asset worth $100,000 under a private annuity arrangement, the annual payment has to equal $16,523 in order to escape estate taxes.

Private annuities are frequently undertaken within families, with the obligor generally someone younger than the annuitant, say, a son or daughter. A family residence and other appreciated real estate are often used to finance the annuity. Sometimes these annuities are used as a method for an employer to pass on his small business to family members or employees, with the business itself funding the annuity.

The deferral of capital gains taxes on appreciated assets is the major advantage of employing a private annuity. Instead of paying such taxes "up front," which is the case when assets are sold to fund a commercial annuity, the tax on the capital gain is paid gradually as the capital is returned to the annuitant. Thus, the tax can be stretched over a period equal to the annuitant's life expectancy.

Besides the deferral of capital gains and the prospect of having regular income over your remaining years, you can have these other advantages by using a private annuity:

The assets can be removed from your estate and thus reduce potential estate taxes and administration costs.

As long as the "present value" of the annuity equals the value of the property transferred plus interest, there will be no gift tax.

The transfer of the property frees you of investment and management responsibilities.

Where the obligor is a relative (but not a child under fourteen) and is in a lower tax bracket than yours, you can lower the family's total tax liability with regard to income generated by the property.

The obligor, too, can reap benefit from such a transaction:

He assumes ownership of the assets and thus can take any tax deductions available on the property (but no deductions for payments to the annuitant).

He can use the assets to provide financial leverage.

He can sell or exchange transferred property without incurring any capital gains.

Proceed Carefully

There are, as we said, some potential disadvantages and opportunities for slip-ups that must be given consideration before committing your assets to a private annuity.

Foremost, the agreement must be carefully and expertly drafted in order to withstand a challenge by the IRS. Because of the complexity of private annuities and this need for careful drafting, you should undertake them only with the advice and help of competent legal and tax counselors.

It is also important for you to realize that you must choose an obligor in whom you have complete trust and confidence. At best, you are exchanging a valuable asset for an unsecured promise on the part of the obligor. If he should go bust or otherwise renege on his promise to repay you, you would have no way to protect yourself or your investment. (You can, however, cover yourself against his untimely death with a life insurance policy separate and apart from the annuity agreement.)

There are ways to avoid or minimize the drawbacks of private annuities, and your counsel can help you incorporate them into your program. In many cases the potential benefits of such private annuities far outweigh the hazards and make them worth the care and effort needed to create them.

CHAPTER 44

Estate Planning

EVEN IF YOU have done a good deal of estate planning—and most of us have done at least some—there's a chance you haven't gone over your program lately. If that's the case, it could well be out of date. An estate plan isn't something you can do and, having done it, say, "That's that." It needs adjustment from time to time to take into account changed conditions in your family and business situations. Furthermore, estate planning must be an ongoing concern regardless of the size of your estate or the seeming simplicity of your individual situation. Finally, your estate is something that quite likely needs the help of a variety of qualified advisors—your attorney, banker, accountant, insurance agent, and investment advisor.

This chapter will give you a starting point for a full-scale review of your own program. It will help you spot areas that need special attention. After this preliminary work, you'll be in a better position to call upon your various advisors for specific application.

The best place to start the review is to find out how much you're worth. Besides determining how much you're currently worth, as we discuss in Chapter 37, you ought to find out how much your estate would be worth. The difference can be substantial, of course, because of proceeds from insurance policies and other death benefits, plus lump-sum distributions from pension and profit-sharing programs where you work.

Net estate worth is the starting point from which estate taxes will be calculated. How much of a bite these taxes— federal and state—take will largely rest on how well you have designed your program. The difference between taxes on an estate subjected to little or no planning and one that is carefully thought out can be staggering.

Keeping Your Will Current

After you find out how much your estate would be worth, you have to think about what you want done with this wealth. The front line of protection in this regard is a will. You do have one, don't you? Is it current?

Dying intestate—that is, without leaving a will—could be one of the most thoughtless, tragic, and expensive errors in your estate planning. It means that the courts, using an impersonal and rigid formula set out by state law, will decide who gets what, regardless of how you or your heirs might have wanted things.

Almost as bad is leaving behind a will that is so far out of date or so carelessly planned as to be inadequate, invalid, or inappropriate to your own current wishes and family's best interests. No matter how simple or clear-cut you think your situation is, you ought to spell out with a will your desires regarding the disposition of your wealth as specifically as possible. Another thought: although you can draw up your own will, there's a better than even chance that such a home-made document will not stand up in court. It's always safest to have the work done by an attorney.

Choosing an Executor

Choosing the right executor is nearly as vital as drafting the proper will. Yet the choice of an executor is too often left to chance and sentiment rather than to common sense. A hasty and ill-considered decision ultimately can undo much of your otherwise careful planning and estate-building efforts.

Many persons almost automatically name their spouse, other close family member, or friend as executor, with little contemplation of the risks that will fall to this individual or the qualifications with which he would confront them.

On the other hand, a bank or trust company or an attorney specializing in estate management might not be as close to the family situation as a relative or friend, and might make decisions quite alien to your own desires or, possibly, to the real needs of the family.

But there is a way to have your cake and eat it too. That is to name your spouse or other relative as coexecutor with a bank or trust company. In such an arrangement, you could give your kin the final say in any decision, thus providing continuity in your family's life-style, while the professional executor would provide the good management, attend to the details, and be available to offer expert counsel.

As with other things, there is a difference in the quality of service between one institution and another. The better you know the bankers in your community, the better you'll be able to decide which one to choose. Your family lawyer can help you, too. Another way many persons get a feel for how a trust department would handle their estate is to establish a living, revocable trust, with the bank as cotrustee. The way the bank handles that trust is a good indication of how it would handle the estate.

An executor's task is not one to be taken lightly. In a small estate, with no major complications, where the will's intentions are clearly spelled out and there is not much property to dispose of or heirs to offer dispute, the job can be relatively easy. But in an estate of any substance, where there are children or elderly dependents and their continuing financial security to consider, or where family quarrels erupt, the job can be far from routine.

In such cases, the availability of an executor could be required over the span of several years. Can you be sure the person of your choice would meet this test? He could die or move away or be otherwise unable to carry on. In this event, a new executor would have to be appointed, at considerable expense to the estate. One way around this eventuality would be to name a successor executor at the time you draw up your will. Unless you designate an alternate choice, a court-appointed replacement might handle the estate, at a variance with your wishes.

Furthermore, an executor should have experience in this type of work. He should have the ability to conserve the estate's assets and administer them prudently. He should also be financially responsible. To be sure, an executor can be held legally responsible for the estate's assets if he carelessly handles them or illegally diverts them. He can be held liable for actions he fails to take as well as for oversights that result in losses. However, if he is financially unable to make restitution, the heirs will be the ultimate losers.

You are in the best position to know who will serve your family's interests well in your stead, if that ever becomes necessary. But you should make the choice only after considerable thought, and possibly with some advice from professionals. Your decision can be as important as the care you take in preparing your will.

Can You Use a Trust?

We mentioned trusts above. Do they have a place in your estate plan? They are not only for the superrich. More and more persons of modest means are using trusts to accomplish a variety of estate planning aims, from lowering taxes to helping charity.

The first step in deciding whether trusts are for you is to determine just what you want them to accomplish. The second is to understand some of the basic differences between various types of trusts.

Here are some of the things trusts can do for you: provide financial support for a relative; divide an estate among heirs; retain family privacy; help minimize estate taxes; provide professional management of assets; protect a family business; make gifts; assure bequests of specific property; help charity.

There are basically two kinds of trusts: those that are in effect while you are alive, or "inter vivos trusts," and those that become operative upon your death, called "testamentary trusts." Living trusts can be revocable (in which you retain control of the assets) or irrevocable (in which you permanently give up control). The distinction is an important one, particularly in estate planning.

Trusts can be used to assure a lifelong stipend for a spouse or other relative from the income generated by the trust assets, with the assets themselves going, say, to a child or grandchild on the income beneficiary's death. This serves two valuable functions. First, it assures an income for someone who might not otherwise possess enough financial acumen to use the capital wisely. Second, it can save a good deal in estate taxes because, in effect, the assets are taxed only once, while serving twice.

Short-term trusts can be used to provide income for an aged parent or other older dependent. These revocable trusts are of no use in reducing your estate, since if you die while one is in force, the assets are counted among your own. This is the case with any revocable trust, that is, any trust which you retain the power to dissolve, or the provisions of which you retain the power to change.

However, if the trust is irrevocable, its assets will not be counted in your estate, because you have given them away totally and permanently. You might find that you incur a gift tax liability when establishing and contributing to such trusts.

Where can you get specific advice about trusts? A good place to begin is with the trust department of your local bank. They can tell you whether your idea has merit, perhaps offer alternatives if it's questionable. They can also give you a picture of total cost. You should also talk with your lawyer early on; you'll need one for just about any kind of trust you set up. You might want to bring your tax counsel into the talks, too. He could have some insights into your financial picture that the lawyer might not have.

Pros and Cons of Joint Ownership

There are many valid reasons for married couples to hold property jointly. If their total estate is so small that taxes would be minimal or avoided entirely, many of the negative effects of joint ownership probably would be nonexistent—and possibly even be more than offset by certain benefits.

Here are some advantages of joint ownership: It can give a sense of family security. It can provide a safe and easy way to maintain and liquidate bank accounts. It can reduce estate administration costs and speed up the settlement of the estate, since property passes at once to the survivor. It can reduce or eliminate the need for probate.

One important thing you should realize about joint ownership is that it does not take the place of a will. Whether you choose joint or separate ownership, each spouse should have a will; that's the only sure way of seeing that your wishes are carried out after death.

There are many types of joint ownership, and a quick review here might prove useful. *Joint tenancy* permits co-ownership of real estate and other types of property, with right of survivorship. In other words, the survivor receives total title of ownership at the death of the other co-owner. *Tenancy by the entirety* is limited to joint ownership by husband and wife, and in many states to real estate only, with the right of survivorship. *Tenancy in common* permits two or more persons to own undivided shares in real or personal property; co-owners' shares pass to their heirs or beneficiaries, not to surviving co-owners. *Community property* is the assumption, in force in eight states, that each partner in marriage has an automatic right to half the couple's assets, regardless of who provided how much. (The eight community property states are Arizona, California, Idaho, Louisiana, Nevada, New Mexico, Texas, and Washington.) Business arrangements such as partnerships, syndicates, and joint ventures are yet other forms of joint ownership.

For most married couples, joint ownership means joint tenancy and/or tenancy by the entirety, where right of survivorship is a principal element. Many couples believe this arrangement is all they need in the way of estate planning.

Here are some reasons why that can be a dangerously short-sighted assumption:

It restricts your estate planning options. Because assets pass automatically from one spouse to the other on death of one, you cannot spell out in a will conditions under which your "share" of the property can be distributed.

It can be inconvenient. Both owners must give their OK to any changes in the property—changing the ownership status, disposing of it, and the like. This means signatures of both will be required when, say, selling jointly held stocks and bonds.

It could increase estate taxes. Although the gift and estate tax laws have been liberalized with regard to the marital deduction and joint ownership, there are circumstances where maximum use of the tax provisions cannot be made because property is held jointly.

What, if anything, can be done to unspring these potential traps? First, it isn't such a bad idea, under most circumstances, to keep the house in joint names. That way, the survivor acquires it at once on the spouse's death. Likewise for a savings account with enough money in it to carry the survivor over the first rough months until the estate is settled, or at least sufficiently organized to permit the disbursement of some funds. Second, you could decide to divide all other property equally, including securities and other real estate, by changing from joint tenancy to tenancy in common, dropping the right of survivorship. This way, each can dispose of his or her share by will. As with other such maneuvers, the guidance of professional counsel is advised.

How Gifts and Estates Are Taxed

Determining how large the taxes on your estate will be should provide ample inspiration for formulating an estate plan which minimizes federal taxes. But before delving into the how-to's of cutting estate taxes, it's important that you have a general understanding of the current estate tax code. Of course, Congress has a habit of updating and changing the rules, which makes it impossible to be too specific here.

The first thing to remember about the federal gift and estate tax structure is that it is progressive. The tax rate is incremental, increasing as a percentage as a taxable estate gets larger. Therefore, even modest efforts to reduce an estate's taxable size can have a significant impact on its total tax liability. This is an important fact to remember as you set about planning your estate.

Because taxpayers have a built-in incentive to reduce the size of their taxable estates, the Internal Revenue Service has evolved a body of rules governing the way in which these reductions can be made. Basically, the IRS wants a share of your estate and forgives taxes on it only begrudgingly. Congress, on the other hand, has become increasingly liberal regarding estate taxation in recent years. It has extensively rewritten the gift and estate tax laws three times since 1975, making it possible for more and more estates to escape taxation altogether.

How has the estate tax code changed? In 1976, Congress scrapped the separate gift and estate tax schedules. It replaced them with a unified tax rate on both and instituted a unified tax credit in place of the separate tax exemptions. In effect, the new unified credit exempted more estates from taxes by raising the minimum level at which taxation begins.

Congress further refined the tax code in 1978. Then, as part of the Economic Recovery Tax Act of 1981, it again made sweeping changes in the estate tax code. The unified credit, which offsets gift and estate taxes on a dollar-for-dollar basis, was again increased. The top estate tax rate was lowered. Joint property rules were simplified and the so-called marital deduction was made unlimited. In sum, the changes make it possible for most estates to be bequeathed tax free to heirs.

Marital Deduction

How you decide to apportion your estate will depend on personal circumstances and wishes. But from a tax savings perspective, primary consideration should be given to an estate plan that employs the unlimited marital deduction. Use of this deduction usually forms the backbone of most couples' estate planning strategies. It allows you to transfer all or part of your estate to your spouse tax free at death. The marital deduction also allows you to make unlimited gifts to your spouse while you are alive. But for an estate to qualify for the deduction, a couple must be married at the time of death of one spouse. Divorced persons may not claim a marital deduction.

An estate plan should not overwork the marital deduction. Sometimes its use can be counterproductive in the long run, saving taxes in your estate only to have substantially larger taxes imposed on your spouse's estate. This is particularly true when each spouse has considerable wealth of his or her own. When planning your estate, don't assume that the spouse with the most property will die first. Above all, your estate plan should be flexible. If you plan to bequeath all or part of your estate to your spouse to make use of the unlimited marital deduction, your will should also contain contingency plans in the event your spouse predeceases you or your deaths are simultaneous.

A well-structured estate plan should make maximum use of both the unlimited marital deduction and the increased unified credit. It's possible to use both techniques to assure the financial security of your surviving spouse while at the same time reducing the total taxes on both estates. Here's an example of how this can be done. Assets of $600,000 are used to fund a testamentary trust benefiting your surviving spouse. The testamentary trust's assets escape taxation in your estate and, upon your spouse's death, pass tax free to your chosen heirs.

The balance of your estate could be left to your spouse in the form of an outright bequest or in a terminable interest trust. Both qualify for the marital deduction in your estate and, when your spouse subsequently dies, for the unified credit in his or her estate. By maximizing use of the unified credit and marital deduction in such a manner, it is possible to bequeath as much as $1.2 million to your heirs tax free.

A Program of Planned Gifts

What else can you do to reduce estate taxes? Individuals with potentially taxable estates should consider making lifetime gifts to their future heirs. Gifts of up to $10,000 per donee per year may be made without incurring a gift tax liability. Married couples can give up to $20,000 per donee. In most cases, gifts made within three years of death are no longer considered made in contemplation of death, and thus are not included in an estate's value for tax purposes.

Remember, too, that both lifetime and testamentary gifts to charity also reduce your taxable estate. A program of planned giving can accomplish noncharitable goals as well. By funding a charitable remainder trust in your will, you can reduce estate taxes while also providing beneficiaries with a lifetime source of income.

Changes in the tax laws, new regulations, and court rulings continually add new shadings to the vast and complicated body of the estate tax code. These changes, as well as the specifics of your family situation, make periodic reviews of your estate plan necessary. Consult your tax advisor for suggestions on how best to meet your planning objectives while minimizing estate taxes.

CHAPTER 45

After Retirement

As YOU APPROACH retirement, you must begin implementing the plans described in Chapter 39 to provide for sufficient income. About a year ahead is not too soon to start making specific arrangements. You're close enough so you can get a fairly accurate reading on how much Social Security income you'll be getting. The same goes for your company's pension plan, if you're included in one. Those two items are pretty much fixed by rules and policies beyond your direct control, but are influenced by your decision to retire before or after age sixty-five. In deploying the assets you've built up in your own private retirement nest egg, you'll need to exercise much more judgment.

Social Security

But before we get into that, let's talk a bit about Social Security. It forms the backbone of the retirement programs of nearly all working Americans. It is frequently the largest single source of retirement income. Company pension plans are often tied directly to it.

For those receiving its retirement benefits, Social Security provides a basic monthly payment for life. It provides extra

473

for a qualifying spouse, and it provides for that spouse after the primary beneficiary's death. It meets certain medical expenses under its Medicare program. It reduces the benefits of recipients who retire early and of those who earn more than a certain amount in retirement.

That much is generally understood. But beyond that, most people's knowledge begins to get hazy. Here is a nutshell description of how your individual benefit level is determined. To qualify for full benefits, you must have at least forty quarters of "covered" service; that means you have to have worked the equivalent of at least ten years in a job where Social Security taxes were deducted from your pay. These days, that means just about everyone except certain public-school teachers and civil servants, who are covered by other plans.

Having thus qualified, you are then subjected to certain rules to determine the amount of benefits to which you are entitled. Your *primary benefit level* is based on your "best" forty quarters. For most of us, that means the most recent ones, because of rising income patterns and a rising wage base on which the Social Security taxes are computed. From these best forty quarters, your individual average monthly wage is computed, and once this has been determined, henceforth and forevermore your Social Security benefits will revolve around this figure. If you choose to retire before the normal retirement age of sixty-five—the rules allow you to start drawing retirement benefits at age sixty-two—your benefits will be set at a lower rate than if you wait until age sixty-five. If you work beyond sixty-five, you can earn higher benefits.

Because the rules and benefit tables are constantly changing, it is impossible here to get very specific about how much your benefit payments will be. So, about a year before your projected retirement date, contact your nearest Social Security office and ask for an estimate of your projected monthly benefit. You should start the actual paperwork involved in getting signed up with your local SS office about three months before retirement.

Then sit down with the people who manage your company's pension program and get a line on what to expect from that source. If you've been keeping tabs over the years, you'll have some general idea, and there should be no shocks or surprises there.

Next, take a pencil and calculator to the family budget to see where and how it will change after your retirement. If you're typical, you should be able to shave between a quarter and a third from your present living expenses. Now, put your expected retirement income figure next to your projected operating budget. You'll probably find a gap. As we mentioned in Chapter 39, it's a gap that's likely to widen with the years, too, because of the persistent rises in prices.

The wherewithal to fill that gap will come from the savings program you have been building and nurturing during your working years. The size of your nest egg will depend largely upon how conscientious you have been in adding to it and making it grow for you. The size of the nest egg in relation to the size of the gap will be a major factor in determining how best to deploy it.

What are your options? Annuities. Bank savings accounts. U.S. Savings Bonds. Bonds and other fixed-income securities. Real estate. Common stocks. Let's take a look, one by one.

Annuities

As you probably detected Chapter 43, we take a generally cautionary stance on the use of annuities as a source of retirement income. The main reason is that you must commit those resources irrevocably to the annuity, and therefore you strip yourself of a considerable amount of financial flexibility. You restrict your opportunities to juggle your assets around to meet changes in your situation. However, annuities have a specific utility as a tax-deferral tactic, as discussed in Chapter 43.

We do concede that there are certain instances where annuities can serve well. So, we offer here some guidance on when and how to choose them. First—when might you consider the use of annuities?

When you want an assured income for life.

When you don't want to or don't feel you can manage your own investments—or if you seek such security for an heir.

When annuity "income" earns more than other investments in the marketplace.

When your health and condition make it likely that you'll live longer than the annuity tables.

Second—when should you not consider annuities?

When your age and other factors make the return on your annuity lower than those available from other securities.

When times are particularly inflationary.

When it appears likely that you won't outlive the annuity tables.

Generally speaking, the older you are when you take out an annuity, the higher the yield will be. That's because the insurance company writing the policy is taking less of a gamble as you advance in age. The return on a policy taken out at age fifty-five would probably be lower than that which those same assets could earn in many other good-quality investment vehicles. However, if you hold out until age seventy-five, an annuity will yield considerably more—but keep in mind that the return is from both principal and interest.

That meshes well with the idea that during your younger retirement years, when you are still physically active and mentally alert, you should retain all the flexibility and control that you can over your assets. Then, as you grow older and less able to perform these tasks, consider placing some emphasis on annuities for your income.

But always remember: once your annuity income payments begin, you cannot change your mind. Unless there is some refund feature, your heirs will receive nothing when you die. All too many annuitants—and heirs—fail to realize this, to their ultimate woe.

One other caution: because annuities so severely limit your financial flexibility once you're committed to them, we firmly recommend that under virtually no circumstances should you convert all of your available assets to them. They should be regarded only as partial answers to your income needs.

In shopping for an annuity for guaranteed retirement income, do not assume that they all pay about the same. In one list of thirty-nine different companies' straight life annuities, there was a 15 percent differential between the highest and lowest figure for monthly payments per $1,000. As you compare, you should also determine whether the companies charge a fee and, if so, how much it is. An unusually large one can significantly affect your return. Check, too, to see which companies offer discounts on larger annuities.

It may seem basic, but be sure that you compare the same type of annuity as you investigate each company. The straight life annuity generally offers the best income return, so that's a good place to begin. But if you feel another type better suits your needs, obtain comparisons on it.

Savings Accounts

Bank savings accounts can play a useful function in your retirement program. They can serve as repositories for funds on their way from one investment to another. They can provide a fund from which you can draw to meet financial emergencies. They can even be used to provide long-term income.

Let's turn our attention for a moment to the latter function. As a rule, the longer you promise to keep your money in a bank account or term certificate, the higher the interest rate you will receive. A notable exception is the short-term money-market account, which under certain interest-rate conditions will provide a better return than some longer-term CDs. Because interest rates that financial institutions pay depositors are no longer regulated, a bank aggressively seeking deposits may sweeten its rates above those of its competition. So shop around for the best rates.

In looking for the best deal, note how the institution compounds interest. The shorter the compounding period, the more generous the yield. But also check when your deposits begin accruing interest—immediately or at the first of the next month? Does the bank impose a fee if the account drops below a certain limit? Are there restrictions on the number of monthly withdrawals? An extra interest point can be easily offset by unfavorable compounding terms, fees, or restrictions.

There are certain advantages to keeping your money in a

savings account. Foremost is safety. The deposits are fully insured; thus there is no loss if the institution should go broke. Second, savings accounts are simple to open—and to close—and there are no sales commissions or other expenses involved when making deposits or withdrawals, as there are when buying and selling securities. Third, they provide you with a source of ready cash when it is needed in an emergency.

But there are some drawbacks, too. Savings institutions impose penalties on time deposits which are withdrawn before the time specified in the agreement. Penalties are no longer regulated, so these too may vary. Be sure to inquire about these fines before investing in a term account. The "penalty" has no stigma attached to it; the money is yours to withdraw at any time, no questions asked. It just means that if you take it out before the agreed-upon interim, you don't get the agreed-upon rate, and you're assessed something for the bank's trouble.

When deciding whether to use savings accounts and/or term certificates, you must compare this return against what you would be able to get elsewhere. Sometimes corporate bonds will pay more and provide virtually the same safety of capital. Sometimes you'll want to link some prospects for capital growth to the income return on your assets, so you'll look at common stocks. Sometimes you'll have an opportunity to reap greater rewards with a real estate investment. We'll examine some of these below.

U.S. Savings Bonds

We discussed the savings aspects of U.S. Savings Bonds in Chapter 35. Now, suppose you have been salting away a $50 E or EE bond each month for the past thirty years or so. As you make plans for your retirement, you'll want to consider the alternatives for turning this substantial savings bundle into a source of continuing income.

For purposes of illustration, suppose by the time you retire you have an even thirty years' worth of bonds purchased monthly—360 of them, at a cost of $37.50 each for the Series

E and $25 for the EEs. Your total cash outlay was $12,525. At retirement, with the accumulated interest, your bonds are worth more than $35,000. Here are four alternatives.

PLAN ONE. Cash in one bond a month, using the oldest ones first. In your first year of retirement your "income" would amount to about $2,100, with around $1,650 representing accrued interest, on which you'd have to pay federal income taxes. (Note than on Savings Bonds, as with most other U.S. Treasury and agency bonds, earnings are exempt from state and local taxation.) The annual income figures would rise somewhat in subsequent years as a result of the higher interest paid on newer bonds. Depending on your life expectancy, you might prefer to accelerate the program by cashing two years of bonds in one year.

PLAN TWO. Convert the E and EE bonds to HH bonds. The tax deferment on the accumulated E or EE bond interest would continue, but the semiannual interest payments from the H or HH bonds would be taxable as received. In converting the entire nest egg, you might have to add some cash in order to make an even exchange (HH bonds come in $500 minimum denominations).

PLAN THREE. Cash in all your Savings Bonds and reinvest the proceeds in better-yielding Treasury securities or corporate bonds. This may or may not be feasible, depending on interest-rate conditions when you retire. Of course, you would immediately incur a tax liability on the $23,000 or so of accrued interest.

PLAN FOUR. Cash in the E and EE bonds and reinvest the proceeds in a common stock portfolio. As in plan three, you'd have an immediate tax liability. The stocks you choose should provide an average annual total return of 11 percent, a performance widely regarded as realistically attainable for well-chosen common stocks held over the long term. By tilting your portfolio toward income stocks, you could obtain, say, 6 percent in dividend yield, with the remaining 5 percent representing capital growth. This would give you, on average, $2,200 in annual income in the early years, but increasing amounts as the years pass. But if your investments appreciate at the aforementioned rate of 5 percent each year, at the end of ten years they will be worth $57,000, and $92,000 in twenty, nicely hedging you against inflation. To do this, you must be aware that you might incur some risk, though that risk is minimized if you stick with investments in the highest-quality companies.

There can be variations of these plans, of course, or they can be employed in some combination. Then, too, the capital need not remain untouched under plans two, three, and four. It can be withdrawn gradually to provide steady income or it can be reserved to meet financial emergencies.

Here is a point to note when redeeming or exchanging E-type bonds. Proper timing of the redemption or exchange can prevent lost income. Unlike daily interest savings accounts, Savings Bonds do not accrue interest between payment dates. Interest is earned and reckoned every six months.

Thus, on a $25 E bond which has been held for twenty years or so, a poorly timed redemption could reduce earned income by as much as $2. Careful planning, especially when a large number of bonds are being cashed or exchanged, can pay off.

Say you have bought an E or EE bond each month over the past several years and now want to swap them for HH bonds to provide retirement income; you can do this most profitably by staggering the exchange over a six-month period. In January, exchange the bonds acquired in January and July of each of the past years; in February, the February and August bonds, etc.

If you start this exchange program six months before you retire, you'll begin receiving interest checks immediately after retirement, thus providing something to help fill the earnings gap right away and not six months down the road.

There's another benefit to employing this gradual exchange tactic. Since HH bond interest is paid semiannually, you not only avoid lost interest by using this serial redemption program, you also establish a schedule that provides you with an income check each month instead of only twice a year.

Corporate Bonds

We discussed corporate bonds extensively in Chapter 8, so by now you're familiar with how they work. But during the years you were building up your retirement fund, you probably did not give them much thought. Now, when income will become your primary investment concern, you may want to add some to your portfolio to provide assured income as well as safety of capital.

That's fine, and as we noted in the earlier chapter, you might even be able to build in inflation protection by acquiring some deeply discounted bonds that you can redeem at par when they mature.

As you consider bonds, look at those with "medium" maturities—those whose maturities aren't too far into the future. As we said earlier, bonds trade on the market near their par as they approach maturity. If you should have to liquidate some along the way, you'll want to do so at par or as close to it as possible.

But because their potential for capital growth is limited, you probably won't want to commit all of your retirement funds to bonds. It depends on what your income needs are, of course, but we tend to believe that 20 percent or so in bonds is about right in most cases.

If you want instant diversification in the bond portion of your retirement portfolio, you can consider some bond funds; we discussed them in Chapter 13.

If you want more opportunity to provide capital growth but you still like the idea of bonds' safety and assured income, you can look at some convertible bonds. They were discussed in Chapter 9. They provide somewhat less yield than straight corporates, and somewhat less opportunity for capital appreciation than common stocks. But that's all part of the trade-offs we've been discussing throughout this book.

Real Estate

Unless you're looking for a new "job," or are willing to lay out money to a manager, the eve of retirement is not the time to start thinking about rental real estate as an investment. But there is this aspect: Rental income is not regarded as "earned" income as far as the Social Security earnings limitation rules are concerned, so no matter how much rental income you earn, it will not reduce your Social Security benefit.

What if you already hold real estate? Should you sell and reinvest the proceeds? Or should you keep the property, use the income, and call its appreciating value your inflation hedge? Several important factors will enter into your decision.

The best starting point would be to determine the true net yield on your investment—the amount realized after paying all expenses, utilizing any tax offsets, and taking into consideration the amount of your own efforts expended in management. Then, compare that yield with the kind of yield the same assets would generate if diverted to other investments. (Remember, there would be some erosion of assets in making any switch—commissions, other sales expenses, etc.—and probably some taxes.)

Next you must determine the future prospects of continued ownership. Will the property continue to gain in value at least as fast as other, comparable real estate? Will rent increases likewise keep pace with inflation? Is there a chance the property could decline in value? Factors such as location, condition of property, and development trends of the community and neighborhood must be studied.

Then you must consider the personal aspects of continued management. Would it tie you down more than you wish? Would the management become too much of a burden as you grow older? Does ownership tie up too much of your wealth, creating the risk of loss in a "distress sale" should you suddenly need to liquidate to obtain funds? Does the real estate constitute too heavy a proportion of your investment portfolio to afford good balance? Would changes in the tax code make the property economically unsound?

Having considered these factors, you then must choose from several alternatives:

Retain the real estate and continue to collect rent.

Sell it all now and reinvest the proceeds in stocks and bonds.

Gradually divest yourself of the property, selling first the least desirable pieces, reinvesting proceeds as received.

Sell the real estate, but write the mortgage yourself. This would give you income as well as a gradual return of capital, while freeing you of the burdens of management and ownership. (Be sure if you choose this option to have the help of competent legal counsel to safeguard your interests.)

Obviously, there is no "right" answer. In general, though, it is our feeling that retirees should make their financial affairs as trouble-free as possible, within the bounds of good sense and sound judgment. It has been our experience that carefully chosen common stocks and bonds go a long way toward providing the sort of returns needed for current income and protection of buying power, while at the same time minimizing the management effort.

Common Stocks

Now you come to your common stock portfolio. During its accumulation years, you have been concentrating on growth, on building its value as much as possible, with little concern for how much income it was generating—or even making a studied effort to avoid income while your salary kept you highly taxed. Now, on the verge of retirement, you suddenly have to shift gears and find investments that will provide income to fill that "gap."

Because it takes time to make an orderly transition, we urge you to move slowly in this regard, as in all other investment decisions. In the first place, a wholesale shifting of "growth" stocks for "income" securities could increase your tax liability and eat heavily into your assets. In the second place, some of your "growth" stocks might also be perfectly good "income" securities, and therefore should be retained.

Don't feel that because you are retiring you must completely divest yourself of common stocks and go entirely into "safe" fixed-income investments. When you think of the impact inflation has on the assets thus deployed, you have to wonder just how "safe" they really are.

On the other hand, wisely chosen common stocks, because they are equity investments, will tend to rise in value right along with—or even well ahead of—the rise in prices. Not only will their asset value rise, but so also should their dividends. Therefore, common stocks should play an important role in your investment picture after retirement, just as they did before.

How, then, does a retiree's investment portfolio look? It will depend, of course, on your own particular situation, but for the purposes of example, here is a fairly conservative approach to deploying a $100,000 nest egg for a couple retiring at age sixty-five:

Amount Invested		Annual Income
$ 15,000	Bank accounts and term certificates for immediate needs and minor emergencies and a money-market certificate or fund for income. Average yield, 8%.	$1,200
65,000	Common stocks. A portfolio with somewhat less emphasis on growth than during the accumulation period, but not entirely committed to income. A representative income yield would be about 6½%.	3,900
20,000	Corporate and government bonds and/or bond funds. Yields will vary according to current market activity, but a representative expectation would be around 10%.	2,000
$100,000	.... TOTALS	$7,100

Consuming Your Capital

Contrary to the old Yankee axiom that it's sinful to dip into principal, it sometimes makes very good sense to do so. The trick is to make the available capital last as long as you'll need it. There's no sure way of foretelling how long that will be, of course, but there are some rules of thumb that you can apply to the task. More on them in a moment.

First, there are some ways you can consume your capital in a rational fashion. One has to do with common stocks, as discussed above. Instead of taking your tax lumps to switch a growth stock to an income issue and then, to boot, paying taxes on the income generated by the new stock (not to mention the in-and-out brokerage commissions), why not sell off a few shares of the appreciated stock as you need the cash? You'll raise the income you require, you'll incur a small tax liability, and you'll still have a good part of your original stake left to continue growing. In terms of the number of dollars invested, you might well stay ahead.

Another way you can do the same thing is to invest in a mutual fund that has a cash withdrawal program. It will send you a regular amount each month, making up the required sum either from earnings on the assets or from the assets themselves. The rate at which the fund is growing and at which you withdraw from it will determine how long your assets will last.

If the combined earnings and appreciation of your stocks or mutual funds equal or exceed the rate at which you're withdrawing, your assets will last forever, of course. But what if you must consume your capital faster than it's growing? To get an idea of how long your capital should last, start by checking longevity figures.

As a safe rule of thumb, about one and a half times the indicated life expectancy should be enough of a cushion for

Life Expectancy Table

Age	Male	Female	Age	Male	Female
50	25.4%	31.1%	68	12.7%	16.6%
51	24.6	30.2	69	12.2	15.9
52	23.8	29.3	70	11.6	15.2
53	23.0	28.4	71	11.1	14.5
54	22.2	27.6	72	10.6	13.9
55	21.4	26.7	73	10.1	13.2
56	20.7	25.9	74	9.6	12.6
57	19.9	25.1	75	9.1	12.0
58	19.2	24.3	76	8.7	11.3
59	18.5	23.4	77	8.2	10.8
60	17.8	22.6	78	7.8	10.2
61	17.1	21.9	79	7.4	9.6
62	16.4	21.1	80	7.0	9.1
63	15.8	20.3	81	6.7	8.6
64	15.1	19.5	82	6.3	8.1
65	14.5	18.8	83	6.0	7.6
66	13.9	18.1	84	5.6	7.2
67	13.3	17.3	85	5.3	6.8

SOURCE: National Center for Health Statistics (1982).

estimating your own longevity. Then, using the following table, determine the number of years your assets will last if they are growing at a slower rate than they are being withdrawn. For example, a widow aged sixty-five with a life expectancy of nineteen years should plan on making her capital last for about twenty-eight years. That means that on assets that are earning and appreciating at a combined 9 percent annual rate, she could safely withdraw 10 percent of her principal each year.

Withdrawal Rate	Annual Growth Rate of Funds									
	5%	6%	7%	8%	9%	10%	11%	12%	13%	14%
6%	36						number of years			
7%	25	33					principal should			
8%	20	23	30				last			
9%	16	18	22	28						
10%	14	15	17	20	26					
11%	12	13	14	16	19	25				
12%	11	11	12	14	15	18	23			
13%	9	10	11	12	13	15	17	21		
14%	9	9	10	11	11	13	14	17	21	
15%	8	8	9	9	10	11	12	14	16	20

In Conclusion

We've covered a lot of alternatives in this chapter, and you can be forgiven if you are somewhat confused by the array of options open to you. Don't panic. But it's because of the number of decisions you'll have to make that we suggested at the outset of the chapter that you start considering them at least a year in front of your retirement date.

We can't tell you exactly how to make these decisions, of course. What we've tried to do here is lay out the options, note their pros and cons, and give you an idea of what they'll do—and won't do—for you.

You have to put together a package you're comfortable with, one that doesn't keep you awake at night worrying about the risks, and one that isn't so complicated that you have to stay up nights managing it. Some people can live with more risk than others, so they won't lose sleep over a plan that would turn the next guy into an insomniac. Others really enjoy a plan that gives them something to do, like managing an investment portfolio or a piece of rental property.

We suggest that you retain as much flexibility as you can in your plan, so you'll be able to roll with any punches that come your way, and so you can change the program to meet any changing needs that come with advancing age.

PART VII

Speaking the Language of the Bulls and the Bears

An extensive glossary of investment, economic, business, legal, and financial terms of importance to investors.

Glossary

acid test   (also known as quick assets ratio or liquidity ratio). The ratio of current assets less inventories to current liabilities. The acid test provides a better test of a firm's current operations than the current ratio, since inventories often do not prove liquid enough to service current debt. *See* **current ratio.**

adjustable rate bond (or adjustable rate preferred stock). A security on which the interest rate (or dividend) is adjusted each payment period in relation to a recognized market rate such as the prime or that on Treasury bills; there may also be a maximum and/or a minimum on the adjustable rate.

advance-decline index.   The net result of all advances and declines which have occurred on the NYSE or other exchange since a particular starting point. The ratio derived from relating advances to declines provides an overbought/oversold index.

advisory service.   An organization offering information, generally buy and sell advice, to investors for a fee.

AMBAC—American Municipal Bond Assurance Corp. A consortium of leading insurance companies which guarantees principal and interest payments on municipal bonds. Evidence of the insurance is printed on or attached to each bond. Since the initials are part of the description of the bond, they should appear on the broker's confirmation and statement.

American Depositary Receipts (ADRs).   Negotiable receipts issued by an American depositary bank stating that a certain number of foreign shares have been deposited with the overseas branch of the depositary or with a custodian. Since foreign stock is often in bearer form, the ADR facilitates such matters as the receipt of dividends by the shareholder.

American Stock Exchange (AMEX).   The second-largest securities exchange, located in New York City. The AMEX's volume is approximately as heavy as that of all the regional exchanges combined.

amortization.   The gradual liquidation annually of the cost of an intangible asset such as a patent or a debt. Amortization is a bookkeeping entry and does not require an outlay of cash.

annual report.   The formal financial statement issued yearly by a corporation to its shareholders.

annuity.   Payment made to an annuitant at some regular interval for either a specified or indefinite length of time. Annuity contracts are sold by life insurance companies. "Annuity" also refers to the contract under which the payments are made.

arbitrage.   The act of purchasing a particular security or commodity in one market and simultaneously selling it in another market at a higher price. The arbitrageur profits when the price differential between the two markets exceeds the cost of the operation. Also, the purchase and sale of related securities—common, options, and convertible bonds or preferreds—for profit on price differentials.

assets.   Physical properties or intangibles of value owned by an individual or a business.

authorized stock.   The maximum amount of stock which can be issued by a corporation according to its certificate of incorporation, which may at any time be amended by stockholders' vote.

balanced fund.   A mutual fund which diversifies its portfolio holdings over common stocks, bonds, preferreds, and possibly other forms of investment. Holdings of defensive securities are proportionately increased when the market outlook appears unfavorable, and aggressive positions are stressed when the market seems to be headed upward.

balance sheet. An accounting statement showing the amount of a company's assets, liabilities, and owners' equity as of a given date.

bar chart. A form of chart used extensively by technicians. The horizontal axis represents time and the vertical axis represents price. Vertical lines are drawn at each time period, with the top and bottom of each bar plotted at the high and low prices for the period. A small horizontal line is drawn across the bar at the closing price. Many charts also include a vertical scale at the bottom depicting trading volume.

basis point. A unit used to measure changes in interest rates and bond yields. One basis point equals .01, or $\frac{1}{100}$ of 1 percent.

bear. One who believes that the market is headed downward. One theory of the term's origin holds that the old proverb "to sell a bear's skin before one has caught the bear" describes what the short seller (bear) is doing, because the short seller does not own the stock he is selling. The terms "bull" and "bear" were both used on the London Stock Exchange in the early eighteenth century. *See* **bull.**

bearer bond. A bond which does not have the name of the owner registered in the books of the issuer, but on which interest and principal are paid to the bearer. Although new bonds have not been issued in bearer form since December 31, 1982 (under terms of the Tax Equity and Fiscal Responsibility Act of 1982), many previously marketed bearer bonds are still outstanding. *See* **coupon bond, registered bond.**

beta. A measure of the sensitivity of a stock's price to fluctuations in a particular average. A volatile stock has a high beta, and a low-risk stock generally has a low beta. If a stock tends to move the same as the average, it has a beta of one.

bid price. The highest amount a prospective buyer is willing to bid or pay for a security at a given time.

Big Board. Another name for the New York Stock Exchange.

blue chip stocks. High-quality stocks of major companies which have long, unbroken records of earnings and dividends, good growth prospects, well-regarded management, and a conservative financial structure.

Blue List. A daily trade publication for dealers in municipal bonds listing the names and amounts of municipal bonds that dealers all over the country are offering for sale.

blue sky laws. Laws various states have enacted to protect the public against securities frauds.

bond. Evidence of a debt on which the issuing company usually promises to pay the bondholders a specified amount of interest for a given length of time, and to repay the loan at the maturity date.

book value. A company's total assets less its liabilities and the liquidating value of its preferred stock. The result is divided by the number of common shares outstanding, to put the measure on a per-share basis.

broad tape. A machine operated by Dow Jones & Co. which prints important financial news on an enlarged form of the ticker tape. *See* **ticker.**

broker. An agent who handles buy and sell orders for securities or commodities for a commission charge.

bull. One who believes that the market is headed upward. One theory of origin holds that the way a bull tosses things up with its horns describes the action of a bull on the exchange. *See* **bear.**

business cycle. Regularly recurring periods of economic activity encompassing prosperity, recession, depression, and recovery.

businessman's risk. The risk involved in securities transactions which a businessman appears able to undertake. The term generally denotes securities entailing greater than average risk, but not so much as speculative issues.

callable. A bond or preferred issue all or part of which may be redeemed by the issuing corporation under definite conditions prior to maturity. Many high-coupon bonds are vulnerable to call in periods of declining interest rates.

call option. A contract which allows its owner to buy a certain number of shares of stock at a specific price, within a given period of time. The term also refers to commodity contracts.

capital gain or capital loss. Profit or loss from the sale of a capital asset. Tax considerations are different from those on ordinary income.

capital goods. Material goods used in the production of other goods.

capitalization. The total amount of securities (bonds, preferred stock, and common stock) issued by a corporation, plus its retained earnings.

cash flow. The reported net income of a corporation plus the amount charged off for depreciation, depletion, amortization, and other charges which are bookkeeping deductions and which do not entail actual payout of dollars and cents.

certificate. The actual piece of paper which is evidence of ownership of stock in a corporation.

certificate of deposit (CD). A certificate for money deposited in a commercial bank for a specified period of time and earning a specific rate of return.

Certified Financial Planner (CFP). A designation conferred by the College for Financial Planning upon individuals who have completed a series of comprehensive exams. Other qualified institutions offer similar study programs.

channels. A technical analysis term. Channels are drawn on a chart by connecting a series of highs and a series of lows to make parallel lines. Characteristically, a stock will trade within ascending and descending channels.

Chartered Financial Analyst (CFA). A professional designation awarded to those financial analysts who have passed a series of three examinations requiring knowledge of accounting, financial statement analysis, economics, and finance, as well as competence in investment management and securities analysis.

Chicago Board Options Exchange (CBOE). A market established in 1973 for the formalized trading of put and call options.

Chicago Board of Trade (CBT). One of the oldest and largest organized commodity exchanges in the U.S. Officially chartered by the Illinois state legislature in 1859, the CBT provides facilities for trading in selected cash and futures markets.

churning. Excessive trading in a customer's account without adequate or proper justification. Churning is usually done to generate additional commissions.

clearing house. A corporation which takes the opposite side of all trades. The clearing house becomes the buyer to all sellers and the seller to all buyers.

Clifford trust. A short-term trust. Assets placed in the trust return to the donor after a specified period, as long as that period extends at least ten years and one day, or upon the death of the beneficiary. Meanwhile, income earned by the assets is taxable to the beneficiary.

coincident indicators. Economic indicators which tend to move directly with the business cycle. *See* **lagging indicators, leading indicators.**

commercial paper. Unsecured short-term negotiable promissory notes of well-known business concerns and finance companies.

commission. The amount paid to a broker or other agent to buy or sell securities or commodities.

commission broker. A broker who owns a seat on the exchange and executes transactions on the floor for customers of his member firms.

commodity contract. A firm legal agreement between the buyer or seller and the commodity exchange's clearing house.

commodity futures market. A market in which contracts for the future delivery of commodities or foreign currency are bought and sold. The most important function of the futures market is that it provides a means of insurance against the risk of adverse price fluctuations between the time of the production of the commodity and its utilization.

Commodity Futures Trading Commission (CFTC). The agency created in 1974 by the federal government to regulate the commodity business, as the SEC oversees the securities industry.

common stock. Securities which represent ownership interest in a corporation. Preferred stock normally has prior claim in regard to dividends and, in the event of liquidation, assets. Stockholders of the common assume greater risk for potentially greater reward.

common stock equivalent. All stock options and warrants, plus all convertible securities which at time of issue have a cash yield of less than two-thirds of the then current prime rate.

confirmation. A formal memo delivered to a client of a brokerage house which bears all data relevant to a securities transaction executed for the client.

conglomerate. A diversified corporation with operations in a number of varied industries.

contractual plan. A plan under which a mutual fund investor signs a contract agreeing to invest a specific sum of money in a particular fund at regular intervals for a definite period of time. Since, according to law, 20 percent of the first year's investment may be deducted as a sales charge, there is a monetary loss in dropping out of the plan prior to completion.

conversion parity. The point at which the price of a convertible security is equal to the value of the common shares into which it can be converted.

conversion value. The worth of a convertible bond, preferred stock, or warrant if it were converted into common stock under the terms of the conversion privilege and if the common stock obtained by conversion were sold at its current market price.

convertible security. A bond, debenture, or preferred stock which may be exchanged by the owner for common stock or another security, usually of the same company.

coupon bond. A bond with interest coupons attached. The coupons are clipped as they come due and are presented by the holder to a bank for payment. *See* **bearer bond, registered bond.**

covered option. An option written against securities already owned. *See* **naked option.**

cumulative preferred. Preferred stock on which unpaid dividends accrue. Dividends in arrears on a cumulative preferred stock must be paid before any common dividend.

current ratio. The ratio of current assets to current liabilities. This measure is used to evaluate a firm's liquidity. *See* **acid test.**

cushion bond. A premium bond, selling above its call price. Because of the possibility of call, it does not tend to rise as much in price as other bonds of a similar maturity when interest rates decline. It therefore does not decline as much when rates rise. Thus price action is cushioned by the call feature.

custodian account. An account—brokerage, bank, Keogh, mutual fund, etc.—held in the name of the custodian for the benefit of another.

cyclical stocks. Stocks of companies whose earnings fluctuate with the business cycle. Cyclical industries include steel, cement, paper, machinery, and autos.

day order. An order to buy or sell which is good for one day only.

dealer. An individual who acts as principal, in contrast to a broker, who acts as an agent. A dealer buys securities for his own account and then sells them to a customer from his own holdings. Profit or loss is the difference between the price he paid for the security and the price at which he sells it.

debenture. A promissory note backed by the general credit of a company and usually not secured by a mortgage or lien on any specific property.

debt to equity ratio. The relationship of long-term debt and other long-term liabilities to common shareholder's equity. This measure is commonly used to indicate leverage.

defensive stocks. Stocks of companies in steady businesses which are relatively unaffected by the ups and downs of the business cycle. Examples of defensive industries are electric and telephone utilities and food suppliers.

deferred annuity. An annuity purchased as a single-premium or annual-premium annuity on which income distributions begin at some future date.

deferred sales charge. Also called a back-end load, this fee is used to discourage investors trading in and out of mutual funds too frequently. The charge declines the longer the shares are held.

depletion. Charges against earnings to reflect the gradual exhaustion of natural resources, such as ore, oil, and timber. It is a bookkeeping entry and does not require a cash outlay.

depreciation. Charges against earnings to write off the cost, less salvage value, of an asset over its estimated useful life. Like depletion, it is a bookkeeping entry.

discount. Amount by which a security may be purchased that is below its redemption value, as in Savings Bonds, Treasury bills, and some corporate bonds.

discount broker. A broker who charges a smaller commission than that of a full-service broker. Generally no investment advice is given by a discount broker.

discount rate. The interest rate the Federal Reserve Board charges member banks for loans.

discretionary account. An account in which the broker determines the timing for buying and selling as well as the selections and number of shares to be bought and sold.

disintermediation. The outflow of money from savings banks and other financial institutions to higher-yielding investments.

diversification. Spreading investments among different companies in a variety of industries, and/or among different types of securities or investments in order to spread risk.

dividend. A payment designated by the board of directors of a corporation to be distributed to shareholders on a pro rata basis.

dividend payout ratio. The percentage of earnings that is paid out in cash dividends.

dollar cost averaging. An investment plan under which an investor purchases an equal dollar amount of a given stock or stocks at regular time intervals.

double tops and bottoms. A technical analysis term which refers to chart formations in which the stock fluctuates, hitting the same top or bottom on two and sometimes three or four successive occasions. The breakout from such a pattern is the clue to the action to be taken.

Dow Jones Industrial Average. An average of thirty blue chip stocks. The average was originally published in 1897, based on twelve stocks. Adjustments in the divisor are currently used to reflect stock splits or stock dividends.

Dow Jones Transportation Average. An average of twenty transportation stocks.

Dow Jones Utility Average. An average of fifteen utility stocks.

Dow Theory. A theory of market analysis based on performance of the Dow Jones Industrial and the Dow Jones Transportation averages. According to the theory, the market is in a basic uptrend if one of these averages advances above a previous important high, accompanied or followed by a similar advance in the other. When the averages drop below previous important lows, a confirmation of a basic downtrend occurs.

downtick. A term which designates a transaction made at a price lower than the preceding transaction in a particular stock.

dual funds. Publicly traded investment companies with two classes of stock—capital shares and income shares. Capital shareholders are entitled to all of the capital appreciation but no income. Income shareholders receive all of the income from the portfolio of holdings.

dual listing. The listing of a stock on the NYSE as well as on another exchange.

efficient market. The theory which holds that stock prices always reflect all available relevant information.

Employee Retirement Income Security Act of 1974 (ERISA). The law which created a uniform federal standard for fiduciary conduct relating to the establishment and maintenance of corporate employee benefit plans.

exchange privilege. The right to exchange shares of one mutual fund for shares of another fund under the same sponsorship at net asset value or at a reduced sales charge.

ex-dividend date. The date when the stock sells "ex," or without the dividend. On or after this date, which is the fourth full business day preceding the record date, the buyer receives the stock "ex," or without the dividend.

federal funds rate. The interest rate charged on overnight loans from one member bank of the Federal Reserve System to another.

Federal Reserve Board. The seven-member board of governors of the Federal Reserve System, the central bank of the United States.

FIFO (first in, first out). The method of inventory valuation in which those goods purchased first are assumed to be sold first. *see* **LIFO.**

financial futures contract. A contract under which an investor agrees to buy or sell a financial asset at a given future date and price.

fiscal policy. The use of a government's spending and revenue-producing activities to achieve certain objectives.

fiscal year. A corporation's accounting year. Because of the nature of their particular business, some companies do not use the calendar year for their bookkeeping. Retailing concerns, for instance, generally end their year on January 31, because of the Christmas rush.

flat. A bond that trades flat is one that trades without interest accruals. Bonds which are in default of interest or principal are traded flat. Income bonds trade flat, since interest is not paid on a regular basis but only when earned. Most bonds trade "plus interest," with the buyer paying the seller the interest that has accrued since the previous payment date.

floating supply. The proportion of the listed capital stock of a corporation available for trading purposes; usually excludes shares closely held by management.

flower bonds. Certain U.S. Treasury bonds which can be purchased at a discount and turned in at par for payment of federal estate taxes if the bonds are actually owned by the decedent at the time of death.

Form 10-K. A report which a corporation must file with the SEC within ninety days after the end of each fiscal year. The 10-K contains certified financial statements and is more detailed than the annual report.

fully diluted earnings. The earnings figure that gives effect to all securities which could be converted into common stock and which would reduce earnings per share. *See* **primary earnings.**

fundamental analysis. The study and evaluation of such basic elements as earnings and dividend growth potential, and the varied impact of economics and politics on the market as a whole or on a particular industry or company.

general obligation bond. A major type of municipal bond backed by the full faith and credit of the issuer.

good-till-canceled (GTC) order. An order to buy or sell which remains in effect until it is either executed or canceled.

Government Retirement Bonds. A special series of U.S. individual retirement bonds issued by the federal government under the provisions of the Second Liberty Bond Act. The government discontinued the sale of these bonds in 1982.

gross national product (GNP). A measure of the nation's total output of goods and services.

growth stock. Stock of a company whose sales and earnings are expanding faster than the general economy. Retained earnings are largely plowed back into the business to facilitate expansion.

head and shoulders. A technical formation whose name is derived from the appearance given by the pattern of a head and right and left shoulders. If a stockholder has not previously sold on the higher, "head" level, he should take advantage of the rally which forms the right shoulder, because price deterioration on reduced volume can set in quickly.

hedge. To try to minimize risk by taking certain steps to offset the risk. In commodities, hedging is taking a position in the futures market that is equal to but opposite from an existing or soon-to-exist position in the cash market.

hedge funds. Mutual funds which always keep a portion of their portfolios in a "short" position.

high-technology companies. Those companies engaged in, or developing products that require, high-level scientific research. Drug, electronic, defense, aerospace, communications, and computer companies are examples.

holding company. A corporation that owns the majority of stock or securities of one or more other corporations for purposes of control rather than investment.

hypothecation. The pledging of customers' securities as collateral for loans to brokers and dealers.

income bond. A bond which promises to repay principal but pays interest only when earned.

income stock. Common stock which pays out a relatively large portion of earnings in dividends, and thus provides a high yield to investors.

indenture. A written agreement under which debt securities are issued. It sets forth the maturity date, interest rate, call provisions, security, and any other factors affecting those bonds.

index funds. Mutual funds whose portfolios either duplicate the structure of the S&P 500 or other selected average or consist of 100 or more S&P issues to track the average. The indexing concept concedes that since it is difficult to beat the average consistently, analysis and investment fees should be reduced and the performance of the average matched.

Indicator Digest Average. Equal dollar investment-type average of all stocks traded on the Big Board.

individual retirement account (IRA). A tax-deferred retirement savings account available to all workers and in limited amount to nonworking spouses and divorced spouses.

insiders. Directors, officers, and principal securities holders of a corporation. Principal holders are those who own 10 percent or more of a publicly traded company's stock. The SEC requires insiders to report their initial position and details of any significant change in their holdings.

institutional investor. An institution, such as a bank, life insurance company, or pension fund, whose investments constitute an important part of overall operations.

intestate. Without a will.

investment banker. The intermediary in the money markets who assists corporations in raising capital from investors. A profit is made on the difference between the price paid to the corporation and that at which the securities are sold to the public.

investment company. A corporation which sells its own securities to the public and invests the proceeds in other securities in keeping with an indicated objective. *See* **mutual fund.**

Investment Company Act of 1940. The basic federal law

governing the registration and regulation of investment companies.

investment tax credit. This credit against taxes is given for the purchase of business equipment. Congress legislates the credit as a means of encouraging spending to spur the economy. When revenue-raising needs become more important than pump priming, Congress limits or withdraws the credit.

joint and survivor annuity. An annuity which pays income over the lifetime of two individuals.

junk bonds. Lower-quality bonds, generally below investment grade, which provide exceptionally high yields with commensurately high risks.

Keogh plan. A retirement plan set up under the Self-Employed Individuals Tax Retirement Act of 1961 (HR-10). Self-employeds and their employees can set aside a stated percentage up to a maximum dollar amount in a tax-sheltered retirement account. The dollar and percentage amounts are altered by Congress from time to time.

lagging indicators. Indicators of economic activity which change direction subsequent to moves in overall economic activity.

leading indicators. A group of indicators of economic activity which tend to turn up or down in advance of general economic activity.

leverage. The effect obtained when borrowed funds are added to invested equity in a financial venture.

liabilities. Claims against the assets of a corporation or individual.

LIFO (last in, first out). The method of inventory valuation in which those goods last acquired are assumed to be sold first. LIFO reduces earnings in periods of rising prices. *See* **FIFO.**

limited partnership. A form of investment often employed because of favorable tax consequences. The limited partnership limits both the risks and the rewards of the investor but puts the planning and decision-making in the hands of a professional management team.

limit order. An order in which the buyer or seller indicates to his broker the specific price at which it is to be executed.

A limit order to buy specifies a price below the market; a limit order to sell indicates a price above the market. *See* **stop order.**

liquidation. The process of converting securities or other property into cash.

liquidity. The cash or near-cash position of a corporation. Also, the term refers to the ability of the market in a particular security to absorb a reasonable amount of buying or selling at reasonable price changes.

listed stock. Stock of a corporation which is traded on a securities exchange.

living trust. A trust which is in effect during the life of the testator, also called an inter vivos trust. A living trust may be revocable (control is retained over assets) or irrevocable (control is permanently forfeited).

load. The sales charge a buyer of mutual funds may have to pay in addition to the actual net asset value of the shares.

management fee. The fee deducted from the gross income of an investment company prior to any distributions to shareholders. Generally it amounts to ½ of 1 percent of the fund's net asset value. Also, the fee charged by an investment counselor for his service.

margin. The value of securities and cash in a brokerage account against which an investor may purchase more stock. Margin requirements in the past twenty years have ranged from 40 percent of the purchase price to 100 percent. In commodity jargon, margin refers to funds put up as security or guarantee of contract fulfillment.

margin call. A call from a broker asking for additional cash in order to bring the equity in a customer's margin account at least up to the margin maintenance requirements stipulated by the exchange. The margin call is made when the value of securities in an account declines.

market order. An order to buy or sell a stated amount of a security at the most advantageous price obtainable after the order is presented on the trading floor.

maturity. The scheduled date for repayment of the principal amount on a bond or other debt instrument.

MBIA—Municipal Bond Investors Assurance. A consortium of leading insurance companies which guarantees principal and interest payments on municipal bonds. Evidence of the insurance is printed on or attached to each bond. Since the initials are part of the description of the bond, they should appear on the broker's confirmation and statement.

monetary policy. The management by a central bank of a nation's money supply to insure the availability of credit in line with national objectives.

money market. The arena in which short-term funds (less than one year) are channeled. Money-market instruments include promissory notes and bills of exchange, commercial paper, bankers' acceptances, Treasury bills, short-term tax-exempts, dealer paper, and negotiable certificates of deposit.

money-market funds. Mutual funds that invest in money-market instruments.

money supply. The sum total of money stock. Common measures are M1, which is currency in circulation plus demand deposits (checking accounts), and M1A, which is adjusted for seasonal variations.

mortgage bonds. Bonds which are secured by a conditional lien on part or all of a corporation's property.

moving average. One of the popular methods for determining market and individual stock strength or weakness. A moving average is obtained by adding up the prices for a certain number of days and dividing the total by the number of days involved. For the next figure, the price for the earliest day or week is dropped and the current one added.

municipal bond. A bond issued by a state or political subdivision, or by a state agency or authority. Interest from most municipal issues is exempt from federal income tax and in some cases from state and local taxes.

mutual fund. An investment company which enables its shareholders to pool their capital into a single professionally managed account. *See* **investment company.**

naked option. An option written against stock which is not currently owned. *See* **covered option.**

NASD (National Association of Securities Dealers). A national organization which provides for the self-regulation of the over-the-counter market.

NASDAQ (National Association of Securities Dealers Automated Quotation system). A computerized communications system that collects, stores, and displays up-to-the-second quotations from a nationwide network of over-the-counter dealers making markets in stocks included in the NASDAQ system. Certain requirements must be met in order for a stock to be included.

net asset value. The total market value of a mutual fund portfolio less liabilities, divided by the number of shares of the fund outstanding.

New York Stock Exchange (NYSE). The largest national securities exchange.

New York Stock Exchange Index. The unweighted average of all stocks listed on the New York Stock Exchange.

odd lot. A trade of fewer than 100 shares. *See* **round lot.**

offering price. The price for which mutual fund shares may be purchased. It includes any load fee.

open-end investment company. An investment company in which the price is determined by the per-share net asset value of the portfolio. There is no fixed number of shares. These funds make a continuous offer of shares for sale to the public, and at any time will buy back outstanding shares at net asset value.

open market operations. The purchase or sale of government bonds in the open market (mostly in New York) by the Federal Reserve Board. Open market operations are the chief stabilizing tool of the Fed.

option. The right to buy or sell specified securities at a set price within a stated time period.

option clearing corporation. The organization which acts as buyer to all sellers and vice versa for all traded options.

over-the-counter market. A negotiation market which has a dollar volume greater than the total of all stock exchanges.

par value. The amount stated on the face of a bond, preferred stock, or common stock. Interest or dividends are often stated as a percentage of par in the case of bonds and preferreds, and bonds are generally redeemed at par on their maturity date. In the case of common stock, however, par value bears no real relationship to the market price or underlying value of the shares.

Pink Sheet. A daily publication of the National Quotation Bureau. Prices on over-the-counter securities are listed along with the names and telephone numbers of those firms which make a market in them. Prices quoted by these firms are not definite bids and offers.

pit. The trading floor of a commodity exchange where traders and brokers stand as they trade in particular commodities.

point and figure chart. A technical chart which shows a compressed picture of significant price changes. These charts are designed to show strength of price movement and to emphasize changes in direction.

portfolio. The total securities held by an institution or a private individual.

preferred stock. A class of stock which has preference over the common stock of a corporation regarding the payment of dividends. In the event of liquidation, preferred shareholders have priority over common shareholders in the distribution of assets.

premium. The amount by which a security, bond, convertible, etc. sells above its redemption or conversion value.

price-earnings multiple. The current market price of a share of stock, divided by earnings per share for a twelve-month period. (Also called price-earnings ratio.)

primary earnings per share. Net income after preferred dividends, divided by common shares outstanding plus the shares that would be outstanding if common stock equivalents were actually converted.

primary issue. The original sale of stock, where proceeds revert to the issuing company.

prime rate. The rate of interest charged by commercial banks for short-term loans extended to their best customers.

private placement. The selling of securities directly to one or more large investors, without the services of an underwriter or an SEC registration.

profit margin (pretax). Pretax income divided by net sales. This figure is a measure of the efficiency of a company, although profit margins vary from industry to industry and company to company.

prospectus. A printed communication which offers a security for sale. The prospectus contains salient parts of the registration statement, which gives all information relevant to the issue.

proxy statement. Information required by the SEC to be given stockholders as a prerequisite to solicitation of proxies for a security subject to requirements of the Securities Exchange Act of 1934.

prudent man rule. The rule which enables a trustee to use his own judgment in making investments as long as he acts in a prudent manner. The rule comes from an 1830 court decision.

put option. A contract giving the right to sell a certain number of shares of stock at a specific price, within a defined time period.

random walk. A theory which states that the size and direction of a stock market or individual stock price action cannot be predicted from the size and direction of previous moves.

ratio writing. Writing calls on more shares than are actually owned.

real estate investment trust (REIT). A professionally managed portfolio of real estate properties and/or mortgages.

record date. The date on which a shareholder must be registered on the books of a corporation to receive a declared dividend or vote on company affairs.

red herring. A preliminary prospectus which does not include the price at which the securities are to be offered to the public. It is issued to obtain an indication of interest in an offer. It gets its name from the statement, printed in red ink on its front cover, that it is a preliminary prospectus.

redemption fee. A 1 percent or 2 percent charge that mutual funds sometimes levy on shares liquidated within the first year of purchase.

refunding. Replacing an outstanding debt obligation with a new obligation.

registered bond. A bond which is recorded on the books of the issuer in the name of the owner. It can be transferred only when endorsed by the registered owner. *See* **bearer bond, coupon bond.**

registered representative. An employee of a securities broker or dealer who, having passed examinations and met other requirements of the SEC and/or NASD, is authorized to receive buy and sell orders for securities from public investors.

registrar. A trust company or bank charged with the responsibility of preventing the issuance of more stock than is authorized by a company.

regular way transaction. A transaction in which delivery of a stock certificate is made at the office of the purchaser on the fifth full business day following the transaction date.

relative strength. The relationship of the price of a stock to the Dow Jones Industrial Average or some other market average. The resulting percentage, multiplied by a factor to bring the plotting closer to the price bars on the chart, shows by the direction of the curve whether the stock is performing better than, worse than, or the same as the market average used.

replacement cost accounting. An accounting concept which espouses valuing assets at their replacement, or current, cost.

repurchase agreement. A cash loan to a bank or broker in exchange for or collateralized by securities (usually U.S. Treasury or agency) which the borrower agrees to repurchase at a specific price on a future date. These are not deposits; therefore they are not insured.

resistance level. A price area which attracts selling sufficient to keep the price of a stock from rising above it on repeated occasions. Once it has been broken through on the upside, the old resistance area becomes a new support level. *See* **support level.**

retained earnings. Profits remaining in the company after payment of preferred and common stock dividends. Retained earnings provide an important internal source of capital for business expansion.

return on equity. Net income available for the common stock divided by the previous year's shareholders' equity.

return on total capital. Earnings before interest and taxes, divided by total capitalization.

revenue bond. A municipal bond on which interest and principal are payable from receipts obtained from the operation of the project they finance rather than from general tax receipts.

revocable trust. A trust in which control of assets is retained.

rights (preemptive). Short-term options granted to existing shareholders of a company to purchase new stock issues, generally at reduced price levels.

ring. *See* **pit.**

round lot. Normally 100 shares of stock; for bonds, $100,000 face value.

Savings Bonds. Nonmarketable bonds issued by the U.S. Treasury. Now sold as Series EE, a discounted bond, and Series HH, a current-interest issue.

Securities Act of 1933. The law which states what information is required in a registration statement and prospectus.

Securities Exchange Act of 1934. The law which created the Securities and Exchange Commission. It requires registration with the SEC of many organizations dealing in securities and sets down rules for hypothecation of customers' securities.

Securities Investor Protection Corporation (SIPC). An insurance corporation organized under the Securities Investor Protection Act of 1970 to protect the assets of brokerage accounts in the event of a brokerage company bankruptcy. Operating funds are provided by assessments on brokerage firms' earnings.

selling against the box. Short selling against stock which is owned by an investor. The short sale may be covered by purchasing additional shares or by delivering the shares already owned.

semilogarithmic chart. A chart drawn on semilogarithmic graph paper. On this paper, the horizontal scale is drawn arithmetically, but the vertical scale is constructed so that equal distances represent equal percentage changes.

serial bonds. A bond issue which is sold with serial maturity dates and commensurate interest rates.

short interest ratio. The figure obtained by relating the monthly short interest (total number of shares sold short) to the average daily trading volume in the period concerned.

short selling. Selling stock which one does not already

own, in the belief that the price will decline. The broker borrows the stock so that he can deliver the shares to the buyer. Later, the short seller must cover his position by buying the same amount of stock borrowed for return to the buyer.

single premium annuity. An annuity contract purchased with only one payment, or premium.

sinking fund. Money set aside by a company to redeem its bonds, debentures, or preferred shares periodically as specified in the indenture or charter.

specialist. An exchange member whose first function is to maintain an orderly market in the stocks in which he is registered as a specialist. To do so, the specialist is expected to buy or sell for his own account when there is a temporary disparity between supply and demand.

special situation. A term which encompasses several types of unusual investment opportunities, including merger or takeover candidates, new-product development, spin-offs, or liquidations.

speculation. The assumption of above-average risk in anticipation of commensurately higher return.

speculative index. The relationship of American Stock Exchange volume to New York Stock Exchange volume expressed as a percentage. Presumably, the lower the figure, the closer the market is to a bottom, and the higher the figure, the closer it is to a peak.

spin-off. The division of an existing corporate entity into two or more separate operating units, with shares of the new company being distributed—"spun off"—to shareholders of the predecessor.

Standard & Poor's 500 Composite Stock Price Index. Average of 500 stocks, consisting of 400 industrial, 40 financial, 40 utility, and 20 transportation stocks.

standing margin (commodities). The amount of money a clearing house member keeps on deposit with the clearing house for each net open position at the end of the trading day.

stock dividend. A dividend paid in securities rather than cash. It may be additional shares of the issuing company or shares of another company (usually a subsidiary) held by the company.

stockholders' equity. *See* **book value.**

stock split. The allotment of additional shares to stockholders to represent their ownership interest in a corporation. Often stock splits are designed to broaden interest in a high-priced stock. A shareholder's proportionate interest in a company is not altered by a stock split.

stop order. An order which specifies a particular price at which a stock should be bought or sold. A stop order to buy specifies a price above the market; a stop order to sell indicates a price below the market. A stop order automatically becomes a market order once the security reaches the specified price.

straddle. The purchase of a put and a call on the same underlying stock having identical striking prices and expiration dates.

straight life annuity. An annuity which provides a predetermined amount of income periodically for the life of the annuitant. *See* **joint and survivor annuity.**

street name. Securities held in the name of a broker instead of the owner's name. Sometimes this arrangement is done for convenience; stocks bought on margin must always be left in a street name.

striking price. The price at which a call or put option is written. In the case of a call option, it is the price at which the stock named in the contract may be bought; in the case of a put, it is the price at which the stock may be sold.

STRIPS. An acronym for Separate Trading of Registered Interest and Principal of Securities. These STRIPS are authorized by the Treasury and are available to individuals through banks.

subordinate debenture. A debt issue whose claim on corporate assets comes after that of debentures in a liquidation.

support level. A technical analysis term which denotes a price area in which there is demand for a stock sufficient to keep the price from dropping below it on repeated occasions. Once there is a break below the area, a new support level is created. *See* **resistance level.**

sweep account. A savings or checking account in which funds over a specified minimum balance are invested in money-market instruments.

syndicate. A group of investment bankers formed to under-write and distribute a securities issue. Also, a group of individuals and/or concerns who combine to undertake a particular investment. *See* **investment banker.**

tax-free rollover. Using an individual retirement account to channel retirement funds from one qualified pension pro-gram to another, with no immediate tax consequences.

tax loopholes. Gaps in the tax structure through which clever taxpayers and special-interest groups can maneuver. Use of tax loopholes is not illegal.

tax shelter. Any means whereby income receives preferen-tial tax treatment.

technical analysis. The study of phenomena internal to the market, such as patterns of price movement, in an attempt to forecast the future movement of the market as a whole or of individual stocks.

tenancy in common. The title jointly held by two people, usually unmarried, to a given piece of property. Each per-son retains control over his individual share of the prop-erty.

tenancy by the entirety. The form of property ownership which exists when the names of both husband and wife appear on the deed to the property, with rights of survivor-ship.

tender offer. An offer by a corporation to buy back its own shares, or an offer to buy up shares in a company by an outsider interested in acquiring control.

ticker. The electronic system which prints prices and vol-ume of security transactions in cities and towns throughout the U.S. and Canada within minutes after each transaction.

"Tiger"—Treasury Investment Growth Receipts. One of several pooled investment vehicles offered by major bro-kerage firms combining the advantages of zero-coupon bonds (no interest payments but assured compounding of yield) with the safety of U.S. Treasury securities of a given maturity.

transfer agent. A bank or trust company that keeps a record of the name of each registered shareowner, his address, and the number of shares owned, and which sees that cer-tificates presented to it for transfer are properly canceled and new certificates issued in the name of the transferee.

Treasury bills. U.S. government securities maturing in one year or less, usually in three months or six months. They are sold at weekly auctions at a discount from par and are redeemed at par.

Treasury bonds. U.S. government securities with a maturity of greater than ten years.

Treasury notes. U.S. government securities with a maturity of two to ten years.

treasury stock. Stock issued by a company but later reacquired by the same company and held in its treasury.

trend line. Line drawn on a chart which indicates the direction in which a particular stock or the general market is trending.

trust. An agreement whereby the person who establishes the trust gives property to a trustee to invest and manage for the advantage of the beneficiary.

trustee. An individual or institution designated to oversee the handling and distribution of a trust fund.

12b(1) plans. Mutual funds using this plan are allowed to cover their marketing and distribution costs and brokerage charges from the fund's assets.

unit trust. An investment entity that issues only redeemable certificates that represent individual interests in a fixed portfolio with a specified life span and no continuing management.

unweighted average. Stock market average in which higher-priced issues do not have more influence on the average than lower-priced issues. This type of average is also called an equal-weighted average. *See* **weighted average.**

upside-downside volume. Tabulation of the shares traded on the New York Stock Exchange at prices higher or lower than the previous day's close.

uptick. A term which designates a transaction made at a price higher than the preceding transaction in a particular stock.

Value Line Index. An equal-weighted average based on equal dollar investments in a list of around 1,700 stocks.

variable annuity. An annuity in which a specified portion of the principal is invested in common stocks.

volume. The number of shares traded in a given market

(unless stated as consolidated, which would aggregate trades from all markets) during a given period of time.

warrant. A certificate giving the holder the right to purchase securities at a stipulated price within a specified time limit or perpetually.

wash sale. A wash sale is said to occur if securities or options to buy them are obtained within thirty days before or after a sale of substantially the same securities. No tax loss may be taken in such cases.

weighted average. An average which gives greater weight to stocks with a higher market value—S&P, NYSE averages. This type of average may also be called a value-weighted average.

"when issued." A new issue of securities that has been authorized but not actually issued to purchasers in a split. Shares are bought and sold in the market, with all transactions settled only when, as, and if the securities are finally issued.

withdrawal plan. An arrangement under which investors in mutual funds can regularly receive monthly or quarterly payments of a specified amount.

working capital. Current assets minus current liabilities. Working-capital needs vary among industries and among firms in the same industry.

yield. The dividends or interest paid on a particular security expressed as a percentage of the current price or as a percentage of cost price, or as related to the maturity of a bond.

yield to maturity. The return earned on a bond if it is held to maturity.

zero-coupon bonds. Bonds on which there are no periodic interest payments prior to maturity, but which are sold at a deep discount from their face value so that the principal payment at maturity provides an effective yield on the amount originally invested.

Index

A or AA bonds, 76–77, 101, 103
Accountant's report, 260–61
Account executive, choosing, 359–361
Accounts payable, 247
Accounts receivable, 245, 253
Accrued expenses, 247
Accrued income taxes, 247
Accumulated depreciation, 245
Acquisitions, capitalizing on, 343–345
Adjustable-rate preferreds, 58
Advance-decline index, 225
Advice, 309–16
  broker and bank, 310
  financial press, 313–14
  government publications, 315
  investment counselors, 315–16
  magazines, 314
  Standard & Poor's and Moody's, 310–11
Advisory services, 311–13
Aerospace industry, 274–75, 347
After retirement, 473–87
  annuities, 475–77
  capital, 484–86
  common stocks, 483–84
  corporate bonds, 481
  real estate, 481–83
  savings accounts, 477–78
  Social Security, 473–75
  U.S. Savings bonds, 478–80
  See also Retirement
Agency marketing, 329
Airline industry, 280
AMBAC Indemnity Corp., 101
American Association of Individual Investors (AAII), 377
American Stock Exchange (AMEX), 330, 331–32
American Stock Exchange Index, 209

Annual-premium annuity, 455
Annual report, 242–61
  accountants' report, 260–61
  analyzing common stock, 257–58
  balance sheet, 244–49
  changes in working capital, 254, 255
  footnotes, 258–60
  intangibles in, 245
  management's analysis of operating results, 254–56
  "other investments" notation in, 245
  source and application of funds statement, 254–55
  statement of retained earnings, 253–54
  statistical summary, 256
  what it will contain, 242–44
Annuities, 455–62
  after retirement, 475–77
  buying privately, 460–62
  decision for, 459–60
  payments and amount of payment, 457–59
  as savings vehicles, 456–57
Astor, John Jacob, 181
Astute Investor, The, 312
"At the market" order, 362
Automobiles and trucks, 264
Averaging, dollar cost, 339–40

Balance sheet, 244–49
  analyzing, 248–49
Bank accounts, 413–14
Bank advice, 310
Banking industry, 293–94, 397–98
Bar chart, 212
Barron's, 314
Barron's Confidence Index, 227
Basic industries, 263–74
BBB-rated bonds, 78–79

Bearer bonds, 75
Bearish investors, 355–57
Berstein, Jacob, 369
Bit-by-bit investing, 41–43
Bond Guide (Standard & Poor's), 310, 311
Bond Investors Guaranty (BIGI), 101
Bonds:
  after retirement, 481
  corporate, 73–81
  federal agency, 92–93
  "flower," 94
  tax-exempts, 95–105, 127
  Treasury, 91–92, 163, 164
  U.S. Savings, 90–91, 389, 393–396, 416–17
Bond Survey (Moody's), 311
Book value, 244
Boston Personal Property Trust, 106
Brokers:
  advice from, 310
  choosing, 359–61, 373–79
  commission rates, 376
  discount, 374–75
  full-service houses, 374
  special programs, 376–77
Bryan, William Jennings, 170
Building a portfolio. *See* Portfolio building
Bullish investors, 355–57
Business Conditions Digest, 315
Business Cycles (Schumpeter), 301–2
Business property, 186–87
Business Week, 314
Butler, Samuel, 170
Buying calls, 351–52
Buying commodity contracts, 364–365
Buying "low," 338

Calendar spread, 356
Call options, 60, 61, 136–38
  buying, 351–52
  risk-rewards of trading (table), 145
Capital:
  after retirement, 484–86
  investing to preserve, 43–45
Capital Changes Reporter, 386

Capital in excess of par value, 247–248
Capital gains distributions, mutual fund reinvestment, 112
Capital gains taxes, 400–401
Capital surplus, 247
Carnegie, Andrew, 181
Cash, 244
  futures market and, 167–69
Cash or deferred arrangement (CODA), 430
Cash refund annuity, 458
Central marketplace, setting up, 332–33
Certificates, stock, 385–87
  as antiques or collectibles, 386–387
  lost or destroyed, 385–86
  obsolete, 387
Changing needs, adjusting for, 46–47
Channels, interpretation of, 231–233
Charts, 211–19
  as aids to investors, 211–13
  and investments, 216–17
  plotting percentages, 217–19
  practical application, 214–15
  use of, 219
  See also Technical analysis
Chemical industry, 265, 347
Chicago Board Options Exchange (CBOE), 135–36, 332
Chicago Board of Trade, 147–48, 163
Chicago Mercantile Exchange, 163
Clearing house, 150–51
Clifford trust, 418
"Clones," 120
Closed-end funds, 109, 120
Coal industry, 266–67
Coinciding indicators, 199–201
College education, 415–18
  custodian accounts, 417
  taxes and, 416–18
  trusts, 418
Colonial Fund, 106
Commissions, 366, 376
Commodities, 146–62
  clearing house, 150–51
  exchanges, 148–50

government regulation of, 161–162

hedging, 156–57

historical evolution, 147–48

leverage, 155

long hedge, 158

margins, 153–55

open interest, 155–56

short hedge, 157, 159

standard contract, 151–53

trading floor, 158–61

Commodity Exchange Act, 161

Commodity Exchange Authority (CEA), 161

Commodity futures, 358–69

buying, selling, and delivery, 364–66

choosing broker and account executive, 359–61

commissions, 366

forms and basic correspondence, 361–62

kinds of orders, 362–64

market quotes and price forecasting, 366–68

speculation factor, 359

trading plan, 368–69

Commodity Futures Trading Commission (CFTC), 161–62

Common stock, 247

after retirement, 483–84

analyzing, 257–58

dividends and rights, 55, 392–93

how to value, 56

for income, 67–72

quality and earnings, 54–55

rights and risks, 53–54, 57

stock splits, 56

Common stock ratio, 249

Community property, 468

Companies, buying the best-known, 321–22

Condominiums, 182

Construction industry, 267–68

Contract, commodity, 151–53

Conversion basis, 83–84

Conversion value, 84

Convertible securities, 82–87

conversion premium, 84–85

how they work, 83–84

how and when to convert, 85–86

uses and limits of, 86–87

Cooperative apartments, 182

Corporate bonds, 73–81

after retirement, 481

drawbacks of, 80–81

mechanics of, 75–76

nature of, 73–74

yields, 76–80

Corporation Records (Standard and Poor's), 310

Cost of goods sold, 250

Creditors, corporation's responsibility to, 53–54

Current assets, 244

Current liabilities, 247

Current (or working capital) ratio, 248

Current yield, 67–68

Custodian accounts, 417

Cyclical indicators. *See* Forecasting

Cycli-Graphs charts, 216, 217–18, 312

Data processing industry, 275–76

Day orders, 335

Day rate, 366

DeAngelis, Tino, 146

Death:

Keogh assets and, 440–41

providing for, 412–13

See also Will

Debentures, 74. *See also* Corporate bonds

Debt-to-equity ratio, 249

Defensive investing, 39–41

Deferred charges, 245–47

Defined-benefit plans, 429–30

Defined-contribution plans, 429–430

Delivery, commodity contracts, 364–66

Department of Commerce, 196

Department of Housing and Urban Development (HUD), 97

Department of Justice, 21, 69

Department of the Treasury, 89, 90, 176, 396

Depreciation, 250

Dines Letter, The, 312

Directory of Obsolete Securities, 386

Disability, providing for, 412–13

Discount brokers, 374–75
Discretionary order, 335
Diversification, 325–27
  mutual fund, 112, 121
  portfolio, 45–46
Dividend payout ratio, 257
Dividend performance, 55
Dividend reinvestment plans, 390–
  391
Dividends, 392–93
  mutual fund reinvestment of, 112
Dividend yield, 257
Dollar cost averaging, 339–40
Dollar currency, gold and, 172–75
Double tops and bottoms (M and
  W formations), 234–35
Dow Jones Industrial Average, 27,
  206–8, 214
Dow Theory, 239–40
Dow Theory Forecasts, 312

Earned surplus, 248
Earnings (in an annual report), 247
Earnings retention rate, 257
Economic Indicators, 315
Economic Recovery Tax Act of
  1981, 470
*Economics of Futures Trading—
  For Commercial and Personal
  Profit* (Hieronymus), 158
Economic trends, growth stocks
  and, 63–64
Electric utilities, 69–70, 297–98
Electronics and electrical
  equipment industries, 276–77,
  347
Employee benefit plans, 427–34
  ERISA standards, 428
  PBGC guarantees, 429
  pensions, 429–34
Employee Retirement Income
  Security Act of 1974, 144, 428
Employee stock ownership plans
  (ESOPs), 430–31
Environmental Protection Agency,
  21
E or EE bonds, 393–96, 416, 417,
  478–80
Equities, advantage of, 424–25
Equity investments, 51–61
  common stock risks, 53–54, 57
  dividend performance, 55

  ownership concept, 51–52
  preferred stocks, 57–59
  puts and calls, 60–61
  quality and earnings, 54–55
  rights and risks, 53–54
  rights and warrants, 59–60
  stock splits, 55, 56
  value, 56
Erdman, Paul, 146
Estate planning, 463–72
  choosing an executor, 464–66
  joint ownership, 468–69
  marital deduction, 470–71
  program of planned gifts, 471–72
  taxes, 469–70
  trusts, 466–67
  will, 464
Exchange privileges, mutual funds,
  112–13
Ex-dividend, 336
Ex-dividend date, 55
Executor, choosing, 464–66
Exercise price, 136
Export-Import Bank, 93
Ex-rights, 337

Fads, avoiding, 323–25
Federal agency bonds, 92–93
Federal Energy Regulatory
  Commission, 299
Federal Farm Credit System, 93
Federal Financing Bank, 92–93
Federal Reserve banks, 395, 396–97
Federal Reserve Board, 89, 214
Federal Trade Commission (FTC),
  21, 278
FIFO (first in, first out), 258
"Fill or kill" (FOK) orders, 335
Financial Accounting Standards
  Board, 260
Financial Guaranty Insurance Co.
  (FGIC), 101
Financial plan, investments and,
  407–87
  after retirement, 473–87
  college education, 415–18
  employee benefit plans, 427–34
  estate planning, 463–72
  IRAs, 442–54
  keeping affairs in order, 407–14
  Keogh plans, 435–41
  retirement, 419–26

Financial press, advice from, 313–314

Financial World, 314

Fixed assets, 245

Floor brokers, 331

"Flower bonds," 94

Food and Drug Administration (FDA), 21, 278

Food processing industry, 285–86

Footnotes, annual report, 258–60

Forbes, 314

Forecasting, 195–202, 366–68
  coinciding indicators, 199–201
  lagging indicators, 201–2
  leading indicators, 196–99

Foreign and Colonial Government Trust, 106

Foreign funds, 123–24

Fort Knox, 172

Fortune, 314

Full faith and credit bonds, 97–98

Fully diluted earnings per share, 251

Fundamental analysis, 220, 367–68

Funds:
  money market, 126–28
  mutual, 106–21
  option income, 144
  for specialized objectives, 122–133

Future, cashing in on, 301–8
  effects of "future shock," 303–4
  "getting there," 307
  guidelines, 308
  innovation versus invention, 302–3
  making money on money, 307–8
  profits in "cleaning up," 306
  watching for trends, 305–6
  why some companies succeed, 304–5

Futures, 163–69
  cash, putting up, 167–69
  entry fee for trading, 165–66
  historical background, 163–64
  informational tools, 166–67

General obligation bonds, 97–98

Gifts:
  to charities, 403–4
  estate planning, 471–72

Ginnie Mae funds, 125–26

Glossary of terms, 491–516

Goals, setting, 320–21

Gold, 21, 170–80
  industrial demand for, 177–78
  investing in, 175–78
  investment outlook, 178–79
  "Kaffirs," 179
  Krugerrands, 180
  popularity of, 170
  runaway inflation and, 171
  and U.S. dollar, 172–75

Gold funds, 123

Gold standard, 170–72

Good till canceled. *See* GTC orders

Government National Mortgage Association (GNMA), 125

Government publications, 315

"Governments," 88–94, 396–97
  bills, notes and bonds, 90–91
  federal agency bonds, 92–93
  how they work, 89–90
  safety of, 88–89
  STRIPS, 91–92
  taxes, 93–94
  "tigers," 91

Grain Futures Act, 161

Gross plant and equipment, 245

Gross profit margin, 252

Growth stocks, 62–66
  and economic trends, 63–64
  table, 66
  timing buys, 64–65
  timing sells, 65–66
  what they are, 62–63

GTC orders (good till canceled), 335, 363–64

"Head and shoulders," interpretation of, 235–36

Health care industry, 277–79

Hedging, 156–57
  long, 158
  with options, 254–55
  short, 157, 159

HH bonds, 91, 394–96
  after retirement, 479, 480

Hieronymus, Thomas A., 158

Hitler, Adolf, 172

Holders of record, 55

"Home-grown" tax-exempts, 104

Home ownership, 181–83

Horizontal spread, 356

Hospital bonds, 103
Hotel and motel industry, 286–87
Housing Acts of 1949, 1965, and
    1968, 182

Illness, providing for, 412–13
Income statement, 249–53
    analyzing, 251–53
    checkbook, 411
Income stocks, 67–72
    current yield and, 67–68
    electric utilities, 69–70
    inflation and, 71–72
    telephone business, 68–69
    water utilities, 70–71
Income taxes. *See* Taxes
Indexes, stock market activity,
    203–10
    approaches and yield results,
        205–6
    building, 204–5
    Dow Jones Industrial Average,
        206–8
    miscellaneous indexes, 209
    S&P 500, 208–9
    usefulness, 209–10
Index funds, 126
Indicator Digest, 312
Indicator Digest indexes, 209
Individual retirement accounts
    (IRAs), 76, 91, 374, 431, 442–
    454
    actuarial table for, 452
    distributions of, 451–52
    employer-sponsored, 446–47
    flexible investment options, 444–
        446
    how they work, 442–43
    new class of, 443–44
    nondeductible contributions and,
        449–51
    penalties, 447–48
    rollovers, 453–54
    taxes, 448–49
Industrial development bonds
    (industrial revenue bonds),
    98
Industries, analyzing. *See* Specific
    industries, analyzing
Inflation, 19, 20, 21, 25, 42, 52, 94
    gold hedge and, 170–80
    and income stocks, 71–72

post–Vietnam War era, 32
    risk of, 32–33
Innovation, profits of, 302–3
Insider trading, 342–43
Installment refund annuity, 458
Insurance, 413
    bondholder's portfolio, 101
    pension plan, 429
Insurance industry, 294–95
Interest expense, 251
Interest-rate risk, 23–35
Intermarket Trading System, 332–
    333
Intermountain Exchange, 332
Internal Revenue Service (IRS),
    105, 445, 446
International Monetary Fund, 176
International Monetary Market
    (IMM), 163
"In the money" trading, 136
Inventories, 245
Inventory and accounts receivable
    turnover ratios, 253
Investment Advisors Act (1940),
    312
Investment alternatives, 51–191
    arcane financial products, 163–
        169
    commodities, 146–62
    common stocks for income, 67–
        72
    convertible securities, 82–87
    corporate bonds, 73–81
    equity, 51–61
    gold, 21, 170–80
    "governments," 88–94, 396–97
    growth stocks, 62–66
    mutual funds, 106–21
    options, 134–45
    real estate, 181–91, 414
    specialized objectives, 122–33
    tax-exempts, 95–105, 127
Investment bankers, role of, 328–
    330
Investment Company Act of 1940,
    108
Investment Company Act of 1970,
    392
Investment counselors, 315–16
Investment funds, special-purpose,
    122–33
    convertible, 122–23

foreign, 123–24
Ginnie Mae, 125–26
gold, 123
index, 126
money-market, 126–28
municipal bond, 128–29
option income, 129–30
sector, 130–31
social-action, 131
unit trusts, 132–33
Investment philosophy, 17–47
    being positive and patient, 22–23
    building a portfolio, 39–47
    "buy good stocks and hold them long," 46
    ideologues and, 20–22
    lessons not learned, 18–19
    planning, 24–30
    positive thinking, 19–20
    risks, 31–38
Investment success:
    alternatives, 51–191
    choosing a broker, 359–61, 373–379
    designing a plan, 389–98
    financial plan, 407–87
    glossary of terms, 491–516
    how to make choices, 195–316
    philosophy, 17–47
    safeguarding securities, 380–88
    strategies and tactics, 319–69
    tax pointers, 399–404
Investor's Quotient, The (Berstein), 369

Joint and survivor annuity, 457
Joint ownership, 468–69
Joint tenancy, 468
Journal of Commerce, The, 314, 367

Keogh, Eugene J., 435
Keogh plans (or HR-10 plans), 76, 91, 374, 435–41
    collecting benefits, 439
    death benefits, 440–41
    how they work, 436–38
    investment alternatives, 438–439
    withdrawal options, 439–40
Krugerrands, 180

Lagging indicators, 201–2
Land, Dr. Edward, 324
Land investment, 183–84
Leading indicators, 196–99
Lettre de faire documents, 148
Leverage, commodity margin, 155
Levine, Dennis B., 342
Levitt, William J., 181
Levittowns, 181
Life annuity with installments certain, 457–58
Life insurance, 417–18
LIFO (last in, first out), 258
Limit orders, 333–34, 362
Line chart, 212
Liquidity ratio or acid test, 248–49
Load funds, 109–10
Loans, corporate bonds as, 73–74
Lodging industry, 286–87
Long hedge, 158
Long term, investing for, 322–23
Long-term debt, 247
Long-term debt due within one year, 247
Low-load funds, 114

Machinery and machine tools industries, 268–69
Magazines, 314
Maintenance margin, 154–55
Management's analysis of operating results, 254–56
Margin call, 155
Margin requirements, options and, 140
Margins, 153–55
Marital deductions, estate planning, 470–71
Marketable securities, 244–45
Market averages, 224
Market order, 333
Market risk, 35
Market's ups and downs, 203–10
    approaches and yield results, 205–6
    "building" an index, 204–5
    Dow Jones Industrial Average, 206–8
    index usefulness, 209–10
    miscellaneous indexes, 209
    S&P 500, 208–9
Marshall Plan, 173

Media General Financial Weekly, The, 314
Media industry, 287–88
Meetings, stockholder, 53
Member firms, 330
Mergers, capitalizing on, 343–45
Metals industry, 269–70
Midwest Stock Exchange (MW), 330, 332
Minority shareholder rights, 387–388
Monetary Trends, 315
Money, making money on, 307–8
Money Magazine, 314
Money market funds, 126–28
Monthly Labor Review, 315
Moody's, advice from, 310, 311
Moody's AA Corporate Bond Composite Index, 76–77
Moody's Investors Service, 78
Mortgage bonds, 74. *See also* Corporate bonds
Motion picture industry, 288–89, 347
Motor Carrier Act of 1980, 282
Moving averages, 236–38
Municipal bonds. *See* Tax-exempts
Mutual Fund Fact Book, 313
Mutual funds, 106–21
  advantages of, 110–13
  closed-ends and clones, 120
  closed-ends vs. open-ends, 109
  concept of, 106–7
  cost of ownership, 113–14
  diversification, 112, 121
  division of risk, 111
  exchange privileges, 112–13
  freedom from emotional involvement, 111
  future and, 119
  housekeeping, 112
  important "don't," 118–19
  information from records, 111
  kinds of, 119–20
  list of good-quality growth funds, 121
  load vs. no-load, 109–10
  low-load vs. no-load, 114
  meaning of, 107–8
  newspaper quotations, 112
  1986 facts (table), 117
  option income, 144

portfolio turnover, 116–17
professional management, 110–111
programs, 391–92
prospectus, 115–16
Mutual Fund Source Book, 313

National Association of Investment Clubs (NAIC), 377
National Association of Securities Dealers, 333
National Futures Association (NFA), 162, 360
Natural gas distributors, 298–99
Net income or net operating income, 251
Net income per common share, 251
Net income profit margin, 252
Net worth, how to find, 408–11
New highs-new lows indicator, 226
New products, capitalizing on, 346–47
New York Futures Exchange, 164
New York Stock Exchange (NYSE), 88–89, 330–31
New York Stock Exchange Composite Stock Index, 209
New York Times, The, 314, 367
Nixon, Richard, 174
No-load funds, 109–10, 114
Notes and loans payable, 247

Odd-lot short sales, 226
Odd-lot trading, 226
Off balance sheet financing, 259–260
Oil industry, 270–71
Old certificates, tracing, 386–87
On close (or on open) orders, 363
One cancels the other (OCO) orders, 363
Open-end funds, 109
Open interest, 155–56
Open orders, 335
Open trades, 361–62
Operating profit margin, 252
Option income funds, 144
Options, 134–45
  attraction of, 60–61
  avoiding unwanted exercise notices, 140–41
  buying and selling, 138–40

call, 136–38, 351–52
CBOE, 135–36
margin requirements, 140
market growth, 143–44
put, 353–54
risk-reward parameters (table),
    145
writing puts, 143
Options Clearing Corporation, 135,
    356–57
Options trading, 350–57
buying calls, 351–52
hedging, 354–55
puts, 353–54
risk versus reward, 357
selling calls, 352–53
spreads, 355–57
Orders, types of, 333–35, 362–64
Organization of Petroleum
    Exporting Countries (OPEC),
    176
Original margin, 154
Outgoing finances, controlling,
    411–12
Outlook (Standard & Poor's), 310,
    312
"Out of the money" trading, 136
Ownership concept, 51–52

Pacific Stock Exchange (P), 330,
    332
Paper and forest products
    industries, 271–73
Par value, 247
Payment date, 55
Pension Benefit Guaranty
    Corporation, 429
Pension plans, 429–34
calculating benefits, 431–32
collecting from, 433–34
"defined-contribution" or
    "defined-benefit," 429–30
insurance, 429
Tax Reform Act of 1986 and,
    432–33
types of employee arrangements,
    431
Percentages, chart, 217–19
Perpendicular spread, 356
Personal care industry, 289–90
Philadelphia Stock Exchange (Ph),
    330, 332

Planning, 24–30
savings, 25–26
stock ownership, 27–28
stock values, 28–30
Point and figure analysis, 239
Portfolio building, 39–47
adjusting for changing needs,
    46–47
bit by bit, 41–43
defensive investing, 39–41
diversification, 45–46
preserving capital, 43–45
record keeping, 47
and selling, 46
Positive thinking, power of, 19–20
Predictor & Tillman Survey, The,
    312
Preemptive rights, 337
Preferred stocks, 57–59
Prepaid expenses, 245
Pretax profit margin, 252
Price-earnings ratio, 257
Price forecasting, market quotes
    and, 366–68
Primary earnings per share, 251
Primary markets, 328–29
Private annuity, 460–62
drawbacks of, 462
Professional advisers, 414
Professional Tape Reader, 312
Profit and loss statement. *See*
    Income statement
Profit-taking, 338–39
Prospectus, mutual fund, 115–16
Public utilities, analyzing, 296–300
Puerto Rico, bonds of, 103
Purchase and sale, 361
Purchasing-distribution, 329
Put options, 60–61, 141–42
buying, 142
risk-rewards of trading (table),
    145
trading, 353–54
writing, 143

Quick ratio, 248–49

Railroad industry, 281–82
Railway and Light Securities
    Company, 106
Ratio-Cator line, 216
Ratio writing, 357

Raw land, 183–84
Real estate, 181–91, 414
  after retirement, 481–83
  business property, 186–87
  home ownership, 181–83
  raw land, 183–84
  REITs, 187
  rental property, 184–85
  successes and failures, 183
  syndicate or group participation,
    189–90
  tax considerations, 190–91
  what can go wrong, 191
Real estate investment trusts
    (REITs), 187
Record keeping, 47, 383–84
  checklist, 413–14
Recreation equipment industry,
    290–91
Registered bonds, 75
Registered traders, 331
Relative strength, 236
Rental property, 184–85
Resistance level, chart as indicator
    of, 230
Retailing industry, 291–92
Retained earnings, 247, 248
Retirement, 419–26
  equities, 424–25
  how much to save, 420–21
  making savings grow, 423–24
  savings alternatives, 421–23
  supplementing income, 425–
    426
  See also After retirement
Return on equity, 252
Revenue bonds, 98
  judging, 102
Reversionary trust, 418
Rights and warrants, 59–60
Rights offerings, 393
Risks, 31–38
  amount of, 36
  common stocks, 53–54, 57
  inflation, 32–33
  interest-rate, 33–35
  market, 35
  options trading, 357
  spreading, 36–38
*Robert D. Fisher Manual of
    Valuable and Worthless
    Securities*, 386

Roosevelt, Franklin D., 172
Rules for investors, 319–27
  avoiding fads, 323–25
  buying best-known companies,
    321–22
  diversification, 325–27
  long term, 322–23

Safe deposit boxes, 413
Safeguarding securities, 380–88
  basic ways of holding, 380–82
  lost or destroyed certificates,
    385–86
  minority shareholder rights,
    387–88
  old certificates, 386–87
  record keeping, 383–84
  SIPC protection, 382–83
Sales, net, 250
Savings, planning, 25–26
Savings accounts, after retirement,
    477–78
Saving alternatives, retirement
    and, 421–23
Savings and loan associations, 295–
    296
Schlicter, Sumner, 32
Schumpeter, Joseph A., 301–2, 303
Scripophily (technique for
    authenticating old certificates),
    387
Secondary market, 330
Securities:
  record keeping, 413–14
  See also Bonds; Common stocks;
    Equities; Preferred stocks
Securities Act of 1933, 115
Securities and Exchange
    Commission (SEC), 21, 163–
    164, 256, 312, 331, 332, 374
Securities Investor Protection
    Corporation (SIPC), 378, 382–
    383
Self-discipline, 398
Self-Employed Individuals Tax
    Retirement Act of 1962. *See*
    Keogh plans
Selling, general, and
    administrative expenses, 250–
    251
Selling, philosophy of, 46–47
Selling calls, 352–53

Selling commodity contracts, 364–366

Selling "high," 338–39

Series E or EE bonds, 91, 393–96, 416, 417
    after retirement, 478–80

Series HH bonds, 91, 394–96

Shakespeare, William, 170

Sharebuilder Program (Merrill Lynch, Pierce, Fenner & Smith), 376–77

Short hedge, 157, 159
    profit-loss effect on, 159

Short interest, 227

Short interest ratio, 227

Short-term trust, 418

Shultz, George, 175

Silver, 21, 146

Simplified Employee Plans (SEPs), 436, 442, 446–47, 449

Single-premium annuity, 455

Social Security, 473–75

Source and application of funds statement, 254

Specialists (exchange members), 330–31

Special-purpose investment funds. *See* Investment funds, special-purpose

Special situations, capitalizing on, 342–49
    investing "at home," 348–49
    mergers, acquisitions, and takeovers, 343–45
    new products, 346–47
    spin-offs and turnarounds, 345–346

Specific industries, analyzing, 262–300
    airlines, railroads, and trucking, 280–83
    automobiles and trucks, 264
    "basic" industries, 263–74
    chemicals, 265, 347
    coal, 266–67
    construction, 267–68
    consumer products and leisure time, 284–92
    financial services, 293–96
    machinery and machine tools, 268–69
    metals, 269–70

oil and natural gas, 270–71
    paper and forest products, 271–73
    public utilities, 296–300
    science and technology, 274–79
    textiles, 273–74
    transportation, 279–83

Special-timing situations, 336–38

Speculative index, 225

Speculator, The, 312

Spin-offs, capitalizing on, 345–46

Spread commission, 366

Spreading the risks, 36–38

Spreads, 355–57

SRC Blue Book of 3-Trend Cycli-Graphs, 216

Standard & Poor's, 78
    advice from, 310–11

Standard & Poor's 500, 208–9

Standby agreements, 329

Standing margin, 153

Statement of account, 361

Statement of retained earnings, 253–54

Stock:
    intrinsic values behind, 28–30
    investment planning, 27–28
    See also Common stock; Preferred stocks

Stock dividend, 55, 392–93

Stock Guide, The (Standard and Poor's), 310–11

Stockholders' equity, 247

Stock market:
    how it works, 328–41
    ups and downs, 203–10
    See also Common stock; *specific names of exchanges*

Stock Reports (Standard and Poor's), 391

Stock rights, 337

Stock splits, 55, 56

Stop limit orders, 335

Stop orders, or stop loss orders, 334–35, 363

Straight life annuity, 457

Strategies and tactics, 319–69
    capitalizing on special situations, 342–49
    commodity futures, 358–69
    how the market works, 328–41
    options, how to use, 350–57
    rules for investors, 319–27

Striking price, 136
STRIPS (Separate Trading of
    Registered Interest and
    Principal of Securities), 91–92
Successful investments. *See*
    Investment success
Supermarket News, 314
Survey of Current Business, 315

Takeovers, capitalizing on, 343–45
Tax Equity and Fiscal
    Responsibility Act of 1982, 75,
    394, 436
Taxes, 414
    estate, 469–70
    on "governments," 93–94
    investing for college and, 416–
        418
    IRA, 448–49
    real estate considerations, 190–
        191
Tax-exempts, 95–105, 127, 417
    deciding what to buy, 103–4
    "home-grown," 104
    insurance, 101
    judging, 102–3
    kinds of bonds, 97–98
    marketability, 100
    new types of, 99
    profitability, 95–97
    when not to use, 104–5
    yield (table), 97
Tax-free rollovers:
    retirement fund and, 453
    rules of, 453–54
Tax pointers, 399–404
    calendar transactions, 402
    capital gains, 400–401
    cardinal rule for, 400
    gifts to charities, 403–4
    loss and saving on income tax,
        402
    wash sale rule, 401–2
    year-end tactics, 403
Tax rate, 253
Tax Reform Act of 1976, 128, 144
Tax Reform Act of 1986, 95, 99,
    102, 189–90, 399, 403–4, 432–
    433, 443, 448, 456
Tax revenue or bond anticipation
    notes, 98
Tax-sheltered accounts, 76

Technical analysis, 220–41, 367,
    368
    definitions, 220–21
    Dow Theory, 239–40
    indicators, 224–27
    interpreting chart patterns, 229–
        239
    irregular forecasting methods,
        228–29
    what it is, 221–24
    See also Charts
Telephone companies, 299–300
Telephone stocks, 68–69, 299–300
Tenancy by the entirety, 468
Tenancy in common, 468
10-Ks, 242
Tennessee Valley Authority, 92
Textile industry, 273–74
Third Market, 332
Three Mile Island nuclear plant,
    298
"Tigers" (TIGR), 91
Time spread, 356
Timing buys, 64–65
Timing sells, 65–66
Toffler, Alvin, 303
Trade confirmation, 361
Trading floor, 158–61
Trading plan, 368–69
Trading volume, 225
Transportation industry, 279–83
Treasury bills, 89, 90–91, 396
Treasury bond futures, 164
Treasury bonds, 91–92, 163, 164
Treasury Investment Growth
    Receipts (TIGR), 91
Treasury notes, 90
Trends, watching for, 305–6
Trucking industry, 282–83
Trust certificates, 74. *See also*
    Corporate bonds
Trusts, 418
    estate planning, 466–67
Turnarounds, capitalizing on, 345–
    346

*United & Babson Investment
    Report,* 27–28, 311–12
United Mutual Fund Selector, 313
U.S. News & World Report, 314
United States Retirement Plan
    bonds, 91

U.S. Savings Bonds, 90–91, 389,
393–96, 416–17, 478–80
after retirement, 478–80
Unit trusts, 132–33
Upside-downside volume, 225
Utilities:
analyzing, 296–300
electric, 69–70, 297–98
preferred stocks, 57–59
water, 70–71

Valuable Extinct Securities, 386
"Value," stock, 56
Value Line Average, 205
Value Line Investment Survey, 311
Variable annuities, 457
Variable hedging, 357
Variation margin, 153
Verne, Jules, 303
Vertical spread, 356

Wall Street Journal, The, 313–14,
367
Warrants, 59–60
Wash sale rule, 401–2

Water utilities, 70–71
Watson, Thomas J., 304
*Wiesenberger Investment
Company Service, The*, 313
Will, 413, 464
choosing the executor, 464–66
keeping current, 464
William I, king of the Netherlands,
106
Women's Wear Daily, 314
Writer (seller) of covered options,
139–40

Yield:
corporate bonds, 76–80
income stocks and, 67–68
indexes and different results,
205–6
tax-exempts and tax bracket, 97
Yield on cost, 79
Yield-to-call, 79, 80
Yield-to-maturity, 79, 80

Zeckendorf, William, 181
Zweig Forecast, 312